A C

A Childhood Psychology

Young Children in Changing Times

Dion Sommer

palgrave
macmillan

First published 2012 by
PALGRAVE MACMILLAN

Palgrave Macmillan in the UK is an imprint of Macmillan Publishers Limited, registered in England, company number 785998, of Houndmills, Basingstoke, Hampshire RG21 6XS.

Palgrave Macmillan in the US is a division of St Martin's Press LLC, 175 Fifth Avenue, New York, NY 10010.

Palgrave Macmillan is the global academic imprint of the above companies and has companies and representatives throughout the world.

Palgrave® and Macmillan® are registered trademarks in the United States, the United Kingdom, Europe and other countries.

ISBN: 978–0–230–36194–2 hardback
ISBN: 978–0–230–25224–0 paperback

This book is printed on paper suitable for recycling and made from fully managed and sustained forest sources. Logging, pulping and manufacturing processes are expected to conform to the environmental regulations of the country of origin.

A catalogue record for this book is available from the British Library.

A catalog record for this book is available from the Library of Congress.

10 9 8 7 6 5 4 3 2 1
21 20 19 18 17 16 15 14 13 12

Printed and bound in Great Britain by
CPI Antony Rowe, Chippenham and Eastbourne

CONTENTS

LIST OF FIGURES AND TABLES

FIGURES

TABLES

ACKNOWLEDGEMENTS

The author and publishers gratefully acknowledge the following for permission to reproduce copyright material:

Elsevier Limited for Figure 1 from Vermeer, H. J. and van Ijzendoorn, M. H. (2006) 'Children's Elevated Cortisol Levels at Daycare: A Review and Meta-Analysis', *Early Childhood Research Quarterly*, 21(3): 390–401.

John Wiley & Sons for Figure 7.2 from Fischer, K. W. and Bidell, T. R. (2006) 'Dynamic Development in Action and Thought', in W. Damon and R. M. Lerner (eds) *Handbook of Child Psychology*, vol. 1: *Theoretical Models of Human Development* (6th edn); Figure 1 from Rothbaum, F., Pott, M., Azuma, H. et al. (2000) 'The Development of Close Relationships in Japan and the United States: Paths of Symbiotic Harmony and Generative Tension', *Child Development*, 71(5): 1121–43.

UNIFEC Innocenti Research Centre, Florence for Figures 2a and 2b in UNICEF (2007) *Child Poverty in Perspective: An Overview of Child's Well-Being in Rich Countries*, Innocenti Report Card 7.

Every effort has been made to trace all the copyright holders, but if any have been inadvertently overlooked the publishers will be pleased to make the necessary arrangements at the first opportunity.

INTRODUCTION: WHY AND HOW A CHILDHOOD PSYCHOLOGY

Perhaps one of the few constants in our times is change. Not only are the endeavours of social science almost perpetually changing, but today's societies and cultures are rapidly changing as well. Consequently, to discuss the childhood realities of the future generation calls for new interpretations and understandings of young children's socialization and development.

A Childhood Psychology is not a traditional textbook. Instead, it is more like a discursive argument; an advanced reader that proposes and contributes to a paradigm shift in the understanding of early childhood and young children who live in a late modern world. However, the magnitude of recent research relevant to this aim is so overwhelming that fragmentation is not only a danger, but a fact. Every year, numerous statistics, articles, reports and books are published worldwide from various disciplines within the social sciences, each contributing their knowledge to the debate. However, merely offering a summary of recent literature can be more bewildering than enlightening, not only because there is too much, but because at present there is very little at hand to integrate this diverse information. Overarching integrative and interdisciplinary approaches are rare, but much needed. Since many studies and approaches have been subjected to limited attempts at integration and remain within the specific boundaries of their discipline, a need has arisen for a presentation that offers not only documentation of the new realities of early childhood, but also an interpretation and a reflective stance. With this current flood of information in mind, *A Childhood Psychology* offers one proposal of how to construct a common frame of reference.

WHY A CHILDHOOD PSYCHOLOGY?

First of all, it is not *the* psychology of childhood. It would be pretentious to attempt to present a definite theory on today's early childhood, and this is not the case. Nor will there be any attempt to monopolize the field, although a particular paradigm of childhood psychology will be endorsed. Monopolization or any attempt to establish *the* new theory would clash with this book's fundamental notion of the temporary nature of knowledge and the possibility that alternative interpretations may always be available, even when based on the same new realities of early childhood. In this book, the theories and methodology concerning children and their development are viewed as knowledge nested in historical contexts. Therefore, this book presents a range of new conceptualizations and ideas, bringing in a perspective that will hopefully inspire others. Needless to say, there are areas important for the understanding of young children's lives in our changing times that are not covered by this book. The book should be viewed as asking some questions and proposing some answers only about the specific topics chosen – as a beginning, not an end.

It is important to say that dealing with the specific topics selected for this book (thus not dealing with numerous other aspects) does not imply any explicit or implicit normality agenda. What, for example, is typical in one developmental context may be untypical in another. The developmental context in this book is mainly a Western late modern – to some extent even a Scandinavian – early childhood. Even within this context, various forms of childhoods are lived that are not covered in this book. In addition, it is not claimed that the range of new concepts developed are necessarily relevant in the understanding of such childhoods. If we extrapolate to global contexts, the enormous complexities of childhoods and the inequalities of young children's lives across and within late modern societies have to be acknowledged. There is an urgent need for new research networks that will address this global imbalance. This should become a future priority for interdisciplinary childhood and child research. In the understanding of global childhoods, research has, until now, just scratched the surface, and as Woodhead (2009, p. 52) says: 'it is fair to say that knowledge of the developmental experiences for the great majority of the world's children has been and still is in very short supply'.

The main source of inspiration in this book is international research drawn from many sources and professional disciplines that are relevant to enhance our understanding of young children's childhoods, their everyday life, socialization and development in late modern society and culture. This book does not join the list of general, psychological developmental theories about young children. Instead, it presents a *contextual new reality discipline*.[1] In a historical perspective, societies change significantly and the focus here is on today's realities – the young child embedded in a late modern era. Even if social scientists disagree on what constitutes the most essential aspects of living in a rapidly changing society, there may be less disagreement about the fact that our current era offers qualitatively different conditions from previous eras.[2] Such societal changes have challenged widely held professional ideas about typical socialization patterns and normal development, as well as commonsense psychological beliefs about which 'normal conditions' lead to a well-developed child. In an understanding of young children's new reality, it is misleading to use top-down, general, universal psychological development principles to explain these recent historical and cultural changes. Such an approach, which later in this book will be positioned as pre-paradigm shift theorizing, has now mainly been discarded (Rogoff, 2003; Woodhead and Montgomery, 2003; Fogel et al., 2006, 2009; Woodhead, 2009; Bornstein, 2010).

Why is such an approach misleading? Because it places the child in a *Procrustean bed*, 'bending and stretching' the child to make them fit into a set of developmental principles.[3] A top-down approach may also lead to unwarranted pessimism and confusion in the assessment of today's young children's 'proper' life and development. The reason is that the new childhood realities do not match previous normal ways of living and established 'law-like' requirements for healthy psychological development. Such pessimism – apart from when there is real cause for concern for children's welfare – may actually turn into a general 'childhood concern'; for example, when mothers, as they do in the child's first years of life, work and leave their child in childcare, thus violating the principle of the primacy of mother–child bonding. Current knowledge about the developmental consequences of growing up simultaneously in family/childcare forces us to draw quite different conclusions about healthy growing up environments.

Several reasons can be found behind an observable shift in international child research in recent decades. First, a rapidly growing number of children live under conditions that require new disciplinary approaches. So, indirectly or directly, new realities open up new research fields. When large numbers of young children started attending childcare, childcare research soon became a new discipline. Second, as a parallel process, developmental research caused considerable changes over time. In the late 1980s, Parke (1989) evaluated this situation. Despite childhood having undergone substantial changes throughout the 20th century up to the 1960s and 70s, this was rarely reflected in child psychology theories or empirical research. Until then, researchers focused mostly on describing general principles that governed children's development, regardless of time and place. Freudian, Piagetian and learning theories were at the forefront in that period.

Changes are becoming increasingly global; for example, the 2007–08 financial crisis has had worldwide consequences for families and children. However, other crucial changes, especially in relation to young children, occurred earlier in the immediate postwar period, with the establishment of welfare systems, consumerism and so on. This was a time when, in some parts of the world, increasing numbers of women joined the labour market. In a Scandinavian context, for example, Langsted and Sommer's (1992) evaluation of empirical evidence and statistics documented almost revolutionary changes in children's conditions during the 1950s and 60s and concluded: 'childhood is not what it used to be'. A recent monograph studying the families and children of today concluded that the process of change had accelerated (Sommer, 2008a). This seems to be a worldwide process, although not necessarily having the same speed or within the same phenomena, due to major cultural and economic differences in different parts of the world (Bornstein, 2010, Part II). Nevertheless, the changing situation produces new realities and substantially restructures early childhood in many parts of the world. The constantly shifting relationship between society, culture and children's childhoods challenges our well-established child psychology knowledge. This highlights the importance of not merely acknowledging change as a fact, but also accepting it by calling for a new set of professional understandings.

The term *childhood* psychology is used in the title of this book instead of the term *child* psychology, because until recently (in Scandinavia at least), the latter term has been closely associated with universal stage theories, precisely the type of general psychological view of children that this book denounces. For example, a standard reference book on education and psychology defines child psychology as: 'a psychological discipline that focuses on typical developmental stages in children' (Jerlang and Jerlang, 2001, p. 31). This definition invokes the image of the young child living in a 'bell jar', an isolated maturing young child, separated from society, culture and everyday life.[4] Hopefully, this book will help clarify the major differences between such a view and an alternative approach based on contemporary research. Despite being presented as state of the art, the above definition seems outdated today, reflecting the inertia of knowledge. Since the beginning of child psychology, more than 100 years ago, stage theories dominated until the late 1960s, influenced by a diversity of theorists, ranging from Freud and Erikson to Piaget. In the above definition, child psychology is defined by a set of fixed typical stages that 'all children go through'. Despite time and place, development is the same for everyone, depending on maturity and ontological age-specific organization.

Child psychology is no longer definable as being synonymous with stage development. Today, the discipline is far too heterogeneous and diverse for stage theories to make up an overarching definitional frame. As a consequence, recent definitions do not acknowledge that ontogenesis is organized by well-defined, qualitatively different, age-specific stages. Some still do, albeit in a modified form compared to the grand classical developmental approach (Berk, 2009).[5] *A Childhood Psychology* does, however, recognize that elements of traditional stage theories may be adapted and incorporated into a comprehensive understanding of children's everyday life in society and culture. For instance, apart from his general and universal drive model, Freud made interesting clinical observations of various defence mechanisms that have proved valid. Although 'denial' is a psychoanalytical clinical construction, it can be observed in relatively common use in everyday life and fulfils many purposes. However, the challenge of extracting useful knowledge from old theories has to be left for later.

But how is the often highly domain-specific new research and theory to be used, approaches that do not deal with young children embedded in a cultural and societal context? One hope is that theoretical purism may gradually give way to creative theoretical interdisciplinarity. The time fighting for purism seems to have gone in the leading research of today. In accordance with Luthar (2006), we should guard against narrow parochial interests that invest more energy in the protection of professional turf than in serving the best interests of children and families based on a broad professional understanding arising from various disciplines. New combinations will hopefully emerge in the future, with various elements taken from multiple theories or far-reaching revisions of the original basis for a given theoretical position, necessitated by new empirical findings and/or changes in children's living conditions. One example of this is the use of the highly domain-specific attachment theory and research. Monotropic, one-to-one attachment is replaced by research into multiple attachments, specifically used to explain the unknown developmental consequences of the young child's new reality of simultaneously growing up in a dual family/childcare context.

Another reason for the use in this book of childhood, together with psychology, is that childhood as a distinct age category is overlooked in much child and developmental psychology. For example, in international textbooks on child and developmental psychology, childhood is sometimes mentioned, but not dealt with in its own right, even in books that emphasize context and culture (for example Berk, 2009). Childhood was recently introduced as a subject of study in its own right by a group of groundbreaking sociologists, who were critical of the dogma of the grand developmental theories in psychology (for an introduction to the field, see Qvortrup et al., 2009). Childhood is defined as an age-specific period with specific characteristics that makes it different from adulthood. In ontogenesis, individual children leave their childhood when entering adolescence. In addition, childhood has some specific properties that are qualitatively different at the level of the individual (Qvortrup, 2009). Childhood is not a uniform age period, but can change, and is perceived and experienced differently between and in societies and cultures, as well as historically. In summary, childhood is constructed and shaped by historical, ideological and social factors – an important dimension in *A Childhood Psychology*. However, a balance is sought. Overemphasizing a historical and sociological approach or using it alone would mean losing sight of the young child's actual psychological development. Hence the childhood dimension is complemented by and integrated with child psychological research.

On the one hand, it is difficult to interpret psychological phenomena, such as thoughts, feelings and behaviour, without examining them in their cultural and social contexts. On the other hand, it is vital to understand society and culture without viewing them as complex 'materialized' products of human agency. The two dimensions – society and culture – as well as the culture-producing human, do not reflect a duality but are complementary and highlight the fundamentally social *Homo sapiens* as influenced by both culture and tradition and being a culture producer (Tomasello, 1999, 2009; Tomasello et al., 2005).

As this is not a classical textbook, but an advanced, reflective reader, the demand to cover all types of psychological domains is reduced. The focus of this book is more on *socioemotional development* in a changing reality and less on children's cognitive development, although this does not infer that the latter is unimportant. Within a contextual frame of reference, to some extent comparable with the paradigm of this book, others have addressed the topic of children's cognitive development (for example Rogoff, 1990, 2003; Cole, 1996; Cole and Cagigas, 2010). Thus many of the developmental principles presented may also apply to cognitive development.

Writing a book about childhood in our times, including an evaluation of professional and commonsense beliefs, one question repeatedly comes to mind: Is professional knowledge about children inherently *normative*? If so, is normativity an inescapable aspect of *A Childhood Psychology*? To some extent, this seems to be the case. Examples will be presented later on how child psychology is permeated, sometimes behind the lines, by ideological contamination and normative claims of how people *ought to live their lives*. Behind the worlds we construe lie the worldviews that give our perceptions of the world their dominant character. This point has an important consequence for the presentation of research-based knowledge; the basic paradigms at work have to be emphasized to the reader, and not remain latent governing conclusions. Despite this, it is perhaps easier to critically judge the 'old paradigms' than the 'new paradigms' – including the ones we adhere to ourselves.

Social science may be in danger of dogma and normativity, but the same science has a healthy tradition of open critique and discussion. It is important here to point out that a researcher must approach potential normative knowledge in a different way from the mass media and the general public. If a journalist writes a story on a specific case, an eye-catching conclusion may be the start of the article (perhaps even the headline), with research information chosen to explain the case and 'prove' the conclusion. A key criterion for a researcher, however, is to establish normative validity by staying normatively impartial, and opinions and assessments are, in principle, not predetermined or mainly subjectively biased. Fundamental beliefs about children develop gradually and emerge as an *essence* of long-time research work; in addition, this perception is, in principle, permanently open to revision.

Present knowledge is temporary, because research is constantly involved in a process of renewal. An established insight is threatened by the fact that our knowledge is insufficient, even when we think it meaningful and adequate. The essence of research is that new findings and insights constantly force a reassessment of previous positions. In addition, young children's childhoods are changing, and thus challenging established knowledge. Therefore, any reader in search of 'hard truths' about young children's new reality will be disappointed with this book. It is crucial to accept the relative nature of research, and the concomitant uncertainty caused by fresh insights. So, *A Childhood Psychology* should be seen more as a process rather than a finished product. Acquiring new knowledge about childhood psychology in our times means going into uncharted territory, travelling like the youngest brother in *Clumsy Hans*, a fairytale by Hans Christian Andersen. The youngest brother was unfamiliar with the route to the castle, unlike his learned brothers. Instead, he had the open mind and confidence that young children possess, which made him to go off the beaten track, seeking and finding inspiration along the way. In the end, he was the one chosen by the princess. Readers are encouraged to approach the book in this spirit.

HOW: OVERVIEW OF THE BOOK

Chapter 1 reviews some of the key paradigm shifts in the perception of the child in international research before, during and after the 1960s. Selected new research generating new perceptions of child development are presented: the movement from family- and mother-centricity towards a growing acknowledgement of the young child's expanded socioemotional world. Furthermore, the important academic shift from the old notion of the exclusively fragile child to the new perception of children as relatively resilient although still susceptible to negative childhood conditions will be dealt with. Then a research-based perception of children's early social competencies is presented. The focus is not on the competent child; instead, competence should be seen as a relative and conditional term. Next, development is argued for without stage concepts and stage theory; instead, development is seen in relation to various contextual levels, as the acquisition of functional competencies in social context, culture and everyday life. Subsequently, development is described as a transactional process, in which simplistic notions of cause and effect are discarded. In closing, the chapter outlines *A Childhood Psychology* as a contextual discipline. This is expressed in nine theses that form the general framework of the book.

Chapter 2 focuses on early childhood in our rapidly changing times and how this provokes established fundamental beliefs and challenges theory. Childhood is constructed, both directly and indirectly, by societal change. The chapter takes its departure in late modernity by summarizing the vital characteristics of this era and the consequences for understanding young children's childhoods. In addition, this is specified by documentation of the importance of the growing phenomenon of working mothers. The relatively new out-of-home care is a reality for families in many parts of the world, indicating that families are not the only caring context for a young generation. Childhood is also created by fundamental beliefs of children that are expressed in a given historical era. Beliefs are defined as 'interpretative filters' that make us 'see' and understand in specific ways. When changes alter the 'natural' ways of living, fundamental beliefs may be challenged and manifested. To illustrate this, documentation from the international childcare debate shows how this new reality has provoked fundamental beliefs of what is assumed best for a child. Recent childcare research is reviewed and conclusions reached about the real developmental consequences of early childcare. In our current late modern times, fundamental academic conceptualizations of childhood and young children's development are challenged. Among this the classical primary/secondary socialization paradigm is critically discussed, and new perspectives are presented – intersubjectivity, companionship, multiple caring and dual socialization.

Chapter 3 lays the foundation for a contemporary theory about the child's culture acquisition. The paradigm of the passive-receptive child is criticized, because it fails to explain 'originality'. As an alternative, the child's active acquisition of culture is connected to the structure of culture – the young child's development of appropriate functional social competencies. A model is presented to describe important relationships between culture and children's development. Here adults are portrayed as mediators of society and culture in the way they organize and share a meaningful everyday life. However, children's role as active participants in their own developmental process is a key axiom. Then selected observations of young children's specific relationship competencies are shown. After that, learning is approached as, in principle, based on human curiosity and a fundamental wish to participate. Everyday learning is highlighted as a situational approach, and the importance of adopting a child perspective is discussed. The chapter closes pointing to a 'developmental duality' in Western late modernity, with its demands for individuality and independence, as well as the cultural need to become a social being who cooperates with others.

Chapter 4 is the first chapter to discuss parenting. It brings in new understandings by elaborating on the theoretical foundation established in Chapter 3. More specifically, it is about emergent themes and trends in parenting, families and caring in late modern early childhood. First, parenting is viewed from a family relationship approach, by seeing the family as a dynamic group where all roles and relationships are taken into consideration. Subsequently, an emergent trend of 'negotiation families' is presented and discussed in detail. Some expected behavioural characteristics of children from such families are also addressed. Next, selected parenting styles are presented, discussed and evaluated for their developmental potential. Then the everyday choreography of active parenting is presented, introducing a proposal for a new understanding of parental practices. Finally, cultural and personal caring is discussed, and care is highlighted, defined and discussed as a specific relationship quality.

Chapter 5 also focuses on parenting, with fathering as a possible emergent trend and father involvement as an important potential developmental resource for the child. First, shared parenting in late modern families with working mothers is raised and discussed. Then, significant professional barriers behind the lack of acceptance of paternal potential for the child is presented – how mothers are mythologized and fathers instrumentalized. Theories on bonding, attachment and infancy as a particularly critical period are presented and critically evaluated. Research on father involvement is presented and discussed to document that fathers have the potential to be just as crucial to children's development as mothers. Finally, the involvement of fathers is situated in its broader context.

Chapter 6 presents a coherent psychological theory on early child development, which is relevant to the paradigm shift in *A Childhood Psychology*. The chapter is not only based on a review, but on a professional discussion of Daniel Stern's groundbreaking theory on self-development in infancy. This theory portrays the human infant as far more socioaffectively competent and developmentally active than previously assumed. This highly creative endeavour, and in many regards unique attempt, combines knowledge from a range of disciplines, including modern psychoanalysis, observational research, philosophy and holistic perception theory. However, *A Childhood Psychology* subjects Stern's theory of self to a somewhat critical review. What does the theory say about contextualism and the role of culture? What consequences can be drawn, understanding core aspects of self? The relationships between cultural differences and panhuman similarities in self-development are evaluated according to Stern's view and discussed in relation to recent cross-cultural research.

Chapter 7 summarizes the main points of the book. First, fundamental changes in theory and research are outlined. After that, important different professional ideas, the pre-paradigm versus *A Childhood Psychology* post-paradigm position, are highlighted. Then a contextual level approach is introduced, summarizing and discussing key elements in the understanding of young children's development in a changing world. This is followed by a section suggesting, arguing for and discussing interdisciplinarity. Examples are given by pointing to some promising 'conceptual stepping stones' identified between childhood sociology and selected main ideas of this book. In closing, the chapter reflects on what affects development in the long run, and the relative importance of the childhood period in the context of the full human life span will be illuminated.

Each chapter aims to offer logical extensions to and elaborate on these preliminary statements. The chapters pursue a number of different themes; two leading perspectives, however, will be present throughout:

1. The perception of *young children as relatively socially competent* – human beings who are equipped from birth (perhaps even during gestation) with potential that directs them towards human communication, ready to engage in and learn through meaningful relationships with others.
2. The premise that knowledge about children has to be seen in its *historical and cultural context* from which knowledge springs and in which it is embedded, and which it even has the potential to influence.

These themes are addressed in a number of ways, directly and indirectly, throughout the book.

1

A CHILDHOOD PSYCHOLOGY: A PARADIGM SHIFT

The past 30–40 years have witnessed significant discoveries in research on children. Theory has changed radically, and new knowledge from a large body of empirical studies has essentially altered researchers' views of children and their development. This change can be regarded as a paradigm shift, which separates time before and after the 1960s. A paradigm is a set of fundamental assumptions, working hypotheses, theories and methods that form the basis of scientific research within a certain field. Paradigm 'shift' means that basic assumptions have undergone a fundamental change. This chapter offers an outline of general features that characterize important shifts in the field; it also functions as an introduction to the approach of *A Childhood Psychology*, and thereby forms the underlying and principal premises of this book. Needless to say, it is beyond the scope of a single chapter to offer an in-depth evaluation of all existing theories and empirical research. However, a broad selection of unconnected theories and research will be presented, provided they have been instrumental in changing the paradigm, as even very different psychological approaches may reflect a correspondent, underlying scientific endeavour, in the sense that they are embedded in a common zeitgeist.

In this chapter, major paradigmatic changes in the perception of children's development will be outlined. This is followed by a discussion of how developmental stage theories have been normatively used as benchmarks for normal development. An alternative is presented, seeing development as a transactional and constructive web. Finally, as guidelines for the book, nine contextual theses are presented.

11

CHANGES IN THE PERCEPTION OF
CHILDREN'S DEVELOPMENT

The recent paradigm shift in theory and research has seen a number of fundamental changes in the perception of children. Even in the late 1980s, it was possible to draw a line in the sand. According to Parke (1989), several shifts occurred within the previous 25 years. One such major shift was the fading ambition to develop general psychological theories with relatively few fundamental, developmental principles and yet wide-ranging explanatory power. Despite major theory differences, the so-called *grand developmental approach* was prevalent before and during the 1960s, which attempted to conceptualize children's development through a limited number of general, universal principles.[6] Examples include the theories presented by Freud and other psychoanalysts, Piaget, social learning theories, as well as bodies of theory within the school of cultural history and Soviet psychology. The grand developmental era resonated with ideas coined in the Age of Enlightenment. Scientists' ambitions were not aimed at construction, but at the discovery of a given phenomenon, by unravelling its inherent logic and general organization and thus revealing inner developmental regularities.

In other words, this powerful paradigm of 'developmentalism' aspired to deduce 'the essence' behind all forms of manifestations and explain 'everything' by building grandiose theories, just as natural science did. Some were also driven by the ambition to outline a normal developmental course by delineating normative, typical stages that children at various ages had to experience (White, 1983; Fischer and Bidell, 2006). Another characteristic of this period was its '-ism tendency' (a sign of the times not merely restricted to psychology) in its struggle to be a hegemonic theory. For example, being 'a Freudian' meant a lifelong involvement with the all-encompassing theory of psychoanalysis; being a 'behaviourist' signified appraising fundamental S-R principles, which claimed to explain all learning; while being a 'Piagetian' involved following his theory of cognitive development, which, as a general epistemology, had far-reaching implications for the understanding of emotions and sociality. Consequently, theories rubber-stamped explanations that were supposed to account for and were used on a wide range of developmental qualities and changes. In their historical tour de force *The Making of Developmental Psychology*, Cairns and Cairns (2006, p. 147) state:

> But none of the models achieved clear dominance, and the science could not claim as its own a unifying theory…Indeed, advances in identifying the contextual events that determined actions and learning raised questions on whether general theory of behavioral development was possible.

This statement has proved to be right during the past 40 years or more, in that it has been increasingly problematic to apply top-down principles on a growing number of empirical studies (Berk, 2009). It is certainly the case with specific developmental domains, which the grand developmental approach is not conceptually equipped to handle, on neither a general level nor in detail. At the same time, doubt about the teleological stance, 'knowing the developmental course beforehand', was sneaking into the humanistic and social sciences. In developmental psychology, this is seen in the stage theories, where the developmental sequence must go from childish immaturity to the final stage of adult maturity.

The growing acknowledgement of the relative openness and continuance of societal, cultural and human change was a process that occurred not only in psychology, but has also been part of a broader paradigmatic shift across a multitude of sciences, as late modernity succeeded classical modernity. Thus, in psychology, the search for underlying universal regularities behind children's development has not become obsolete per se, but the top-down, grand developmental approach has gradually been superseded by 'bottom-up' inferences made on the basis of empirical evidence. One illuminating example of this trend is the empirically driven controversy of early ontogenetic knowledge about the properties of the physical world. Is an infant's surprise in an experiment when a solid thing (a toy car) goes through another solid thing (a wall) – inferring that it should not be possible – explained by an innate 'core knowledge', or a 'fast-learning mechanism' (Spelke et al., 1992; Baillargeon, 1994; Spelke and Kinzler, 2007)? This is just one example of the increasing specialization in developmental psychology that has led to a rapid increase in *mini theories*.[7] Unlike the broad grand developmental approach, these aim to explain specific aspects of children's development.

Therefore, the overall assessment of development since the 1960s is that while the grand theories have lost their interpretative power and appeal, there is now a requirement for theories to offer relatively detailed conceptualization and explanation of specific aspects of children's development. Combinations of detailed knowledge from different disciplines were seen during this period, for example Shantz's (1983) early integration of cognition research and knowledge about children's social development led to the discipline of social cognition. A recent example of an integrative discipline is the combination of intentionality, imitation, early language acquisition, cognition and evolution (Tomasello, 1999, 2005, 2009; Charman, 2006).

Nevertheless, the field has been increasingly influenced by domain-specific theories, that is, development of knowledge that is limited to clearly defined domains of children's development.[8] Parke (1989) concluded that despite integrative efforts, the scope of these theoretical endeavours was strictly limited in relation to the situation before and during the 1960s, although there was a growing interest in contextualist thinking in developmental psychology in the 1970s and 80s (for example Reese, 1991). Luthar (2006) warns that what she calls the excessive splintering of psychology as a field has been deplored. In the future, it will be ill-advised to remain insulated from other people's research that clearly overlaps with one's own. This sentiment is endorsed in this book. But the problem is what the next step should be, which is still unanswered. In a recent evaluation of the still fragmented situation and as a potential solution, Witherington (2007) advocates a unifying metatheory for developmental psychology to be found in the dynamic systems perspective. What remains, however, is the hugely difficult task of combining the dynamic systems approach (divided between a pure contextualist and an organismic contextualist orientation) with the growing multitude of domain-specific research. Nonetheless, as presented later in this chapter, the dynamic systems approach has proved inspiring and useful. Therefore, in this context, it will be interwoven with *A Childhood Psychology* stance. Furthermore, until the 1960s, child and developmental psychology were only moderately interested in studying children's lives and development across cultures and history. This will also be remedied in this book.

Childhood has changed, and so have the scientific views of children and their development. Below, selected crucial elements of the child paradigm are introduced. It is important to say that the following is an outline; the themes introduced here will be elaborated and used later in the book.

From family- and mother-centricity to the expanded world of the child

Prior to the paradigm shift, the socialization theories widely used in social psychology and developmental psychology undisputedly assumed that so-called *primary socialization* took place within the family (the site of basic personality formation). This point of view had a significant impact on the perception of the nature of the child and their need to be socialized. In his classic text, Brown (1965, p. 193) stated:

> The American sociologist, Talcott Parsons, has called the birth of new generations of children a recurrent barbarian invasion. He does not mean barbarian in the sense of Neolithic humans living by hunting and fishing but in the familiar popular sense which holds a barbarian to be an uncultured or non-socialized person. Human infants do not possess culture at birth; they do not have a conception of the world, a language, or a morality. All of these things must be acquired by them, and the process of acquisition is called socialization.

In other words, the belief at this time was that the child was perceived as a barbarian or savage who was essentially non-social by nature and had to be turned into a social person through the process of primary socialization. As will be shown in Chapter 2, this belief has been undermined by subsequent research. The above understanding is rooted in empirical research and theories concerning the traditional pre-1960s nuclear family (females as housewives, males as breadwinners). During the 1960s and since, this family set-up ceased to be the typical early childhood in many societies (Dencik et al., 2008). When placed in their proper context, that is, situated in time and place, traditional socialization concepts attempt to explain the relatively brief historical period when the gender-segregated, nuclear family formed the functional normal setting for children's first years of life. However, such a theory has lost its legitimacy in a late modern world, by losing the ability to interpret contemporary children's real lives and experiences.

Nevertheless, this conditioned and relative knowledge is still presented as generally applicable insights in textbooks, for example in social psychology. Despite living in a family/childcare context where the majority of children's typical social geography is greatly expanded, Katzenelson (1994, p. 177, translated for this edition) defines primary socialization as:

> Primary childhood socialization normally takes place in the bosom of the family, the general seat of basic formation and reinforcement of person and personality. This occurs through profound influences from significant others, who during this period incarnate the child's entire cultural world with their attitudes, role expectations and role performances.

This classical definition has no theoretical consideration for the eventual positive/negative impact of experiences that infants encounter in contexts *outside the family*. So can we assume that children's childcare and preschool experiences have no significant developmental impact during the early years of life? Research based on contemporary lifestyles documents that although the family is still crucial, childcare has a profound influence on young children's development during the first years of their lives (NICHD Early Child Care Research Network, 2005; Clarke-Stewart and Allhusen, 2005). Similarly, there is ample evidence of the existence of fundamental socializing factors besides the family in contemporary childhood, which makes it difficult to reserve the term 'primary socialization' to a particular developmental period that, normatively speaking, takes place within the family. In all, the problem is that the classic socialization paradigm does not acknowledge important personality-forming factors, apart from the family, during the child's first years of life, which is reminiscent of the *family-centric* pre-paradigm shift period.

The implications of family-centrism are both substantial and negative. The family is considered sine qua none for the child's development, and, at best, other factors may only play a secondary role. Some presentations based on classical socialization perceptions regard any competition to the primary position of the family as cause for concern. This is often referred to as the 'family being stripped of its functions', that is, the late modern family has lost its primary functions – caring and socialization (Sommer, 2008b).[9] This argument has been opposed not only by research that depicts the consequences for children who live in family and childcare contexts, but also by theoretical reformulations. As a replacement of the classical understanding of socialization, Chapter 2 presents the 'dual socialization butterfly', a contextual holistic model that visualizes the complementary socializing impact of children's actual developmental settings of today. Furthermore, the model integrates and explains present and future empirical findings.

Prior to the paradigm shift, with only a few exceptions, child and developmental psychology was distinctly *mother-centric*. As early as the 1980s, it was concluded that theory together with empirical studies had narrowed the infant's social world down to being an exclusive mother–infant relationship with no room for other significant persons (Scarr and Dunn, 1987). Freud was not the only one to celebrate a mother's unique status. However, he did play a key role as the theoretical leader of a generation of psychoanalysts, who, in the grand developmental era, had a tremendous impact on child psychology. Freud's contribution to mother-centricity is expressed in his elevated description of the mother: [She is] 'unique, without equal, established unchanged through a life time as the first and strongest object of love, as a prototype for all other love affairs – for both sexes' (Freud, 1975, p. 188).

As will be discussed later on, mother-centricity is linked to a historical idealization of motherhood that goes back several centuries. Furthermore, examples are given of the way in which mother-centricity is reproduced even in relatively modern child theories. Here, suffice to say that psychoanalytical and ethological approaches (early attachment theory) in the mid-20th century had a strong influence on the view of motherhood (and childhood). At the time, child psychology considered early personality formation as practically synonymous with descriptions of the early mother–infant relationship (Haavind, 1987; Phoenix et al., 1991; Eyer, 1993).

Alternatives to the narrow mother-centric view of early development are found within the growing number of empirical studies of infants' relationships to other people apart from the mother. International research into fathers and infants began in the mid-1970s and constitutes one of the earliest examples of the growing criticism of the mother-centric point of view (Lamb, 1976a; Parke, 1996). Subsequently, research has included a variety of human relationships that occur in children's real environments – mothers, fathers, siblings, grandparents, peers, childcare staff, teachers and so on. So the 1990s witnessed a drive to establish a more comprehensive and profound psychological understanding of the child's *multipersonal world* (Pianta, 1992).

Again, it should be kept in mind that children's cultural embeddedness plays an important role in the interpretation of research, including research into fundamental aspects of development. Examples of this are caring and attachment that vary with children's cultural backgrounds, and one should be cautious of deducing general principles from research on the quality of children's social contacts (Jackson, 1993; Rothbaum et al., 2000; Kagitcibasi, 2007). As Chapter 2 will show, studies of the infant's multipersonal world have shed new and surprising light on children's early social and emotional competencies, and this knowledge poses serious challenges to the mother-centric paradigm, which dominated prior to the 1960s. From then onwards, the prevailing view was that *provided children received quality care*, they would develop competencies that enabled them to thrive in an expanded social world from a young age (Schaffer, 1990).

Children: fragile or resilient?

Concurrent with these attempts at studying children in their actual social worlds, there was a shift in the way some researchers viewed children, based on a growing acknowledgement of infants' ability to develop in a socially expanding world. A widely held perception of children among profession-als prior to the paradigm shift may be summarized by the phrase *the frag-ile child*. Various theoretical perceptions converged in a belief about the child's ontological 'dependency' and fundamental 'vulnerability'. Clinical and psychoanalytical perceptions dominated internationally in the 1960s, and consequently a *psychopathological perception* of even normal children was dominant.[10] The professional agenda at the time focused mostly on children as victims of deprivation and trauma, and conflicts governing childhood development. This idea is illustrated in Figure 1.1.

First, a direct connection is seen between early critical phases and later pathology or normality. This means that every phase has its own distinct and direct contribution to later developmental functioning. For example, a later

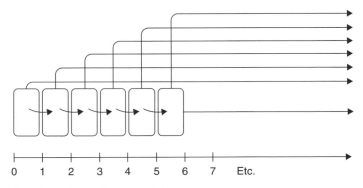

Figure 1.1   The critical phase model

indulgence in, for example, alcohol or substance abuse will be explained by a 'fixation' on an early oral stage. Second, a more indirect relationship is seen between early and later development, indicating that specific, stage-bound conflict 'solutions' influence the next stage and so on.

In this approach, developmental deficiencies or disorders were widely generalized and applied to normal development. An underlying premise was that the difference between pathological and normal function was only a matter of degree, and hence it became legitimate to apply theory concerning disorders and deficiencies to the field of normal development. However, there is a weak basis for assuming that children's normal development and functioning including pathological processes can be explained by conceptualizations stemming from psychopathology. Thus, the concept of the fragile child relates to pre-paradigm shift beliefs, a top-down ontology rather than a realistic understanding of the child. In his look back at the hegemonic period of psychoanalysis, Stern (2006) states that developmental theories, such as those of Freud, Mahler and Erikson, were inspired by and based on fantasies about the nature of the infant. In other words, they constructed a child in the eye of the beholder as a 'psychoanalytic projection on the child'.

However, the paradigmatic dominance of the fragile child position has weakened since the 1960s. Researchers have increasingly been involved in studying infants' and children's *relative resilience* (Sommer, 2011). Today, it is generally acknowledged that the pre-1960s paradigm exaggerated children's vulnerability and underestimated their capabilities. This shift in perspective springs from a number of sources. Recent developmental studies have not focused on pathology and selected problem cases, but on what was expected as typically occurring phenomena. This has uncovered considerable, hitherto unrecognized capacities in children generally, and an ability to compensate for early developmental deficiencies in particular (Schaffer, 1990; Luthar et al., 2000; Luthar, 2006; Masten, 2007). There has been a growing awareness of children's relative mental flexibility and psychological capacity for coping with stress.

This has removed focus from the one-sided study of developmental deficiencies towards a much broader view of the developmental process. To mention just one example of the revolutionary work in the field, early maternal deprivation, which in the 1960s was considered as sine qua none for the development of later emotional disturbances, was being strongly criticized in light of new empirical research in the 1970s (Rutter, 1972), and this approach has now been discarded (Rutter, 1991, 2008). Assessments of children's future prospects have to incorporate the child's entire social world and experiences over time (Bronfenbrenner, 1979). Isolated trauma and negative incidents are important when they occur, but do not necessarily predict children's long-term prospects, although long-term stress and negative influences throughout childhood may adversely influence the development process. Thus, after the paradigm shift, it still has to be acknowledged that there are limits to children's flexibility and adaptability. Admittedly, a child may have the capacity to adapt to change during ontogenesis (Rutter, 2008).

By questioning the concept of the fragile child, one should steer clear of the polarized notion of the 'robust child'. For example, it is rarely meaningful to discuss absolute vulnerability or absolute robustness in children. Instead, the development process may be characterized by relative and varying relations between exposure to environmental influences and the ability to compensate for relatively stressful conditions. Thus critics of the fragility paradigm still have to acknowledge that infants, toddlers and older children may be both vulnerable and fragile, and that good quality care is needed throughout childhood.

The challenge to the old paradigm is that the one-sided focus on fragility, developmental crises and risks makes it difficult to grasp the complex development potential and the child's ability to regenerate. The classical view in which the infant is regarded purely as a dependent, passive and vulnerable being, whose main need is protection from danger, detracts from infants' capacities and resources, which recent research has so amply documented. The move away from the one-sided focus on vulnerability is noticeable. In a textbook about infancy, the shift in perspective is coined as follows:

> Traditionally, there has been a clear tendency to focus more on vulnerability and psychopathology and little interest in the large group of at-risk children who do well despite poor care. In recent years, there has been a growing emphasis on factors that may protect development. (Smith and Ulvund, 1999, pp. 19–20, translated for this edition)

In developmental psychology, the fragility concept has been replaced by the subtler professional term *resilience*. Resilience has a range of meanings, including elasticity and the ability to rebound or recoil after pressure. Consequently, it is more appropriate than the previously applied term fragility. Expected normal development may be envisioned as an 'elastic membrane'. In its resting state, the membrane maintains its normal shape, but external pressures may push it out of shape. If the pressure is relatively brief, the membrane quickly returns to its original shape. If, however, the pressure is sustained over time, it will take longer for the membrane to return to its normal state. With the inherent limitations of any metaphor, this image serves to illustrate relative developmental flexibility, elasticity and regenerative potential.

This paradigm is supported by research, which shows that some (but not all) people are able to recover after relatively serious and difficult childhood conditions (Schaffer, 1990; Cicchetti and Garmezy, 1993; Rutter and Rutter, 1993; Sameroff, 2007). However, the capacity to recover is only one side of the coin. The membrane metaphor also illustrates possible chronic developmental damage that occurs over time. Constant and sustained pressure may eventually cause the membrane to freeze in an abnormal position. With time, it becomes increasingly possible that the membrane loses the flexibility to return to its normal state. Thus permanent disorders rarely occur over night, but over time, negative developmental life conditions and experiences may result in *abnormal stability*. The membrane metaphor also allows for the possibility that extreme, sudden external pressure may cause the membrane to burst. Furthermore, the metaphor allows for the possibility that individual children are more or less sensitive. For example, some membranes may be thinner or thicker, reflecting individual variations in sensitivity to negative environmental pressures. Examples of particularly vulnerable children may include temperamentally sensitive children, children with birth and/or brain defects and children born prematurely (Schaffer, 1990; Berk, 2009). But even in this context, it is essential to focus on vulnerable children's dynamic (albeit different and perhaps typical) interaction with their environment in order to understand their developmental course, because seeking explanations in personality factors and endogenous vulnerability is only one facet of the whole picture.

The resilience concept has more connotations than the concept of the exclusively vulnerable child and the opposite notion of children's absolute 'invulnerability' and 'robustness'. The term 'resilience' embraces meanings that are helpful in avoiding stereotypes and any absolute labelling of children and their development process. This view was expressed by Luthar et al. (2000) when they outlined the history of the resilience concept. Perceptions about resilience as absolute or global, in contrast to resilience as something relative and contingent, have changed considerably over the years. In some earlier books and articles, children who coped well with many risk factors were labelled as 'invulnerable'. This was misleading because the avoidance of risk was absolute and unchangeable. As research improved, it became clear that positive adaptation, despite the exposure to adversity, implies a developmental progression in a way that new types of vulnerability and/or strength follow as a consequence of changed living conditions. Thus, it is not a question of either accepting the paradigm of the child's inherent vulnerability or, in naive optimism, exaggerating late modern children's robustness and powers of regeneration.

Polarized views do not promote good professional dialogue or research. Both extremes are constantly present as complementary dimensions in the lifelong development process. For some children, vulnerability dominates at certain times in their lives, while it may be less dominant at other times. For other children, it remains relatively constant throughout life. Humans differ in the way they encounter and cope with living conditions, which can also change over time. This makes it difficult to clearly define 'identical environmental factors' and their impact. These arguments make it a complex matter to understand how humans change over time, and how susceptible they are throughout their lifetime. However, this reflects the challenging situation of how the complexities of development cannot be expressed in a simple formula.

Researchers look for regularities and patterns in this complexity, and in this search, the concept of resilience is currently an acknowledged professional term in international developmental psychology, although it is also the subject of debate in the search for improvement and refinement (see the discussion in Waters et al., 2000a, 2000b). Through the years, resilience has not been understood in the same way. Some researchers have used it to define particular personality features in children, such as charm, autonomy, optimism, confidence and a tendency to forget the past, qualities that are believed to protect children who grow up in adverse environments (Masten and Garmezy, 1985). These and other protective personality features have been referred to as *ego-resilience* (Block and Block, 1980). A perhaps unintended implication of this view may give the impression that some individuals simply 'have what it takes' to overcome difficult conditions, while others are bound to fail. This view would imply that the untapped resources lie not in the difficult environment, but rather within the intrinsic personality of a child.

A Scandinavian example of this decontextualized approach is the term 'dandelion child'. This metaphor celebrates the idea that some children from underprivileged environments have the personal strength to thrive, despite adverse childhood conditions. Equally, the metaphor implies that some children defy conditions and perhaps even gain nourishment from them by flourishing, resembling another one-dimensional phrase – 'the ironing effect'. This means that exposure to adverse conditions in life hardens children, making them invulnerable to later stress. The term 'mould-breaker' also has similarities with the term ego-resilience, by implying that there are particular qualities and strengths within the individual that make it possible for them to thrive despite a difficult background (Sommer, 2010). These views carry problematic implications in the understanding of the developmental process, but if the term 'mould-breaker' is rephrased as 'mould-breaking', the specific relationship between a child and their surroundings has to be included – a relationship that explains how and why a positive outcome is possible even in an expected negative development process for some children, but not for others.

A terminology is not appropriate that regards surprisingly positive development processes as something caused mainly by children's inner qualities and robustness. In recent years, focus has shifted from the child's inner protective factors to the context of the child's life. In other words, there is also a paradigmatic shift from the early focus on ego-resilience, that is, a primary focus on someone's internal personality features, to *resilience as a term that denotes and explains the dynamic development process that individuals engage in with the full range of their strengths and vulnerabilities*. It should be acknowledged that even the most robust individual cannot handle an adverse environment indefinitely, unless the environment also contains protective resources – factors that interact with and promote the child's relative degree of ego-resilience; for example, a supportive grandmother who cares for a child whose mother is incapable of doing so due to substance abuse, a caring and supportive school teacher and so on. Attempts are pursued to identify and understand the underlying protective processes in the child's environment. Thus the term resilience has increasingly been applied to a complex dynamic process involving both child and environment. In addition, resilience refers to a dynamic process that entails positive adaption within the framework of considerable negative exposure (Luthar et al., 2000). This recent approach is in line with the relational perspective of *A Childhood Psychology*, which aims to bring together various professional disciplines that specialize in the typical childhood, children and the child.

It may seem strange to use the term resilience in a book that does not investigate major adverse environmental exposure, but instead attempts to construct a contemporary theory on what constitutes 'typical' childhood. The argument is that the resiliency paradigm is particularly useful in explaining the relationship between child/infant and environment in development processes when major normative and non-normative life events occur in the process of growing up. Consequently, the resilience perspective should not be reserved exclusively for children in particularly disadvantaged environments but can also be used (to varying degrees) to characterize all children who have to adjust to the demands and challenges of life. So resilience also applies to the vast majority of children who face challenging, but typical transitions in their life – birth, going to nursery, the transition from nursery to school, leaving home as a teenager and so on. Throughout life, the adaptive capacities of humans are repeatedly tested (for the transitional life span perspective, see Baltes et al., 2006). In conclusion, resilience is not established once and for all, because it is:

1. *Situationally dependent:* In dynamic interactions with their environment and living conditions, a child may display a high degree of resilience in one situation but not necessarily in another, depending on the relationship between the individual and the particular situation.
2. *Age-dependent:* In dynamic interactions with their environment and conditions, children may be more resilient or vulnerable at one time in their lives than in another. Thus, humans are not necessarily either vulnerable or resilient throughout their life.
3. *Individually dependent:* Some children (for example 'inhibited' and sensitive children) are highly susceptible in the dynamic interactions with their environment. Other children are only affected when faced with much stronger influences. Thus the 'same' external pressures may be perceived differently, depending on the individual's frustration threshold and interpretation of the situation. Therefore it is important that professionals

are familiar with the individual child's developmental history and relative degree of resilience.

Children: novices or competent?

A similarly distinct shift in perspective has occurred with regard to the perception of the *child as a novice*. The idea of the novice or the incompetent child varies in expression and rationale with various theories.

During the era of the grand theories, the concept was reflected in social learning theories with their 'tabula rasa' (blank slate) argument, where the child was merely a passive recipient, as the environmental stylus inscribed the child's personality on the slate of life. A similar idea was evident in socialization theories that supported the paradigm of a child being moulded by their upbringing. The very concept of socialization implies that the child is a novice to be moulded by primary and secondary others.[11] Classical psychoanalytical theories also understand the child as an organism, motivated by internal drives and with no primary competencies for establishing genuine personal and social communication. However, numerous subsequent studies of infants and older children have demonstrated that they are equipped with a staggering range of competencies. For example, babies as young as three or four months have constructed global categories for mammals (Quinn and Oates, 2004), and at the same time they are capable of 'triadic' communication in the family (Stern, 2006). A huge number of studies since the 1970s have described children's perceptual, emotional, cognitive and social competencies, and this research has revolutionized our perception of children's psychosocial capacities. This research allows us to argue that babies are born with the prerequisite for actively engaging in genuine interpersonal interactions from the beginning of life (Stern, 2004; Bråten, 2007).

Acknowledging children's active participation in their own developmental process makes it difficult to describe development as the exclusive result of external environmental influences, which are either imposed upon or transferred to the child through caring and upbringing. However, it would be a simplification to assert that the environment merely activates a preset biological programme within the child. Instead, development occurs in the reciprocal interaction of various agents. In other words, competent children's relationship with their social environment is characterized by active participation and, over time, the necessary *personal relationships* develop (Stern, 2006). In some interactionist rhetoric, development is described as the result of interactions between two protagonists; yet development is more than interactions with others. Gradually during ontogenesis, each individual establishes a unique fount of social and personal experience, and the individual's historical continuity becomes the key element that separates interactions from personal relationships with others.

But what is competence, and how does it relate to the concept of *the competent child*? Essentially, competence denotes skill and ability. The word comes from the Latin word *competentia*. However, professional terms such as competence and competent child should be used with caution, as the words have different meanings, depending on context. In psychological terminology, competence is often used to refer to one of three aspects:

1. *Competencies as potentials:* Abilities that have yet to emerge or are not yet fully developed. References to children's competencies in this sense imply some inherent, not acquired, possibilities, for example a capacity for tuning in to motherese, imitating mouth protrusion, a primary intersubjectivity, an innate fear response. Competence as potential is especially useful in discussions of basic human nature. Research into the fetal stage and very early infancy, in particular, may produce surprising knowledge about the child's potential, and it may also stimulate philosophical discussions about human developmental potential.

2. *Competencies as acquired abilities:* This means that a child develops abilities or functions as various potentials (possibilities) come to fruition. The perspective implies that the child is born with certain innate abilities – basic competencies. During childhood, abilities and skills develop within all developmental domains – motor, emotional, social and cognitive. For example, through an extensive process of learning, a baby gradually acquires fine motor skills and comes to master the complicated pincer grip. Developing this skill does not mean, however, that the baby will use the pincer grip exclusively. Another example is when the infant's spontaneous smile evokes a response from the adult, which gradually makes the child's smile a more conscious socioemotional skill – a 'smile-back'. A third example is how, over time, the child develops the ability to communicate with others through language. Later, this skill evolves to include the ability to tell coherent stories (narratives). An important feature of this perspective of competencies is that certain basic abilities may be present from birth (that is, facial imitation), while the vast majority are acquired. The point is that a child 'possesses' many more competencies than they actively apply. This makes sense, as it would otherwise be impossible to act in any specific situation. For instance, a child uses a large number of competencies during play with their peers. However, when eating with adults, the play competencies are put aside, and only the contextually relevant competencies are used.

3. *Competencies in the sense of performance and accomplishments:* Competence is also used to refer to qualified performance or accomplishments in practice. Thus a child's level of competence is assessed on the basis of what the child *does.* When the child displays skills in external actions or behaviour, the competencies are directly observable.

Although these three meanings of competence are interrelated, they are also distinctly different. Thus, the claim that 'children are competent' may mean different things, depending on the underlying definition. It is important to realize that there is a huge difference between the useful, but general discourse regarding aspect 1, children's 'potential competencies' – their many inherent possibilities – and aspect 3, the notion of children's 'skill-based competencies', that is, the ability to act in actual everyday practice. Additionally, important distinctions have to be made between cultural competencies (see Chapter 3), social competencies (see Chapters 3 and 5), emotional competencies (see Chapters 3 and 6) and cognitive competencies.

As argued, competencies include potentials, acquired abilities and qualified performance, yet this does not preclude children from being completely incompetent in a number of developmental areas. Admittedly, research has demonstrated that contrary to previous beliefs, even young infants possess potentials, acquired competencies and practical skills. However, much remains to be developed during childhood. If competencies were fully developed early in life, there would be no room for learning, influences and development later in life. Thus, when leading researchers' claim that infants and young children are competent, this should be seen in the context of a pre-paradigm shift understanding of children's abilities. For example, in contrast to the pre-paradigmatic period, infants are now believed to own 'primary and secondary intersubjectivity' (Reddy et al., 1997; Trevarthen and Aitken, 2001). From early on in life, infants seem to display an innate social directedness and attention (Slater and Butterworth, 1997; Bråten, 2007). Apparently, from birth (and probably before) human infants possess innate *basic competencies* required to engage in, affect and learn about the physical world (Karmiloff-Smith, 1995).

This unique social readiness probably originates from generic human genetics, which developed throughout *Homo sapiens'* millennia-long evolution (Fogel, 2004; Stern, 2004; Tomasello, 1999, 2009). Even newborn babies consider their environment 'interesting'. Activity and action are essential human manifestations of life (Field, 1990). Furthermore, humans appear to be 'sense-making' beings, as, from the very beginning of life, infants attempt to 'construe meaning' by looking for connections between events. Thus humans prefer not to navigate in chaos but instead constantly strive to structure both the physical and social environments in ways that make personal sense (Bruner, 1990). This endeavour develops *qualitatively different competencies, depending on ontogenetic time.* Thus there are major differences in the competence levels that characterize babies, toddlers, older children and adolescents, where meaning is constructed in qualitatively different ways.

A distinction has to be made between *basic protocompetencies* (innate) and *later acquired competencies* (learned). Basic social, emotional and cognitive competencies constitute the foundation for taking the first steps forward in a year-long developmental process. New competencies develop along the way, others disappear and existing ones are expanded and refined. Consequently, it is possible to be simultaneously competent in certain relational areas and incompetent in others, and human competencies are both conditioned and relative. Even the most accomplished person is not fully competent in all areas. Mozart was unquestionably a musical genius but also had a reputation for lacking social manners.

By advocating children's competencies, the paradigm has affected both social and educational theory. Some caution should be exercised, however, when extrapolating from this new perception of children. For example, the research network Nordic Childhood Perceptions states: 'The perception of children as competent, autonomous and strong is crucial to our understanding of childhood in many contexts' (Brembeck, 2000, p. 11, translated for this edition). Here, the competence perspective is linked to the generalized view that children are both autonomous and strong. However, Brembeck refers to resilience rather than competence, and it should be remembered that even the most competent child may be anything but strong and autonomous in every possible context. In fact, the two phenomena are relatively unrelated and should not be confused – competence (potential, knowledge, skill and ability) is not the same as personal strength and autonomy. The psychological paradigm of the competent child may have other unintended implications. The competence perspective has been used to explain major power changes in relationships between adults and children. Thus, Brembeck (2000, p. 11, translated for this edition) writes: 'The view of children as competent also requires adults to relinquish some of their authority and to establish an equality, peer-like relationship with the child.' This statement exemplifies a trend of rendering the *adult–child relationship symmetrical*, that is, characterized by an equal distribution of responsibility, decision-making and authority. The view expressed by Brembeck implies a questionable link between the psychological concept of the competent child and the notion that children and adults should be equals. A peer-like relationship in power and authority downplays child and adult differences in both competence and power. A symmetrical relationship between children and adults – implying a loss of adult authority – should not be legitimized with reference to the competence paradigm. Instead, the equalization of authority approach may be inspired by equality-oriented trends in postwar, anti-authoritarian societies (Esping-Andersen et al., 2003). This has led to democratic and equality-oriented views in education and parenting that question the legitimacy of adults' authority and responsibility in relation to autonomous children.

But what are the factors that increase competencies in relatively competent children? In her review of research, Maccoby (1992) stresses the developmental potential of an *asymmetrical relationship* between child and adult, that is, a relationship based on accepting major differences in authority.

It should be emphasized that 'authority' and 'authority relation' are not synonymous with an 'authoritarian' or a 'dictatorial' power adult–child relationship, instead the *authoritative adult* manages a delicate balance between articulating demands and expectations, and being able in a 'democratic' way to empathize with the child and also adopt the child's perspective (Sommer et al., 2010). This balanced and complementary approach is closely related to competence development in children (Baumrind, 1988). Similarly, Rogoff's (1990) theory of apprenticeship does not claim that children's competencies are symmetrical. Instead, a key criterion for understanding adult–child relationships is that adults are typically more competent and act as 'guides' in reciprocal participation processes in everyday situations. Such considerations underscore what should be implied and interpreted on the basis of well-founded, post-paradigm shift ideas of the competent child. (Chapter 4 addresses the particular asymmetric role of adults in greater detail.)

The competence perspective implies an educational principle. *Children's autonomy and responsibility* are not fixed aspects that are automatically legitimized by children's assumed competence. Instead, adults *gradually involve children* and *delegate autonomy and authority* to children, as they develop their necessary competencies. Dam (1999) has pointed out the danger of overinterpreting new psychological theories and studies on children's competence and the perception of children as active participants who influence their own development process. These psychologically well-founded concepts may become linked to a current, westernized trend that calls for individuation, early independence, rapid competence development and a high degree of early personal responsibility. For example, in Scandinavia, there has been a tendency to adopt the competent child perspective to legitimize educational principles of autonomy, responsibility for one's own learning and development, self-socialization and similar ideas. This may place excessive demands on young children, demands that children cannot grasp or have not yet become competent to handle.

In a Scandinavian context (although this transcends national borders), national and local planners have embraced new management phrases about 'play, learning and competence development' as a means of preparing the next generation for the challenges of globalization, by using a lifelong educational perspective, that is, not just in primary school and beyond, but also in early development. However, this is not solely a Scandinavian way of presenting the problem. In a distinctive pronouncement, 102 leading international child researchers have drawn attention to this growing global situation, stating that 'the education of young children has become an international priority' (Santiago Declaration, www.jsmf.org/declaration). While acknowledging that 'high-quality early childhood education better prepares children for the transition to formal education', they urge caution in the methods used to achieve this aim.

One should be careful, however, not to adopt the relatively new research-based psychological terminology about children's competencies in order to legitimize the early training of human resources and thereby maintain global competitiveness. A key notion in this book is the paradigm of the *relatively* competent child. Very early in life, humans spontaneously seek, initiate, respond to and change through ongoing, varied human contact. The emphasis on competencies may, however, be seen as a promotion of a current ideal of 'the flexible individual'. Although this chapter emphasizes human potential and its relative but not absolute plasticity, the limits of human adaptability are also highlighted. However, by acknowledging the difficulties in separating time-specific, research-based knowledge from cultural perceptions, the competent child paradigm will be upheld as the most scientifically and well-documented understanding of children.

To sum up the discussion so far:

1. The change from family- and mother-centricity was described.
2. It was shown how the resilience and competence concepts are widely used in international child research and increasingly so since the 1960s.
3. The ideas of resilience and competence were presented, based on decades-long empirical research of children's emotional and social worlds. It has been demonstrated that children display a multitude of skills and resources that pre-paradigm child psychology failed to explain, which is one of the main reasons behind the significant weakening of the grand developmental theories.

DEVELOPMENTAL STAGES AS BENCHMARKS

Previously, development was often defined on the basis of prescribed stages. The stage perspective seeks to conceptualize children's development by establishing age-specific developmental periods that children must go through in a given order, more or less rapidly, and more or less successfully.

This perspective holds that:

1. development follows a forward, stepwise progression
2. each step is fixed and qualitatively unique, with corresponding types of thinking, feeling and sociality
3. there are developmental 'plateaus', where assimilation dominates, and developmental progression, where accommodation and new learning take place
4. each developmental step is mainly regulated by organismic maturation, which is a universal phenomenon
5. the child 'starts' at the bottom of the developmental ladder when born and 'finishes' at the top when an adult.

Thus ontogenesis is outlined in a stepwise, age-bound logic. Piaget's (1977) influential cognitive and developmental model is an example of the ladder model, but other theories, such as Freud's oral, anal, phallic, latency and genital psychosexual phases, share the same characteristics. In principle, it is feasible to describe children's development in stages, and there has been a strong tradition for this approach in classical developmental psychology, a tradition that continues to some extent as reminiscent of the grand developmental era.

Creative researchers may develop stages as heuristic models that enable the categorization of developmental periods, but somehow this categorization comes to be reified as true and necessary steps in normal development (Burman, 2008a). Despite the fact that stage models are not objective reality, they can be perceived as working metaphors that are useful in practice. 'Stage ordering' allows a description of changes that occur in relationships between adults and children over time in a culture. Indeed, they can guide parents and educators, as stage-like generalizations may help explain what is historically and culturally expected of children at various ages. For example, in terms of being successful in school, in middle childhood, it is beneficial not to stay too long in a Piagetian 'preoperational' mode of thinking. A major problem with developmental stage theories is, however, that they have become 'scientific', in other words, objectified and converted into universal, guiding norms for development, known as *benchmarks*. This issue is reflected in the following criticism of traditional stage theories in developmental psychology:

> Developmental psychology establishes a yardstick for good and bad upbringing. A good upbringing is one that addresses the child's developmental stage – a bad upbringing is one that fails to do so. (Ellegaard, 1995, p. 47, translated for this edition)

This is, to a degree, caused by the tendency for *teleological thinking* that stems from the pre-paradigm shift period. Teleology is a philosophical principle, according to which a phenomenon is determined by its purpose, and it considers developmental change as being bound for a given end goal (finality). This more or less implicit notion has been predominant in social studies and the humanities (including psychology) until recently. It characterizes an evolutionary perspective on society, where change is viewed as a single uninterrupted progressive line of development, as societies move from simpler to more complex and better developed types. This is a classical modernity perception based on 17th-century philosophical thinking, far removed from recent concepts of change in a late modern reality. The classical concept of development in psychology has been closely associated with the idea that human development is an orderly, progressive and time-bound movement towards higher and more complex forms of thought, emotion and social adjustment (Fischer and Bidell, 2006). A teleological view can be integrated so intimately with developmental thinking that the very concept of finality (the idea of an end goal) and the essential perception of development merge into one. For example, a given stage theory, with its built-in, step-by-step developmental logic, may leave the impression that there is a specific and definite level and an end goal to reach during ontogenesis.

The ontogenetic stepwise progression towards this goal comes to be seen as the normal development route, while any movement away from this optimum end goal or any stagnation along the way is construed as deficient development. There are several reasons why, since the 1960s, the stage model has lost so much ground in international developmental psychology. According to Stern (2006, p. xii):

> The classical Freudian model of psychosexual stages (replete with fixations) had not fulfilled its predictive promise for linkage with later psychopathology, even after three-quarters of a century; it was not productive of new ideas and had become less persuasive and less interesting... Piaget's stage model... was inadequate to conceptualize the encounter with the richer and more complicated social-emotion human world.

The concept of teleological finality has distinct negative implications for the understanding of childhood. According to Näsman (1995), it *reduces childhood to a transitional period*. Children are viewed as immature, relatively incompetent beings, who are meant to develop into something they have not yet become. In classical developmental theory, childhood (with its substages) may be acknowledged as crucial, but it is also considered as a transitory state on the way to the fully matured competencies of the adult.[12] As a consequence, adult development sets the optimum goal for the child:

> developmental theories focus on the way that children progress through certain given stages, or the way they develop by being socialized into society by various agents. Thus, childhood is described as a path leading out of immaturity, ignorance and inability. The perspective of developmental psychology may be said to aim for creating optimum conditions for the child to follow the path of normal development without deviation. (Näsman, 1995, p. 286, translated for this edition)

The influence of teleological thinking on child and developmental psychology has been an important reason why the non-stage-bound character of development and its embeddedness in time and space has not been fully acknowledged until recently. Importantly, this line of argument should not be confused with the discussion as to whether or not development occurs in *qualitative leaps*. Even classical stage theory (such as Piaget's that clearly highlights the important role of qualitative leaps in development and thus supports discontinuous transitions) still generally perceives human development as having a *predetermined overall direction or plan.* A contemporary perspective increasingly acknowledges the relatively open-ended character of development and the need for cautious interpretations of the future (Bornstein, 2010).

The criticism of the teleological perspective of development, including the growing doubt about grand, reassuring narratives of order, regularity and pure objectivity proposed by science, has led sociology, psychology and the humanities, as interpreters of human life, into a new and unsettling universe. As a vital part of social science and the humanities, child and developmental psychology is embedded in this overall historical and cultural scenario, which continues to bring surprising changes, not expected or predicted by experts. So in this regard, child and developmental psychology as a discipline should not take a disinterested or neutral stance. When society, history, culture and families change, not only rapidly but also unpredictably, classical theorizing of children's development and socialization is also under pressure to change (Kojima, 2003; Kagitcibasi, 2007).

However, in their claim for conceptual universality, the grand developmental theories did not in any way address this altered reality. Both now and in the long run, this considerably weakens the theories' interpretive power and their applicability. It may be thought-provoking (and disturbing) to some psychologists that sociology and childhood sociology have threatened psychology in recent decades. One key reason for this is that recent *sociological* theories have offered a timely and meaningful interpretation, not only at the macro-level of contemporary society, but also at the micro-level of social life, which includes dealing with the substantial personal implications of living in, for example, late modernity, the risk society and the information society. Increasingly, sociology has encroached on privileged areas normally held by child and developmental psychology. Cultural and educational studies are increasingly incorporated into the study of childhood at the possible expense of developmental psychology.

In summary, attempts to explain humans' place in history, society, culture, family and personal relationships as something that is governed by purpose and end goals have given way to more modest, specific and temporary interpretations, based partly on specific studies of human change across the life span.

DEVELOPMENT AS A TRANSACTIONAL WEB

A number of approaches have been suggested in order to reach a newer understanding of the developmental process. A promising view inspired by late attachment theory is the understanding of the child's development as a process that follows *a variety of possible developmental paths* (Smith and

Ulvund, 1999; Berk, 2009). The future holds a number of possible and potential paths, which are partly influenced by children's starting points at birth and in early childhood, but also by later life events. A growing body of longitudinal studies has demonstrated that it is relatively difficult (on behalf of the individual child) to predict the later development of children who are raised under similar adverse conditions. Potential risk does not determine the future prospects of the child, but enhances the relative probability of developmental disorders (Rutter and Rutter, 1993; Gottlieb, 2003). The early longitudinal Hawaiian study of the probability for developmental risk and resilience in children who grow up in adverse settings was groundbreaking in this regard (Werner et al., 1971; Werner and Smith, 1977). This study initiated the change of the paradigmatic approach to development (Luthar et al., 2000).

It has proved particularly hard to predict how children will fare in the future, especially with respect to following *individual children's* development over time. Some children develop close to the expected, while others defy expectations, for better or for worse. Such types of research-based knowledge, and a growing frustration about fragmentation and specialization, have led to the introduction of a promising integrative, developmental metatheory – the *transactional perspective* inspired by dynamic systems theory (Sameroff, 1987, 1991; Sameroff and MacKenzie, 2003; Lerner, 2006; Thelen and Smith, 2006; Witherington, 2007).

The model indicates that ontogenetic development is not a linear, unidirectional process, because the individual and their environment constantly and interdependently change over time. Although the model is rather general and does not fully appreciate the complexities within child and environment, important developmental principles can be deduced from it. First, environmental influences alone (for example the behaviour of the mother or other adults) cannot predict a child's developmental future; the child's unique behaviour also has to be included. Similarly, development cannot be explained by the child's characteristics alone (for example temperament, sociability, biological maturity) or by mother–child interactions at any one point in time. Characteristics do not reside solely in the individual but in the adaptiveness of the relationship between the individual and context (Sameroff and MacKenzie, 2003). Predictors can be found, however, in the *complex and changing interactions between child and environment over time*, that is, a transactional process, where actions over time change both child and mother and, consequently, their mutual relationship.

The concept of transaction is different from the commonly used term 'interaction', as the latter only applies to co-action between two parties, not indicating whether or how this changes or develops the involved parties. The transactional process can be described as a progressive process, in which each message affects the recipient, so that every response is a product of the totality of previous messages and responses. This means that a developmental chain is formed as a function of time. According to Sameroff and MacKenzie (2003, p. 617):

> Transactions are documented where the activity of one element changes the usual activity of another, either quantitatively, by increasing or decreasing the level of the usual response, or qualitatively, by eliciting or initiating a new response, for example when a smile is reciprocated by a frown, which may elicit confusion, negativity, or even increased anxious positivity.

This perspective enables us to understand how childhood development may be relatively predictable for some children. But this need not always be the case, depending on whether children encounter one or more so-called positive or negative developmental 'turning points' during their life course, which may eventually change their developmental path, for better or for worse (Rutter and Rutter, 1993). In line with the idea of ontogenetic pathways and the transactional model is the constructive web model (Figure 1.2).

Instead of approaching change as a process of ladder-like, age-bound stages, the developmental web model illustrates it as a wide range of

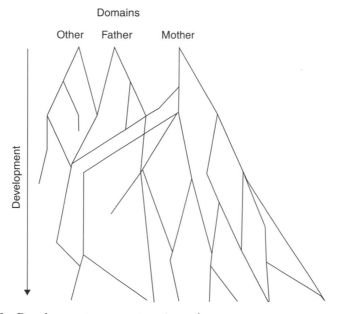

Figure 1.2   Development as a constructive web

Source: Adapted from Fischer and Bidell, 2006

prospective routes. This branching network moves in different directions, some of which are interconnected while others are not.

A given location in the web indicates a certain potential competence and situates the individual in a specific 'place' in their development. The various directions of connections indicate important and potential variations in developmental pathways. Connections across imply a change of course in development (important developmental shifts). The network expands as the child grows older. This means that the child's competencies increase both in number and complexity. The web model also shows that although multiple possibilities are open, development is not chaotic, arbitrary or completely open-ended. There is a (temporary) order in the web, including similar orderings of spatial positions for some strands, separations and junctions of strands, and related starting and ending points of some strands (Fischer and Bidell, 2006, p. 319).

As time goes by, dramatic shifts in a person's developmental course become increasingly unlikely. But this model does not clearly capture the influence of *culture*, which will be discussed later (see Figure 6.3 and the related discussion in Chapter 6). Furthermore, it does not explain how the child's developmental web is affected by the different *contextual levels* in which the child is embedded (for more information, see Figure 7.1 and the discussion in Chapter 7). Thus, the general models of the transactional nature of development and the developmental web have to be combined with other types of models and theories that specify the contexts of childhood and the individual child.

Pursuing *A Childhood Psychology* paradigm, the transaction process has to be combined with children's specific everyday personal relations and interactions with other people. Cicourel's thesis (see Douglas, 1970) expands on this view. Children gradually acquire cultural competence through interactional experiences by developing a *sense of social structure* as they improve their grasp of the meaning of social practices. Hence, developmental research should study the ways that members of a society or a culture acquire this sense of social structure, thereby enabling them to negotiate and participate in everyday activities. Individuals are active interpreters, learners who continuously expand their competencies with a view to ever more sophisticated social involvement (Sommer et al., 2010).

Developing from a newcomer to this world into an experienced participant in social and cultural events requires a childhood where the child is involved daily in a variety of personal, social and cognitive experiential processes. Thus, as a starting point, the development process should be described and explained along with the child's gradual acquisition of social and cultural competencies (see Chapter 3). Interacting individuals continuously affect each other's actions in unfolding social events and processes. This ranges from the first silent exchange of gazes between the newborn baby and the parents to the highly evolved dialogue with a teenager. The attentive observer will notice that children engaged in play, for example, constantly practise and rehearse their grasp of social structure, often in ways that resemble an adult actor rehearsing for a play. Thus competencies not only have to be acquired, they must also be maintained and improved. Studying competencies means:

1. Observing what children routinely participate in and do as part of every-day activities.
2. Conceptualizing these activities and actions.
3. Exploring the child's interactions with all individuals in the child's life.
4. Assessing children's competencies on the basis of their social and cultural function.

A starting point could be to conceptualize the many different types of com-petencies that happen in *routine activities and interactions taking place in the flow of everyday events.* Chapters 3 and 4 will elaborate on this developmental paradigm.

A CHILDHOOD PSYCHOLOGY: NINE CONTEXTUAL THESES

The significantly reduced dominance of the grand developmental theories has today resulted in a profession that is, on the upside, highly diverse and specialized, but on the downside, highly fragmented, because a vast number of studies and domain-specific theories have entered the scene. Although a metatheory for developmental psychology based on systems theory has recently been proposed (Thelen and Smith, 2006: Witherington, 2007), no one should expect a comprehensive grand theory of the type seen before the 1960s to rise from the proverbial ashes. Nevertheless, there is a growing need to integrate some of this diversity in a consistent pattern of paradigms or theses. This is not, however, an easy endeavour, perhaps even impossible. Several propositions and routes are, in fact, possible, with the relevant basis in selected recent research. The nine theses listed below originate from the particular paradigm shift that occurred, and will be discussed in *A Childhood Psychology* as one discipline among others:

- Thesis 1: *Development is contextually constructed in time and space.* Context is defined as any historical, physical, ideological and social characteristic of human activity in a culture. Universal theses concerning children are not to be launched as theoretical preludes but rather as possible postludes evaluated or constructed by studies and discussions of inter- and intra-cultural similarities and differences. A supplementary principle is that altered living conditions for children not only challenge old paradigms but require new ones. This is particularly vital in order to understand the full professional consequences of studying children in contemporary and rapidly changing societies.

- Thesis 2: *The child is embedded in everyday life in a complex system of social situations and lives in various developmental arenas.* Top-down theorizing about the abstract child, detached from context, should not be construed or applied. Furthermore, the developmental contexts for the individual child will have both direct and indirect influences. Contexts involve human activity and its derived 'products', ranging from the cultural macro-level to the intimate micro-level of which the child is a part.

- Thesis 3: *Children's actions, will power, independence and self-reliance do not necessarily carry the same meaning in different cultures.* This principle applies across cultures and subcultures. Within a specific culture, families and schools may differ in their cultural definitions of apparently identical acts, for instance differences in views between childcare workers and school teachers in relation to within culture minority and ethnic parents.

- Thesis 4: *Culture, emotion, cognition, sociality and action are interrelated phenomena.* The study of children's emotions, thinking and sociability becomes an integrated part of the study of various aspects of social and cultural practices. All acts, mental and physical, are concrete, in the sense that any act described out of context becomes an abstraction, a product of analysis rather than observation.

- Thesis 5: *Child development as culture acquisition.* This takes place through routine forms of social interactions that gradually enhance the child's ability to read and manage cultural systems of meaning in specific everyday situations.

- Thesis 6: *Competence development relies on the options a given culture offers the child for acquiring and practising competencies.* Traditions and routines, as repeated behaviours and expectations in given situations, are perpetuated by culturally competent and significant individuals (adults and other children). These people act as guides for the child in important everyday social interactions. However, the child does not merely replicate and perpetuate culture but also acts as a sense-making agent in these interactions. The child is active in processing impressions, acting and producing change in everyday social communities.

- Thesis 7: *Competencies are tied to local contexts.* Essentially, competencies develop as experiences in a local and contextual manner, that is, as skills that apply to particular situations and contexts. Therefore, competencies are not abstract skills that can be applied freely across situations and developmental arenas. For example, in order to study the way a young child develops competencies, one has to study the infant in clearly defined cultural, social and physical contexts, and in specific types of activity. Children acquire so-called 'domain-specific competencies' based on knowledge obtained from well-known situations. New experiences and skills build on this foundation. As children grow up, they become increasingly adept at generalizing and applying local experiences and competencies across situations.

- Thesis 8: *Competencies reflect their cultural function.* Developmental assessments of children's activities are the result of social evaluation. Assessments are mediated by cultural tradition, commonsense experience and academic positions. This principle of cultural function means that the child is not perceived in relation to a theoretically defined, developmental level. Psychological assessments of children are the result of written and unwritten pragmatic cultural agreements, which address the child's personal, social and intellectual function. These assessments rest on cultural standards for and experiences concerning what can and should be expected. Developmental norms are neither constant nor universal, as standards change over time.

  Normative assessments also rely on the person(s) carrying out the assessment and on the purpose of the assessment. This means that, in principle, an assessment of normality versus deficiency should not be determined through a universal yardstick – it will invariably be both *relative* and *functional*. Current Western standards for development are supposed to be relatively high. This is reflected in the growing application of psychological know-how, as psychologists are asked to assess the cultural functionality of given competencies (even though this may not be the way these professionals would choose to describe their role).[13]

- Thesis 9: *Professional knowledge about children is contextual.* Knowledge of children (theories, empirical findings and so on) should not be isolated from its subject, that is, a source of distant, objective explanations. Professional knowledge may also be contextual, and knowledge of children may be both relative and temporary. Nevertheless, knowledge may possess ecological validity, that is, offer systematic and well-documented insights capable of capturing, interpreting and making sense of important aspects of children's lives and development in our age and culture. By grasping and conceptualizing children's sense-making efforts, child psychology as a cultural and ideological source of information may even alter its subject.[14]

Does the shift from the grand developmental paradigm to contextualism prevent generalizations of children's development across culture and context? Is there only 'local specificity' and no universal human features? The contextual principle of embedding development in time and space and the requirement of studying development in the context of everyday life do not imply a rejection of general developmental principles. Everyday relationships between children and adults may simultaneously display universal panhuman commonalities (that is, communicating by using a symbolic tool – language), and specific historical and cultural manifestations (that is, conversation in their native language). To some extent, the issue of universal versus culturally specific features depends on the level of abstraction. For example, few would deny that spoken language (a complex system of sounds with assigned meanings within a given language community) has universal presence as a human form of communication and has held this position for millennia. However, specific languages, such as Chinese and English, display considerable culturally conditioned differences.

Thus, the challenges to the universality of classical child and developmental psychology do not aim to discard universalism as such, rather they question the pre-paradigmatic and some contemporary tendencies towards a priori universalism, that is, the more or less hidden assumption that a theory, without documentation or rationale, is universal by claiming it has 'identified' developmental regularities. This view has lost ground, and claims of universality are difficult to accept without considering historical and culturally specific aspects. *A Childhood Psychology* is in line with this 'both/and' perspective:

> The direction of development is channelled by specific as well as the universal givens of the human physical and social endowment. That is, all humans share a great deal of universal activity because of the biological and cultural heritage that we have in common as a species (for example two legs, communication through language, helpless infancy, organization in groups, and capacity to invent tools), and at the same time, each of us varies because of differences in our physical and interpersonal circumstances (for example, visual acuity, strength, family constellation, means of making a living, familiarities with specific languages). (Rogoff, 1990, p. 11)

In place of a priori assumptions of universality, the goal of *A Childhood Psychology* should be a consistent striving to explain the complexity of development in terms of panhuman universalities, as well as historical and cultural similarities and differences. This task becomes no less daunting when one considers that it includes exploring the relationships between universal and specific features.

On the basis of the discussion so far, the concept of development in a contextually anchored childhood psychology may be summarized as follows. Development characterizes the qualitative and quantitative transitions that gradually enable children to handle the competence requirements encountered in the social dynamics of everyday life. The development process may be either facilitated or hampered by the complex interaction of cultural features, social interactions and the individual child's potential and limitations.

2

A CHANGING YOUNG CHILDHOOD: BELIEFS PROVOKED AND THEORY CHALLENGED

Two of the nine theses mentioned in Chapter 1 that propose a paradigm shift are of specific relevance to this chapter:

- Thesis 1: an understanding of childhood needs to include the historical, ideological and social characteristics within societies and cultures.
- Thesis 9: professional knowledge about children is ecologically contextualized, and one should therefore attempt to make sense of important changes in contemporary children's lives and development. Knowledge and beliefs about children – professional and commonsense folk psychology – constitute a cultural and ideological force. As a consequence, both scientific and commonsense beliefs about children and their life worlds are objects of professional studies in their own right.

Beliefs may be private and not communicated to others, but in this context they refer to various publicly distributed ideas, assumptions, truisms and assessments concerning childhood. Growing knowledge about children and their childhoods has contributed to our cultural base of expertise and theory, while research has, directly or indirectly, affected social policies, legislation and other practical areas. Furthermore, magazines, newspapers, TV and other media routinely report on issues relating to children, which indicate that children are on the public agenda. Therefore, professional and widely distributed beliefs about children and their childhoods seem to present a potential influence on both society and families. Knowledge about children has become an important source of cultural capital that may even act as a 'developer', having the potential to positively and negatively influence parental beliefs and practices (Furedi, 2001; Stern, 2006). However, unanimous interpretations of childhood are not to be expected, as experts and laypeople alike represent a wide range of views and beliefs. Public opinion differs considerably when it comes to the evaluation of 'the good and bad of childhood', so today's children and their upbringing have clearly been the object of ideological strife (Börjeson, 1995; Kamerman and Moss, 2009). Ultimately, an underlying premise of this chapter is that in times of rapid change in fundamental developmental arenas and relationships, for example the role of the family and mothers, 'self-evident' beliefs rooted in the time before these changes will be challenged.

But what changes? In order to answer this, Chapter 2 will start briefly by embedding contemporary childhood in its late modernity context, thereby underlining the concomitant restructuring of societies. Then the focus will be on a changing early childhood. A point of departure is a selected description and documentation of two interrelated contemporary, widespread phenomena, which have restructured early childhood, provoked deeply held beliefs and challenged theory. They are the dramatic rise in the number of working mothers and the childcare revolution. The reason behind this presentation is to base the subsequent discussion of beliefs and theory in substantiated, rapidly changing realities. Growing up for today's typical young child has, in several ways, become qualitatively different from previous generations (Dencik et al., 2008), and it is important to back this up with empirical research. However, if the developmental consequences are to be understood, creating new concepts and theory is also relevant. Using theories from the grand developmental approach may lead to misinterpretation because of their contextual insensitivity (Burman, 2008a), rooted as they are in a time before the changes occurred.

In a critical evaluation of the underlying assumptions in child psychology, Scarr and Dunn (1987) stated that there exists a developmental psychology for 'keeping women/mothers at home' and a developmental psychology to 'let women/mothers work' without damaging the child. The first theory has its roots in the pre-paradigm shift time and the second is based on research compiled during the paradigm shift. Scarr and Dunn highlight the polarity between two underlying *zeitgeists* – divergent undercurrent beliefs in surmised objective child research (see also Eyer, 1993). When used top down and without contextual sensitivity, the interpretation of the consequences of secular change may become misleading. A changed and still changing childhood, however, calls for a reorientation rooted in facts, conceptual interpretations and reflections embedded in recent research developed after the paradigm shift.

In a discussion of how changing childhoods provoke beliefs, the relative rigidity and malleability of beliefs has to be acknowledged. Beliefs can lag behind changes, while perceptions may change considerably if they are allowed some time to react or mature.

Rapidly changing childhoods have challenged well-established theory as well. More specifically, this will be apparent in a critical discussion of the classical concepts of primary/secondary socialization. Subsequently, new groundbreaking research about the intersubjective infant and young child is introduced. Children are not non-social novices, but have a deep motive for social companionship. This leads to the presentation of recent research on multiple attachments and caring, followed by a suggested, updated redefinition of socialization. Finally, a new framework, 'the dual socialization butterfly', will be presented, and then the interpretative potential of the model will be discussed.

LATE MODERNITY AS A CHILDHOOD CONTEXT

Late modern society's significance to human beings and the individual has been described and discussed by sociologists. The phrase 'late modernity' denotes that societies, despite new developments, have not turned into a discrete state beyond modernism, that is, postmodernity. This book is in line with that argument. For example, the growing emphasis after the Second World War on child-friendly ideas is not a postwar or a late modern invention; these ideas have their historic roots in humanistic philosophy developed long before that. Despite the widely held emphasis in Scandinavian parental beliefs that it is good for young children to be 'self-reliant' and not entirely subordinate to adult regimes, there's still a belief that 'good manners' and 'obedience' are valued. There are clear socioeconomic differences behind such parental belief systems (Sommer, 2008b). As this chapter looks at contemporary children, it is relevant to outline some selected special characteristics of our time and place (Box 2.1).

Box 2.1   Late modernity as a context for young children

- *Constant change:* Innovation is a characteristic of changing late modern societies. This has dual consequences as it opens up new possibilities as well as ambiguity and insecurity. For example, how are the next generation to be raised to prepare it for a future where conventional ways of life are changing? What kind of socialization will qualify young children to handle a future that is in many ways unknown to present socializers?
- *Complexity:* Society is hypercomplex with its numerous decentralized and loosely connected systems. Values and expectations related to one socialization/learning system (e.g. childcare, family, peer groups) are not necessarily consistent with other systems. Hence, today in young childhood, it is developmentally functional to learn how to socially navigate in different system contexts.
- *Detraditionalization and norm pluralism:* Impairment of tradition occurs pari passu with popular superstition, social norms and conventional values being

---

challenged. Norm pluralism includes a plurality of norm and value systems. In principle, innovation makes anything negotiable, open for discussion and reflection. Alternative perspectives, within and across societies, on 'the child', 'the family', 'mother's/father's role' and 'gender' may continuously challenge existing dominant norms. So, young children commuting between family and childcare may daily experience different norm systems in their two socializing arenas.

- *Individualization, humanization and child centredness:* The young child is regarded as a unique subject with its own needs. The humanization idea indicates that children are humans with inviolable rights. These ideas can be signalled, being reflected in public documents (for example the UN's Declaration of the Rights of the Child) as well as in educational notions such as 'care is a personal relationship'; 'self-direction'; 'learning and socialization, an active process involving the child'. All in all, these tendencies show that authoritarian discipline seems to be in decline to the benefit of child centredness.

These characteristics apply mainly to so-called democratic and Western societies. However, even within this context, emphasis is placed differently on the various characteristics, as, for instance, individualization, child humanization and child-centred approaches can vary considerably within society (Sommer et al., 2010). So there's not just one late modern society.

The late modern characteristics are interwoven and driven by a complicated relationship between material, economic, historical, social and cultural factors. Behind a number of these characteristics lies increasing *globalization*. It sets the agenda, directly or indirectly, and locally, in a number of areas, resulting in the curious term 'glocal society'. Late modern society has particular features in comparison to previous societies, and can be denoted with several names, depending on which features the focus emphasizes. Especially noticeable is science's success not only in garnering huge amounts of new knowledge (*knowledge society*), but also with the number of technological inventions that have revolutionized late modern life, for example cars, TVs, mobile phones and the internet (*technology and information society*). This is also an epoch with unprecedented possibilities in the West for constant consumption (*consumer society*). However, the flip side of late modern society is the *risk society* (Beck, 1997), with its nuclear bombs, terrorism, global climate change and global financial crisis. In other words, the late modern world is complex, ambiguous, unpredictable and even brutal to humans. In addition, as seen both across and within societies, some have benefited from living in late modern times, whereas many others definitely have not.

To avoid misinterpretation of Box 2.1, it must be said that despite today's children growing up in a late modern context, they are not all influenced by it in the same way. Rather, late modern contexts constitute common 'sounding boards' for many specific lives, in which children act and which they perceive as meaningful. Importantly, each characteristic in Box 2.1 can be handled in several different ways by different societies, families and institutions. Thus, the possibilities for acting and development consequences are manifold. Late modernity does not 'enter directly into' children, there has to be selection, described by the educational and sociological term as *complexity reduction*. Significant adults (parents, nursery teachers and teachers) and other children (siblings and friends) mediate, extract and filter selected parts of late modernity's characteristics for children. This interacts with perception of values, educational background and a number of other factors. Furthermore, children also filter and actively process the information they receive. Therefore it is hardly surprising that the selfsame reality is perceived, experienced and understood quite differently by people living in various socioeconomic, cultural and gendered contexts.

On the other hand, there are also a number of common features that characterize human beings in any given time and society. This makes communality and diversity two dimensions of late modern life. Thus human beings do not uncritically adopt the society of which they are a part, on the contrary, they relate to it. For example, in Scandinavia's egalitarian societies, parents reduce the enormous complexity of values in late modernity by not applying the same upbringing values. Although some values are similar, significantly different upbringing values are also practised. Hence, the same late modern values are not simply transferred to the next generation (Sommer, 2003).

Not only is late modernity communicated to children, it also works in reverse: children quickly learn not merely selected parts of their culture and society through a process of mediation, but also actively reproduce this culture. For example, a child knows certain habitual ways of being with others in specific situations and expects others to behave accordingly. This relationship between mediating for the child and the child's active reproduction will be discussed in later chapters.

THE EARLY CHILDHOOD REVOLUTION: WORKING MOTHERS AND YOUNG CHILDREN IN OUT-OF-HOME CARE

For more than 40 years, Scandinavian societies have experienced the consequences of 'a large-scale natural experiment' – the rapid, dramatic rise in mothers going out to work, and a concomitant sharp rise in the proportion of young children in out-of-home care. This revolution has caused important changes in family life patterns, rising divorce rates and falling birth rates, although mainly at the beginning of the period. In Denmark, the breakdown of family structure did not happen and the majority of Scandinavian children still grow up in an intact nuclear family with two biological parents.

Furthermore, an ongoing decline in birth rate and increase in maladaptive child behaviour have mainly been absent (Dencik et al., 2008). Children's wellbeing in the Nordic countries is documented as being among the highest in the OECD countries (UNICEF, 2007).

Initially, the fast changes caused much concern and heated debates. Yet after more than a generation, the phenomenon of working mothers and children in childcare is seen as the accepted normal childhood condition in most professional and public discourses in today's Scandinavian societies (Sommer et al., 2010). Interpretations of this can differ, however. Dencik (2008), in a social psychological analysis, mainly reviews the 'new situation' in a positive light. Haavind and Magnusson (2005), on the other hand, in their 'The Nordic Countries: Welfare Paradises for Women and Children?', discuss the changed situation more critically from a feminist perspective. Nevertheless, there is agreement that, compared to earlier times, living conditions for many more children have improved considerably.

Despite increasing global competition from various countries and regions such as China and Eastern Europe, Scandinavian welfare societies have not only maintained but also increased their international trade, and since the mid-1990s, their economic growth has been well above the average for Western Europe. The gross national product is well above the general level in Western Europe and, indeed, most countries in the world (Statistics Denmark, 2006). Thus, Scandinavian children grow up in societies that can be characterized as highly affluent. Socioeconomic differences do exist but are relatively modest from a global perspective (Dencik et al., 2008). But it is important to note that the global economic crisis may modify this picture in the future.

Although Scandinavia may have gained experience of the consequences of having children predominantly in childcare on a large scale for a longer period than other parts of the world, there is overwhelming evidence that working mothers and out-of-home care have also become a truly widespread phenomenon in the rest of the world (UNICEF, 2008). Therefore, a wider outlook is required, in order to document a rising, widespread tendency and highlight the challenges this poses for the reconceptualization of childhood.

Maternal employment

After the Second World War, and since the early 1960s in particular, the lives of families and children in Scandinavia have changed considerably. A main catalyst for these changes was strong economic growth in the postwar years. In the 1940s, few Scandinavian women had joined the workforce, and this situation remained the same for most of the 1960s. In terms of recent overall employment rates for women, Denmark and Sweden top the list of the 24 EU countries (Statistisk Årbog, 2007). Thus, the change in women's role in society has happened considerably faster and been much more pronounced and pervasive in Nordic countries than in most other nations in Europe or, for that matter, around the world. But recent statistics show that many countries are now catching up. Data – from 35 countries in Europe, Asia, North America, Australia and the Nordic countries regarding maternal employment rates by age of youngest child – shows that, on average, nearly 60% of mothers with children under three are in employment (OECD, n.d.), while maternal employment rates of mothers with three- to five-year-olds is above 60%. The Nordic countries feature at the top, but Slovenia, the Netherlands, Estonia, France, Germany, Canada and the US are above the average. Apart from Turkey, the countries with the lowest maternal employment are not lower than 30% (OECD, n.d.). The Nordic countries, which were already somewhat egalitarian, witnessed a complex and rapid change in thinking and practice concerning traditional gender roles within the family (Haavind and Magnusson, 2005). The Nordic countries quickly became established welfare models that enabled families to function after women had joined the workforce. In most southern European and some Eastern European countries, women have not entered the job market in equally large numbers, and many countries do not offer widespread public childcare services. Dencik et al. (2008) summarize the relatively fast decennium changes in women's employment patterns in a Scandinavian country:

- *In the 1950s:* Few mothers worked outside the home. They ran the home and looked after the children. The fathers were the sole providers, thus the typical pattern was the 'dad-provider family'.
- *In the 1960s:* Women began to work outside the home but typically took a break while the children were young.
- *In the 1970s and 80s:* More and more mothers worked away from home but usually part time. With fathers still working full time, many families had by now become a 'one-and-a-half working family'.
- *In the 1990s and into the 21st century:* More and more mothers work full time, but now while the children are young. Today, typical Scandinavian families have two incomes. The 'dual-earner family' has become much more prevalent.

So, in today's Scandinavia, the housewife has largely left the private family arena, a fact reflected not only in statistics (only 1% of Danish women are categorized as housewives) but also in daily language use. The terms 'housewife' and 'homemaker' are almost exclusively used rhetorically in reference to a historical phenomenon, that is, the natural role for women in the role-dichotomized nuclear family as it was before the major changes took place in the 1960s. Today, the term is rarely used in the social sciences, since it is a phenomenon that no longer has a widespread empirical basis in contemporary society.

Despite some differences between countries, it has been documented here that maternal employment is frequent in many countries in the world and this accounts for mothers with young children too. Maternal employment as a driving force in the restructuring of early care raises the question: Who looks after the infants and young children while the parents are at work?

The childcare revolution: a developing generation's reality

After centuries of being a family responsibility, the care of very young children is now becoming an out-of-home activity. Today in OECD countries, a new generation is the first in which the majority of children are not cared for in their homes during the day. Instead, young children are situated in some type of childcare. Approximately 80% of the rich world's three- to six-year-olds are now in some form of early childhood education or care. Across the industrialized nations, out-of-home care is a fact of life for even more children at an earlier age and for even longer hours. This revolution has been driven mainly by economic changes and new challenges, such as the growing demands of a highly competitive, knowledge-based global economy, rather than parental choice. It is also a fact that among millions of families in OECD countries, two adults raising two children need a minimum of one full-time and one part-time job to stay above the poverty line. Such pressures reflect new requirements for early out-of-home care and education (UNICEF, 2008).

The 'Scandinavian natural experiment' may serve as an example of how countries can embrace the idea that it is in the best interests of both families and society to provide qualified, widely available childcare to support dual-earner families. Along with the fact that the majority of families ceased to be the exclusive arena for children's primary socialization, a culture of 'shared responsibility' developed (Dencik et al., 2008). In Figure 2.1, Denmark serves as an example of the changes in external care attendance.

Figure 2.1 shows that, during a relatively brief period, there has been a dramatic increase in the number of children in childcare, from around 50% in 1983 up to around 80% today. The remaining 20% include the youngest infants who stay at home with their mothers during their maternity leave. The slightly older preschoolers now spend as much time in public facilities as school children. In 2006, 96% of children aged three to five years attended kindergarten or some other childcare facility. The average Danish preschooler attends nursery from 8am until 3.30pm, a total of 7.5 hours a day (Statistics Denmark, 2007).

This fundamental restructuring of daily life sees the separation of young children's lives into family time and childcare time, and dramatically expands the range of people close to the child in the early years and alters their daily experiences. Initially, this revolution was not driven by the public goal of educating or socializing children at an even younger age. What

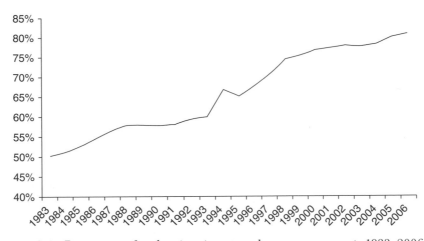

Figure 2.1 Percentage of under sixes in external care arrangements 1983–2006
Source: Statistics Denmark, 2007

made childcare a growing and widespread phenomenon in the mid-1960s was Scandinavian societies' response to a simple necessity: an urgent need to take care of large numbers of young children whose mothers went out to work. This necessity was reflected in the Danish term *fremmedpasning* (stranger care), which was common at the time. The word signals the underlying ideological view that placing young children outside the family was unusual. Over time, this term was replaced by the neutral term 'childcare', which, despite its neutrality, still implies a fundamentally different everyday life for the current generation of Scandinavian (and other) children in comparison to earlier generations of preschoolers. As mentioned, this is not solely a Scandinavian phenomenon, and Figures 2.2 and 2.3 provide a recent picture of childcare in selected OECD countries.[15]

As Figure 2.2 shows, the attendance of under fours in childcare varies among OECD countries, with Scandinavia having the highest percentage. However, in the UK, for instance, the majority of mothers now return to full- or part-time work within 12 months of having their child. In the US, more than 50% of children under one year of age are in some form of childcare – three-quarters of them from four months or earlier and for an average of 28 hours a week (UNICEF, 2008).

For three- to six-year-olds in early education, the number of children in out-of-home care is generally much higher, with the OECD average over 60% (Figure 2.3). This indicates a fundamental restructuring of early education, learning and primary care. Massive preschool attendance as an instrument for early education and care has become a widespread global phenomenon. For example, the percentage of three- to five-year-olds in publicly supported care is between 90% and 100% in France, Belgium, Italy, Denmark and Sweden, the last two topping the table (Lamb and Ahnert, 2006).

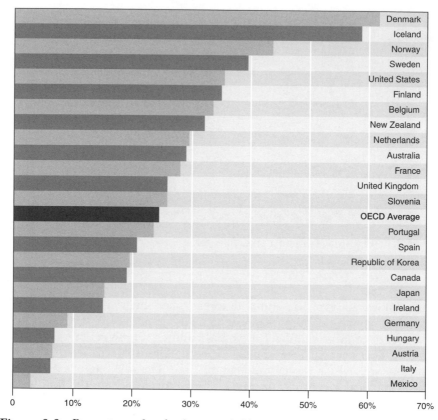

Figure 2.2   Percentage of under fours in childcare in selected OECD countries
Source: UNICEF, 2008

Strategies for handling the consequences for children as women join the labour force vary considerably internationally. The large number of women joining the workforce places great pressure on societies to provide out-of-home care (UNICEF, 2008). In the US and the UK, for example, this situation has led to major problems in securing widespread, qualified care for preschoolers while both parents are at work. Also, this is ideologically considered a 'private matter', solely the family's responsibility (Clarke-Stewart and Allhusen, 2005), although in the Scandinavian welfare approach, it is considered a joint responsibility between state, local government and family.

The study by the NICHD Early Child Care Research Network (2005, p. 432) illuminates the situation in the US:

the fact is that child care in the United States is highly fragmented and erratic ... the vast majority of child care is of unacceptably low quality, and

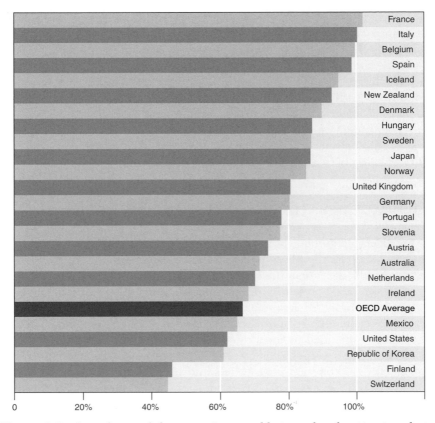

Figure 2.3 Attendance of three- to six-year-olds in early education in selected OECD countries

Source: UNICEF, 2008

in the first 3 years of life it does not meet even minimal recommended guidelines.

This is not the case in many European societies, but in a report on the childcare conditions in Germany, Bertram (2006) concluded that a strong and pervasive ideology regarding the natural obligations of mothers to their family and young children has considerably slowed down early out-of-home care. In other words, 'family-centrism' and 'mother-centrism' (see Chapter 1) are still potent beliefs in a modern society confronted with the enormous practical consequences of the changes impinging on families, women and young children.[16]

In contrast to the UK and the US, the Scandinavian countries strongly believe in the role of the state as being co-responsible for childcare (Leira, 1992), which has led to the establishment of a nationwide childcare system.

Thus, the old theories about the mother as the child's sole carer rarely work as explanatory models to enhance the understanding of the social complexities of early childhood today. Nor do they fit women's dual functions in both the private and social arenas in society. According to Leira's (1992) feminist analysis, this relatively new situation not only undermines the rationale behind traditional sociological and psychological views of motherhood, but also poses problems for this dualist idea: the woman as *either* mother *or* wage earner, dependent on whether the focus of study is the family or the labour market. This private/social sphere division fails to capture the everyday reality of being both a mother and an employee.

CHILDCARE DEBATES AND INTERPRETATIVE FILTERS

The considerable number of young children in daycare has had a profound impact not only family life but also on the development of young children. Fundamental beliefs about the assumed importance of parents may be challenged by the new non-family developmental arena. According to Phoenix et al. (1991), rapid societal change opens up ideological controversies because concepts such as 'motherhood', 'family', 'child' and 'childhood' are inextricably embedded in social ideologies that act as mental and cultural institutions. The changes documented previously may threaten political, professional and commonsense beliefs and give rise to concerns and criticism, as vital belief systems come under attack.[17] Professional and public debates may be seen as a clash of values to define the child's best interests. Therefore, an analysis of fundamental, widely held beliefs about children is a relevant research subject in itself, because the 'problematization' of children and childhood has become an active discursive part of how childhood should be construed (Rosier, 2009).

With reference to the chapter heading 'beliefs provoked', this section analyses media debates about childcare as a presumed problematic developmental arena. As evidenced by Singer and Singer (2001), the media (newspapers, magazines, TV, radio and the internet) influence not only children but also parental beliefs. However, this is rarely touched upon by developmentalists. The subject is nonexistent in most mainstream developmental psychological textbooks (for example Papalia et al., 2002; Bee and Boyd, 2007; Harwood et al., 2008) or is only briefly touched upon in others (Bukato and Daehler, 2004; Kail, 2007; Berk, 2009; Boyd and Bee, 2010). When it is discussed, it is about the impact of media (TV, computer games and the internet) on the child, which is important, but media influences on parental beliefs and socialization practices are not touched upon. Why is this issue important? Because, in various ways, media communication and debates do in fact influence public opinions as well as parents' self-evaluation (Singer and Singer, 2001). Content analysis studies consistently indicate that some media represent a distorted view of reality, in particular with regard to gender roles (Signorelli, 1989). A meta-analysis of 31 studies (total number of respondents 12,597) of the media effect on gender stereotypes and socialization concluded that the media are indeed powerful (Oppliger, 2007). In addition, a clear relationship has been documented between socialization beliefs and practices and how they affect the child's prosocial development (Eisenberg and Valiente, 2002).

In view of massive media exposure, one may speculate if the power of the media has a stronger impact on people's beliefs than family and child research. As will be demonstrated, childcare debates are often rooted in selected research, which is, in turn, interpreted by so-called 'experts' who are not researchers.

People hold certain beliefs about what constitutes appropriate or inappropriate behaviour, perceptions of what a child essentially is and what constitutes good parenting and caring. These perceptions function as *interpretative filters* that seem influential in constructing the child. Interpretative filters change over time. Fuller (2008) examined the political and cultural struggles over early education and care and the major historical contests over early childcare. He showed that controversies based on idealized views and ideologies regarding young childhood go back many years, and controversies continue today, creating new challenges. In a summary of childcare research and its concomitant opinions, Rutter (2008) concluded that the controversies over childcare have not gone away, and one may add, they probably never will.

In the discussion that follows, there is no underlying assumption that *all* infants have to be in out-of-home care, only the knowledge based on facts that very many are. In addition, in some debates, the realities of childcare are vital, for example when low quality is a frequent criticism. This is an important fact not to be ignored. But an extrapolation made from the negative consequences of low quality to the abandonment altogether of childcare, as seen in some critiques of early childcare, is problematic. In comparison, who would abandon the family as an important social institution on the basis of reported violence and maltreatment in some families?

In what follows, repeatedly articulated arguments in public childcare debates will be presented and evaluated according to which interpretative filters are at work; however, it should be noted that they are not necessarily representative. After presentation and categorization of the debates, recent childcare research will be presented as a base for reflection, finally reaching a conclusion. It is beyond the scope of this discussion to show the worldwide prevalence of the childcare debate. The arguments in this section are mainly drawn from material written in English. However, as the types of argument, published in English and other languages, are surprisingly alike, it is relatively easy to categorize them under similar headings. Rapid changes in young children's lives stir up controversies, of which New Zealand is an illuminating case, where, in recent years, a rising number of mothers of children under three have joined the workforce, creating a need for more extensive early out-of-home care.[18] This situation has caused much debate and stirred up fears about early childcare. Kamerman and Moss (2009), in reviewing the politics about parental leave (and childcare) in several countries, even call the debates 'value wars'. So, both manifest and latent beliefs in the debates are a basis for analysis, together with material from other countries with similar debates to the UK, Australia and the US.

The arguments below are categorized into three groups: family- and mother-centricity, the problem behaviour argument, and the cortisol debate.

Family- and mother-centric filters

Chapter 1 defined *family-centrism* as a belief that the only important primary socialization of preschoolers took place in the family. The notion that in societies with growing early out-of-home care, the family has been 'stripped of its functions' or 'functionally emptied', thus weakening the importance of the family in society, is based on Parsons and Bales (1955). They consider young children's socialization within the nuclear family as the sine qua non of healthy development , advocating a family-centric paradigm for preschoolers. When the developmental change implies a delegation of early care and socialization to other arenas, this is becomes a threat to the family's primary role. As pointed out in Chapter 1, this has led to childcare being ignored or denied as a socialization arena.

The critique of the family-centric stance does not argue that the family has become irrelevant. (Chapter 4 will prove the contrary.) But in the contemporary developmental ecology of early childhood, the family has become one (special) socializing agent among others. With a growing number of children in early out-of-home care, it becomes problematic to apply a family-centric filter to understand the consequences for a child growing up in two arenas, family and childcare. In a later section, some professional challenges to classical socialization theory will be discussed, followed by an alternative definition and a presentation of the dual socialization model.

Family-centrism is in play both directly and indirectly in the childcare debate. This is seen in the relative overimportance of the (negative) impact of childcare as opposed to the family. This is articulated when serious short- and long-term consequences are emphasized. For example:

> research shows that child care – unless done incredible well – can be psychologically damaging for babies. It may lead to poor social attachment and arrested emotional development – unhappy kids who have learnt to switch off. (Porter, quoted in McCrone, 2009, p. 1)

Dr Simon Rowley's 'home is best for babies' message, as he believes that parents should 'actually be parents – not absentee parents', stirred a fierce debate about the dangers and negative importance of early childcare (see Woulfe, 2009). Similarly, John McCrone (2009) asked if they had been building 'politically correct orphanages? Sterile baby barns that will turn out emotionally stunted children?' Taking childcare as a serious developmental threat is rooted in an underlying belief of what 'normality' should be – the primacy of the family in early care and development. If the family is the primary socializing agent in young childhood, childcare threatens and competes with the fundamental role of the family in society. But instead of ignoring or underscoring the impact of childcare, as in the underimportance approach, potential dangers are exaggerated in order to install the family as the proper place to grow up in early childhood.

A pure mother-centric position claims that only in a one-to-one intimate relationship between the natural mother and her young child is proper care and development possible. In Chapter 1, this position was traced back to pre-paradigm shift professional views in developmental psychology – as seen in early attachment theory, where Bowlby coined his 'monotropy' concept.[19] If warnings about early childcare as a threat are to be substantiated, they should be derived from an unbiased use of the available research. A review of the childcare debates, however, shows that this rarely happens. When research is referred to, the impression is that it is selectively used for the underlying purpose of claiming a mother-centric position. For instance, Steve Biddulph, Australian psychologist, debater and family guru, has been influential in debating the dangers of early childcare.[20] In a UNICEF report (2008), Biddulph is quoted as saying:

> The first three years of life are those when children are too vulnerable, too much in need of intimate care and all it can offer, to be left to group care by strangers. (p. 19)

When reading the report, it is clear that the opposite of strangers solely responsible for fulfilling the child's need of intimate care is the natural mother and, to a certain extent, the father too. The emotive words 'left to group care by strangers' do not appreciate that the child obviously becomes acquainted with the staff, and that within quality childcare, it is also possible to develop personal relationships (Clarke-Stewart and Allhusen, 2005).

In the UNICEF (2008) report, Oxford psychotherapist Sue Gerhardt's (2004a) book, *Why Love Matters: How Affection Shapes a Baby's Brain,* is cited.[21] Here she points to the necessity of a one-to-one relationship. But which adult is responsible for what happens in the one-to-one relationship?:

> The baby's mother is primed to do these things for her baby by her own hormones, and is more likely (than others) to have the intense

identification with the baby's feelings that is needed, provided she has the inner resources to do so. (UNICEF, 2008, p. 19)

This statement is partly legitimized by referring to new neurobiological research, which will be discussed in a later section. Gerhardt clearly demonstrates the naturalization of motherhood using a mother-centric interpretative filter. Even when hormones are at play, which they are, it seems that the hormone argument is influenced by bonding research, which has turned out to be a fallacy (Eyer, 1993), and maternal bonding is not part of current attachment research (Cassidy and Shaver, 2008). So it is misleading to conclude that only a mother is primed to do these things. In her criticism of early childcare, psychotherapist Elisabeth Muir provides a pure mother-centric stance:

If you say a mother and a caregiver are interchangeable, what are you saying? You are saying that anyone can mother a baby and it's cheap at the price. Well, I disagree. The cost in societal and ultimately in human terms is very high. (quoted in Feeney and Porter, 2009)

A recent and somewhat extreme mother-centric argument comes from Dr Dennis Friedman (2010). His book *An Unsolicited Gift* caused debate in England, claiming, as it did, that baby boys who have had a nanny turn into 'womanizers', and baby girls, who have had a nanny or au pair, are filled with an internal feeling of emptiness, which they will later compensate for with oral fixating behaviours such as drinking, taking drugs and being sexually addicted. Friedman said that the baby has a right, too – the right to have a relationship with a mother who is '100 per cent connected' (see Rollo, 2010). The arguments are built on a traditional, pre-paradigm shift, Freudian stance from child psychology with the Oedipal conflict in top-down use. In addition, empirical verification is missing. Thus, falling short of research-based arguments for his stance, an interesting question is why Friedman's classical psychoanalysis, a professional voice from yesteryear, can provoke public debate today? It may be that underlying feelings of guilt in working mothers are stimulated, and that still held gender naturalization ideologies in society about maternal responsibilities and roles are legitimized.

These examples of the mother-centric interpretative filter are rooted in pre-paradigm shift theories. Young children need a mutual core relationship with someone, including their mothers, but research has shown that it seems not to be a fundamental need to be with the mother 24 hours a day (Howes and Spieker, 2008). Assessed with the interpretative filter of mother-centricity – claiming a 'must be' and totally devoted relationship – many young children's actual lives clearly deviate from such an underlying benchmark of normality.

The problem behaviour argument

A second problem raised by the impact of childcare is the 'problem behaviour' argument. In contrast to warnings based on family-centric and mother-centric interpretative filters, the problem behaviour argument is based on sober, but seemingly exaggerated interpretations of research findings (to be discussed later). Warnings about bad behaviour and aggressiveness have been widely disseminated:

> The strongest research findings are that full-time care during the first and second years is strongly linked to later behaviour problems. These are children that are 'mean' to others, who hit and blame other children. They are likely to be less cooperative and more intolerant of frustration. To me, these are all capacities which suggest poor development of the 'social brain'. (Gerhardt, 2004b, p. 21)

The UNICEF report (2008) also links very young children's full-time childcare with behavioural problems and aggression later in life. As noted in an article in the New Zealand *Little Treasures* magazine (2009, p. 9), the problem behaviour argument is directly linked to specific research:

> The more children spend in child care from birth to age four and a half, the less likely they are to get along with others and the more aggressive and disobedient they are, found one of the biggest studies on ECE [early childhood education], the National Institute of Child Health and Human Development (NICHD).

It is reasonable enough to mention, the only moderation of the media claims at hand, that the differences between aggressive, disobedient children and other children were small. Furthermore, if they experienced good parenting as well, they suffered no major negative effects. In their evaluation of the childcare research, Clarke-Stewart and Allhusen (2005) devoted a section to 'Behaviour problems'. They concluded that 'Child care can apparently be a venue for learning social graces or a breeding ground for aggression' (p. 91). The message about the link between early full-time childcare exposure and behaviour problems seems to have spread in the public debate about childcare as a threat. There is a tendency, however, to exaggerate the findings and their long-term importance. The relative strength, degree and generalization of the childcare problem behaviour findings will be discussed later in the chapter.

The cortisol argument: new warnings

Will research findings settle the childcare debate once and for all? Hardly, because the undercurrent of ideological controversies is too strong to put to rest. As mentioned earlier, in a time of rapid change, polarization is expected to occur. The latest controversy and the concomitant critique of childcare claim documentation in 'hard' neurobiological evidence – more specifically, recent studies on the stress hormone cortisol. Why the preoccupation with cortisol? Because it is an important hormonal indicator related to stress. Cortisol is a steroid hormone produced by the adrenal gland, which is released in response to stress. Increases in salivary cortisol levels are used as biological markers of stress and emotional reactions, and chronic exposure to stress in early childhood may be a risk for later affective and cognitive functioning (Vermeer and Ijzendorn, 2006).

The media have been powerful in dissipating the cortisol research, serving a vital function in public education and knowledge. In a sample from the written media regarding the neurobiological arguments, very few active researchers are interviewed; instead various so-called 'experts' and organizations construe the message from new research. Clearly, extrapolations about the consequences show that seemingly non-communicated interpretative filters are at work, too. For example, under the headline 'Home Best for Babies Says Doctor' (Woulfe, 2009), neonatal paediatrician Dr Simon Rowley is cited as having advised parents to do all they can not to put their young children in childcare, as it could permanently harm their brains. One parent (obviously the mother) should stay at home with the child, at least for the first two years:

> I think the evidence is increasing that it's best for the child to be with a single caregiver if possible, or you know, with family. (Rowley, quoted in Woulfe, 2009)

Regarding 'the evidence is increasing', these wide-ranging family- and mother-centric-based recommendations are founded on a single cortisol study on childcare (the importance of the cortisol findings will be scrutinized later). In *The Press* (see McCrone, 2009) under the heading 'Daycare Debate', Lauren Porter, social worker and leader of New Zealand's Christchurch Centre for Attachment, explained that the dangers of early childcare can lead to the stress hormone cortisol being found in childcare babies. Furthermore, a presumed developmental link between exposure to stress early in life and later behavioural problems is established. Under the headline 'Fear in the Blood', *The Family in America* (2003) cited new cortisol research:

> When mothers leave their toddler-age children in day care rather than care for them at home, they expose them to stress severe enough to adversely affect their body chemistry. The troubling biochemical effects of childcare recently received attention from a team of child-development experts at the University of Minnesota, who worry that day-care stress in young children may translate into serious later psychological problems.

However, the researchers themselves admit not knowing if there are adverse effects on the developing brain from the elevated cortisol levels found in toddlers attending daycare. They acknowledged that 'we do not know... whether early experiences of mild repeated neuroendocrine stress such as that observed in the present study for toddlers have any influence on the developing brain'. The serious warning above is based on only one small study.

A sample of newspaper and magazine articles reveals that intense international media exposure followed in the wake of a book made popular with its 'translation' of the esoteric language of neurobiological science. As previously mentioned in connection with the neurobiological argument, Gerhardt (2004b) wrote an article in *The Guardian*, 'Cradle of Civilisation', with the subtitle 'In order to develop a "social brain", babies need loving one-to-one care'. Without specifically using the cortisol childcare studies, Gerhardt concluded the following, extrapolating from neuropsychology:

> Babies can only cope with about 10 hours a week of daycare, before it may start to affect their emotional development, particularly if the care is of low quality. The strongest research findings are that full-time care during the first and second years is strongly linked to later behaviour problems. (Gerhardt, 2004b)

The evidence behind the child's presumed need for loving *one-to-one care* will be evaluated in a later section.

The 2008 UNICEF report *The Child Care Transition* briefly summarizes new neuroscience research. This is not, however, based on primary sources, but on three second-hand reviews using basic non-applied research with a 'what-can-we-do?' purpose, for example in the education of preschoolers and in policy matters (see UNICEF, 2008, p. 7). By using research in this way, gaps have to be filled with inferences and conclusions that do not derive from the said research. The reason being that basic neurobiological research does not deal with applied consequences. In other words, this widely disseminated and often cited UNICEF report builds on a rather shaky foundation. In spite of this, far-reaching theoretical claims are made. For example, we see a renaissance of the developmental fixed stage statement, not in a Piagetian way, but in neurobiological terms:

> A... core concept is the sequential development of the human brain. Each of these periods is associated with specific areas of neurobiological circuitry and with specific human abilities. And each builds on the circuits and skills laid down in the previous period. It is this process that sets the stage for all future cognitive and emotional development – a stage that is either sturdy or shaky depending on the kind and quality of interactions with primary caregivers in the earliest months and years of life. (UNICEF, 2008, p. 6)

Although there are some evolutionary-based time schedules involved in building the brain, this neural fixed stage paradigm is not a matter of fact, but is debated and questioned by leading researchers (Rutter, 2008). Little in development seems to be predetermined or permanently fixed – including the brain and even some gene development (Karmiloff-Smith 2010); rather epigenesis seems to be probabilistic, and both brain development and gene expression are *activity dependent* (Majdan and Schatz, 2006 Gottlieb, 2007).

The 2008 UNICEF report also claims that there is evidence that a *persistent elevation* of the stress hormone cortisol is known to be damaging to the delicate architecture of the developing brain, and is linked to stress-related illnesses later in life. This is an important and plausible statement, but as will be documented later, children in early childcare do not seem to have elevated cortisol levels all the time, only in the afternoon.

Using the neurobiological argument and additional findings of reported behaviour problems seemingly arising from early childcare experience, the following statement was made: 'Overall, there is a broad consensus that child care that is "too early and too long" can be damaging' (UNICEF, 2008, p. 12). Obviously, early childcare is not necessarily a must, and longer maternity and paternity leave policies, similar to the ones in Scandinavia, will be beneficial. Such cautiousness may be well directed; let the doubt be to the potential benefit of the infant. But does this seemingly broad consensus have a solid, confirmed research base? In order to answer this question, let us take a careful, unbiased look at the present research evidence and its implications for practice (for example Ramey, 2005), instead of making premature conclusions based on unwarranted extrapolations of selected examples.

RECENT CHILDCARE RESEARCH

The intention here is to present a relatively balanced and reflective position, although even the high-quality research presented may prove insufficient to solve this matter definitively. However, research is undoubtedly the best navigator in this rough territory to establish fairly solid ground upon which conclusions about the potential benefits and drawbacks of early childcare can be drawn.

Findings presented and discussed

For several decades, evidence has accumulated about the developmental benefits of *high-quality* early childcare and education in a number of countries (UNICEF, 2005; Clarke-Stewart and Allhusen, 2005; The NIHCD Early Child Care Research Network, 2005). Children from disadvantaged families and less well educated parents seem to benefit the most, whereas the effect on children from more privileged families is less prominent (Fuller, 2008). Balancing the evidence, positive developmental gains outscore negative findings. In addition, family factors significantly outweigh the childcare factors (NIHCD Early Child Care Research Network, 2005).

Research on the impact of childcare has continued into the 21st century. The debate for and against childcare has been replaced by more sophisticated insights into which aspects of childcare and its interaction with the family can affect the children. In Scandinavia, which has more than 40 years' experience of universal childcare of a relatively high quality, the focus today is not on an either/or debate arguing for the family and against childcare. Childcare is seen as being normal; instead discussions are about maintaining quality in times of global economic crisis.

The infant childcare debate was in full swing when the high-quality, longitudinal NICHD Study of Early Child Care and Youth Development started (Howes and Spieker, 2008). Here an impressive group of leading developmentalists joined together to examine the short- and long-term impact of childcare on 1,300 children in the US.[22] The children were observed from the age of six months throughout their school years. The important main findings relevant for the childcare debate are:

1. *The family's emotional importance for children's development is not reduced:* A consistent finding is that family factors, for example the quality of the mother–child relationship, have a major impact on children's early and later development. This is found for children who have attended childcare from a very young age.
2. *The emotional, social and physical qualities of childcare are moderately related to children's social and emotional development:* This may relate to the quality of the interactions with adults in childcare, for example positive interactions between teacher and child. Thus, some children in low-quality childcare do not experience optimum conditions. Their relationship with their mother is less harmonious, they display more behavioural problems and poorer language comprehension than children in higher quality facilities.
3. *Contact with childcare staff neither spoiled nor improved children's emotional connection with their mothers:* There were some exceptions. Infants who spent more than 10 hours a week in low-quality childcare facilities, or who switched repeatedly between facilities during their first 18 months, had less secure attachments to adults. This was only seen, however, when the mothers were simultaneously assessed as less sensitive. So, the quality of both the mother–child relationship and the childcare facility appear to lead to attachment issues for these children.
4. *Childcare quality has an effect on children's development:* Examples include staff–child ratio, group size, staff education, beliefs and relationships. The higher the number of quality indicators, the fewer behavioural problems

reported. This also relates to better language comprehension and readiness for school.

5. *A relationship, although a moderate one, is seen between the hours spent in childcare during the first six months of life and maternal sensitivity:* At 36 months, such children display less positive engagement in interactions with the mother. However, family factors, for example mothers' educational background and maternal wellbeing, better explained the quality of the mother–child relationship from the child's sixth month of life than the number of hours spent in childcare.

6. *A significant relationship exists between the number of weekly hours spent in childcare and the occurrence of behavioural problems:* This was found both for four- and five-year-old children and, later, when they reached primary school. More than 30 hours a week in childcare predicted more behavioural problems – increased aggression, more fighting, more disobedience and more bullying behaviour. But not all children develop antisocial behaviour by spending more than 30 hours a week in childcare. The differences relating to the number of hours spent in childcare were also found in high-quality childcare.

These are some of the facts behind the warnings seen in the childcare debate, for example how to interpret the gravity of the childcare problem behaviour argument. Some moderations must be raised:

1. The relationship found only shows small effect sizes. So, in giving 'parental advice', it should be made clear that on the individual child level, there is no need to worry that a child will become aggressive. However, the findings may prove relevant in large-scale policy matters (NICHD, 2005).

2. The elevated behavioural problems are not seen to be pathological.

3. There is little evidence that increased childcare aggression will continue, for example, into adolescence.

4. Children's behavioural problems equal the amount in society in general. But the results point to the fact that some US children will not benefit from spending many hours in childcare.

The above findings appear to be robust, at least in a US context. A UK longitudinal study of more than 3,000 children showed similar results, and before the age of three, early childcare experience was associated with higher levels of antisocial behaviour at age three (Sylva et al., 2003). The degree to which such findings are relevant to countries other than the US and the UK is debatable (UNICEF, 2008). It is an open question whether the findings arising from children sampled from a relatively larger number of lower than high-quality out-of-home care can be generalized. Do the findings of greater behavioural problems occur in a Scandinavian context, for example, with its universal, relatively high-quality childcare system? A Swedish longitudinal study (Andersson, 1989, 1992) did not find that the number of hours spent in childcare were associated with problematic behaviour.

In a Danish longitudinal survey of children, 6,000 children were followed from five months to fifteen years of age (www.sfi.dk). Among a wide range of developmentally important dimensions, the study explored the developmental consequences of the amount of time spent in childcare. A relatively small number of Danish children spend large amounts of time in childcare (more than 40 hours) a week. But many children are above the critical 30-hour limit, which the US study emphasized. For a randomly selected sample of children of 3.5 years of age, a range of emotional and social characteristics were examined. These included ratings of externalization/internalization, sadness, nervousness, anxiety, confidence, temperament, impulsivity, aggression, hyperactivity, ability to concentrate and social skills. Was there a significant relationship between a higher negative temperament profile and the amount of time spent in childcare?[23] Figure 2.4 shows the results.

As can be seen, a non-significant relationship was found in children who spent up to 38 hours a week in childcare and their temperament profile. From 38 to 45 hours, a rise in odds ratio frequencies, although still non-significant, was observed. From 45 hours, the relationship became significant. Interestingly, 3.5-year-olds, who are in Danish childcare for 48 hours a week, are 0.8 times more prone to manifest a negative temperament profile than those in childcare for 30 hours a week. A simple linear connection

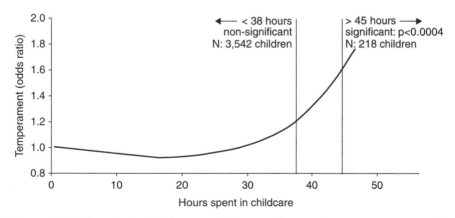

Figure 2.4 The relationship between 3.5-year-olds negative temperament profile and weekly hours in childcare

Source: Dencik et al., 2008

between time spent in childcare and temperament does not seem to be the case, however. Additional analyses showed the following:

1. *No developmental differences were found between children who were in their mothers' care and children in childcare:* Unlike the findings of the Swedish study, this means that the early influence of childcare is neutral, neither positive nor negative, for Danish children. Thus, there is no support for viewing childcare as a general threat or benefit.
2. *No gender differences were detectable in relation to time spent in childcare:* The same number of boys and girls showed negative behaviour when analysed in relation to an increasing number of childcare hours.
3. *No discernible difference was found between children who had been looked after by others for 0–30, 30–35 or 35–45 hours a week:* Bearing in mind the large sample, even minor developmental differences will show up. In the sample, recruited from all parts of the country and from a wide range of childcare facilities, unlike the US and UK studies, this one does not support the finding that more than 30 hours a week spent in childcare poses a risk in terms of developing behavioural problems. However, a gradual increase in temperament difficulties and behavioural problems is seen for the 3.5-year-olds who spend more than 38–39 hours weekly in childcare.
4. *Spending more than 45 hours in childcare a week is associated with a significant increase in both temperament difficulties and behavioural problems* ($p < 0.0004$): This applied to 1.3% of the sample. But time spent in childcare is not the only explanatory factor. Additional analyses showed that these children came from difficult family backgrounds. More often than the majority of the sample, these children have experienced a divorce, and live with a single mother, who is more prone to depression. In addition, these mothers work far more hours per week than the rest of the mothers in the sample. Thus, an extremely high number of hours spent in childcare per week is not the only explanation behind the negative temperament and behavioural characteristics found in the Danish study. Rather, it is a combination of both family and childcare factors. More than 45 hours per week spent in childcare, however, should be viewed as a contributing risk factor.

Apart from this longitudinal Danish study, Scandinavian studies of the long-term developmental effects of spending time in organized childcare are rare. There is, however, the groundbreaking Swedish study of early childcare and its consequences later on in childhood. The study attracted international attention, as it revealed distinct effects of growing up in public childcare of generally high quality (Andersson, 1989). A number of positive effects of early childcare were found, benefits that remained discernible into later school age. This does not necessarily mean that these effects will last beyond that age. Are there any long-term effects of early childcare experiences, or are they gradually erased by experiences in school and later childhood? In other words: Are children aged 13 different because they spent part of their early life in childcare of relatively high quality? If they are, which group does better?

The second part of the Swedish study followed children until the age of 13. Andersson (1992) examined the social, emotional and cognitive status and the academic performance of children, who, as preschoolers, had:

1. spent time in childcare before the age of one
2. gone to childcare after the age of one
3. spent their childhood with their mother.

To avoid any bias, analysts were not told which group any one child belonged to. The findings were striking. Many years later, early childcare experiences had a clearly discernible effect. Children with early and full-time childcare experiences were regarded as socially competent by teachers and peers alike. They had better academic performances compared to those who had been looked after at home. The Swedish study showed no signs of negative emotional effects of early childcare experiences. On the contrary, at the age of 13, children with extensive early childcare experience were found to be less aggressive, more independent and less anxious, compared to those who either started later in childcare or stayed at home in their early childhood.

In some political contexts, however, sometimes even the best research, highlighting the developmental benefits of childcare, cannot move legislators. But what if public investment in early child development pays off in a society's economy in the long run? For example, what provides the best pay-off for a society that, by law, is obliged to help at-risk children? The World Bank has dealt with that. Examining the evidence from public childcare and other out-of-family arrangements, Grunewald and Rolnick (2007, p. 29), two leading economists, concluded that:

> The evidence is clear that investment in ECD [early child development] for at-risk children pays a high public return (17 dollars in return for each dollars invested). Compared with the billions of dollars spent each year on high risk economic developmental schemes, an investment in ECD is a far better and far more secure economic development tool. Now it is time to capitalize on this knowledge.

How is this possible? In reviewing the research evidence, Young and Richardson (2007) concluded that money spent by society in the early years significantly reduces later costs. The subsequent risk of getting into later problems reduces for at risk-children who grow up in a childcare arrangement in their young childhood compared to not being in early child-care. The risk is significantly reduced concerning engaging in criminality, becoming a school dropout, needing special education, having teenage pregnancies and receiving social support. Fewer were sent to prison in ado-lescence and adulthood. In addition, more went on to secondary school and vocational training, and more became employed, so not living on welfare; instead, they actively contributed to society by paying taxes. When the cost of running a preschool was compared with the expense these children might incur if they ended up as school dropouts and social delinquents, the difference was strikingly in favour of the early preschoolers (Grunewald and Rolnick, 2007). The conclusion is that an early child developmental arrange-ment is, in the long run, probably the cheapest and most efficient long-term countermeasure to teenage delinquency within a high-risk population.

Such findings appear to be even better in societies that, on a broader scale, invest in public welfare. In an analysis of the connection between the welfare state and the family, Andersson (1992) argued that childcare in Sweden constitutes a safety net, offering vital support to dual-income Scandinavian families. Furthermore, a young childhood in Sweden, with its universal high-quality childcare and, by international comparison, generous maternal and paternal leave arrangements, has these distinct characteristics:

- young children generally thrive in childcare
- they do not suffer from their mothers' absence and fathers have become increasingly involved in caring for the next generation.

Three main conclusions can be drawn now:

1. Any relationship between 30 hours of childcare and a significant rise in negative behaviour was not found in two Scandinavian longitudinal studies.
2. The effect sizes in the NICHD study were small, indicating that the chances for an individual child to suffer behavioural problems are low.
3. The behavioural problems depicted in the NICHD study were not pathological and they equalled children's behavioural problems in society in general.

What is known?: the cortisol studies

Here, the results of cortisol studies will be presented, interpreted and dis-cussed. Vermeer and van Ijzendorn's (2006) paper is highly relevant, because all the cortisol studies are mentioned, evaluated or used in a meta-analysis, combining all the data. Furthermore, the results and the implications, known and unknown, are seriously discussed. Their only agenda is to reach sober conclusions based on the research at hand.

So, what is known at the present time? Studies using urine sampling have not shown elevated cortisol excretion, whereas four using saliva samples did. A meta-analysis of those showed a characteristic pattern of diurnal cortisol in children in childcare compared to children at home, as shown in Figure 2.5.

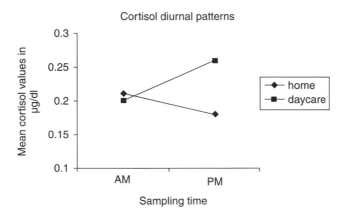

Figure 2.5   Diurnal changes in cortisol levels between mid-morning and mid-afternoon at home and in childcare

Source: Vermeer and van Ijzendorn, 2006

A mid-afternoon raised cortisol level is seen in childcare children, but not in children at home. With the home cortisol level assumed to be the norm, there is a marked deviation from the expected.[24]

In order to interpret such findings, four questions have to be answered:

1. How strong are the findings?
2. Are elevations chronic or temporary during a day/night and week cycle?
3. Does context matter?
4. Do the studies show whether the rise in cortisol is developmentally harmful as claimed in new warnings?

Let us examine each question in detail.

1. *How strong are the findings?* Discussing effect sizes may seem trivial and technical, but it is relevant in order to reach a clear interpretation of the results. Correlations alone are not sufficiently informative. The combined effect size for seven studies was $r = 0.18$. Leaving out two urinary cortisol

estimating studies that did not show any effects, the effect size became $r = 0.23$. The effect of childcare on cortisol production was especially noticeable in children younger than three: $r = 0.25$. For children older than three, the combined effect size was not significant: $r = 0.08$. This seems to indicate that with increasing age and childcare experience, cortisol levels normalize. Vermeer and van Ijzendorn (2006) themselves state that all *effects are small*. Technically speaking, they account for only a minor part of the variance accounted for. In other words, a huge range of unexplained factors that may potentially contribute to the findings are unknown. Small effect sizes indicate that the effects on 'my child' are absent or minor. But when experienced by many children, it may have some implications for large-scale policy issues.

2. *Chronic or temporary?* Short-term increases in stress hormone levels can be positive, whereas chronic exposure is not (Hart, 2006). What do the cortisol studies tell us? What is known and what is not known? The measured elevations in childcare children are obviously not chronic during a 24-hour period, as they occur mid-afternoon. It is known that in the morning, cortisol production is the same for both children at home and in childcare. It is also known that in childcare during the afternoon, it is higher than expected in a family context. It is not known, however, whether cortisol levels are raised in childcare children at home in the late afternoon, or in the evening and during the night. But living in a well-functioning family seems to keep stress at normal levels compared with the distress of children living in families with major problems.[25]

   Based on that, a plausible hypothesis may be that childcare children's cortisol levels return to normal when the children are back with their family in the late afternoon (or earlier) after childcare. If this is so, childcare children (without stress in the family) would, over a 24-hour period, have normal cortisol levels for probably 18–20 hours. Thus, the raised afternoon cortisol levels are not chronic on a 24-hour scale, but rather a functional contextual adaptation to the fears (for some) and excitements (for others) in childcare. As a whole, there is a weak basis in the cortisol studies to conclude that childcare children are exposed to chronically raised cortisol levels. This conclusion can obviously not be drawn from the meta-analysis (Vermeer and van Ijzendorn, 2006).

3. *Does context matter?* Short-term stress is beneficial because it helps individuals cope with demanding situations. Vermeer and van Ijzendorn (2006) speculate whether stressful encounters in peer groups may explain elevated hormone production. Peer group experience may be more uncontrollable and frightening for the under threes. This 'peer group as stressor hypothesis' seems plausible. If confirmed, small children's peer group encounters (although dependent on size and type of interaction) may, in principle, function in the same way in several contexts. One can take this one step further regarding some non-childcare children's developmental ecology. Although not interacting with their peers in childcare, many

one- to three-year-olds experience extensive peer contact in playgrounds, organized activities, clubs or neighbours' gardens, with parents watching, but not directly involved. Afternoon cortisol production has not been measured in these contexts. One hypothesis is that during excited group playing, cortisol will be elevated in one- to three-year-olds, compared to children staying at home without peer contact. For some children with elevated cortisol levels, peer group interactions may be experienced as exciting, not as threatening. For example, when happy rough-and-tumble play occurs, a corresponding short-term rise in cortisol production is to be expected, that is, an adaptive context-specific response.

4. *Developmentally harmful?* New warnings have repeatedly used the cortisol studies as hard proof to support arguments that early childcare threatens children's development. But can this be inferred from the present studies? In a specific discussion on this question, Vermeer and van Ijzendorn (2006, p. 398) conclude what is not known:

> none of the included studies were designed to examine the impact of the (small) increases of cortisol levels on child development. Therefore, it is not known whether the reported elevated cortisol levels at child-care are an adaptive context specific response to the stresses of group life... However, there is no empirical evidence that the elevated cortisol levels at childcare would have adverse implications for children's later development.

This may be supported by the important finding that after three years of age, there was no significant rise in cortisol in childcare children. The childcare cortisol effect seems to fade when children get older and have had more childcare experience.

Does childcare quality matter? The cortisol debate has to be connected to the quality dimension and at the present time this is an unresolved discussion. The childcare quality dimension is important, because Vermeer and van Ijzendorn (2006) did find evidence of raised cortisol levels even in high-quality settings. However, this was not uniform, as cortisol levels changed with group size, child–carer ratio, number of adults in the group, characteristics of the carer team, areas of indoor space and playrooms, and available space per child. So, even within childcare centres of relatively high quality, the specific ways of running the centre can have consequences for children's stress levels. All together, however, it seems that childcare quality, not in general but under specific conditions, may be an important modifier of elevated stress hormone levels:

> Child care quality is associated with children's cortisol levels. Children who received more attention and stimulation from their caregivers in child care have lower cortisol levels over the course of the day; their cortisol levels looked just like those of children who stayed in the peaceful environment of their own homes. (Clarke-Stewart and Allhusen, 2005, p. 107)

Conclusions and future perspectives

Evaluating the childcare debates, one is left with the impression that the more heated the arguments, the less room for an unbiased, research-based voice. Ideologies and fundamental beliefs about families, mothers and children show interpretative filters at work that are easily detectable. Such convictions, however, seldom stand alone in the debate, the authority of research is frequently used as a fig leaf, presumably to legitimize preconceived conclusions.

Evaluated on the basis of recent high-quality research, there is little support for family- and mother-centric-based warnings about the threats of childcare. However, the realistic warnings about possible behavioural problems should not be overlooked, or exaggerated. Although the effect sizes are small and therefore do not pose a problem to the individual child, the link between many hours spent in childcare and the occurrence of aggression and bullying behaviour does exist, despite childcare quality. Although this correlation is not found in Scandinavian studies, it has been manifest in UK and US samples. It remains an open question as to how to interpret this difference.

Some recent, widely distributed warnings against full-time, early childcare attendance presented by the mass media have been based on neurobiological warnings. The cortisol childcare studies especially have been used as 'evidence' of serious short- and long-term negative consequences for young children's brains and socioemotional development. Claiming 'hardwired' neurobiological evidence is a powerful tool in the hands of public commentators and child experts. Yet used in the polemic, as demonstrated earlier, it may throw some babies out with the bathwater. Complexity and multifactorial explanations face hard times here, and an impression is that the fewer factors drawn into an argument (or selected from a study), the more important each of them appear to be.

So, regarding the growing 'practical' and 'advisory' use of neurobiological research in the criticism of early childcare and the claims of pure family- and mother-centric positions, some warnings must be given. Neurobiological research is a promising and rapidly growing field that contributes to developmental studies. But the relative weight of neuroscientific arguments has to be evaluated in their proper context. In a review chapter on the implications of attachment theory and research for childcare policies, the distinguished researcher Rutter (2008) looked explicitly at the implications of 'natural underpinnings'. The research evidence behind the last decades' outpouring of claims regarding the supposed effects of experiences on the brain is evaluated:

It is important to emphasize (1) that these claims (often) represent speculative extrapolations from the findings of neuroscience, and not empirically demonstrated causal connections; and (2) that the supposition that all the 'action' with respect to brain development takes place in the first 3 years is simply wrong. (Rutter, 2008, p. 964)

On the basis of the evaluation and discussion of present research, it can be concluded that the cortisol card has been wildly overplayed in the child-care debate. As we have seen, the cortisol warnings have been a hot issue, widespread in the media, and even appeared in the influential UNICEF (2008) report that warns against the hazards of early childcare. This is counter-argued in a recent report dealing with advantages and problems in the education and care of infants and toddlers (Carroll-Lind and Angus, 2011). There may be many arguments for or against early childcare, but the present research-based knowledge from neuroscience in general and the cortisol studies in specific does not support the warnings against early childcare.

The relatively small rise in cortisol levels for some hours in afternoon childcare can be interpreted as a relatively short-term adaptive response to stimulation and excitement in peer playgroups. Obviously, it is not separation from the mother that is at play as a mother-centric argument may suggest. If it were, then elevated cortisol levels would be found in children from when they started their day in childcare.

In other words, there is not one or even a few factors to explain this. In a discussion of the results, and pointing to the future, Vermeer and van Ijzendorn (2006, p. 399) embrace this contextual and multifactor interpretation:

> In our view, the most plausible explanation lies in the complex interaction between the quantity of child care attendance (both length of the day and hours a week), the quality of the child care setting, and characteristics of the child itself.

To this a wide range of family stressors and non-stressors can be added that directly or indirectly are interwoven with the childcare setting.

Numerous questions have been raised but remain unsolved. More research is clearly needed to obtain a better understanding of whether childcare produces chronic stress that can lead to illness or whether it is more about positive, temporary, contextual adaptation. Studies dealing with variations in stress hormone production in childcare children during a typical week are needed, and it would require measuring and comparing childcare and home children's cortisol levels, not only on a 24-hour basis, but also on a seven-day week basis. Furthermore, longitudinal studies of the potential later developmental effects of early raised stress hormone levels are needed, despite the findings that after three years of age, the levels are normal.

THEORY CHALLENGED IN CHANGED
REALITIES AND NEW RESEARCH

Classic socialization theory has greatly contributed to the understanding of children in social and developmental psychology. Chapter 1 briefly outlined the basic view in classic socialization theory by focusing on primary and secondary socialization According to the theory, primary socialization occurs exclusively in the family where the preschool child's fundamental personality development and sociality are established. Despite the paradigm shift within developmental psychology, specific critical evaluations of socialization theory have been mostly absent, with the notable exception of the so-called 'deconstructivist' approach (Burman, 2008a). But it was mainly the childhood sociologists who, in the 1990s, began to question some underlying basic assumptions behind the concept of socialization. The Parsonian approach especially presented an influential perspective on how the child becomes a social being. But does this type of understanding play any role in today's social theory? Sociologist Chris Jenks (1996, p. 29) has pointed to its immense influence in his discussion of Parson's socialization theory: 'the paradigms. ... established have, to a very large extent, captured and monopolized the child in social theory'.

'To become' and 'to make' social: socialization
paradigms challenged

Here the focus will be on highlighting the basic understanding of the non-social child in classical socialization theory. It will demonstrate that from the beginning of theory construction, a belief in how a biological foundation was transformed into a human being was an implicit assumption.

From where does this type of thinking originate? A historical perspective can localize it as being influenced by specific societal conditions, family life, gender roles and children's upbringing in pre-1960s Western cultures and, more precisely, in the 1940s and 50s postwar context. Embedded in this historical, specific reality, classical socialization theory constituted a meaningful, specialist narrative at a time when there was a dichotomy between the societal tasks of men and women. The woman/mother was (and should be) at home, looking after the children, and thus her societal task was devoted to her reproductive function. In contrast, the man/father was attached to society's productive sphere and his task was to provide the necessary material foundation for his family's survival. At the time, psychology regarded the father's role as insignificant in the early years of the child's life. He was, however, of significant and increasing importance as a role model, educator and authority figure as the children grew up. In primary socialization, non-family members (other adults, peers, friends) are considered to be without significance in socialization. It was only when children went to school – secondary socialization – that the social circle expanded significantly. This classical understanding of socialization has been influential in sociology, social and developmental psychology. But it can only be so as long as adults and children live in the type of family that classical socialization theory more or less implicitly presupposes. The problem is they do not live like that, and have not done so for decades.

What is the core meaning of the word 'socialization'? Socialization means *to become and to make social* (Katzenelson, 1994). Thus, it is implicit in the very term that human beings must *become* something, which they are not originally, and also that something or somebody must *make* them into this. In other words, the concept of socialization presupposes a 'to become' for the non-social human being. This basic view originates from various connected earlier theories. For example, when Freud's classical psychoanalytical theory was prominent, it was not uncommon to apply his metatheory as the general psychological basis and validation of classical socialization theory. The basic view about human beings' primary asociality found (and still finds) support in classical psychoanalysis. The drive-controlled, irrational, asocial 'id' must, gradually, with the help of care, upbringing and socialization, be superimposed by reality, represented by the 'ego'. The installment of the psychic representative of social order, the 'superego', was seen as a result of successful socialization and adaptation (the internalization of parents' morals) in a number of 1950s and 60s prominent international handbooks on social psychology (see for example Brown, 1965). George Herbert Mead's influential socialization theory presupposes secondary sociality and is based on this interpretative filter:

> Through a social process, then, the biological individual of proper organic stuff gets a mind and a self. Through society the impulsive animal becomes a rational animal, a man. (Mead, 1934, p. xxv)

The psyche and the self do not exist, not even in early shapes from the beginning of life, but come into existence as a reflexive process. In other words, self and sociality do not exist until this is in place in the ontogenesis.

However, psychoanalysis – which inspired Mead[26] – was (is) far from being the only theory that emphasized human beings' fundamental asociality (see Chapter 1). Additionally, sociality was (is) an acquired, secondary developmental process. A common idea behind the notion that children must be socialized is founded on the historically dominant perception that children basically were (are) incomplete adults. They were defined by what they did not know and were unable to do. The smaller the children were, the further they were from rationality. This is a basic view whose origins can be traced back to the Age of Enlightenment. Subsequently, on the basis of this philosophical foundation, psychological and pedagogical theories were developed about upbringing, which would 'bring the child up' to the desirable, socialized state, as defined by adults. The theories were and are numerous, but the above more or less implicit view of children has applied until recently (Gopnik et al., 1999).

Socialization ideas were also closely connected to the classical modern developmental ideal about striving for the 'enlightened human being'. In this connection, socialization became synonymous with civilization, development and modelling of immature, uneducated and basically uncivilized people. It was natural then to start with the children, before it was too late; to bring them up, *raise* them to the enlightened adults' level. This was not merely a matter for psychology but also for pedagogy. According to Gopnik et al. (1999), oddly, this general, historically conditioned perception of children was rarely substantiated by systematic proof. Theorists (initially philosophers) did not make the effort to examine what children really knew about the world – what they started with and what they learned later on. This did not happen (with a few exceptions) until modern child and developmental psychology systematically began to study small and older children's competencies. According to Gopnik et al. (1999), recent developmental research has proved that the historical consensus about children was quite wrong.

From the non-social novice to intersubjectivity and companionship

Today's research-based interpretative filters are far removed from Mead's impulsive and non-social animal. The paradigm was relatively representative of the period and has been repeated in standard textbooks in social psychology from the 1960s (for example Brown, 1965). As mentioned in Chapter 1, decades of research into infancy have, for some, revolutionized our psychological knowledge about human nature. This is an inevitable conclusion that must be drawn on the basis of a number of groundbreaking empirical studies of children's early competencies (see Parke, 1989; Field, 1990; Legerstee, 1992; Spelke et al., 1995; Karmiloff-Smith, 1995; Slater and Butterworth, 1997; Reddy et al., 1997; Tomasello, 1999, 2009; Bråten, 2007; Tomasello et al., 2005; Gopnik, 2009). For example, even shortly after birth, a baby can, in a non-reflexive manner, imitate adults who poke their tongues out – and not just mothers but also males (Field, 1990). Different facial expressions can also be imitated from a very early age. Soon after, the baby is capable of 'deferred imitation', which indicates that their memory has stored previous interactions, which have then obtained the status of experience. The baby is also particularly sensitive to the human voice and reacts rhythmically with their body according to the voice's intonation and volume (Condon, 1982).

'Still face' studies, in which mothers are instructed not to respond as they normally would but to remain unresponsive and expressionless, initially create energetic 'social invitations' from the baby to the mother, and if she still does not respond, the baby becomes unsettled or passive. These studies suggest that very early in life, human beings *expect* that repeated activities with another person quickly assume their own typical social and emotional dynamics. The baby becomes familiar with the code for interaction, and tries actively to influence it, for example by socially and emotionally reacting as they normally do in specific situations. However, if the expectations are disappointed, as in the 'still face' studies, frustration occurs, that is, the baby expresses negative emotions, and their attention shifts focus or they remain passive. This can be interpreted as a sign that very early on in ontogenesis, human beings develop representations and knowledge of a number of everyday social episodes.

In the mid-1990s, Reddy et al. (1997) examined the research and reached the conclusion that preverbal *intersubjectivity* is possible through (social) activation of emotions and attention. Intersubjectivity is an unconscious or a conscious recognition of how social connections exist between two or more people's worlds of experience, first as the immediate sense of it and later as a conscious reflection that 'there is not just an *I* but also *other Is* unlike *me*, with whom I can share experiences'. These connections between the baby and adults are quite different from the ones between older children and adults, or among adults. Nonetheless, a number of studies have demonstrated that from birth onwards, babies are particularly sensitive to human communication – they actually start life with both the physical and mental prerequisites for involved social communication. Reddy et al. (1997) draw extensive, theoretical conclusions from this new knowledge. They argue that basic ideas about human nature should be turned upside down; that we must accept that human beings enter the world ready for social communication – from the beginning of ontogenesis, a deeply social creature appears. This human being expresses a particular *motive for companionship*. Human beings seemingly spontaneously want to be cooperative from very early on in life (Tomasello, 2009). This fundamental motivation to be with another is a different conceptualization from that of attachment theory, which believes that the child's need for attachment to others (anxiety reduction and need for protection) supersedes the motive for being together with another person. The attachment motive is, according to Reddy et al. (1997), either a motivation system developed later that originates from the early companionship motive, or attachment may possibly constitute a specific, independent motivation system for protection. Attachment theory is important in explaining human connectedness, but it is not enough. The implication of research is thus a recognition of human beings' *primary sociality*, which is not gradually replaced but is superseded by a more advanced intersubjectivity. Therefore, this is not a *secondary sociality* – that the child must be included in a year-long process of socialization, which will eventually make them social. The human child appears to be social from the beginning of ontogenesis.

In summary, the following far-reaching conclusions about an infant's nature can be drawn, which show a significant discrepancy with the idea of the non-social child, who must necessarily be made social:

- *Intersubjectivity:* The human child is capable of social mutuality very early in life.
- *Action:* The infant actively tries to influence their interaction partners.
- *Mental organization:* Extremely early in ontogenesis, human beings are mentally organized. They remember, expect, recognize and express delight in interactions.

Before the child learns the use of symbols and speech, emotions and gestures together constitute a powerful 'first language'. The nonverbal child uses this efficiently to communicate their inner states to other people, that is, intentions are converted into behaviour.

Although research on infants' remarkable competencies regarding intersubjectivity and companionship is relatively separate from research on caring, there are substantial links between them. Infants' fundamental ability to intuitively feel and know 'other minds' points to capacities of relatedness vis-à-vis other persons (Bråten, 2007). Also, infants' complex cognitive, social and mental organization and activity opens up the possibility of developing, not only a single working mother model, but various models constructed in actual social encounters with various people. In addition, new research on human beings' intrinsic motivation, not only for protection but also for social companionship, supports ideas of multiple caring.

One-to-one and multiple caring

The one-to-one argument, as seen in the childcare debates, implies that infants' healthy development is based on an intimate, interpersonal relationship between the child and their mother (their primary carer). Underlying this is the core belief that infants are not capable of more than one-to-one mutuality. In the childcare debate referred to earlier, the child's other person (directly as well as indirectly inferred) is clearly the biological mother. In principle, the one-to-one position opens up an acceptance of father–infant intimate encounters, or an adoptive parent, but this is rarely the case.[27] In construing the one-to-one relationship in this version, two mutually supportive, interpretative filters are at work. On the one hand, we are dealing with the mythology of motherhood (Eyer, 1993) – the mother-centric stance. On the other hand, we are producing a socially restricted infant, who is only capable of interacting with one person. Yet recent attachment theory and empirical research have challenged this idea. Although mother and infant, in many parts of the world, begin to form their relationship shortly after birth, many persons can care for the child from very early on in life. Potential (positive/ negative) influential attachment figures can be fathers, grandparents, other relatives in the extended family, adoptive and foster parents, and carers.

The evidence indicating the child's innate capacities for developing multiple relationships, even intimate ones, does not doom mothers to be irrelevant. Maternal characteristics were previously documented as more important for the young child's development than any other childcare characteristic. With this in mind, we can now investigate the infant's and young child's capacity for multiple attachments (for recent research overviews, see Grossmann et al., 2005; Cassidy and Shaver, 2008; Howes and Spieker, 2008).

The father of attachment theory, John Bowlby has, perhaps unfairly, been held responsible for the so-called *monotropic idea*. This idea holds that early attachment is established only in the one-to-one relationship with a mother figure, not necessarily the natural mother, but to only one person. This idea has now been undermined by longitudinal childcare research (for example Sagi-Schwartz and Aviezer, 2005). Clearly, there were signs of the monotropic idea in Bowlby's writings. What may be less well known is his later acknowledgement that a child develops a hierarchy of attachments – although first with the mother as the primary carer (Bowlby, 1969). From Bowlby till today, attachment research has flourished and become one of the main domains in developmental psychology. Recent studies in multiple attachment relationships have made great contributions to the paradigm shift. In a recent review of the research, Howes and Spieker (2008, p. 317) conclude:

> As research on multiple attachment relationships has become more common, there is little dispute that children form attachment relationships with childcare providers, and that child-mother and child-other attachments are independent in antecedents and quality.

This research, in itself a serious blow to pure family- and mother-centric positions, also underscores the importance of families and mothers.

It seems that the formation of the toddler–childcare provider attachment relationship is, in some ways, comparable to infant–mother attachment formation. At the start of childcare, children direct their attachment behaviours at carers. With more childcare experience, the interaction with the carer becomes more stable and organized. Both previous and actual sensitive non-maternal caring is related to children's secure attachments both as individuals and in groups (Howes and Spieker, 2008). However, there seems to be a distinct difference in the organization of attachment relationships, for example being secure or insecure, which depends on the carer being around and being a stable figure. Therefore, relationship continuity with loving and responsive carers is an important factor in establishing stable attachments (Clarke-Stewart and Allhusen, 2005).

As previously discussed, the NICHD study (2005) investigated the relative importance of the family vis-à-vis childcare. Howes and Spieker (2008) placed considerably weight on this study, as opposed to earlier studies, because of its size and the quality of the data. Among other subjects, the potential threat of public care to the primacy of the family was investigated. A main family function in society is to be an 'intimacy zone' (Dencik et al., 2008). Will childcare threaten that? The NICHD study reached two conclusions. The general worry that childcare would not give mothers and children sufficient time to get to know each other, and therefore not establish a quality attachment, was not supported. But extensive hours of childcare time can, when interwoven with family characteristics, be related to less maternal sensitivity and less positive child engagement with the mother. However, as pointed out earlier, the overall conclusion is that repeated NICHD analyses have consistently demonstrated important family effects, stating that internal family influences are stronger than any childcare factor in determining the quality of mother–child attachment. For some children, however, *dual risk effects* have been found, that is, children with difficult relationships with their mothers combined with long hours in low-quality childcare suffer an increased risk of attachment problems (Howes and Spieker, 2008).

To summarize, research on attachment has demonstrated that the reality of young children's life experiences is not merely that they live in multiple caring environments in, for example, both families and childcare, but that they are also able of creating important multiple personal relationships from early on in life, thus developing various context-dependent working models, for example hierarchical, integrated or separated (Bretherton, 2005; Bretherton and Munholland, 2008). In addition, recent evolutionary research comparing primates and humans also stresses the reality of multiple care among humans (Tomasello 2009; Hrdy, 2009):

> It is a startling fact that among all the great-ape species except humans, the mother provides 100 per cent of child care. Among humans, across traditional and modern societies, the average figure is closer to 50 per cent. In a cooperative breeding scenario, helpers – all who are not the mother – often engage in a variety of pro-social behaviors such as basic food provisioning and basic child care. (Tomasello, 2009, p. 84)

So, to have multipersonal care has been and still is a fact not to be ignored. With up-to-date knowledge about the formation of personal relationships early in life, we are better equipped to accept, understand and realistically evaluate both the qualities and risks for young children living in their multipersonal worlds. It is now well known from research that young children are capable of responding positively and negatively to multiple caring. They are able to form multiple secure attachments to sensitive carers, as well as insecure attachments to less sensitive carers. It is even possible to have a secure attachment to the mother and not the father or vice versa and to carers. So multiple caring is, in principle, neither good nor bad – just like a one-to-one relationship, it simply depends on the caring quality.

Carefully reviewing the growing research on multipersonal care, Howes and Spieker (2008) make this clear non-mother-centric conclusion (although with an important place for mothers as well). Most children grow and develop within a changing network of attachment figures, which includes some enduring attachment figures and some that change with time and circumstances. The evidence shows that:

> children construct relationships with mothers and residential fathers within the same family. Children come and go between home and child care facilities...However, child-parent and child-caregiver attachment relationships are largely independent in quality and may have different antecedents. (Howes and Spieker, 2008, p. 328)

A redefinition of socialization

One may wonder why, given the conclusions reached above, new paradigms are less often appropriated by social psychology than developmental psychology. It has not been common to revise the concept of socialization, regardless of the fact that several of its classical, fundamental beliefs seem to have collapsed. However, Dencik (1999, p. 12, translated for this edition) has suggested *active self-socializations* or *auto-socialization* as an alternative to the classical paradigm:

> this is not so much about *becoming* socialized as socializing *oneself*. The child is not merely a passive receiver of influences, but, so to speak, from the beginning an active co-creator of his/her own world of him- or herself. Children seem to be deeply involved in a process, which could be called *the child's active self-socialization or auto-socialization.*

Dencik's concept of auto-socialization constitutes an important revision of the classical understanding of passivity. In this new definition, the child is regarded as actively involved in creating their own world and themselves. However, this definition only solves one of the problems, that is, that the child in their development and learning is not originally passive-receptive, but the quintessence of activity. It is still implied – or at least not clearly separated from the other basic view – that the child is originally an asocial creature. In other words, even though it is a necessary step in the right direction, it is not enough to place prefixes like 'auto' or 'active self' in front of socialization. Although the child fundamentally – and in perfect accord with recent psychology – is seen as an active participant in the process of becoming social, socialization still signals the implicit, primary asociality. Can this problem can be solved?

This calls for a closer look at whether it is possible to adapt the fundamental, etymological meaning of socialization to the paradigm of action.

Previously, socialization's 'to become social' was discussed as the first of two classic, basic meanings. The second aspect focuses on 'to make social'. On the basis of the shift in perspective from passive to active, it has become problematic to apply the concept of socialization in its second basic meaning *to make social*. In light of classic socialization's idea regarding 'to make social' as a basic notion, this implies that others, apart from the child, do something to the child – expressing a passive-receptive idea about socialization. To solve this problem, one can redirect 'to make social' in socialization to the following. Socialization must also include the child's 'active involvement', that is, participation in their own process of transformation. However, this does not solve the previously mentioned problem: that a (supposedly) originally asocial organism, for example in the shape of Mead's 'impulsive animal', needs to be made social. In adapting socialization's classic basic view to the new basic view, another problem appears as *action presupposes sociality*. In other words, it does not make sense to claim that the child as an agent for their own socialization cooperates with the adult to make themselves social. How can you actively make yourself social through cooperation? The child must inevitably already be that, otherwise it would not be logical to talk about cooperation. This indicates that the word 'socialization' in its second classic, basic meaning 'to make social' is difficult to combine and adapt to more recent basic views within psychology.

Obviously, in many ways socialization ideas have to be considered problematic when applied in an ahistorical and generalized form. However, some alternative perspectives and new conceptions of the child have been discussed, which make it possible to redefine socialization:

> Socialization entails the social human being's active mastery of the society and culture in which they grow up.

On the one hand, socialization involves a growing awareness and mastery of the complex social order and, on the other hand, it implies creative possibilities for 'cultural reproduction' (Corsaro, 2005). This is possible, first, because of the relative unpredictability of human action and cooperation. Second, late modern society and culture changes relatively quickly while the next generation is undergoing socialization. This causes some 'breaches' that will influence the process of socialization in unpredictable directions. However, the acquisition of culture cannot lead to just anything, because socialization still occurs within the framework of relatively stable customs, consensual frameworks and the use of cultural, communicative and historically established tools (Fogel, 1993). Socialization is not something the individual can actively acquire in their own 'auto-socialization', nor can others stamp it on the individual.

From primary socialization to dual socialization

Revolutionary changes in the developmental ecology of early childhood were documented in the beginning of this chapter. In addition, new research has seriously challenged the paradigm of the non-social child who becomes social through a socialization process. A redefinition of socialization was suggested, building on the new child paradigm. But a model is still missing, which can integrate contemporary young children's two developmental arenas into one configuration. The research challenge is to create an adequate, contextually sensitive, conceptual framework, interpreting the developmental and socializing consequences of growing up in both a family and childcare. Like researchers in the past who studied middle childhood and constructed a school age period, early socialization and developmental researchers have to invent new models in order to grasp and interpret this relatively new and developmentally unusual situation.

A vast amount of out-of-context understandings have been left behind by contemporary reality. Empirical documentation of the changed ecological situation has been updated and empirical research of childcare is flourishing. Nevertheless, the creation of new concepts and theories is scarce. Influential, international 'state-of-the-art' textbooks do perhaps embrace the importance of context, yet do not include the full consequences of this challenge (for example Berk, 2009). Instead, there is a tendency to split research on infants and young children into either family or childcare research (consequently, textbooks devote separate sections or chapters to family and childcare research). Similarly, interpretative filters of practitioners and laypeople may handle this by 'dividing the child into two' – the family child and the childcare child. The arguments presented in the sections about childcare as a threat clearly showed this. But in doing so, a perhaps trivial, but obvious fact is overlooked – the daily life for a rapidly increasing number of young children is to experience *both* developmental, socializing arenas.

So, in order to grasp this relatively new, dual context early childhood, a conceptual model called 'the dual socialization butterfly' is presented.[28] The model has been constructed in order to grasp the situation for a typical Scandinavian young childhood – infants and young children who grow up in family relationships and childcare relationships where they interact with a multitude of adults and peers (Figure 2.6). The point is that the two socializing contexts represent the experiential realities of a growing number of young children in the same early ontogenetic period of life. So the model can also work well in other parts of the world where the family/childcare context has or will become the main arena for young children as they grow up.

Dual means complementary, because the meaning of the relationships may be experienced differently by the target child. For example, relationships with parents carry other meanings than relationships with childcare personnel, thus having potentially different socializing and developmental

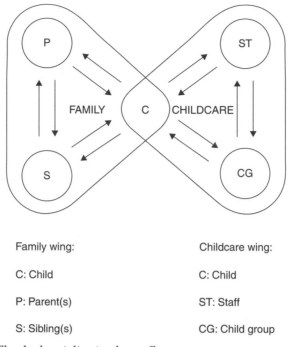

Family wing: Childcare wing:

C: Child   C: Child

P: Parent(s)   ST: Staff

S: Sibling(s)   CG: Child group

Figure 2.6   The dual socialization butterfly

functions. Mother–child, father–child and staff–child relationships seem to fulfil diverse functions. As mentioned earlier, child–mother and child–other attachments are independent in antecedents and the impact of quality.

A key consequence of 'dual socialization thinking' is that the possible impact on the child, who lives in the two worlds, cannot be reduced to its parts. With the child embedded in the middle, a phenomenological configuration is emphasized. It is important to stress that, in principle, the model is neutral regarding eventual developmental gains or losses. The dual socialization model is an interpretative tool to use when confronted with the fact that for young children, in many countries worldwide, an increasingly normal situation is to live in both family and non-family caring and socializing systems. However, there are numerous developmental pathways and outcomes for young children depending on the quality of the specific relationships they have within the configuration, therefore several possible scenarios can be discussed using the dual socialization butterfly.[29]

3

Young Children's Culture Acquisition: Competencies and Learning

Chapter 3 offers a more detailed look at several of the nine theses about culture embeddedness stipulated in Chapter 1. The fundamental question is: How is everyday cultural experience and competence acquired in young childhood? To answer this, Chapter 3 will focus on the relationships between contemporary culture and the young child's acquisition of culture and learning.

Why is it important to highlight the connection between culture and children's learning? Bruner (1990) used a metaphor to explain the relationship between culture and man: when humans begin their lives, it is like entering a scene in order to perform in an already ongoing show or play. This may seem like a fixed structuralist understanding of culture, but it is not. The metaphor opens up the possibility that the scene has been constructed by someone and the performance has been written by an individual or individuals in collaboration. Even the roles of the actors may be open to improvisation. Adults (parents, preschool educators and teachers) are the key agents in the child's social and culture acquisition process. They 'set the scene' and the 'show' that is already in play as the child enters the world. In other words, adults are development agents, mediating society and culture to the child (Cole, 1996). This happens in childcare, parenting and teaching, mediated and practised in everyday routines and relationships. Seen in a broader perspective, this underlines the importance of 'the greatness in the trivial'. The child's developmental changes happen in front of our eyes while people are engaged in what they usually do.

However, young children's culture acquisition is hard to discover without considering the widespread late modernity fact that the family is not the only arena for young children's socialization. The family shares this with childcare and other out-of-home arenas, coined as the new dual socialization seen in young childhood (Chapter 2). The increased role of a public, structural reorganization of childhood and the pervasive scheduling and supervision that it entails are relatively new phenomena (Qvortrup, 2009). This restructuring has been especially revolutionary in relation to infants and young children and this change challenges not only socialization theory and the non-social child paradigm, but also culture acquisition theory. In Chapter 2, the classical view of the nuclear family as the primary socialization arena was noted as being counterproductive to a current understanding of young children's socialization. A significant consequence of this restructuring of early childhood into dual arenas has been the ontogenetically early *expansion of the social horizon.* The child has to develop multiple relationship skills, that is, the ability to decode social situations and move between a wide variety of adult and peer contexts as an active participant. Living in both families and out-of-home arenas, with their multitude of relationships, makes the everyday culture acquisition process markedly different from previous times and probably more diverse.

The life worlds that young children construct are the result of a process of culture acquisition, based on the construction of meaning in everyday social practices (Corsaro, 2009). It is important that children (and adults) make sense of everyday practices and routines when being together, because this connects the child with their culture (Bruner, 1990). Young children's cultural competence is gradually acquired through practical engagement in communication in a multitude of social encounters in various arenas – family, childcare, neighbourhood and school. A key underlying function of these settings is their contribution to the 'exoticizing of experience', that is, allowing the young child to comprehend a multitude of cultural codes. For some young children experiencing dual socialization, family codes may be quite different from childcare codes. A growing number of young children now face the formidable task of learning to decode a multitude of cultural 'texts' and 'subtexts'. Furthermore, they are actively and continuously editing these in exchanges with other people and groups, reproducing everyday culture. Corsaro (1997) made detailed observations and interpretations of this cultural reproduction process in his analysis of five-year-old Italian children in childcare playgroups, who showed surprisingly elaborate interactive skills. (Later on in this chapter, case examples from a Nordic study will be presented that elaborate and qualify such competencies.)

ORIGINALITY: THE POSSIBILITY OF CHANGE

Chapters 1 and 2 described how fundamental beliefs of the child as a non-social novice in a world of educated adults have dominated both sociology and psychology. Despite its obvious shortcomings, the paradigm of the passive-receptive child was, until recently, common in both developmental psychology and classical socialization theories (Woodhead, 2009). According to this mainly pre-paradigm shift view, the mature generation, parents and teachers, hand over the 'cultural baton', with its customs, beliefs and 'how to dos', to the next generation. The child, being a novice, gradually internalizes the codes of the prevailing culture through established upbringing and teaching. According to Valsiner's critique (1987), the culturally competent adult who has served their cultural apprenticeship is portrayed as the only organizer and purveyor of knowledge. The passive-receptive paradigm of culture acquisition seems illogical.[30] If the child is a mere passive recipient and the adult the agent, at what age does a human being acquire the capacity for agency to influence other people? At 18 years, crossing the crucial line between childhood and adulthood? The *gradual and early manifestations of children's agency* are not addressed in the passive-receptive paradigm. In addition, this paradigm also fails to address when and how the passive-receptive child turns into a social being. Furthermore, the paradigm holds the tacit assumption that children are not fully matured before adulthood, which downplays childhood as a unique period in its own right.

'Originality' is not possible in the passive-receptive paradigm because of the inherently static nature of knowledge and experience that adults convey to children. In this model, the child is portrayed as an organism that does not actively process incoming information, but only receives and acquires some information, while distorting the information they fail to grasp. However, we live in an age of constant change, so a culture acquisition approach has to be open to the phenomenon of 'originality'. The following demonstrates the problem inherent in the passive-receptive, one-way perspective of the relationship between the generations, as well as the fact that inventions can be created by the younger generation. One can start by asking: Do fathers always know more than sons? Yes, according to the passive-receptive paradigm. No, if what really happens is that actual change creates originality. For example, was it James Watt's father who invented the steam engine or taught him to do so? No, it was James himself, inspired by new ideas of his time. Was it Einstein's father, engulfed in the classical Newtonian world, who taught his son the principles of relativism? No, it was his son, influenced by the revolutionary cosmology ideas of the time. Today, great inventions are still produced; but changes also take place in more modest ways, which create new ways to live. For example, Chapter 2 demonstrated that not only have early childhood conditions changed surprisingly quickly, but also fundamental research-based beliefs about the child.

So, how is innovation and change possible in the younger generation if culture transmission is a matter of one-way communication from parents and teachers to children? The passive-recipient approach makes it impossible to explain ongoing social and cultural renewal in the competence-building institutions of family, childcare and school. To remedy this, alternative approaches will be presented in the following sections.

THE AFFORDANCE STRUCTURE OF CULTURE ACQUISITION AND LEARNING

Why is it necessary for small children to learn and impossible for them not to learn? It may be that human beings' fundamental motivation to explore the social and physical world supplies the answer. One could add that the child's pleasure in activity, alone and with others, not merely creates learning, but also produces changes in the environment. Thereby the child is seen as both producer and product of its own learning activity.

Furthermore, all situations are potential learning situations in which children auto-socialize (Dencik, 1999). This perspective, although essential, is not completely adequate. In principle, children are capable, through their own learning activities, of far more than is deemed important in a given time and culture. Thus, the learning potential is far greater than the learning end product. This unique capacity for learning ensures that children, over time and in many societal and cultural contexts, have been able to acquire the competencies that were crucial for reproduction in the specific era in which they grew up. Consequently, not everything that children learn is appreciated and supported in a given culture – so-called 'framing' occurs. Framing manifests itself to the child in the way that others make demands on them. Only part of the knowledge and experience that children acquire is deemed significant. Non-functional learning experience 'wilts' and dies if it is not reinforced or encouraged.

In other words, a selection process has started in which certain types of learning are reinforced through social acknowledgement in everyday life, or learning becomes institutionalized, in childcare settings and in school. For instance, in literate cultures, it is functionally useful that 10-year-olds are able to read and write and they learn this at an institution of learning (school). However, this is irrelevant to a 10-year-old Indian boy in the Amazon jungle. For him, a detailed, practical knowledge of hunting and cognitive mapping of the jungle's geography are essential requirements for survival.

Immediately after birth, human beings' development potential is culturally influenced and channelled to such an extent that both 'close relations' and the 'self' are constructed in significantly different ways in Eastern and Western cultures (Markus and Kitayama, 1991; Rothbaum et al., 2000). The same applies to what and how small children are expected to learn in society and cultures in different historical periods. Thus, the reality we grow up in demands certain skills of the next generation. How these demands become a part of and frame a child's learning environment is difficult to account for, and remains a complex matter. However, adults (and other children) play a decisive role as 'mediators', who bring culture and society into children's life worlds (Cole, 1996). As a consequence, learning is channelled into an already established context, which children need to react to, experience and acquire knowledge about; a reality which they themselves can only influence to a limited extent.

Learning becomes *functionally useful* when it directly or indirectly qualifies children to participate in the society and culture in which they grow up. This means that children, through social practice with adults and other children, acquire knowledge of social conventions. Yet this is not merely about the development of specific skills and abilities in the here and now. More generally, it is also about children's gradual integration into culture and society. Babies apparently enter the world with amazing learning capabilities. However, despite this, they must laboriously learn to decode the cultural significance of other people's acts, in order to become valued members of society in the long term. This is illustrated in Figure 3.1.

Integration means inclusion in a broader entity. The child's integration into the greater entity C (culture) is connected to the actual learning

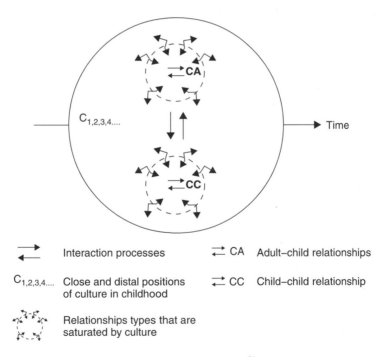

Figure 3.1 The child's complementary integration[31]

that happens in the child's small world in its social relations with other people, who function as societal and cultural mediators. This integration is complementary, because the two categories, CC (child–child) and CA (child–adult), each constitute structurally different learning contexts. Whereas CC denotes an egalitarian, symmetrical relation, CA is the unequal, asymmetrical relation. However, they are both unique learning contexts, which, in their own way, constitute significant engines for the development of children's competencies. Importantly, both are essential for developing all the necessary aspects of a child's functionally useful competencies. The word complementary also implies that, although the two types of social contexts are structurally dissimilar, in terms of learning, they still complement each other.[32]

It may seem surprising that the passive-receptive perspective has held such sway in our view of culture acquisition, as it is clearly too simplistic. Culture acquisition, however, takes place in the processes of interpersonal verbal and nonverbal dialogues – development is a relational process where meanings, definitions and interpretations of what is going on are negotiated. In reciprocal social transactions, agents create meaning and test their own perceptions against others. Culture does not exist in a vacuum nor is it a fixed set of customs; it is related to specific traditions and recurrent practices that characterize social institutions in society. This anchors the child's identity and self in everyday interactions within cultural institutions (family, childcare and school). Thus, it is misleading to talk about identity and a self independent of a child's specific cultural context.[33]

However, the dialogue and negotiation process has two sides. On the one hand, it facilitates young children's culture acquisition and helps them understand their world, and on the other, culture is constantly produced and reproduced. More than two decades ago, Bruner (1990) declared that the pure structuralist approach to human culture had been discarded. Structuralism views culture as established, systematically interconnected customs and codes of conduct that are passed on to the next generation. Instead, the understanding of culture is that *culture is implicit and loosely connected experience and knowledge* (Bruner, 1990). Culture acquisition, developing appropriate sets of skills, stems partially from the internalization of external values and codes of conduct. It also has much to do with gaining experience in the negotiation processes in interpersonal situations in family and other culture-saturated settings. A key premise here is that people strive for personally satisfying and meaningful ways of relating to other people, making shared or conflicting understandings. In this sense, society's culture is locally produced in a multitude of microcultures; events have unpredictable and unclear effects on the macroculture, which in turn affects the microcultures in a constant reciprocal transformation. This approach is indebted to the transactional perspective inspired by dynamic systems theory, as presented in Chapter 1.

Tomasello (2009, p. 99) describes the origin of culture as the result of cooperative human activities: 'Humans putting their heads together in shared cooperative activities are...the originators of human culture.' But in order to create culture, here-and-now activity has to be strengthened and with time turns into habits. Building on Tomasello's thesis, culture will, in this context, be understood as a highly complex system of routines – including norms, customs and practices – that participants are engaged in and find meaningful. The challenging task of interpreting a multilayered text may be used as a metaphor to illustrate what it is like to manoeuvre in a changing culture. Although culture is a product of living social processes, created here and now, it must be remembered that culture, using Bruner's theatre metaphor, also includes a stage that was constructed before the play began. So culture is not only made in the here and now, but also comprises relatively solid, materialized products of routines negotiated in earlier times. This is seen in various *traditions* that are still observed in rapidly changing cultures; for example, in most families and childcare institutions, celebrating children's birthdays and giving gifts remains a tradition. As long as traditions hold important latent functions for society, culture and individuals, they are expected to survive.

The structuralist approach to culture, as a fixed entity that was given as a blueprint to the next generation, also described an authoritarian, premodern society. However, the structuralist paradigm lost its function as an adequate interpreter when cultures faced rapid transformations. It is interesting to note that recent research in Scandinavia and other countries has observed a non-authoritarian type of late modern family – the 'negotiation family', where the child is respected and allowed a voice, a presence and a say (Dencik et al., 2008). One may wonder why this is so. The answer may be that society is not what it used to be: the 'negotiation culture' has turned out to be a growing although not universal characteristic of late modernity, observable in many contexts. (Characteristics contributing to this were illustrated in Box 2.1.) Non-authoritarian, negotiated outcomes are seen in the way legislation and regulations are made, for example as the result of democratic compromise where political conflicts are handled during negotiation. Another example are the unwritten, but practice-based codes of manners that regulate behaviour in public and private companies, schools and other social settings where cultural actors meet. (In Chapter 4, this negotiation phenomenon will be elaborated on, dealing specifically with the growing tendency in late modern families for negotiation relationships between parents and even young children.)

As mentioned before, not everything is open to negotiation. Dependable products of routines negotiated previously in history, culture and society set 'the stage' and frame, but do not determine, interactive practices. Besides, even after the demise of the authoritarian society, obviously not all groups or individuals possess equal negotiation powers. So it is necessary to modify approaches that exclusively perceive culture as the product of shared negotiated interactive practices, thus ignoring existing institutional and individual power conditions. For example, the relationship between adults and children is not equal (symmetric) regarding decision-making, it is asymmetrical. The *balance of power relationships*, that is, the degree to which individuals, groups and institutions influence others, has to be considered. This is also the case in democratic, late modern 'negotiation cultures', where power relations are less overtly visible than in authoritarian societies.

Culture acquisition: assessing participation competence

In traditional developmental psychology, the assessment of young children's development of culture acquisition has usually been detached from everyday practices, based on defined stages. However, this is not the case in this context, nor will it be measured in a standardized test tradition. Instead, another approach is suggested. The development of competence in participation is mainly a matter of qualifying for social and cultural membership. Thus, through social encounters, children gradually learn to act efficiently, responsibly and appropriately in a multitude of microcultural contexts. Culture acquisition and participation require learning competencies that enable a child to engage in meaningful interactions in specific situations that are regulated by often implicit culturally defined codes of conduct. Instead of being value free, social exchange and individual expression are valued. Competence development is therefore anchored in everyday social relations, with their rules and manners, and is, consequently, assessed in specific contexts. How can a given competence in participation be evaluated as relatively developed? The child's cultural participation and competence development may be assessed by observing social relationships characterized by the following:

- *Elaborated reciprocity:* The young child obtains an increasing knowledge about social exchange rules and contributes in a well-adjusted manner to the underlying meanings and expectations that regulate specific social encounters.
- *Increased responsibility:* Personal responsibility increasingly guides interactions, showing growing skills in perspective-taking. The child regulates their own actions by taking in responses from other agents.
- *Cultural functionality:* Acts that are not culturally useful will wither away, whereas acts that work well are expected to be strengthened through the process of culture reproduction (Corsaro, 1997). With time, the young child is expected to act with growing competence in cultural exchanges with other people.
- *Positive motivation:* An everyday culture that appraises the young child's growing reciprocity, personal responsibility, together with a child's experience of 'what I do' functions, fosters positive motivation.

Gradually increased social reciprocity, responsibility, cultural functionality and motivation are viewed as developmental progression. This highlights the ways in which children become active social participants in everyday culture. This approach may be further specified and included in educational considerations about *learning*. For example: Which social tasks and activities of a culturally integrative nature will it be useful to involve children in to enhance their culture acquisition? How might these processes be structured to increase reciprocity, personal responsibility, cultural functionality and positive motivation? Which specific communicative abilities and skills do we want young children to develop in order to support their culture acquisition?[34]

EVERYDAY ROUTINES AND 'PLAIN TRADITIONS': BASES FOR CULTURE ACQUISITION AND LEARNING

In Chapter 2, the changes in young children's developmental ecologies were given the term 'late modern childhood' to describe the present state of affairs and its impact on early childhood. Although societal and cultural changes have happened throughout human history, the pace has accelerated and transformed people lives, especially in our times (Cunningham, 1995). As said in the Introduction, the most constant phenomenon in our times seems to be change.

However, in many respects, the changes have been studied on a macro-societal, sociological level, for example in terms of changes in maternal employment, rising out-of-home care rates, divorce statistics, birth rates, and changes in family structure. As seen earlier, data has documented a wide range of important and rapid structural changes in society that have reshaped young childhood. But the macro-level research evidence of rapid change may also give an impression of the young child's life as characterized by *constant change* and *unpredictability*. If this is the case, it may have serious negative consequences for the child's development. One example of a situation for a young child experiencing dual socialization may be that they are frequently confronted by new strangers in childcare because of high staff turnover, while experiencing instability in the family because of impending divorce.

Bruner (1990) coined the young child's self, not as an inner core, but as a *distributed self*. This is a relationship self that has been constructed and is constantly in the making in actual social processes in social arenas. If developmentally sensitive arenas are characterized by change, this implies negative consequences for the young child who is constantly required to adjust to variability and unpredictability. Developmental psychology also reaches the same conclusion. Systematic research of child development shows that *stable caring and parenting practices* are crucial for healthy development. Even in critical life events, the child is usually protected as long as some fundamental positive routines remain stable (Schaffer, 1990).

The distributed self functions as a kind of gyroscope that detects and responds sensitively to sudden change. Consequently, it is important to clarify if inferences made from macro-level changes – apart from their important restructuring effects – are useful or not on a micro-level. They probably are not. Although it is a fact for some young children, change and unpredictability seem to be the exception, not the rule, seen from an everyday life perspective. Why do many young children's everyday lives not descend into chaos, despite the changes that have considerably altered young childhood in late modernity? To answer this question, further elaboration is needed of the theoretical framework presented earlier in this book.

Leaving the framing macro-level (despite its strong indirect impact on the child through mediators), we now turn to the level of everyday life – the sphere where people strive to create stability, order and gradual change. Ethnologists have pointed out that cultural routinization of everyday life is a foundation for meaningful culture acquisition, and seen in a larger perspective, this ensures the reproduction and reconstruction of culture across generations. Without day-to-day continuity in relationships, traditions and habits, both the child's socialization and the stability of culture are at risk. Thus, *everyday routines and plain traditions*[35] are key theoretical concepts that enable us to grasp the importance and relatively independent nature of a micro-level where people are involved in getting things done and are striving to make their everyday life function in meaningful ways.

Routines are reoccurring ways of being together in specific activities and situations and they function as 'plain traditions' by being potential buffers[36] against the possible threats of rapid societal and cultural changes. The term 'plain traditions' is used to set the concept apart from the ethnological concept of cultural traditions, which refer to holidays, celebrations and ritual rites of passage. Plain traditions are small daily routines that are performed without much conscious awareness. The young child's ability to engage in and understand the meaning of these activities and interactive routines is an important indicator of both the child's everyday cultural knowledge and social development. The codes for 'how to be together' have to be acquired in childhood, although it is not uncommon to observe a child who has not fully grasped the tacit rules in a social situation and thus has to be told.

Socializing arenas such as the family and childcare have the potential to make their own plain traditions of care and learning in everyday life function as buffers against rapid change, unforeseen by the young child. Despite the turbulence and perceived instability of late modern life, people's everyday life is not necessarily characterized by disruption and unpredictability. In fact, everyday interactions are highly repetitive.[37] *Repetition* is a typical pattern in family, childcare and in everyday life, for children and adults alike. In families, the early morning period may be filled with regular activities. For example, many young Scandinavian children and parents get up around the same time every morning, get washed and dressed, have their breakfast together in the kitchen, put on their shoes and coats and head off for childcare and work. The pattern may vary; in some families children dress after breakfast, in other families before. The interactions may vary a great deal in both tone and content. But families develop their own way of managing the relationships in their own plain traditions.[38] Explaining how such patterns arose usually elicits the answer: 'It just happened that way, it seems to be the way it works for us.' This acknowledges that despite families' routines starting as the result of spontaneous here-and-now processes, with time, they develop into habits and 'what-we-usually-do' routines.

Childcare is a developmental arena heavily structured around routines. The schedule may fluctuate between various types of adult-organized, collective activities and child-organized forms dominated by play and interactions with other children (Pramling-Samuelsson and Asplund-Carlsson, 2005). The typical day may also vary between indoor and outdoor activities. This everyday, fluctuating rhythm forms a pattern that does not determine but structures activities and children's experiences. Repeated social and cultural routines seem to be the rule, not the exception.

In a larger perspective of cultural integration and acquisition, routines may be seen as 'frozen negotiations', that is, ways to do things whose meaning was constructed in previous negotiations. The production of routines reflects certain tacit interpersonal 'traffic rules' (Rogoff, 1990). When people regularly meet around activities, routines gradually develop, establishing norms and cultural expectations for interpersonal relationships. For example, at a staff meeting for the first time, people choose a chair and sit down to allow the meeting to begin. At the next meeting, the likelihood of taking the same chair is relatively high. The third time, the 'everybody-sits-where-they-sat-previously' norm is established as an implicit rule – a routine. Another example is the often highly routine and regulated way of putting a young child to bed. Unpredictable deviations from, for example, the bedtime story and the good night kiss, may make the routine-experienced young child protest, demanding a return to the 'what-we-usually-do' procedures.

With time, routines, although often based on complex behaviours, become subconscious and automatic, which allows for new events and information in social exchange situations. When seen in a larger perspective, establishing and structuring routines fosters a sense of security and predictability in an otherwise variable, fragmented, late modern society. A related concept describing this is formulated in the need for sensing 'basic trust' in relation to systems, as well as persons (Giddens, 1990). On a bus, people are not expected to fight, in busy streets, there are rules of how to move forwards; while in workplaces, in families and in childcare, the relationships among adults and adults and children are highly regulated and routinized. Without a certain degree of routinization, chaos may interfere with everyday life.[39] Routines are not necessarily impersonal, but are enacted in a personal way that is either meaningful or at least necessary for the individual. To feel that this is what I do together with others makes intuitive sense.[40] Consequently, culturally framed expectations of behaviour are connected to the individual's motivation to engage in routines.[41]

Routinization: rigidity, flexibility and developmental progression

Routinization and children's culture acquisition and development are closely interwoven. The everyday routines the child is involved in are the basis for their culture acquisition and social competence development. Thus, regular everyday activities are an integral aspect of situated social interactions: getting up in the morning, having breakfast together, saying hello and goodbye to parents and childcare teachers, playing with peers in childcare and having lunch together.

As a period in human life, early childhood is characterized by change. The foundations that make this development possible have to acknowledge this fact. In addition, societal and environmental change are inherent characteristics of late modernity. Everyday routinization is one way to deal with rapid change and make it 'digestible' for children. Repetitive, fixed habits are, however, not beneficial to young children's development.[42] In fact, rigid routines are the essence of developmental stagnation, while developmental progression requires flexible routines and vice versa. In order to facilitate a young child's development, routines and social relationships have to be attuned to a child's actual competence level and gradually make room for the child to engage in increasingly elaborate, interpersonal communication. Thus to promote child development, everyday routines have to strike a balance between monotonous routine and flexible change. There is a fine balance between monotony and change – a balance that varies with age and children's growing capacity to adapt to new experiences.

Both extremes, total monotony and constant change, may be harmful; the first because it prevents children from acquiring new skills and managing various situations with different people, whereas constant change can be harmful because it exceeds the child's capacity to take in new information and thereby makes for confusion (Schaffer, 1990). Seen in this perspective, the development of cultural competence means that children will gradually master regular situations and activities, which in turn enables them to engage efficiently in everyday routines, as well as affecting them.

RELATIONSHIP COMPETENCE: FIVE-YEAR-OLDS' PEER PLAY[43]

The acquisition of everyday culture is inseparable from participation in social exchanges with other humans. During early and young childhood, this process becomes increasingly sophisticated. The twin partner in complex everyday cultural knowledge and skills is *relationship competence*. Relationship competence includes a range of factors and can be studied in many different contexts – in the family, in childcare, in school, in the playground, between children and adults and among children. Another important context is young children's peer interactions. Successful interactions in groups of young children require particular social skills, and children who do not master these skills may be in danger of exclusion (Pramling-Samuelsson and Asplund-Carlson, 2005).

Apparently, it is not enough simply to be a follower who submits to a group's rules. Observations indicate that popular children are capable of social empathy but they also exhibit independent, but socially attuned initiatives in peer play (Sommer, 2003, Ch. 6). Young children's initiatives, ideas and active influence are more frequent and elaborated in child–child contexts than in adult–child contexts. This may be due to *symmetry/equality* in peer groups, as opposed to relationships with adults that are structured by *asymmetry/inequality*. In fact, children's groups are a developmental arena that is open for observing potential relationship competencies in full bloom, acted out in everyday social processes in childcare routines allowing 'free playtime'.[44]

The peer group has been compared to a 'flight simulator'. Before flying a real plane, training in a realistic simulator is required. Experiences in peer groups function as a kind of *natural simulator* for practising and developing important social and communicative competencies (Frønes, 1994). Tomasello (2009) also links young children's pretend play to symbolic communication and argues that 'the acting out scenes for others' is inherently social. To this, Corsaro (1997) adds another important function of peer play: it promotes young children's culture reproduction and acquisition.

In the following, thematically organized examples of the vicissitudes of relationships competencies will be presented, drawn from an observational study of five-year-olds observed in Nordic childcare settings (see the whole study in Sommer, 2003, Ch. 6). In the first example, Martin observes the activities of a group of children for a while.

Social context

The children are playing indoors. Martin is not engaged with anyone. He watches a boy (B) and a girl (G), who have initiated a play activity with some chairs that are lined up in rows. They are presumably playing 'bus drivers'. No teachers are around.

Social episode

Martin observes G and B playing for a few minutes. Then he approaches them, asking: 'What are you doing on the bus?' G and B do not reply but continue to play. Then Martin says: 'If you were going to fly, I could be the pilot.' No reply from B and G. They do not look in his direction. Martin sticks around, scratches his head and puts his finger in his mouth. He retreats and begins to play with some toy cars for a while. Meanwhile, he continues to look at G and B and their activity. A minute passes, whereupon Martin quickly gets up, walks over to B, who is sitting on the front chair, apparently being the bus driver. Martin asks whether they have a 'ticket collector' on the bus. B turns to Martin and looks at him and says: 'Then you can be that guy, the collector.' So Martin joins their play, and stamps G's ticket.

After a while, there are no more tickets to stamp, and it seems like the bus driver play fades out. B is now moving down from his front chair, whereupon Martin says: 'If we are going to the moon, this could be a spaceship.' Pointing at B, Martin says: 'And you are the moon king that shall return to your kingdom with your queen.' B and G nod and shortly after Martin is in the front chair, apparently flying his two passengers to the moon.

How does an outsider enter a social group? It may be achieved by *social decoding*, that is, the ability to read and understand specific social episodes and act in accordance with them. This episode shows that to be allowed in as a participant in an already ongoing play, knowing and interpreting the roles in play is essential. In his first, self-articulated proposal of being the pilot of an aeroplane, Martin seems to make two misinterpretations of the situation. First, he redefines the play before becoming a participant. Second, he places himself in the leading role (pilot), thus undermining B's position (bus driver). This is followed by a strategy of ignorance – the non-member is not to be looked at. Martin's attuned interpretation, however, is expressed in his second attempt. From a distance, he seems to 'reread' the type of play, causing him to adopt a new strategy. He invents a 'role for sale' that does not challenge B's status and makes sense in relation to G, the passenger. So his new role is integrated into the play theme (driving a bus) and therefore it is easy to accommodate him as a new group member. Later on, when the play fades out, he elaborately reinvents his previous suggestion of being a pilot. By nominating B and G new, high-status roles (king and queen), he obtains access to what he wants, to be a pilot on a spaceship.

Martin's second effective social decoding seemingly maintains his intentions; he restrains his impulses and accommodates the implicit rules of the game. Such well-adapted strategies do not apparently develop spontaneously. The case of Martin indicates that this is a trial-and-error process, making and correcting mistakes when entering a group and subsequently being granted membership.

To decipher social codes requires a large repertoire of knowledge based on a wide range of previous experiences with other children. Repeated peer group experience gives extensive interactive training. Five-year-old Martin has attended childcare for most of his life and is thus a highly experienced peer player. In Scandinavia, as well as many other societies, contemporary five-year-olds acquire daily practice in the learning of social decoding through their social activities and routines. Thereby, childcare, compared to the growing number of one- and two-child families, may function as an extended educational 'natural social simulator'.[45]

The episode also illustrates an example of *culture reproduction*. The actual play theme is clearly rooted in a contemporary society where transportation is collectivized and driving a bus is what adults and children do. Roles are enacted and their interrelatedness are in play – without a driver, no passengers and with no passengers, sooner or later no driver or ticket collector. Also the spaceship theme is within cultural realism, spiced up with clearly imaginative roles and actions – taking the king and queen back to their kingdom, the moon.

Setting the stage: how to manage a circus performance

The beginning of this chapter introduced Bruner's (1990) culture metaphor: when the human infant is born, they enter a 'stage' already set. This means that other, older people have created a social forum that needs performers to act out roles and interactions. Five-year-olds are active constructors of stages, which can be seen in their peer play activities.

In a peer group, some agents regulate relationships by acting in ways that can be characterized as 'setting the stage'. Like a film director, a child may demonstrate competencies in arranging, directing, rehearsing and performing complex social processes involving other children as active participants. Setting the stage may take on a multitude of forms. In the following example, Mary is an initiator and director of a 'circus performance', in which all the performers and spectators are children.

Social context

The children are in a large common room. Adults pass through the room from time to time but do not interfere. Five children besides Mary are singing and playing imaginary musical instruments, when she shouts: 'We are going to play circus.' Mary divides the children into spectators and performers.

Social episode

Facing the audience and her fellow performers, Mary loudly sings an improvised tune: 'We are all in the ring, holding hands, we're sisters and brothers, and we love one another. Our God is our father; the earth is our table, and you are all with us, you bet!' All the children clap their hands, and yell: 'Baa, baa, black sheep.' Everybody is laughing loudly and clapping their hands.

Now, two younger children (a boy and a girl) enter as 'clowns'. They stand in the middle of the floor (the circus ring), bump into each other and begin to fight for fun. 'That's it, yes, what a good show!', Mary says loudly. Everyone applauds, and Mary asks the two children to do the act one more time. They do. This time, the play becomes rougher, suddenly the girl falls down, and the boy falls on top of her. 'Owee!', cries the girl, 'that actually hurt.' 'Carry on now, little ones', says Mary. The audience of children is laughing and clapping their hands. 'Yes, but he stepped on my foot', says the girl, weeping, 'it really hurts.' After a short silence, Mary says to the girl: 'Then you just tumble onto him, too.' This she does, and both tumble down acting like clumsy clowns. Everybody laughs, and the show goes on.

Mary is highly active in performing her role as stage director, deciding who the audience is and who the performers are, partly through direct instruction. Through her opening song, seemingly *a sense of group spirit* is created. She also demonstrates a sense of a higher purpose ('the show must go on'), as a conflict threatens to stop the game when the boy and girl bump into each other, and the girl is hurt. Mary manages this unexpected and play-stopping event as a part of the game – as crazy 'little clowns', they bump into one another. Maintaining a balance, Mary arranges it so that it is the girl's turn to fall on top of the boy. A delicate balance is observed between Mary's articulation of her 'management' of the other children and the show, as well as her social awareness of the needs and demands involved in playing circus.

On reflection, setting the stage and performing a circus show in a peer group may act as a natural social simulator that may fulfil more general functions. Complex relationship competencies acquired in the learning arena of childcare may become functional and useful in other social arenas, and perhaps later in the child's life. For example, for appropriate and harmonious class behaviour in school, it is useful to know a multitude of behavioural codes beforehand.

Defining and elaborating themes and relationships

'What shall we play?' Young children are actively involved in suggesting activities, defining play themes, structuring the meaning of being together. This determines roles and relationships and allows further negotiations and elaborations of games. However, proposing a particular play theme is only a start. Sooner or later, even the best game becomes boring if it is not developed and new dimensions added. Hence, young children who contribute to *elaborating a play theme* hold a crucial position in the group. This may be achieved by articulating their own intentions, ideas and suggestions, balanced with due consideration for the actual social context. To be acceptable to a group, suggested themes and ideas for elaborating a theme have to appeal to the other participants.

Defining a theme by making play suggestions occurs frequently in peer groups, and among three- to six-year-olds, imaginative and symbolic play flourishes (Berk, 2009). A young child who is imaginative and sufficiently creative to produce a wide range of suggestions will earn a relatively more central position than a child who is merely a follower (Sommer, 2003, Ch. 6). To obtain approval for a proposed play theme also means that the initiator is the agent in structuring roles and framing the conditions of the performance. For example, 'father-mother-child' play implies both specific participant roles that must be assumed by someone, as well as awareness that no role can exist without the other. To be a father and a mother, one must have a child and visa versa. But when the play theme has set the stage, and the appropriate roles are distributed, the performance and activity can be elaborated and lead in many directions.

A play theme is not necessarily decided upon through an explicit decision in a peer group, although that may be the case. Instead, a sudden initiative in the process of playing may cause an 'outburst' of a new type of play that everybody immediately becomes engrossed in. For example, a group of children sit on a big mattress on the floor pretending to be pirates sailing across the ocean in search of ships to board. Suddenly, one child rolls off onto the floor screaming 'sharks'. Immediately, the pirate boat is turned into a rescue vessel and the pirates into rescue personnel, throwing life jackets to the man overboard and poking and yelling at the imaginary shark.

Perhaps an accepted play proposal is the one with the best 'contextual fit', that is, an idea that is intuitively familiar to the specific contextual mix of resources, interests and the participating individuals in the group. Anna is a five-year-old, high-status peer. She is observed in many situations acting in imaginative ways, showing both mental and social flexibility. She adapts her perspective to what is going on, and easily switches from producing ideas to joining the stream of play. In the following observation, Anna and three other children perform a puppet show.

Social context

Anna is enacting a puppet show in cooperation with three other children. They are in the living room, which has a large opening into an adjacent room. An adult is in the adjacent room, drawing large pictures for a later activity. The adult and the children can see and hear each other, but Anna and the three other children are absorbed in their activity and appear to take no notice of the adult. Assuming the role and voice of a puppet, the arms and posture of the doll are moved in accordance with the situation and the children's vocal tones are dramatically altered regarding how they normally speak.

Social episode

Anna goes to the front of the stage to watch the other children's performance with the hand puppets. She talks to the puppets, asks who they are and what they are doing. The puppets reply, through the voices of the children. This continues for a few minutes. Then she goes behind the stage. She puts a puppet on her hand and introduces it on stage. She asks the three other children, who are now watching, what their names are. They answer loudly, all at once. Anna's puppet says 'Hello' to each of them and asks them where they live. The puppet waits and 'listens' to each of the children. The conversation via the puppet continues, and now the puppet 'says' that they should have a birthday party. Anna's puppet asks if it can have some birthday cake. 'Yes', the others say. Meanwhile, one of the other children stands up with her puppet on her hand. Through her doll, she asks Anna's puppet: 'Is your name Teddy?' But quickly she says through her puppet: 'No, you're not, cos I am.' Anna looks at her, but her puppet does not reply. Suddenly, the playhouse tumbles over. The adult next door tells them to be careful not to break the playhouse. The children put the playhouse back up and continue playing. Anna now has a puppet on each hand. She moves the puppets slowly through the air as if they were flying in front of the audience, silently. Then the flying puppets get into a fight, and everybody laughs. A child in the audience leans forward and tries to grab a puppet. The puppet flies away. Suddenly, the adult comes in and tells them to tidy up as it is time for lunch. The play stops.

This game evolved spontaneously. No pre-existing rules defined the theme or content or determined who was in charge of performing the active role of a puppeteer. An ongoing process happened in the 'stage setting' within the puppet show, with subordinate invented play themes as to who they are and where they live, having a birthday, flying puppets. This is elaborated in a continuous unfolding flow through the participants' intuitive, coordinated social involvement. Anna has a profound influence on defining and elaborating themes. She articulates initiatives through puppet role-playing, actions that move the game along and change it. It is noticeable how she moves smoothly between periods of observer status and active participation, as well as performing either as audience or puppeteer. Her puppet displays 'conversational turns', that is, she makes it initiate a conversation, then pauses, waiting for a response before starting again. This is an example of play that practises *impulse control* through suspended self-assertion. Impulse control is a vital prerequisite for the development of social competencies in young childhood. In this play process, cultural conventions are also integrated, for example having a birthday party with birthday cake and having polite conversations about names. The flying puppet theme is a product of a shared imagination that everybody finds meaningful; a cultural reproduction, perhaps inspired by cartoons or other media experiences that stimulate young children's fantasy production.

LEARNING THROUGH CURIOSITY AND PARTICIPATION

In order to discover where human being's need to learn originates from, one must start at the beginning, that is, when the human being is born, or even earlier. The desire to learn – or the fundamental motivation to acquire new experiences – is apparently based on the child's natural preference for new information about the social and physical surroundings (Berk, 2009). For instance, a baby expresses a limited interest in a uniform, unchanging environment. In this environment, the baby does not look at anything in particular and does not turn their head towards anything. The introduction of a colourful mobile results in the baby turning their head towards the object and staring at it intensely. Alternatively, when a father or mother approaches the cot, significant activity occurs in the baby's body – they gesticulate energetically with their arms and legs, and their facial expression changes to wide eyes and open mouth. This basic focusing on the surroundings, which is observable even in newborns, can be assumed to be innate.

The child's focus is channelled and selects certain 'areas', which in the short or long term can be assumed to be of the greatest value to the child's survival and adjustment to their physical and social environment. This presupposes that the child has a particular, inherent interest in new objects and events, and also that there is a particular attraction and early preference for social contact. In addition to this, there is also motivation to draw active experiences from interactions with the surroundings, thus the desire to learn is a fundamental characteristic of human beings from the beginning of life. So straightaway, learning is an active process of acquisition.[46] Human beings' formidable ability to survive and adjust throughout an incredibly changeable ontogenesis is closely linked to their ability to create culture and their natural interest in learning. Seen in a historical developmental perspective, a variety of learning strategies are used and cultural competencies learned during upbringing. The readiness for culture is a part of human biology and the drive to learn is one of our most important, basic drives (Tomasello, 2009).[47]

Basic knowledge about the social world?

The ability to learn is a fundamental characteristic of *Homo sapiens* (Stern, 2006). But how early in ontogenesis are human beings capable of entering meaningful social communication with others, which is not only essential for our basic caring for others, but also for our learning? Contrary to previous ideas, recent research indicates that through active observation of other people, infants gain experience extremely early on. As early as an hour after birth, a newborn can spontaneously imitate adults' facial expressions, for example surprise (Field, 1990), thus:

1. the baby is capable not only of perceiving another person's face, but also sensing that it 'expresses something'
2. the baby quickly learns how to associate the adult's expression with their own.

Newborns are also capable of imitating head movements, as has been observed in many ethnic groups and cultures (Meltzoff and Kuhl, 1990). Furthermore, they also react with interest when they hear human voices[48] (Floccia et al., 1997); apparently, they have also learned to recognize their mother's voice, which they have heard in the womb. After studying the relevant research, Krøjgaard (2002 p. 134, translated for this edition) concluded that: 'infants appear to be predisposed for a world full of people. Infants also seem to be preprogrammed for dialogue.'

The early learning processes that build on observation and imitation seemingly occur quite spontaneously, and can be assumed to have their foundation in the desire and predisposition for learning, which is useful for the survival of the species. This also includes an important perspective for future and continuous learning. From the beginning of life, crucial social interactions are under construction with adults, who will serve as the child's key learning agents.

Basic knowledge about the physical world?

According to recent research, the interest in how the environment is organized begins extremely early in human life. A simple example of this is that stripes and patterns have a 'mesmerising power' over newborns. They can stare intensely at a striped shopping bag or a pattern on their mother's top. Newborns will typically direct their attention towards complex patterns with contrasts as opposed to simple patterns with little contrast. Movements in the room are also of particular interest (Gopnik et al., 1999). The development of cognition starts before birth and continues in the newborn child, and a leading researcher in the area suggests that cognitive development starts in the womb (Karmiloff-Smith, 1995). For a long time, researchers were unaware of the range of early learning. But recent new methods (for example 'habituation' studies) exploring what babies prefer to look at and listen to brought to light unexpected capacities among newborns and babies (Karmiloff-Smith, 1995). In the first few months of their lives, babies treat inanimate and animate objects differently (Krøjgaard, 2002). They have seemingly created some mental experience regarding the basic differences between objects and human beings – between the physical and the social worlds.

One controversy in developmental psychology involves core knowledge. According to Spelke et al. (1992, 1995) and Spelke and Kinzler (2007), human beings arrive in the world with 'core knowledge' about fundamentals in the organization of the physical world, such as 'solidity' – a solid object (toy car) cannot go through another solid object (wall). One the other hand, Baillargeon's (1994) thesis is that the child enters the world equipped with some 'fast learning mechanisms', which enable them to grasp the basic rules of the physical world. These two positions disagree as to the existence of innate knowledge. Yet they are similar in that they both attribute significance (although in different ways) to innate dispositions with regards to children's knowledge of the physical world. The Spelke position about innateness holds that important core knowledge is already there at birth, developed during evolution. The Baillargeon position holds that no innate knowledge exists, but evolution has equipped humans with impressive abilities to experience fast learning. Their studies of infants' perceptions of objects support the fact that babies enter the world with innate knowledge. Piaget (1977), on the other hand, believed that the newborn had no cognitive schema of basic knowledge about the physical (and social) world. Thereby, knowledge is acquired from experience gained by exercising the child's active learning in the environment (constructivism). In the sensorimotor stage, the small child gradually becomes familiar, according to this view, with the particular characteristics and regularities of objects. In summary, environmentally created experience is essential to what a child knows at any given time. Naturally, this perception is correct insofar as children need to acquire a number of experiences, but it has turned out to be problematic as a general statement pertaining to all types of early knowledge about the physical world. The Piagetian pre-paradigm shift position underestimates the capacities of infants, thus it has lost impetus in the light of recent empirical research (Spelke and Kinzler, 2007).

EVERYDAY LEARNING: A SITUATIONAL-RELATIONAL APPROACH

Dewey's famous principle 'learning by doing' undoubtedly applies to small children. According to Dewey, all cognition is situated, that is, it happens in a specific context. Furthermore, learning does not happen through passive observation but through participation (Brinkmann, 2006). Thus, the starting point is what the learner does and not think. Young children use objects before they fully understand them; so it is a reciprocal process, because when they recognize objects after practice and experience, they can also apply their knowledge to other objects. With time, children establish a growing store of experience, which enables them, in more and more advanced ways, to handle their social and physical world. The continuous, active creation of experience and habits during everyday activities and practice is the key to understanding what and how small children learn.

Small children's immediate and explorative 'being-in-the-world' develops an efficient, situational, practical and physically embedded intelligence.[49] Although it is important to know what the child is thinking, attention should be directed at their actions, as this is where inner intentions and emotional moods are externalized. Thus, children's actions offer the possibility of interpreting what they 'want' (intentionality), together with 'whom' (sociality), how they are 'moved' (emotionality) and how the process involves 'changes in behavioural patterns' (learning).

In later years, relationship theory has entered developmental psychology. Today, focus on interhuman processes must be said to be a particularly crucial thesis in understanding how children change. A relationship can be defined as a personally experienced connection of a certain duration among social agents. In order for relationships to have some duration, and thereby become significant to learning, the development of insight into other minds is required, as well as an ability to adjust one's intentions and actions to one's current social context. As previously shown, frequent relational experiences in a group can be influential in both articulating and developing relationship competence. In principle, however, the interaction is open not just to social learning but to all types of learning experiences – entirely dependent on what the child's intentions are.

The relational perspective also constitutes a basic new element in the paradigm shift. With the relation as the turning point, the focus moves from the individual child to the educational, social processes in which they are involved. Therefore, when a child is called 'competent', this does not refer to an isolated individual's abilities, but to their capability of acting together with others in 'competent relations'. Competence is created in the learning process as a product of relationships. However, it is important not to abstract relations from the situational context in which they are embedded. In principle, a relation does not exist without a situation. Situations, such as everyday routine interactions, organize and regulate connections among people involved in a non-determined manner. As a matter of fact, most situations allow for different actions 'within the situation'.

Human beings are socially advanced animals who are not controlled by instincts but regulated by habits. Therefore, learning can also be regarded as practice and experience, with the acquisition of a number of specific habits that are linked to specific situations in everyday life. To highlight the principle, the regular, everyday routine of the meal has been selected as a specific situation. Meal situations are highly significant, studied as cultural, structured learning and socialization processes (Ochs and Shohet, 2006).

In a childcare setting, when adults call, 'Lunchtime!', cultural customs are activated. Without further reflection, children begin to 'act mealtime'. They wash their hands, sit down at the table, wait for the food to arrive, talk to the child next to them and share the food with the other children. Eating together is, like other regular situations in everyday life, a learning arena, which contains a number of implicit behavioural codes. The rules for 'good table manners' have, however, changed significantly over time. For instance, a generation ago, children were not allowed to talk with food in their mouths and they were to be 'seen and not heard'. In today's negotiation culture where children are both 'seen and heard', mealtimes are an opportunity to learn the rules for conversation (for example taking turns), which is far more important than externally controlled training in good manners. The point is that specific rules for what one ought to learn change over time, whereas the everyday life situation survives as a significant learning context.

ADULT PERSPECTIVES AND CHILDREN'S PERSPECTIVES ON WHAT IS LEARNED

Approaches favouring children's perspectives on their own learning have flourished and a child perspective will be a vital part of this book's approach to young children's learning (for an introduction and discussion, see Sommer et al., 2010).

For the purpose of learning, childcare teachers organize 'situations' for young children each day. Huge amounts of knowledge are taught, coached and communicated in the knowledge society. Perhaps this only results in a limited amount of in-depth learning? The actual criterion for learning is lasting changes in patterns of actions, experience construction and understanding. This is best achieved through the young child's own active processing rather than through purposeful adult-structured activities. Thus the child's own perspective on the world becomes a central turning point in an understanding of learning. *A Childhood Psychology*'s view on learning therefore also includes both 'children's perspectives' and 'child perspectives'. But the terms should not be applied interchangeably because they relate to different positions. *Children's perspective* relates to children as subjects: they are, in comparison to adults, qualitatively different in their understanding and approach to the social and physical world to which they constantly relate. In contrast, *a child perspective* relates to the adult's empathic understanding of children's worlds of experience. The following is an example of how different a father's and son's perceptions of the 'same' phenomenon can be:

> Father and five-year-old Martin are on their way to childcare. The sunshine is reflected in a small puddle of oil, spilled on the road. The father

points and says: 'Look, an oil puddle.' Martin replies: 'No, Dad. It's a dead
rainbow.' (adapted from Sommer et al., 2010, p. ix)

Here, the father directs Martin's attention towards the physical phenomenon
and calls it an 'oil puddle', as this natural product is actually called. In this
way, the father translates the visual impression into the everyday concept of
an 'oil puddle'.[50] Martin's spontaneous reaction, by contrast, is based on a
five-year-old's direct visual perception of the world. The sun's reflection in
the oil creates a rainbow effect, which presumably inspires associations –
that the rainbow is on the ground and not in the sky must mean that it has
'fallen down'. It is therefore logical for Martin to suggest that it is 'dead'.[51]
Martin's father adopts a child perspective by describing the phenomenon
in such a way that it can be understood by any five-year-old.[52] In contrast,
Martin's perspective on spilled oil expresses a five-year-old's experience of
the same phenomenon.

A central thesis about learning in *A Childhood Psychology* can be formulated thus: as opposed to surface learning, in-depth learning leads to a
relatively long-lasting change of knowledge. Lasting learning primarily
occurs through the child's active, subjective processing of, and experiences with, the social and physical surroundings. Adults' perceptions of
the child's perception are also significant but, as mentioned, not the same
as the child's experience. To highlight some consequences for learning
caused by this distinction, an example of five-year-old Sarah's social
experiences in childcare will be included. According to an interview with
the teacher, Sarah is dominated by her friend Emily, and needs help from
the adults to handle the issue. Based on the interview with Sarah, another
experience emerges. Box 3.1 gives an extract of the two interviews.

Box 3.1   What Sarah learns about dominance[53]

Adult perspective (according to interview)

Child perspective (according to interview)

The two friends, Sarah (S) and Emily
(E), often eat together. E is a picky
eater and she decides what S can eat.
The adult (A) tells S not to let E decide
for her. A thinks that even though S
says that E is not deciding for her, S is
glad that A has interfered. Today, the
adults have decided that S and E cannot eat together because of the 'dominance problem' – they say that S needs
the company of other children.

S says that E wants to have the final
say over her, which E should not
hear. S tells this to the adults who
then scold E. S says that in case of
'problems', she often calls the adults
so that they can come and scold and
leave again. It is important, says S, to
obey the adults. Also when the adults
have decided that the two friends are
not allowed to eat together.

To explain the interaction further:

- *The adult's perspective – comment:* The basic intention to 'intervene is to help' originates from the nursery teacher's idea that Sarah has a problem with dominance. The nursery teacher performs two interventions:
    - *verbally restricts:* says that Sarah must not let Emily decide
    - *socially structures:* separates the friends because Sarah should expand her social range of contact.
- *The child's perspective – comment:* It may seem contradictory that according to the nursery teacher, Sarah denies that Emily dominates, as she says the opposite when she speaks to the researcher. However, in the lunch episode, Emily is present and cannot be told of the decision (presumably because of negative consequences).[54] Sarah's perception of authority is permeated by how adults indisputably decide. Thus it is legitimate that they intervene when she calls them. Yet what has Sarah learned? Her experience is that adults yet again decide and that in turn diminishes her self-regulation of peer relations. Paradoxically, the adult, unaware, through her 'help' unintentionally confirms and supports Sarah's perception. The nursery teacher legitimizes her intervention in the relationship between the friends: 'Sarah looks happy about the intervention.' This may be the case, but it is not the point. The point is that the intervention has, to a limited extent, its starting point in the child's own perspective, and so does not solve Sarah's problem with dominance. Perhaps the dependence on the friend lessens; however, it is achieved by subordination to adult authority. Sarah experiences that the world is divided into 'decision-makers' and 'non-decision-makers'. Her style of decision-making is limited, calling the adults who will then exercise their authority (tell off).

An educator's understanding of the same situation and the same relationship can therefore be significantly different from the socially involved child's. Adults regulate and influence children's relations to a great extent, but it is the child's particular perception of the situation that ultimately constitutes the learning outcome. Similarly, in the example of Sarah, she experiences something quite different from what the adults believe she has learned.

Children's perspective on their world should be central, which is far from being the case in various theories and learning programmes. The paradigm shift in developmental psychology, as presented in Chapter 1, does not in itself make it professionally easier to understand children's particular perspective on their life world. Much of the new research mostly focuses on an 'objectified' child. This is important, but for adults who are eager to understand how children's learning really happens, it is also a matter of how children experience and acquire knowledge, including how the child, as a subject, experiences, senses and understands their surroundings.

TOP DOWN VERSUS BOTTOM UP:
OPPOSITE LEARNING VIEWS

Pedagogy and education offer a number of paradigms, which all represent different learning views. This chapter's first section discussed some definitions. The conclusion was that the choice of concepts is a relevant activity. Key concepts within sociology, psychology and pedagogy not only represent professional knowledge, they are also constitutive, in the sense that they create the world in their own image (Dahlgren and Hultqvist, 1995; Burman, 2008a). This applies not only to specific concepts but also to constructing theories that create different interpretations of human beings and their relations to the world. With the need to be well educated in order to progress in today's world, the choice and use of pedagogical paradigms has intensified within childcare pedagogy and learning. In many countries, including Scandinavia, learning plans are developed, implemented, documented and evaluated. The debates about and choice of pedagogical and educational theories and methods have become a professional necessity. Such a choice is binding, not only because it constitutes the pedagogical reality, but also because it has crucial consequences for practitioners' work, as well as on how children's learning is perceived and planned.

As will be made clear in the next section, a new global educational and pedagogical agenda dominates our time. With global competition among knowledge societies, toddlers can be expected to receive increased attention as the first stage in gaining lifelong qualifications in preparation for the new global reality. Therefore it is to be expected that increasing pressure will be put on childcare institutions (and families) for small children to learn certain skills before they go to school. Thus toddlers will be included as the first stage of lifelong learning and education.

Learning happens through active experience in everyday routines and relations. Young children probably learn most when they are allowed spontaneously to examine their surroundings in a not too tightly organized and adult-controlled environment with fixed learning targets. *A Childhood Psychology*'s view on learning opposes top-down pedagogy, recognizing a bottom-up approach, partly influenced by situated learning theory.[55] Everyday life practices are crucial, instead of focusing on the end goal, actual, process-oriented events and occurrences act as fuel to children's learning. Pedagogical professionalism involves using the ability to reflect on one's own practice in order to be able to change it. Table 3.1 shows two perceptions with regard to their fundamentally different pedagogical and educational starting points and consequences.

In the structured learning programme's pure version, the adults are in control.[56] They set clear boundaries for the children and give instructions according to a goal-oriented plan. Playing is allowed but occurs either before or after 'the lesson'; or play is included only so that the child can learn

Table 3.1   *Two opposite views on young children's learning*

Top down	Bottom up
Goal-directed didactics	Everyday life and its practices are central
Planning of learning according to definite goals	Learning in playing-learning social contexts
Learning is 'externally steered' by specific plans	Child perspective and children's activity in focus
Eagerness to plan and organize	From planning to reflection: the reflective practitioner
Planned 'relevant learning' is controlled/documented by means of forms or tests	Everyday life contains learning structure and practices (can be described and documented)
Evaluation according to preset developmental goals: passing or failing?	Evaluation: discussing and reflecting on learning practice and experiences. Finding your feet in the process. Where are we going?

specific things (didactic play). The teachers are consistent in their approach to the children. They clearly explain to the children – and parents – their targets for the interaction. The children are involved in task-oriented activities, aimed at the practice of specific skills. It is relatively easy to evaluate the activity's effect regarding selected abilities over time. In this situation, children's opportunities to choose their activity and act on their own initiative are limited, as are the opportunities to have spontaneous, informal interactions with other children and adults. In the US, this top-down model is used in childcare institutions that have ambitious targets for stimulating small children's cognitive learning (Clarke-Stewart and Allhusen, 2005).[57] By contrast, others are more broadly developmentally oriented, with an approach similar to the bottom-up model. This allows children to pursue their own interests, while the adults guide and support the children but are reluctant to control the activities. All developmental areas are emphasized, including the cognitive; however, their social development is given a higher priority than in the top-down approach. This offers unique opportunities for research to evaluate how the two types of pedagogy influence children, not only during the toddler years but also long term, during later school years. This will be pursued in the next section.

As mentioned, these two models have significantly different consequences for working with children's learning. There is literature about the theories and methods supporting both specialist perspectives. But what works and what does not promote children's early learning? Which ways of learning in early and young childhood endure when children start school and later on in life? Let's turn to that.

WHICH TYPE OF LEARNING POINTS FORWARD?

The basic condition for learning is enduring changes in patterns of acting based on experience, understanding and practice that leads to 'knowing'. It is tempting to think that all changes are beneficial. However, there are changes that are uninteresting when it comes to the long-term consequences of learning. For example, one can learn something that is useful now for a specific purpose, but it is without any long-term significance, because later in life different qualifications are required. In order to educate the next generation, learning should not just be seen as a here-and-now requirement. What children learn in a pedagogical setting is framed. This is because learning should have a so-called 'carry-forward value'. This does not mean that everything that is learned needs to be seen with respect to future usefulness. However, this prerequisite – more or less consciously formulated – is based on the whole progression idea in many educational systems. What pupils learn in the early years constitutes the foundation for what they are capable of acquiring later on. For instance, you need to know the alphabet first before you can combine letters into words and then sentences. But which type of learning in early childhood has the best carry-forward value, that is, is functionally useful in the long term?

In Denmark, the Globalisation Council's report (2006), the OECD Programme for International Student Assessment (PISA), the introduction of tests in primary schools and the language test for three-year-olds are Scandinavian examples of a globalized, educational and pedagogical agenda. Toddlers (and early childhood) can be expected to receive increased attention and there is an anticipated, increasing pressure on childcare institutions (and families) to give young ones an 'early start'. This idea of an 'early start' argues that early scholastic stimulation (for example counting, learning the alphabet, measuring and so on, and practising logical reasoning) will provide children with a head start. In other words, this linear time idea is cherished: what is acquired initially is stored as knowledge and experience and what is acquired subsequently is based on previous knowledge. The logical consequence is that the earlier you start in life, for example by learning the alphabet and counting, the more time you have to learn throughout your life span. The opposite idea can be formulated as 'early starter, later loser'. This means that early systematic learning results in pressures on the child, who in the 'unsystematic play age' learns spontaneous, unstructured interactions with other people. In other words, their learning style is not compatible with the scholastic idea, whereby what is to be learned becomes surface skills, rather than in-depth knowledge. Early scholastic teaching means, according to this view, that the young child loses their learning motivation. They will then fall behind their peers in the long term, who have not been exposed to an early, structured, scholastically oriented influence.

What does research have to say about this current and important problem? Which view of learning gains support? In a themed issue of *New Directions for Child Development* (Rescorla et al., 1991), the consequences for toddlers of an early, relatively systematic learning process were studied in several independent research projects. These are the main conclusions:

- Environments that emphasize teaching small children 'academic skills' have no long-term effect. Young children can learn early on what they are being taught, for example numbers and letters. However, the advantages of early learning wears off over time as their peers catch up.
- Young children with parents who have high expectations for them to be clever display more performance anxiety and fear of failure, as opposed to children who are not pressurized by high expectations. Family values are therefore important in this area.
- Scholastically oriented environments also have certain negative consequences for young children's development. Children are relatively less creative, have more 'test anxiety' and display negative attitudes towards starting school.
- Warm, developmentally oriented environments seem to be more successful at maintaining young children's desire to learn than scholastic environments.

However, is this supported by further research? One study followed 461 children for seven years, from before they started school until the first years in school (ReadyWeb Virtual Library Archives, n.d.). The main conclusion was that early, systematic practice in formal, scholastic learning programmes (including the ones where it is supposed to be fun to learn numbers and letters) negatively contributes to children's successful transition into school. On the other hand, if in the toddler years, children have participated in child-oriented activities adapted to children's development and interests, nine-year-old pupils perform better in maths, reading, writing and languages than those who have participated in scholastic 'early start' programmes. Boys especially benefited later in school from having attended childcare institutions that emphasized socioemotional development. The conclusion of this study is that successful school preparation is undermined by exposing young children to structured 'school-relevant' learning.

The results from a longitudinal project of scientific quality also need be presented. Curtis and Nelson (2003) summarize the results from the ambitious Head Start programme in the US, which began in the 1960s and ran for many years. The purpose was to give small children from underprivileged backgrounds a head start. This was achieved through a systematic learning programme, which focused particularly on early practice of children's language and thinking. Furthermore, it sought to influence families' attitudes to and support of the children's learning and performance motivation.

Various intelligence tests were included in tests of the children's performances. Among other things, the researchers were interested in whether early,
systematic scholastic practice could result in a relatively lasting improvement in children's thinking. The results were as follows:

1. The programme increased children's intelligence and other abilities
   considerably, *as long as they were in the programme.*
2. Around 12 years of age, the effect was non-existent. Research showed
   that systematic practice of school-relevant skills through early childhood
   does not create relatively lasting changes, for example in intelligence
   (Curtis and Nelson, 2003).

Clarke-Stewart and Allhusen (2005) summarized results from a number
of studies that compared structured childcare educational programmes to
unstructured and moderately structured ones. They concluded that children
involved in adult-structured programmes expressed more negative emotions,
were less cooperative, and were more often disciplined by adults. Children
also showed more stress and had less confidence in their own abilities. For
example, in one childcare institution, the children were divided into small
groups of five or six with a teacher. In three 20-minute sessions a day, they
had to learn to read, speak and do maths according to a structured method,
particularly developed for small children. For the remainder of the day, the
children could occupy themselves freely with activities of their own choice.
These children quickly showed remarkable progress in intelligence and at
the end of nursery, they were noticeably better than their peers with regard
to sentence production, maths, vocabulary and the ability to persevere with
a difficult task. However, three years later, at the age of eight, they fared
significantly worse than their peers in intelligence tests, spelling, numbers,
semantic understanding, creativity and curiosity. Again it can be concluded
that *preschool progress had not only vanished, but the gains had disappeared as well.*
Even many years later, for example in secondary school, the children, who
as small children had participated in structured, top-down learning activities, were less socially competent, less academically motivated and less
interested in learning (Clarke-Stewart and Allhusen, 2005).

The other extreme is to choose a totally unstructured environment, where
children spend most of the day playing with their peers, adults delegate learning to make it the children's responsibility, and children's free choices solely
create the everyday structure. However, the best option seems to be a pedagogy and learning environment that alternates between *moderate adult structuring and children's opportunities to explore* in a rich environment consisting of
friends and toys without adult control (Clarke-Stewart and Allhusen, 2005).

In summary, it can be concluded that early scholastically oriented
learning – whether it is practised in the family or in childcare – has no
lasting effect and even a direct negative effect on young children's development of knowledge and intelligence. It also threatens development in

other areas, for example the motivation to learn. Even though there may be political/ideological interest in involving children early on in adult-structured, purpose-specific learning, there are limited research-based reasons for doing so. Small children who early in life enter into structured, didactic learning environments experience it more as a pressure than as a challenge. They seem neither physically nor mentally prepared for structured learning. To sit still for more than 10 minutes for a five-year-old can be more tiring than running and jumping. Furthermore, the ability to focus attention is limited to only a few minutes.

Young children will themselves seek the challenges they need, with the necessary guidance from adults. In-depth learning, that is, relatively long-lasting changes of action patterns, experience formation and understanding, occurs through direct, practical contact with the physical and social surroundings in a moderately adult-structured learning environment. One can conclude that a scholastic 'early start' attitude to educating children does not find support, whereas the 'early start, later loser' attitude finds more support.

However, this presents a dilemma, as research has also shown that before three years of age, significant differences in children's development can be detected, and they are socioeconomically founded in the family (NICHD Early Child Care Research Network, 2005). If these socially determined differences are ignored or even accepted throughout early childhood, then the differences among children will be even more significant at the beginning of school. So existing socioeconomic differences, which have existed for generations, that affect the acquisition of knowledge will be reproduced in early childhood. Also, research shows that high-quality childcare institutions, in terms of teaching and resources, can make a difference to children from disadvantaged families, that is, can compensate for deficiencies in the family. However, this requires well-educated teachers and an adult–child ratio that makes possible a focused effort (Clarke-Stewart and Allhusen, 2005).

The following important conclusion can now be deduced. In order to meet the late modernity challenges of globalization, human beings' lifelong learning and acquisition of qualifications will have a better start if children are allowed to actively examine and experience the world at their own speed in child-centred, developmentally oriented environments. This is available today, based on new research about small children's learning, which takes its starting point in young children's particular way of understanding and acquiring knowledge of the world (Sommer et al., 2010). A gradually increasing focus through the early years on 'learning through play', which happens in a non-scholastic play and learning environment, is a vital part of this comprehensive pedagogy (see Pramling-Samuelsson and Asplund-Carlsson, 2005).

Creativity, ingenuity, social competence, the ability to cooperate and an interest in learning are crucial qualities for coping with the innovation society of the future. The learning through play point of view is not against the gradually increasing focus on acquiring academic knowledge in the latter part of early childhood and in school:

- Whether planned or not, all social relationships among children, their parents, siblings and people in childcare will have a certain element of learning.
- All social situations and relationships can be stored as experience and therefore have great potential as learning situations.

To preserve people's short- and long-term interest in learning will be the challenge for learning environments in the future (Johansen and Sommer, 2006). This is necessary in order that people gain qualifications for their future participation in a global economy.

In the Santiago Declaration (2007), a number of internationally recognized researchers in child development 'urge that policies, standards, curricula, and to the extent possible, commercial ventures be based on the best scientific research and be sensitive to evidence-based practice' (www.jsmf. org/santiagodeclaration/). Politicians and social debaters are encouraged to include the present social and behavioural research, as there is currently a huge gap between action and knowledge: 'Scientific data and evidence-based practice must be integral to the ongoing global dialogue.'

SELF-ASSERTIVENESS AND OTHER-RELATING: DUAL AFFORDANCES IN LATE MODERN WESTERN CULTURE

Historically, Western societies have moved towards increasing individualization. Since the beginning of the Renaissance, modern man has become increasingly autonomous. The human subject has attained relative supremacy over kin and tradition and thus is left to individualization (Verhave and Hoorn 1981; Ward, 2003; Dencik et al., 2008). This has caused a problem as to how to value the success of cultural integration in late modern Western societies, that is, stressing either individualized self-assertiveness or social cooperation (Kitayama and Markus, 1994). As argued in Chapters 1 and 2, there is a functional connection – although not a simple one-to-one correlation – between the beliefs and ideologies held by society and important child values held by parents and educators. As a consequence, the implications for the education and socialization of the next generation should not be overlooked. Living in a global information society demands the ability to move between a variety of real, and virtual, social and cultural arenas. Individual (Western) self-assertiveness may be an essential way of handling this.[58] In order that this does not turn into selfishness, however, self-assertiveness has to be adapted to the situation and social context. This requires relationship

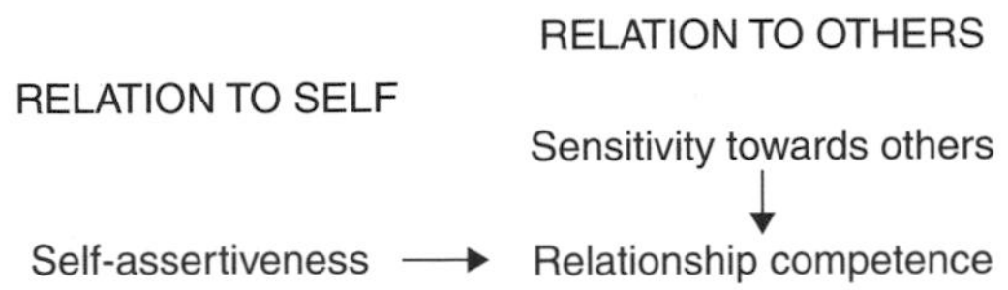

RELATION TO OTHERS

RELATION TO SELF

Sensitivity towards others
↓

Self-assertiveness ⟶ Relationship competence

Figure 3.2 Relationship competence, self and others

competence, that is, the ability to be both *individually driven and tuned in socially*. This is illustrated in Figure 3.2.

Relationship competence requires two abilities:

1. that young children can state their intentions, leaving a personal mark on what is going on in social encounters
2. that children are able to act in accordance with other people's stated intentions and motives (we have seen observations and interpretations of this in the peer play of five-years-olds).

In summary, they are skilled in understanding and adapting to the social meaning of the relationships they are engaged in, and in organizing, maintaining and negotiating such relationships.

Individualized cultures are more likely to appreciate and socialize young children's self-assertiveness at the expense of the child's other-adapted orientation (there is more about cultural differences in Chapter 6). The socialization of individual self- and other-directed competencies seems to have a complementary nature – an expectation that the individual child can establish *a sense of belonging* to other individuals and groups, which stresses the importance of gaining social competencies, but by the same token, there are strong demands for developing *independence* and *autonomy*. Socially competent five-year-olds, as shown earlier, seem to have the capacity to handle these contradictory demands. But there is evidence that young children at that age do not balance this duality very well, either showing self-assertiveness, with little concern for others, or conformity and compliance, thus not showing the 'I' dimension of self (Sommer, 2003, Ch. 6). Families and social institutions seemingly expect early individuality in young children, because of the positive value that Western cultures attribute to personal independence. Family, childcare and school are faced with how to promote and socialize both individuality and social connectedness, ensuring an optimum balance between social bonds and individuality[59] (Shulman, 1993). This may be vital in a broader perspective: developing personal qualities to handle close and intimate relations, on the one hand, and individuality and independence, on the other, within the context of social bonds. In ensuring this, parenting is important, and is dealt with in Chapters 4 and 5.

4

PARENTING I: EMERGENT THEMES AND TRENDS

Parenting is a huge, well-researched subject, including a five-volume handbook, covering all main areas within the field (Bornstein, 2002a). Obviously, parenting is a highly complex matter that changes with culture and over time. Pre-paradigm shift, parenting was not commonly used as a scientific concept. Instead, it was the focus of classical socialization and developmental theory that explained the parent's (mother's) influence on her relatively passive-receptive young child.

The purpose of this chapter is to present a perspective on parenting and caring that places it in its contemporary late modern context, and its cultural and everyday contexts. The aim is to expand and elaborate on the new paradigm of mutual relationships and the axiom of the active and socially competent young child introduced in Chapters 1 and 2. This chapter will also build on the acquisition of culture presented in Chapter 3.

When mentioning parenting, the family often follows. Parenting and families come in multiple combinations. There is an enormous variation in the practice of parenting, in the definitions of a family, and in the differences in living conditions of children and families in contemporary societies and cultures. It is impossible to cover the diversity of families in one book, and the important social conditions of parenting and families, ethnic and minority parenting in various cultures, and parents and children in poverty have been extensively covered elsewhere. (A whole volume of the *Handbook of Parenting* (Bornstein, 2002b) is devoted to these issues.)

The family has been much harder to define, especially in late modernity, because of the number of family forms. For example, in Scandinavia, there are a range of acknowledged family types, besides the classical nuclear family of two parents, father and mother, and children. Divorce and remarriage have led to families with quite complicated relationships and along with single-parent families and the dual-earner family form the patchwork of context in which contemporary children grow up (Dencik et al., 2008). Of course, this is not unique to Scandinavia because these changes in family composition and structure have occurred on a global scale. For example, the UK charity Family and Parenting Institute provoked a debate in 2010 by declaring that emergent trends show that the traditional family pattern is in rapid transition and the classic nuclear family, with a married couple as the basis, has become only one among many other cohabitation types.[60]

The central issue in this chapter is family and early childhood in late modernity with its specific characteristics (see Box 2.1). However, late modernity is not a template for parenting, but this context makes it possible to grasp some emergent trends in our rapidly changing times. This chapter focuses on families with young children, because the book is about early childhood, and particularly dual-income families, motivated by empirical facts outlined in Chapter 2 that this type of family is an emerging global phenomenon. Scandinavian countries have experienced more than 50 years of rapid changes in the female role in society and families, with a concomitant change in family structure and type. As emphasized in Chapter 2, out-of-home childcare for young children has become far more common in many countries worldwide, creating the dual socialization situation.

In Denmark, 70% of children live with two parents, that percentage being lower in other European countries (Jensen, 2009). In her sociological analysis of the pluralization of family forms, Jensen highlights a heightened fragility and instability in contemporary children's family life. Despite these changes, the two-income family, with a father, mother and children living together in a household, is still the most common family type in most countries, even in Scandinavia where the changes started. So this type of family will be the focus here, while acknowledging that there are other types of family. *A Childhood Psychology* deals with what changes but also what remains typical in our changing times. Discussing the typical nuclear family is not, however, to be interpreted as meaning that this is what a 'real' family should be, or that the fulfilment of life is to live in some kind of family. The pathways of human development are diverse and 'normality' comes in many variations.

This chapter will discuss some newer trends in late modernity that impinge on parenting and family life, for example a tendency towards relatively more equal power relationships, which are observable in families of this generation. Negotiating, discussing, compromising and balancing needs and interests between spouses, in parenting and in communicating with children is a growing trend. In surveying recent trends in fatherhood in the EU, O'Brien (2004, p. 140) documents an important 'general movement away from paternal authority as a major organizing principle in family life in most European societies'. Concurrent with the postwar fall of the strict authoritarian society and corresponding changes in beliefs, the rapid growth in maternal employment has also been influential in this. This is clear when comparing parenting today with that in authoritarian Western societies some generations ago. Another theme is the emerging trend towards 'active fathering', legitimized in part by new paternity legislation in several countries (Kamerman and Moss, 2009) and by the UN Convention on the Rights of the Child (1989). Here both maternal and paternal rights and obligations are underlined.

Parenting Young Children: A Family Relationship Approach

In order to come to terms with the contexts of parenting, a basic framework will be presented, situating parenting within the complexities of family relationships. Relationship and transactional approaches were presented in Chapter 1 as part of the paradigm shift. In order to grasp the complexity of the levels, roles and processes within a dual-earner family with young children, the following principle will be used: the developmental impact of parenting derives from the joint pattern of relationships of all persons involved over time. Today, research focuses on the dynamics of close relationships rather than on personality constructs, or the action impact of one individual on the other (Collins and Roisman, 2006). For instance, this is five-year-old Martin's experience of a specific communicative style and pathway in his family: 'When my little sister yells a lot, my father begins to argue angrily with my mother. Then my mother yells at me: "Why on earth haven't you cleaned your messy room?"'

There are multiple direct and indirect communication pathways in family relationships. In more recent developmental psychology, the family is perceived as a holistic social system. Berk (2009) defines the family as an independent system of interactions, although influenced by the greater social context outside the family. The term 'family system' implies a network of mutually dependent personal connections among all family members (Parke and Buriel, 1998; Lerner et al., 2002). This chapter will consider the family and its members as involved in relational processes, which are regulated by and also regulate *specific situations*. One such situation could be 'leaving for work and childcare in the morning', which produces a number of routine actions among family members – washing, dressing, breakfasting and so on. These everyday family situations have evolved into interaction processes and, over time, have become regular practice.

For several years, research has been preoccupied with the question: How do children develop the basic foundation of experiences and knowledge that enables them meaningfully to handle social relations? As noted earlier, since the paradigm shift, the focus has been on the 'socially competent child'; however, this competence exists only in a rudimentary form at the beginning of life. The 'basic alphabet', which enables children to enter social communication, is probably innate. In spite of this, there are still an incredible number of social, emotional and cognitive competencies that children need to acquire in their childhood. It requires years of care and upbringing before a child fully masters living together with others in the complicated world of everyday life. Young children's early experiences of family relations are based on and also further develop the original social basis. Therefore, the study of families with children and the processes in the private arena are crucial if we are to understand the development of children.

The relational view can account for the complex direct and indirect processes among *all family members*. For instance, the mother–child relationship involves more than one relation, as it is significantly influenced by the quality of the parents' relationship, the father's attitude to how mother and children should interact, the child's relation to their sibling(s) and so on. Thus, it is complicated to understand a family's different dynamic processes and their relations to each other, but it is a professional necessity. In this connection, the focus is on how children in a family learn to regulate their feelings, because this is sine qua non to the development of relationship competence.

Even though the family is mentioned as an entity – *the family* – when we look at it as a private arena, the attention turns to an individual family member's relationship to another. This manifests itself not just in everyday psychological jargon, but also professionally. In older developmental psychology, the focus was on the mother–child relationship. This narrow starting point was later supplemented with research on the father–child relationship, extending family interactions to two people in two separate dyads. This does not mean that focusing on a two-person interaction is not important in order to understand what happens in a family, but that it is insufficient when the family is regarded as a relational entity.

THE FAMILY AS A DYNAMIC GROUP

Until recently, an understanding of families as a complex multiperson entity – in which the ways to influence something can be both direct and indirect – has been relatively rare in research on children (Fivaz-Depeursinge and Corboz-Warnery, 1999). This was because developmental psychology did not attribute young children with competencies that enabled them to enter into any social entities that were bigger and more complex than the relationship with another individual. However, until it becomes professionally realistic to regard the family as a dynamic group, one central question has to be answered: When does the child's ability to enter into triangular relations occur? When are small children capable of participating in meaningful encounters with both parents at the same time or with a parent and a sibling? Even to talk about the family as a social entity presupposes that *all parties* are capable of perceiving others, relating to them, influencing them and being influenced in return. As adults, we consider this a matter of fact, while this does not necessarily apply to children – especially very young children.

According to pre-paradigm shift developmental psychology, children were not capable of establishing personal connections with other people apart from their mother until they were three (Eyer, 1993). This was formulated early on by Bowlby, with his monotropic construct. New research indicates, as will be apparent in Chapter 5, that fathers can be important interaction partners early in life (Lamb, 2000, 2004; Day and Lamb, 2004a). However, a child is still perceived as only being able to handle being with one person at a time. In order to participate in a family, 'triadic competencies' are required of the child (Fivaz-Depeursinge and Corboz-Warnery, 1999), that is, participating in a three-person group with both parents. The point in time when a child is psychologically capable of living with more people has far-reaching consequences to our perception of how developmental influences are 'converted' in the family. Furthermore, to what extent and when the child has competencies to relate to small groups is also relevant to society's reproduction (Tomasello, 2009). The fact that many mothers work outside the home necessitates care outside the family, but it would be detrimental to the development of the next generation if the small child does not, early in life, have the mental capacity to establish and thrive in small face-to-face social groups. Research now indicates that even infants demonstrate triangular competencies early on in life. For instance, Stern (2006) notes the child's sense of 'self-together-with-others', which is part of the family triad. He points out that growing research indicates that, from the age of three months, children begin to establish expectations and mental representations about themselves as a part of a triadic constellation. This is not surprising, as a lot of time is spent in triads as well as dyads.

Developmental psychology has only recently begun to study the child in the whole family and not just the child 'with another' – 'child with mother' and 'child with father'. There are several reasons for this delay:

1. There has been a long tradition in psychology to have the individual as the starting point rather than the social group to which they belong.
2. For decades, the mother-centrism of psychoanalytical and early attachment theories locked children's development to the mother as the primary carer.
3. There was a professional revolution, around the 1970s, when it became possible to document that fathers are also significant to children.

Thereafter, families could be seen as a dynamic entity that affects everybody's development. As early as three months of age, babies are capable of actively participating with both their mother and father. For instance, they react with smiles and eye contact to the mother, then connect to the father, mimicking body movements, and then resume the dialogue with their mother. The child also observes and reacts to the mother–father relationship. Research shows that mothers and fathers, with their different styles of interaction, spend time with their child in different ways (Parke, 1996, 2002). Therefore, children experience early in life that they can be with people in different ways. However, the early triadic competence is relatively limited, and is refined and extended over time to become triadic expertise through thousands of interactions in the family's private arena.

Many young children grow up and have social experiences in a family that is more socially complex than a three-person group. The dual-earner family, which is the pivotal concern in this chapter, may have only one child, although it is also quite common for many children to grow up with one or more siblings (Zukow-Goldring, 2002).

The family is a group that consists of small groups, each with their relational characteristics. In the family, young children need to learn to act in several family arenas, in which they must gradually develop different social competencies. This requires the development of not merely triadic, but also *tetradic competencies*, that is, the ability for simultaneous participation with three others. This probably happens in the first half of the toddler years, but here family research is still inadequate and finds it hard to explain the complex social reality in many families.

In principle, the family is constructed by family members' relations over time in three *constellations* (dyads, triads and tetrads), which include eleven *combinations*.

Table 4.1 visualizes a family with two adults and two children. It is chosen to demonstrate the principle in the relations model, as there are families with both fewer and more children. For example, one-child families are more common in southern Europe than in Scandinavia. The single-income family, with one parent and one or more children, also constitutes a family, but in relation to Table 4.1, it will consist of fewer subgroups, in that the couple relationship is missing, and therefore there are fewer possibilities for interactions in the single-parent family. Naturally, there are also families with five or more people, where the group constellations and combinations will be more complex than illustrated in Table 4.1.

The group structure of families can be understood by naming the different subgroup relationships: *mother–child relationship, father–child relationship, the couple's relationship* and *siblings' relationship*. In principle, each subgroup has its own qualitative characteristics determined by the age, gender and personality of each person. For example, daughter Mia's relationship with her mother Anna is, in principle, different from Mia's relationship with her father; even though Mia is the 'same girl', emotions and moods will differ in interactions with parents of different genders and personalities. Mia

Table 4.1   *Group structures in a four-person family*

Group constellations	Group combinations
Dyads	Mother–Father
	Mother–Child1
	Mother–Child2
	Father–Child1
	Father–Child2
	Child1–Child2
Triads	Mother–Father–Child1
	Mother–Father–Child2
	Mother–Child1–Child2
	Father–Child1–Child2
Tetrads	Mother–Father–Child1–Child2

does certain things with her mother and other things with her father. New multipersonal attachment research, as presented in Chapter 2, has also documented that the child's relationships with their mother and father can be quite different (Howes and Spieker, 2008).

The ages and gender differences of siblings also play a role, as does the number of siblings. To Mia, it is developmentally significant if she is the big sister or the baby sister, whether she has an older or younger brother, or whether she is the middle child in a family. Research into sibling caring has proved that sibling relationships are an independent, developmental force in the family (Zukow-Goldring, 2002). In this light, families influence the course of development in both children and adults in a multitude of ways.

To reiterate, various group combinations in the family each have their characteristics, not only because of the social entities' different sizes and thereby varying possibilities for interaction, but also because of the specific persons involved – their personality, gender, age and role position in the family. At the same time, the many group constellations influence each other in complex ways, both as direct and indirect influences among the family's subgroups. Children's opportunities to have social experiences with their different family members in various group constellations can vary considerably, even in same-size families. This depends on a number of factors outside and inside the family, for example parents' working hours influence when parents are accessible for participation in family life. The distribution of family tasks also regulates who is together, for how long and when. In addition, there are personal preferences, habits and attitudes to the interactions in family life.

This chapter cannot discuss each and every group constellation or combination, because research has not yet examined all of them. Nor has research thrown sufficient light on the many complicated relationships that exist *among* the subgroups. To illustrate this with a single example, Table 4.1

shows that siblings are together in all three group constellations and in many of the group combinations. Although the sibling relationship can be studied directly in the Child1–Child2 dyad, this is not enough from a family dynamic perspective. Siblings alternate between being with all members of the family in the tetrad and with mother/father in the triad, while they are also together as siblings.

So, although empirical research still cannot explain all social constellations and combinations, the model can be used as a 'professional reminder' to those who try to understand and explain social processes in a family. The model draws attention to the fact that there are rarely simple explanations of parenting or the family's influence on children. A number of complex answers must be found for this.

DOES PARENTING MATTER?

As discussed in Chapter 1, the new perception of children as relatively competent, self-determined and resilient individuals does not imply that caring and parenting have lost their importance, despite children experiencing many hours in daily childcare. For young children, the relative importance of parents seems to prevail despite the demise of classic family-centric socialization and despite the claim that childcare has stripped the family of its function. Parenting is still seen as important to young children's development (Clarke-Stewart and Dunn, 2006). The new dual socialization model, presented in Chapter 2, underlines the importance of parenting and family in early childhood without denying the influence of childcare.

Despite this, there may still be some doubt about the importance of family and parenting in a contemporary world with many carers and other individuals around young children. The debates and themes presented and discussed in Chapter 2 can be seen as a warning sign of such concerns. This section offers a closer look at a professional counterclaim that parenting either does not matter or only 'has to be good enough'. This claim will be compared with recent evidence and a final conclusion will be reached.

One might believe that in professional circles there is fundamental consensus that parents are essential to young children's development. However, some researchers argue directly against the 'truism' that parents create the environment that means the most to their children's development (Scarr, 1992; Harris, 1998). These thought-provoking critics minimize parents' importance, and emphasize three factors: heredity, child culture and functional emptying of the family.

Scarr (1992) argues that within the framework of the average family environment, genes mean more than parents. Through the realization of a 'good enough environment', parents do matter, not as a environmental influence but by passing their genes on to their children. Furthermore, the child's genetic disposition organizes the child's 'evocative behaviour', so that it will look for and create the environments that suit its genetically controlled tendencies. Scarr tries to substantiate her point with twin studies. The arguments and the evidence have, however, faced fierce criticism (see the debate in Scarr, 1992; Baumrind, 1993; Joseph, 2003).

Harris (1998) caused a stir with the conclusion that parents have little influence on their children's development. Evidence is presented that siblings who grow up in the same family apparently share no resemblance – in either temperament or personality. By contrast, they are more similar to their friends than their siblings. According to Harris, siblings' 'non-shared' different genetic make-up as well as different experiences in peer groups overshadow parental influence. However, it is simplistic to think that genes function as a 'blueprint' controlling the child, which Scarr and Harris assume. The gene–environment causality has become too simple a way of perceiving this relationship, which is further highlighted when the two are combined with an underlying axiom about the passive-receptive child. There is a complicated and reciprocal connection between genes and environment formulated in the term 'probabilistic epigenesis' (Karmiloff-Smith, 2010). Epigenesis is probabilistic and both brain development and gene expression are environmentally activity dependent (Gottlieb, 2003; Majdan and Schatz, 2006). This undermines Scarr and Harris's blueprint idea about 'genes outdoing parents'.

Furthermore, this chapter's approach to the family as a dynamic group explains why same-parent siblings become different, and why similarities among siblings are probably more often the exception and not the rule. Also, Harris's argument about the importance of peers in young children's socialization can be incorporated into dual socialization – not as a group that overrides the parents' importance, but as a significant part of early childhood socialization. For instance, research into peer groups in childcare has found no evidence that they are more important than parental influence (Clarke-Stewart and Allhusen, 2005).

The third objection to parents' importance in bringing up children originates from classical socialization theory (see Chapter 2), which claims that after the mothers' entry into the workplace gained momentum in the 1960s and 70s, society's institutions – crèches, nurseries, schools – and people – friends and adults other than parents – have, over time, reduced the modern family's functions. According to this view, this delegation of bringing up children has undermined families' reproductive function in society. Dencik et al. (2008) disagree with this view of families, instead they emphasize the family's function as an 'zone of emotional stability' that has become intensified in today's society, that is, the importance of parents is highlighted. However, does this counterargument of the thesis about the functional emptying of the family express a normatively based *wish* for the importance of the family – that it ought to be the child's protector and emotional guarantee in a time marked by break-up and rapid change? That the family should necessarily function as the essential buffer and retreat from the stress of everyday life in late modern society? Is this a wish or a reality? Does the family matter in our turbulent times? Can research answer such questions?

In other words: Is there a research-based foundation for saying that parenting, that is, bringing up children, does take place, and does it mean anything to children's development? There are a number of well-documented answers to these fundamental questions. Berk (2009) summarized research that refutes the argument about parents' minimal significance, and up-to-date documentation can also be found in Clarke-Stewart and Dunn (2006). (For a review of dual-earner families and the impact of maternal employment on parenting, see Gottfried et al., 2002.) Here are some important conclusions:

- *Parents' influence on their children's development is substantial:* For instance, there is a strong relationship between authoritative parenting and children's social responsibility. Parents' monitoring of the child combined with loving care are closely connected to the absence of antisocial behaviour. Direct behaviour regulation by parents is significant for the development of children's social competencies.
- *Parents influence their children differently:* That Harris (1998) could claim a modest resemblance between sibling personalities is not necessarily because parents fail to make a difference. Research shows that parents respond differently to each child in their family. Adults adjust their interactions according to the children's differences and they are thereby treated as the unique people they are. This research supports this chapter's relational view that the family's different dyads and tetrads can each be influenced by their distinct relations.
- *Over a long period, parental influence matters:* Longitudinal studies have shown that parents' influence on their children is significant, as is the importance of early genetic influence, for example temperament.
- *Growing up in a dual-earner family does not generally diminish the parental importance of bringing up children:* Relationship quality with mothers and the developmental importance of mothering has changed little despite the increase in maternal employment. In addition, there is consistent and overwhelming evidence that fathers become more involved in childcare and activities with their children when mothers are employed. The more hours mothers work, the more father involvement in the dual-earner family. (Chapter 5 is devoted to the developmental importance of this emergent trend in fatherhood.)
- *Systematic change in raising children causes change in children's behaviour:* Arguments in favour of parents' significance stem from intervention experiments, in which parents have been helped to make positive changes

to their parenting style. When the parenting changes for the better, an equally positive change can be observed in children's behaviour.

- *Parents influence their children's relations with their friends:* When they are toddlers, parents regulate their children's contact with their peers, who they spend time with and when. The beliefs that parents communicate to their older children also influence their choice of friends.

The relational view is important for avoiding an 'either/or', genes or environment polarization. Genetic factors (such as intensity of emotions/temperament) and children's experiences in peer group interactions can be assumed to have a certain influence on how children develop. Thus parents do not influence in isolation but in conjunction with a number of other factors. In addition, there is the active contribution from children to interactions, as well as experiences in social arenas outside the family.

In light of existing evidence, it does seem that the argument about parents' minimal importance is not supported. Parenting by a mother and/or a father generally still seems to matter, when evaluated in the complexity of young children's multiple social worlds.

The family remains an essential developmental arena for the child, but is no longer a closed circuit consisting of fully developed adults who affect their children, as may be portrayed in traditional personality psychology (Datan and Ginsberg, 1975). Parenting skills only partially rely on the parents' personalities and previous childhood experiences. Parents' competencies are continuously influenced by negative and positive life events, which in turn affect their interactions with their children. A family's inner life and its relationships with both close and distant external environments are essential to young children's development in late modern society. The following factors are deemed to be important:

- *In the eye of the beholder – parent's perceptions of children:* Child-rearing philosophy and interpretative filters concerning what a child is in general are key factors. Parents' perceptions of children have a strong influence on parenting practices and may either hamper or promote the child's development (Goodnow and Collins 1990; Goodnow, 2002). If mothers and fathers have conflicting and non-negotiable perceptions of their child, this may have a negative influence on family relationships. If spouses fail to negotiate a mutual acceptance of each other's views or are unable to develop shared views, this may hamper positive parenting in various ways (Sommer, 2001).
- *Parent–child relationship quality:* The quality of caring/parenting practices in the family is of special importance. In Western cultures, adults' empathy with and realistic interpretation of the child's needs have a considerable positive impact on the child's development. Caring in the form of sensitive interactions with children is essential (Stern, 2006). Parents can

function as developmental engines and instructive guides by adjusting their actions to keep up with and anticipate their child's developmental level. In parents' interactions with their child, their parenting style is important – especially with regard to their ability to make balanced demands on the child. This parenting style is neither authoritarian nor laissez-faire, rather, it can be described as 'authoritative parenting', which respects both adults' and children's rights (Baumrind, 1988).[61]

- *Parental mental health and wellbeing:* Are the mother and the father content, or are there serious concerns? The mental health status of mothers and fathers is closely linked to children's wellbeing (Rutter, 2008). For example, infants with depressed mothers may initiate joyful interactions, but with time their facial expressions reveal diminished joy, surprise or social interest, and they begin to look as sad as their mothers (Pickens and Field, 1993). Although this book deals mainly with so-called typical development, it is noteworthy in such a context that parental mental wellbeing establishes the basis for developing positive relationships.

- *Parental conflict and harmony:* The mutual parental relationship is important, especially in terms of their ability to cooperate and resolve conflicts concerning the child. A relatively harmonious relationship between spouses seems to be a prerequisite for a positive developmental pathway for young children. In modern dual-earner families (and in others), arguments and conflicts between individuals living together are a part of normal life. Research, however, has consistently shown that intense long-term conflict and disharmony between spouses does not always predispose children to deviancy. But intense, unresolved long-term conflicts are risk factors for the development of disorders (Rutter, 2008). Studies of long-term before and after effects of divorce have found that a child can be negatively affected years before a divorce actually happens (Schaffer, 1990). The point is that a disturbed family relationship seems to be more than or just as important as the potential negative after effect of a divorce on the child.

- *The young child's perspective and sense-making:* Although recent theory stresses the developmental importance of relationships, individual interpretation must be accounted for as well. The young child's subjective and personal approach and contribution to their own development, socialization and learning has evoked increasing interest (Sommer et al., 2010). Infants and young children show remarkable individual responses depending on the meaning they attach to interactions with others (Berk, 2009; Gopnik, 2009). In addition, young children differ individually in response to conflict and stress, some showing more resilience than others (Masten and Gewirtz, 2006). The ability to cope with anxiety and aggression varies from one child to another. Individual expectations and the child's personal sense-making efforts are an important part of this.

- *Extrafamilial networks:* Grandparents, friends, colleagues and childcare staff may strengthen or weaken parenting and conflict management competencies (Lerner et al., 2002). Furthermore, a well-functioning network may provide practical support during stressful times. Networks may also have an important indirect influence on young children's development as maternal satisfaction with network support correlates with the mother's impression of how easy it is to handle the child. A small network that offers modest support to parents, however, seemingly makes it difficult for the mother to care for the child (Melson et al., 1993). The same also seems to go for fathers. So even though the family is a main source of caring and upbringing, it is also affected by the larger social context.

NEGOTIATION FAMILIES: AN EMERGENT PHENOMENON

An important emergent trend has appeared in the wake of the almost universal increase in female employment and changes in cultural and societal beliefs. Not only has the number of dual-earner families risen, but they are becoming the norm in many countries. Also, core beliefs about male and female family roles have changed quickly, with vital consequences for parenting. In an article in *Time* magazine, Nancy Gibbs (2009) called these changes in family life 'a quiet revolution', stating that 49.8% of jobs were held by women and 50.2% by men in 2009. The current economic crisis, with thousands of lost jobs, has hit men harder than women, and 'it's [soon] expected that...for the first time in history, the majority of workers in the U.S. will be women'. As a part of this scenario, more and more women are becoming primary breadwinners (Gibbs, 2009). In order to investigate this, 'the Rockefeller Foundation, in collaboration with *Time*, conducted a landmark survey of gender issues'. In general, female participation in the workforce is now widely approved as a positive thing. Relevant to this chapter was the finding that '84% affirm that husbands and wives negotiate the rules, relationships and responsibilities more than those of earlier generations did' (Gibbs, 2009).

In a longitudinal Scandinavian-based study, 73% of a representative selection of Danish parents replied that in order to solve an argument, they used discussion to reach agreement. A small percentage reported that the male had the last word, and a small percentage stated that they failed to reach agreement when there had been an argument (Sommer, 2001). There are several ways of having a discussion and resolving a disagreement. Nevertheless, arguments, discussions and talks with the partner seem to be the most common approach in many contemporary families. For Dad to put his foot down, because he is the 'head of the family' appears to be an anachronistic idea far removed from the realities of many late modern families. Research has consistently proved a more pronounced role balance between mothers and fathers in dual-earner families than in families with a male breadwinner (Gottfried et al., 2002).

In the systemic and functionalist approach used in the relationship between family and society, it is expected that families are, to some extent, influenced by the zeitgeist. Recent studies from other countries show a growing trend towards more equal roles among males and females. Some of this has been explained by connecting specific changes in late modernity's consensus-seeking culture with the life of the individual who lives in such a culture (Esping-Andersen et al., 2003), while others relate it to the emerging paternal involvement in children's upbringing (Haavind, 2006). Some point to the impact and growing societal shift in parts of the world towards humanism and democracy, which also changes fundamental beliefs about children's best interests (Sommer et al., 2010).

The fundamental gender beliefs about how to manage a family's inner affairs and the power balance in relationships with even young children seem to have changed surprisingly fast. A general parental attitude and ambition seems to be governed by negotiation and not by undisputed male superiority.[62] *Explaining, debating* and *reasoning* play a growing role in the way parents relate to their children. For example, many contemporary fathers and mothers have become – through education and profession – skilled in a conversation and negotiation culture, which they use as a benchmark in the relationship with their children. In other words, both mothers and fathers are influenced by a set of occupational conditions that have implications for how they interact with and socialize their children (Crouter, 2006).

In dealing with this emerging family phenomenon, some reservations should be made clear. Not all families and their relationships are covered. Nor can it be claimed that everybody lives in a context where negotiation is the main relationship rule. In fact, an international study of the extent and content of the phenomenon is missing. Negotiation *families*, not *the negotiation family* are addressed here. So, it is not *the* late modern family stereotype, but rather a description of an emerging trend towards a 'negotiation culture'. Nor does this section claim to portray 'today's children' in general or all modern children. Again, the point is to highlight some current trends that may characterize individual children to a greater or lesser extent.

Clearly, as a way of including and interacting with children, negotiation is a relatively recent historical phenomenon. Some children are included in decision-making processes about family affairs and the parents pay attention to their opinion.[63] The days when 'the child's will lies in the father's pocket' or when 'children must be seen and not heard' seem to have gone.[64] For example, a modern father in a dual-earner family probably does not have first choice or the best cuts of meat, as he may have done in the past when, as the sole provider, his physical strength and mental energy were needed.

So inclusion and the delegation of influence are vital characteristics of families referred to as negotiation families. In today's world, authority is less a given, instead it has to be earned. It no longer automatically follows rank or status. The democratization of the way people interact in late modern culture, described in Chapters 2 and 3, has had a substantial influence on the way parents perceive themselves and their children.

Negotiation relationships between parents and children assume many forms and have various consequences for children. But in general there seem to be some positive consequences. Dunn and Brown (1991) note that young children who are most emotionally well balanced are the ones whose parents include them in conversations and discussions about their emotions and relationships. In addition, children of parents who use a democratic authoritarian approach function well in a range of developmental domains (Baumrind, 1978, 1988, 1991). (Baumrind's groundbreaking research will be presented later in this chapter and evaluated with regard to its relevance for understanding parent–child negotiation relationships.) Here, suffice it to say that being included in discussions and in balanced decision-making processes is closely related to young children's development of personal and social competencies. Tomasello (2009) also relates non-authoritarian parenting to young children's more advanced social cooperative skills.

Negotiating and arguing with a young child may be seen as a hard route to follow – giving in to the child's will, bargaining over meals and bedtime – where the child is attempting to manipulate and control adults. This may, in special cases, be the result of the way parents handle this, perhaps being defensive, non-involved and delegating decision-making to a young child who cannot handle the situation. But is it so in general? In her book on commonsense myths and misunderstandings about child development, Mercer (2010, p. 160) discussed this claim in light of research: 'Preschoolers who try to bargain with their parents really want to manipulate and control adults, and they should not be allowed to negotiate.' The claim seems unjustified because repeated negotiation experience in childhood appears to enhance children's perspective-taking, thus knowing the mind of another. Furthermore, an internal working model of trustworthy relationships seems to be fostered. In addition, complex language skills are developed, because negotiation requires verbal competency. Mercer (2010, p. 162) points to this potential long-term benefit: 'the experience of bargaining with adults is an excellent way to practise negotiation and compromise skills that will be beneficial in the future'.

Thus parents' inclusion of children is a crucial factor in understanding important aspects of contemporary young children's development. But which factors and developments lead to the emergence of negotiation families? Chapter 3 established the basis in terms of presenting vital cultural conditions that resulted in the late modern family, that culture is not a rigid system of rules and conventions that the child is socialized into. Instead, culture is a communicative product of human activity on many levels, produced by actors through 'negotiation' (Fogel, 1993). Seen in the perspective

NEGOTIATION

HUMANIZATION

- Being seen and heard
- Being included
- Having personal importance
- Being unique
- Having unique needs

DEMOCRATIZATION

- Rules are changeable
- Individuals have a say
- Children have rights
- Seeking social participation
- Demanding to be seen and heard as a person
- Weakened acceptance of authority figures

INDIVIDUATION

Figure 4.1   Negotiation families: trends and beliefs

of dual socialization introduced in Chapter 2, the family is still an important arena for socialization, and thus the negotiation principle has to apply to families' internal interactions. In order to constitute a negotiation family, however, a series of external cultural and internal family factors have to be present. This is illustrated in Figure 4.1, where all the dimensions need to be seen as each other's prerequisites as well as consequences. The humanization and democratization dimensions in the model, as well as the principle of individuation, are important late modernity (Western) ideas (see Box 2.1).

It is important to say that this is a *speculative model* invented in order to stimulate new research of specific relevance to deepen our understanding of the relatively recent negotiation phenomenon. (This also means that in many other family contexts the model will be irrelevant.) A longitudinal, representative study of parents and their way of handling conflict shows that 'negotiating' is, in fact, the preferred mode when solving conflicts, as the vast majority of couples say they discuss and negotiate, choosing between various alternatives. In addition, this specific way of handling conflict was strongly related to the child's positive wellbeing (Sommer, 2001). But much more empirical research is needed in order to confirm or change the model and its hypothesis for children's development (Figure 4.1).

Along with a multitude of factors, three cultural phenomena in particular have been the driving forces behind the making and emergence of a culture of negotiation: humanization, democratization and individuation. There is no one way, but a multitude of ways to implement negotiation relationships in a negotiation family. The following will offer illuminating examples of how this may occur. It is a closer examination of how, in principle, humanization, democratization and individuation may be 'seen' in families characterized by negotiation relationships.

Humanization (the left side of Figure 4.1) characterizes the culturally late modern belief that children are human beings who deserve consideration. Children have rights like everybody else and should be treated with respect. Humanization may be expressed in negotiation families in the following ways:

- *Being seen and heard:* Children are not expected to be invisible in the family, instead they are expected to be both 'seen and heard'. This belief may be expressed in a wide range of situations, from parental pride in the baby's first babbling and first insecure steps, to listening to the young child about what to wear before heading off for childcare.
- *Being included:* From a relatively early age, children are included in decision-making that affects themselves and the family. Being included characterizes the child's relationship with adults and may well start early in life. For example, in the infant–adult context, inclusion means that the adult makes sure that the child feels they are participating, understand what is going on, and are actively allowed to contribute to the relationship. Later in childhood, parents may include children by asking what they would like for dinner. The phenomenon may also be observed when a parent and a child negotiate deals, perhaps making compromises, reaching a final decision or when the child tries to twist family rules.
- *Having personal importance, being unique, and having unique needs:* Individuation is, as stated earlier, a profound and recent phenomenon in late modern Western societies. The concomitant belief in every person's uniqueness is transferred to young humans and individuation penetrates family life in many ways. Living together in a small group of individuals in a family glued together by 'pure relationships' – by love and devotion – opens the way for intimacy, binding reciprocity and appreciation of the individual. For example, as many modern families have become smaller with fewer siblings, the tendency to categorize 'children as just children' (that is, as an age category) gives way to a more detailed view of each young child as unique. In addition, the invention of birth control has made it possible to have plan when to have children, so contemporary parents are more likely to love the child they have actively chosen to have. Parental love is a uniquely strong sentiment, and the object of that

affection is given tremendous personal importance in the life of the adult. Furthermore, the humanization trend has had a strong influence on the perception of today's children as unique beings with unique needs that adults should accommodate.

Democratization (the right side of Figure 4.1) as a part of everyday life means that children 'have a say' in decisions that concern them and perhaps the family as a whole. In a micro-societal context, democratization has a less lofty ring than it often has because it denotes a specific practical way of living together. Democratization as a process in ontogenesis is essentially about the development of attitudes and competencies that are essential to act and live in a culture of cooperation – in a here-and-now social context where conflict and strife are not settled by violence or authoritarian rules. This requires participants to gradually learn to balance their individuality – the 'I-am-unique' approach – with cooperative concerns; for example, by being personally visible and using arguments and reasoning as tools in a social negotiation process with a common goal of compromising.[65] This democratic attitude is a particularly important childhood experience with far-reaching consequences to children's culture acquisition and their way of being together with other people. Democratization may be reflected in negotiation families in the following ways:

- *Rules are changeable:* Unlike an authoritarian regime, a basic implicit code in negotiation families is that rules and decisions are not laid down by God, the president or the family male. Children involved in negotiation and decision-making learn at a early stage that rules may be open to change. Authority in a negotiable context is, in principle, delegated to family members who are invited to express their opinions. This may seem an uncontrollable avenue for giving in to children's whims, who then bargain and manipulate the adults. But this does not generally seem to be the case, especially if parents are attuned to the child's level of understanding and define some non-negotiation zones.
- *Children have a say and rights:* As a consequence of being included and involved in negotiating rules, children experience that they have a say. Being involved in decision-making should be understood in a down-to-earth way – children are allowed a say and are included in decision-making when parents think it is appropriate. This has important perspectives, since involvement in decision-making is a fundamental aspect of any democratic social group. The gradual development of the negotiation competencies needed to participate in democratic groups is an important developmental task, not just for the family but also for extra-familial childcare settings. Young children's first-hand experience with age-appropriate democracy constitutes their first tentative steps towards full participation in the negotiation culture and is thus a vital part of the

culture acquisition process. Closely connected to having a say is that children are given rights as well. This is connected to postwar changes towards negotiation culture, humanism and child centredness as vital societal values (Sommer et al., 2010). That children have rights has even been institutionalized in the UN Convention on the Rights of the Child (1989). But negotiation families are not simply copying societal ideas and laws. Living in contemporary society, the socialization practices of such families are influenced by the zeitgeist as well as contributing to it.

- *Seeking social participation:* Repeated experiences of being seen and heard, being included, being of personal importance and having a say in interactions with others seem to strengthen a child's personal sense of mastery. Mastery is closely related to feelings of relationship security and self-esteem (Berk, 2009). This is crucial for young children living in their various socialization arenas with their many complex social relationships. Mastery combined with a sense of relationship security and relationship confidence also motivates the child to be socially engaged. The child wants to contribute to the 'give-and-take' encounters this requires. The so-called authoritative parenting style, to be discussed in more detail later, seems to be especially important for the development of mastery and the desire to engage in social participation. Baumrind's research (1978, 1988) suggests that the parental *balancing* of demands and being responsive to children's needs, and not permissiveness, facilitates the development of personal confidence and social motivation.

- *Demanding to be seen and heard as a person:* One consequence of treating young children as individuals who deserve to be listened to is that they may demand to be seen and heard. To be treated as anonymous members of a group of children will probably not be acceptable. This individual-ized attitude is not necessarily the same as egotism (although it may turn into that, depending on parenting style); it is a consequence of being included and allowed to have a say in public. A child who has taken part in democratic power-sharing and grows up as an experienced negotiator may well show some social audacity.

- *Weakened acceptance of authority figures:* Children with years of experience in a negotiation culture may develop a low acceptance of adult authority. This is a logical consequence of 'allowing children in' – giving them a participatory role in families. Adults may from time to time need to be on their toes to meet the arguments, protests and alternative suggestions from their 'negotiation-experienced child', who may have developed some sophisticated ways of gaining influence. Adult authority (in the sense of evoking positive respect and responsiveness in children) may be necessary, but is not granted – authority has to be 'earned' and legit-imized in relationships. For example, at nursery, a new member of staff, who has not yet established their authority, may have a hard time to begin with in getting such a child to cooperate and participate.

Negotiation-experienced children in non-family contexts

But how do negotiation-experienced young children, who move between their family and non-family contexts, behave outside the family? This has rarely been researched, although it is important for the contextual understanding of early childhood. It is unknown territory and it may be beyond what can be substantiated professionally. However, this will be investigated based on previous theorizing in this book and supplemented by relevant research, although more research is needed. In this section, family socialization based on negotiation relationships will be discussed in relation to potential 'spillover' consequences for the child's social behaviour in non-family contexts.[66] This will highlight some structural differences between families and non-family socializing contexts that may explain (not condemn) whether young children of this generation seem self-centred, impulse-driven and without much respect for adults. In the supermarket queue, a young child may be heard demanding sweets, seeing them displayed in front of their nose, or impatiently asking 'why isn't it our turn now?' This may be frowned upon and seen as an example of a spoiled generation that arose as an upshot of the changes documented in Chapter 2. Rapid and unforeseen changes also provoke fundamental beliefs. In Scandinavia, with its 50 years' experience, child stereotyping flourished in the 1990s. Books were published launching popular generalizations, such as 'the new selfish child'; 'radar children' – scanning situations to manipulate others; 'curling children' – having busy parents clearing away obstacles on their child's developmental pathway. Such stereotypes were often followed by 'good advice' to parents about how to fix the problems[67] (for a 1990s review, see Smånyt [Small News], 1996).

Clearly, parenting has much to do with a child's bad behaviour, but the workings of 'an invisible structuring hand' behind the parents' backs may also, as will be apparent, be in play. By arguing that negotiations and compromises have been a deep and recurrent experience in the socialization process in early childhood, it may have some 'spillover' consequences for the child's attitude and behaviour in non-family contexts. An underlying premise is that what is experienced and learned in family conversations is generalized and also used as a meaningful and useful matrix for subsequent encounters in non-family contexts. Seemingly this proposition is supported by recent research and relationship family theory (Milardo and Duck, 2000; Clarke-Stewart and Dunn, 2006). As documented in Chapter 2, despite time spent in daily childcare, the relative weight and developmental importance of the family has not been weakened. In addition, there exist important reciprocal relationships between family and childcare. For example, in the dual socialization configuration, secure/insecure attachment is not explained solely by childcare factors such as staff–child ratio and quality of nursery teacher–child relationship, or by family factors such as maternal sensitivity, but by a mixture of both.

So fundamental styles of parenting and upbringing have important consequences for how young children 'orient' themselves outside their family. To be treated as an individual, a unique person, 'seen and heard' and involved in decision-making in the family may have profound influences on the way a young child relates to others in public spaces. A childcare setting filled with negotiation-experienced young children poses challenges. Each child seemingly considers 'I' as a special, important person, a human being that stands tall, with their own needs and cravings that do not necessarily match teacher's or other children's perspectives.

Young children raised in a negotiation culture with secure relationships with their parents may tend to address public spaces with self-reliance and self-determination. In addition, they may have an inquisitive attitude and be socially motivated – eager to learn, slightly undisciplined, keen to discuss, expecting attention and to be listened to, and showing limited respect for adult authority per se. This may conflict with the way the individual is contextualized in public socialization and learning arenas like childcare settings and school.

In Western societies, in the social worlds of childcare and school, the child is, in principle, acknowledged as an individual. Compared with the child's unique and personal position in the family, the child's status as 'the only social one' is less apparent when acting in public arenas. Despite the fact that school and childcare settings set educational goals for children and define the developmental meaning of daily relationships, a structural group-organized feature is the tendency to perceive the young child as a member of an age category, a peer group member. This is not only structurally different from the young child's position in the family, but it may result in different relationship practices. In the family, with its generous adult–child ratio, parents have better opportunities to establish personalized accommodations to a young child than a teacher does. If so, family and non-family contexts will turn out to have qualitatively different socialization functions in late modern early childhood – as indirectly stated by the term 'dual' socialization, they are not additive, but complementary.

A second key structural difference between families and non-family child arenas is the child–child ratio. For example, in childcare, school or neighbourhood playgrounds, there are many more children than in a family, where living with a sister/brother is of significant developmental importance (Zukow-Goldring, 2002). In preschool and school, however, the child engages with large groups of children, and this experience in peer groups also has important developmental functions (Clarke-Stewart and Allhusen, 2005). Child–child socialization is different and fulfils different functions for the young child in their daily living in both family and non-family arenas.

A third crucial difference is that most parents love their children – a strong sentiment that has established the family as an unchallenged 'zone of emotional intimacy' (Dencik et al., 2008). In public learning and socialization environments, the young child encounters professionals who do not need to be emotionally involved – a civilized, friendly tone is sufficient. Again the socializing functions of parenting are markedly different from the socioemotional socialization function in non-family contexts.

In summary, profound socialization differences between families and public spaces (childcare and school) exist, which work as complementary developmental arenas. However, this is admittedly rather sketchy and speculative. Empirical research is urgently needed in order to determine how this complexity is managed by young children growing up in negotiation relationships. Interestingly, much early preschool pedagogy is, more or less implicitly, based on some of the same cultural beliefs of humanization and democratization. This was discussed in Chapter 2 as key markers of late modernity and in this chapter specified as an important cultural context behind the emergence of the negotiation family phenomenon. Today's pedagogy and teaching are rarely based on authoritarian relationships between adults and children. Instead, conversations, reciprocity and balanced relationships are – despite specific curricula – common reference points of being together (Clarke-Stewart and Allhusen, 2005). In Scandinavia, this is in the forefront of early pedagogy and care, and is also part of the many early childhood education programmes worldwide (see www.omep.org.uk; Sommer et al., 2010). This indicates that many young children of this generation live in dual negotiation contexts, with 'spillover' effects from the family and the non-family context.

These ideas have important *consequences for professional practice.* For example, like millions of other young children in the world, five-year-old Mary and Mike live in and are influenced by their dual socialization world – family and childcare. Let us say that Mike represents 'a problem' in his childcare. Based on observations in social encounters, he is too impulse-driven and aggressive, creating conflicts. In a systems approach endorsed by this book, Mike's behaviour cannot be explained by referring to personality traits. Nor can Mike's family be the basic cause of the problem – the approach labelled as family-centrism. Instead, focus should be on the potential consequences of Mike living in two distinctively different social arenas. Several explanations are possible here, but they need to be based on careful observation and information-seeking. Perhaps Mike's conflicting behaviour occurs because he is perceived and treated differently in the family and childcare contexts. In addition, there may be no cooperation between parents and childcare staff in order to deal with Mike's problem in a collaborative way. Consequently, in order to deal with this relatively new early childhood situation, professionals have to be educated to meet the particular challenges of this situation. Children who grow up in negotiation families have particular expectations of the interactions they engage in, and they want to be treated and heard as individuals: 'Hey, listen to me – see what I can do!'

This trend towards having negotiation relationships in contemporary families is probably irreversible as it reflects deep changes in culture and society. Context-sensitive care, learning and education should, as a point of departure, adapt to the real-life situations of the young child who moves between family, childcare or school.[68]

PARENTING STYLES AND UPBRINGING

The long-term task for adults is to help the child acquire the moral and social 'maps' that make it possible to navigate in the social geography of late modern life. As the child grows up, primary personalized care is reduced and gradually changes into upbringing. Even though newborn babies are surprisingly competent, morals and knowledge of the social ground rules are not hardwired. Therefore, the child has to learn to navigate the world on the basis of a huge number of explicit and implicit rules defining social and moral acts. This is similar to what was said in Chapter 3 about the acquisition of cultural codes. Upbringing is an everyday term for this process.

Direct parenting is important, as expressed in the particular ways that adults influence children. How might one best characterize late modern adults' various parenting styles, and how do these different approaches affect the child's competence development? Only recently have researchers begun to study the effect of parents' and other adults' perceptions and upbringing approaches on children's competence development (Smetana, 1994). Even though much of this research describes upbringing as constant and detached from everyday events, it is a step in the right direction. Now, we can begin to narrow down the specific effects on children's development of various approaches to upbringing.

A typology of parenting

Some years ago, an influential model based on empirical findings describing parenting and its consequences for children was developed by Baumrind (1978, 1988, 1991). Her model has been widely used in child psychology textbooks, proving that it has become a kind of 'state of the art' (see Berk, 2009). For *A Childhood Psychology*, Baumrind's typology and those who have subsequently extended her work are of special interest in the understanding of socialization within the late modern family. Although she does not refer to or specify temporal context, the concepts make sense for understanding the types of late modern parental upbringing strategies.

According to Baumrind, parents' different ways of relating to their children can be assessed along two main dimensions:

- A *demand/non-demand dimension:* some parents either set relatively high standards for children or demand very little.

- A *responsive/non-responsive dimension:* parents either show warmth, acceptance and empathy, or are low in acceptance and warmth.[69]

When combining the two dimensions, four types of parenting arise, and each is discussed below.

Authoritative parenting

Authoritative parenting sets relatively high aspirations on behalf of the child. Parents are responsive and child-oriented – this is a rational and democratic style that respects and balances the interests of adults and children. Parents appear adult-centric and child-centric. Baumrind identified a group of children that were characterized by significantly more vitality, joy of life, cooperation and confidence in their mastery of new tasks than other groups. Furthermore, these children were less involved in socially destructive activities. When their personal and social competencies were matched with family backgrounds, their parents were found to practise an authoritative style. Authoritative adults are characterized as making developmental demands and setting clear boundaries for behaviour, while showing understanding for the child. They take an interest in the child's activities and display personal affection. These adults listen to the child's point of view and reason with them by *encouraging involvement in the family's decision-making processes.*[70] In this respect, this clearly resembles what happens in negotiation families. Longitudinal studies following Baumrind's groundbreaking research have emphasized several important long-term positive developmental gains (Hart et al., 2003). Others have documented developmental gains by linking authoritative parenting with the absence of delinquency in adolescence (Laird et al., 2003).

An interesting point in the definition of the authoritative parent is that it underlines demands *and* empathy as conditions of qualified parenting. This is a solution to the problematic idea that good parenting is an either/or matter presented as a *choice between empathy and demands.*[71] Children of authoritative parents relate to other people by arguing, compromising and making alternative suggestions. This negotiation style is an inevitable consequence of including children and showing respect for their opinions. Unlike the permissive style (see below), the authoritarian style is mentally to contain and be responsive to a child's eventual resistance, arguments and protests. Thus this approach sees both children and adults as active participants and offers children a measured level of influence on those aspects of everyday life that affect them.

Authoritarian parenting

Authoritarian parenting makes great demands on the child but is non-responsive, and can be characterized as mainly adult-centric. Parents set relatively high aspirations on behalf of their child, like their authoritative counterparts, but demands are more non-negotiable. Parental emphasis is on conformity and obedience, which makes them less tolerant of the child's perspective. When conflict arises, the parents' aim is to make the child comply; little time is devoted to engaging in dialogue. Fixed rules that are not open to discussion are laid down by the adults once and for all, and so the child's expressions of independence are considered signs of disobedience. Baumrind found that children exposed to authoritarian parenting were more anxious, nervous, sad and socially withdrawn than other children. In interactions with peers with a low degree of adult control, however, they were more likely to respond to frustration with anger and aggression. Boys, in particular, were hostile, while girls were more dependent and avoided challenges, perhaps as a result of low self-confidence. This parenting style is obviously far from what happens in the negotiation family, and has little concern for children as active participants. Inclusion is not on the agenda, children are to be obedient, with parents as active agents. What a child is supposed to learn is handed down to them from adults.

Permissive parenting

Permissive parenting is primarily responsive to the child's needs but avoids making demands, and is child-centred. In other words, this is an overly tolerant attitude to children and a child-rearing practice that hesitates to intervene when the child violates codes of moral behaviour. Children of permissive parents are routinely included in decision-making and predominantly have their own way. This parental style, which misses the adult-centric balance, may well provoke situations that are too complex for a young child to grasp. The child's desires and impulses are given priority over the adults'. In Baumrind's study, children of permissive parenting were characterized as impulse-driven, and had difficulty curbing their immediate desires and following someone else's lead. They protested when asked to do something they did not want to do. Compared to other children, they were relatively more demanding and dependent on adults. When handling tasks that required persistence, they gave up sooner than other children; restlessness and a lack of concentration in relation to tasks were particularly characteristic of boys.[72] This parenting style takes the view of the child's self-agency to the extreme.

Uninvolved parenting

Uninvolved parenting is relatively rare, and avoids demands and is non-responsive. Thereby, it is neither adult-centric nor child-centric, but appears indifferent. Apart from making sure the child is fed and clothed, this approach expresses a limited interest in the child's wellbeing. The uninvolved parenting style may be practised by adults who are under a great deal of pressure, feeling overwhelmed by the task of bringing up a child. Conflicts and interventions are avoided, and long-term attempts at involving the child in committed and empathic activities and interactions are vague. Parents with depression and emotional detachment may have difficulties meeting the demands of bringing up a child. One example from childcare could be the overworked preschool teacher who suffers from burnout, making her unprepared to engage with the individual child. In the uninvolved pattern, a child and an adult may live parallel lives with sporadic intersection points, with children left mainly on their own. Children living with uninvolved parents for extended periods of time are affected negatively in a range of developmental domains. In extreme cases, the uninvolved pattern may constitute *neglect* and a need for outside assistance, support or intervention (Berk, 2009).

Later in this chapter, the four styles will be elaborated. This will be done by combining the essence of Baumrind's and her followers' research with some relevant concepts presented in this book in order to make the concepts workable in the interpretation of dimensions in late modern parenting. But first, some reservations have to be made, as there are risks inherent in the construction of typologies.

Parenting typology: some limitations

Typology characterizations of parenting and their relationship to child behaviour have a tendency for categorization and leave little room for nuances; either you are an 'authoritarian parented child' or you are not. In addition, a cause-and-effect direction from parent–child rhetoric may sneak in, despite the fact that all studies are based on correlations.

Typologies can be useful only to the point that they can contribute to the understanding of important and different ways of parenting. But in everyday practice, there are far less clear-cut stylistic ways of being a parent. The four distinct styles outlined above are *models* of reality, which clearly simplify the complexities of parenting in the adult–child relationship. Nevertheless, Baumrind's influential model does capture recognizable, essential ways of influencing children, albeit in a prototypical form. In the following, an attempt will be made to add some modifying nuances to the clear-cut categories of the model.

In her review of studies on parenting styles, Smetana (1994) evaluates Baumrind's model in the context of subsequent research. In fact, research has confirmed that the model does identify dimensions seen in parenting approaches. A main objection, however, is that the four styles are general and decontextualized, and they fail to address and identify specific situations in parent–child relationships that will modify or weaken the prototypical classification. As distinct types, the four categories seem problematic, because they infer that a parent 'typically' and across a multitude of situations reacts in a uniform way: the indulgent parent is always permissive and overly tolerant; the authoritarian parent is always demanding and insensitive; while the authoritative style is consistently 'perfect parenting' and always able to strike the right balance between developmental demands that are in step with the child's needs.

By observing everyday parenting practice, however, these four different portraits seem not nearly so clear-cut. The individual parent may, in fact, use different parenting styles, depending on the choice made between conflicting concerns. A choice of disciplinarian strategy does, as a minimum, depend on timing, situation and the seriousness of the child's disobedience. The time of day can also affect the balance between demands and permissiveness. For example, in a busy dual-earner family with a toddler, there is much to done before leaving for childcare and work. Time is of the essence in the morning, and things have to 'run smoothly', which may lead to a lowering of parental discipline, resulting in relative permissiveness in order to avoid conflict and encourage the child to be cooperative. But at other times of the day (that is, afternoon and evening), time pressure may be less of an issue, so the parents may shift the balance and increase demands and lower permissiveness. Then the parenting style may revolve around more authoritative strategies, with age-appropriate challenges that involve the young child in dialogue, reasoning and negotiation. To illustrate that parental situational flexibility is not always the case, let us take another example. Serious disobedience – the child suddenly leaves the parent and runs across a busy street – will be met with an immediate and strict sanction even from 'permissive' or 'authoritative' parents. Less serious wrongdoing, however, is more likely to be addressed in a dialogue about rules, fairness and the reasons behind them by authoritative parents.

This indicates that parenting is a complex of flexible strategies, balancing numerous conflicting demands that are inherent in everyday situations, instead of being a cross-cutting upbringing style laid down on children. 'Strategy' does not necessarily mean that parenting is a calm, carefully planned occurrence, and that acting out a strategy is not necessarily very conscious either. Rather, strategies are adapted to specific situations based on repeated experience from numerous daily encounters. The accumulated repertoire and implicit knowledge about 'what works' and 'what does not work' make parenting function, effectively and competently. This interpretation is in line with the functionalist approach presented in Chapter 1 as one core approach in *A Childhood Psychology*.

So it would seem that parents are much less consistent in their approach to upbringing than the parental style model suggests. Competent parenting

can, generally, be described in the way that different situations lead to flexible, contextual responses.[73] The next section will elaborate further on this.

Although here-and-now situational demands, pressures and opportunities
are relevant to the understanding of parental practice, another important
dimension in explaining actual parenting has to be considered. Adults' *long-
term goals* for their child also play an important role in parenting. Smetana
(1994) highlighted a study showing that mothers with long-term developmental goals took a more relaxed approach to disciplining their children
compared to mothers with short-term goals. This suggests that adults are not
only guided by the requirements of the immediate situation, and that long-
term goal orientation is associated with here-and-now parenting. Having
long-term developmental goals may function as navigation marks that
enable the parent to evaluate and put into a larger perspective the child's
actual behaviour, and not be engulfed in solving conflicts on the spot.

As a consequence of this evaluation of Baumrind's typology, it may be
refined while still keeping its fundamental prototypes. Figure 4.2 offers a
fresh look at the four parenting styles. They are not seen as categorical styles,
but as a departure from the four 'pure styles' positioned at the extreme ends
of a continuum. This allows parenting and upbringing to have a multitude of
variations depending on their relative placement in four dimensions.

As shown in Figure 4.2, the four 'pure styles' – demanding versus non-
demanding, responsive versus non-responsive – are placed at the extreme
ends, functioning as opposite poles. Although an empirical study has to

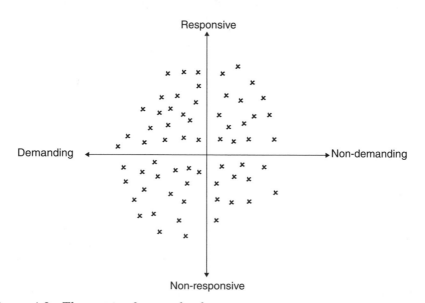

Figure 4.2 The matrix of parental styles

confirm this, one hypothesis is that observations compiled during morning, afternoon, evening, at weekends and leisure times will show that *the same parents* will be located differently in the matrix regarding time and the specific situation on a typical day. For example, as noted earlier, in a dual-earner family where mother, father and child have less time together in the morning because all have to leave for work and childcare, demands on the child may be more pronounced than in the afternoon when all have returned home. Perhaps demands are lessened in weekends and holidays when having more leisure time together.

Figure 4.2 indicates that few parents are expected to be as dichotomized as in Baumrind's model, that is, demanding or responsive, demanding or non-responsive. Instead, parents are more likely to be characterized by being so in various degrees. One hypothesis is that when parenting is observed in many families over time, it will be possible to plot each parent on the matrix. Some may be 'shifting' depending on time and context, where others may show a more 'rigid' position. For example, it may be expected that the relatively few parents who are highly demanding/non-responsive or highly non-demanding/non-responsive show a more rigid parenting pattern than other parents. If it is possible to locate various 'parenting positions', it will be possible to identify and differentiate a specific family regarding its relative upbringing *tendency* and its various placements in a day and in relation to other families.

Models like Baumrind's are not temporally contextualized. So is the parental prototype typology useful in understanding emergent trends in parenting and families in late modernity? Interestingly, her authoritative type bears a clear similarity to parenting within late modern negotiation families. However, this model is embedded in contemporary cultural humanization, individualization and democratization processes, which the parental model clearly is not. The shared decision-making and democratic processes that characterize emergent negotiation families are based on particular parental beliefs about children, such as 'being seen and heard', 'being included', 'having personal importance' and 'being unique'. Combining the practice in negotiation families with the key understanding behind being relatively authoritarian oriented on the whole – with the many contextual exceptions accounted for – this kind of parenting can be seen as a growing late modern phenomenon. Specific research on negotiation families is sparse, however. Nevertheless, the positive developmental findings mentioned earlier arising from research on authoritarian parenting following Baumrind's ground-breaking research are a starting point transferable to negotiation families.

A final problem with the parental model is that it seems to infer that parenting is *the* factor that determines child development, thus being an example of the passive-receptive child paradigm in pre-paradigm shift socialization. This conclusion can be derived from the model, but cannot be based on the empirical findings. The interpretations of the findings are founded on (significant) correlations between parenting style and the specifics of child development. The child's agency is clearly missing in the parental style model, as not much is said about 'child activating the parental style'. Today, parenting research is clearly based on more mutual action paradigms discarding the passive-receptive model. However, by interpreting Baumrind's data differently, allowing her significant correlations to indicate some possible bidirectional associations, her study can support an approach that children's actions and ways of behaving to some extent affect the way that adults respond to them.

In summary, if authoritative, authoritarian, indulgent and uninvolved parenting are contextualized as historically and culturally specific types that are open to functional and normative perceptions, parental typology research – despite some major limitations – can be useful in the identification of important patterns of parenting in late modern childhood. However, the specific strategies and parental competencies shown in everyday life are missing in the typology approach. The next section will explore this.[74] New concepts will also be introduced. In addition, used in an everyday context, two of Baumrind's important dimensions will be expanded – the demanding and responsive dimensions.

THE CHOREOGRAPHY OF PARENTING: SOME STRATEGIES[75]

This section starts with the presentation of a paradigm explaining how competent parenting practice can be grasped as more than direct care and intervention. In fact, direct parenting cannot take place successfully in everyday encounters unless 'an invisible hand' has made time, space and opportunity for that to happen. Successful parenting demands much more than just 'being there' as the intimate mother and the rough-and-tumble playful father. A parenting paradigm has to encompass and explain the underlying organizational aspects of parenting. After presenting such an understanding, three distinct parental strategies are elaborated on in order to flesh out the paradigm presented.

Parenting has been explored as a direct influence, expressed in various parenting styles – a 'what parents do' approach. The *Handbook of Parenting* shows that the majority of research deals with explicit parenting (Bornstein, 2002a). Much upbringing, however, goes beyond control, intervention, guiding, positive feedback and so on imposed by adults.[76] Upbringing is also a process in which the child is exposed to ground rules of social practices through everyday interaction routines with others. This process teaches the child how to behave in specific situations. Situations have a 'behavioural affordance character' – for example getting up in the morning and being put to bed are full of implicit rules and codes for behaviour.

As mentioned in Chapter 3, socializing, upbringing and learning in everyday contexts lead to the young child's culture acquisition. The parental role in this is that parents use their environmentally given possibilities while accommodating their restraints in an effort to create developmentally beneficial settings for their children. The process of 'choosing settings' and adjusting to restraints is ongoing and renegotiated in family contexts in response to the changing needs of parents themselves, children and the changing environment. Thereby families are active constructors of their own world of meaning, and not merely recipients of and reactors to external contingencies. Parents behaving as constructors can be described in many ways, for example through their direct parenting strategies, such as caring, comforting and sanctioning. Seen in a broader perspective, however, a vital part of everyday parenting has to do with organization:

> Furthermore, the ways the parents organize settings and activities for their children, interact with them, and talk about them are clearly a part of an integrated system, although one that may require frequent adjustments to keep the various elements in harmony with each other. (Harkness and Super, 2002, p. 272)

This means that when direct interaction occurs, for instance parents talking to their children, such activities are organized and embedded in a broader parenting context. The structure of everyday life is not only 'bits and pieces', elements of situations, habits and routines. It becomes an integrated system, *frequently adjusted by parents* in their continuous efforts to construct a day that is considered meaningful to all family members. Behind the phrase 'frequently adjusted' lay a host of unspecified parental skills and strategies. To be able to adjust in order to create harmony between the various and sometimes conflicting elements of everyday demands, a repertoire of skills are necessary. For example, a mother is able, at one and the same time, to be engrossed in a here-and-now routine, with the implicit knowledge of what comes next and why. The description of such skills will reveal some parental resources and competencies.

A heuristic name for this can be the 'choreography' of parenting. Choreography as a metaphor of competent parenting denotes a skilled and complex composition of a meaningful everyday life with a child. But how does the choreography of parenting take place as a process? To answer this requires a further step into this overlooked territory by using an everyday, 'down-to-earth' approach.

As shown in Chapter 3, everyday routines contain a multitude of implicit behavioural guidelines. Eating dinner is, like many routines, a social situation with implicit behavioural guidelines and rules that children and adults unconsciously adhere to. Few skilled young diners jump vigorously on their chair or run around the table (implicit rule: 'behave yourself'), empty the serving dishes (implicit rule: 'share with your fellow diners') or throw food around (implicit rule: 'respect the food'). When talking during dinner, conversations are conducted in a moderate voice and by taking turns (implicit rule: 'be civilized'; 'be heard and hear the other'). Should this not be so, which obviously happens in some families with young children, they may be seen as temporary exceptions from the expected or an immature phase of development. If deviations from routines are too frequent according to parental judgement of what is tolerable, discipline is likely to follow. Interestingly, most invisible rules embedded in routines are not articulated and brought to light before they are violated. So, by sanctioning deviations from 'what we usually do and are expected to do', parents further confirm and legitimize everyday situation-regulated normality.

Young children are not passive, however; they become active participants as routine upholders. If a father forgets or is too busy for the usual bedtime story routine, he will probably be reminded, told of his duties or asked for a good reason for this omission. Routines become habits, and routine-experienced young children seem to be conventionalists, because doing meaningful regular things together with close relatives establishes a sense of trust. In a broader micro-sociological interpretation, having a secure base in everyday family life may be a buffer against the turbulence of living in a world of rapid change (Dencik et al., 2008).

The development of socially acceptable behaviour is often a result of direct parental interventions, especially in early childhood, but gradually, everyday routines take over. Routines are constructed and maintained by relationships, and more and more social rules are internalized and taken for granted as implicit agendas behind interaction. Thus parenting is also about involving the child in the acquisition of implicit and indirect codes embedded in everyday interpersonal interactions. In some situations, direct upbringing will dominate, for example when the child is told what is right and wrong or the adult is guiding the child. In other contexts, the impact of routines is predominant.[77] As children grow older, they actively maintain and take part in routines, which can be expressed in a number of ways.

Everyday competent parenting, with its possibilities, resources, efforts and specific strategies, has, with exceptions, not been described in detail by research.[78] As referred to earlier, strategies do not imply an explicitly planned, goal-oriented approach by parents. Strategies are more often based on gut feelings of how to react, which originate from an accumulated store of experiences with hundreds of previous everyday family occurrences. Parents and other adults who spend time with young children gradually acquire competence as functional 'everyday planners' – they have learned what works and what does not work, and this guides them in their actions.

The pre-paradigm shift top-down developmental and socialization approaches presented in Chapter 1 are too abstract to capture the *micro-social reality* of everyday life. They fail to describe parental practice and especially parents' actual repertoire of strategies in the active maintenance of social routine-based rules with young children. Parents have to consider a complex array of conditions that influence their parenting. A host of external and internal constraints and possibilities have to be dealt with and managed by negotiation family parents, functioning as the main actors in children's present and future upbringing. An example of an externally imposed restraint on family life that is relatively non-negotiable is parents' working hours. This structures the time children spend with their parents and the times they will be in a non-family caring context. But it does not determine their relationship or how they interact together. Working hours also structure the timing of routines and situations in the family, such as when it is time to get up in the morning and when it is time to go to bed for a young child in order to have a good night's sleep. A more negotiable external constraint is shopping time. With greater flexibility, shopping can be postponed to the following day, the child can be taken on the shopping trip and so on. Not everything outside the family constitutes constraints, however; external possibilities are many, including a voluntary neighbourhood network involving parents and children in joint activities, parks and playgrounds.

Parents as choreographers of everyday life have to incorporate and handle a complex array of constraints and possibilities by inventing strategies that are workable in – to use two Baumrind dimensions – balancing being demanding with being responsive. In the *demand mode*, the child is seen as 'becoming somebody' who is growing up and is on the road through childhood with all the long-term goal expectations this implies. Through demands, parents try to pursue the child's best long-term interests. Through the daily implementation of long-term strategies in everyday routines and situations, it is communicated to the child that there are (age-appropriate) duties and responsibilities in life. In very ordinary terms, parents expect that there is a time when children have to be resourceful, such as dressing themselves without adult assistance, handling their own utensils and so on. As children grow up, demands are progressively raised, such as children's self-control and impulse regulation – two- or three-year-olds may be allowed to yell quite frequently, but not six-year-olds. More articulated words are expected at that age. At the end of early childhood, adults usually have higher aspirations for the child's cognitive functioning, favouring skills that are conducive to starting school.

The *responsive mode*, by contrast, communicates a sensitive departure in the child's subjective meaning-making efforts. This seems for a long time to have been a part of sensitive and competent mothering, probably in place long before the turn to the child-sensitive period that started with the scientific study of infants and young children (Bråten, 2007; Sommer et al., 2010).

Expanding Baumrind's parental responsive dimension to an everyday context, to be responsive may be to respect and accept the fact that sometimes – in a relatively strict day schedule with many inherent 'must dos' – the child needs a refuge. The 'let the child be a child' saying reflects the acknowledgment that a young child needs to be shielded from too many external demands. The parental management of responsiveness is shown in many ways, for example by allowing free playtime without didactic purpose, allowing the child to do nothing in particular, watching TV together, just having fun with someone. Competent parenting can be described as – on behalf of the young child – creating a balance between demands and responsiveness in the changing rhythm of everyday life.

The following sections present three selected parenting strategies: *continuous forethought, defensive compliance* and *buffering/shielding*. This is not an exhaustive description and analysis of everyday parental strategies, rather, it is a proposal, presenting highlighted examples of some parental strategies rarely previously described in detail.

Continuous forethought

Families living together have a day that is structured and organized by routines and people doing specific meaningful things together. It makes one wonder how this is possible. There are numerous explanations behind why people construct routines. According to a recent evolutionary outlook, it has to do with humans' lack of instinct-organizing behaviour and our natural tendency to establish habit and culture (Tomasello et al., 2005; Tomasello, 2009).

In a specific late modern context dealing with dual-earner families, some external obligations are important, as previously mentioned. Parents' work hours structure the day, and what has to be done in the morning between getting up and leaving the house is structured by this external reality. This indicates that despite the fact that the clock does not determine relationships, time has a profound impact on what is done when and for how long.[79] A young child who mainly lives in the present is probably not too bothered about whether the family is on time or not. Strategies about 'keeping time', 'dwelling in the situation', as well as knowing 'when it is time to move onto the next daily chore' require a sophisticated temporal outlook that is far beyond that of young children.

Continuous forethought has to do with the experienced parents' complex sense of the best way to devise a viable structure for a meaningful everyday life in the family. For example, it feels right to spend time together at certain times of day and to be engaged in separate activities at other times. Parents also place implicit limits on the duration of a given social activity in the family to keep it from colliding with other types of desirable interactions. The Nordic study (see above) analysed the organization of timing of everyday events and routines. The study found that breakfast never dragged on for hours, although no one actually looked at a clock and said, 'Right, time to go'. Instead a parent begins to put the dishes in the dishwasher. Taking too long over breakfast would impinge on subsequent chores and activities, suggesting that the rules for the length of a meal are inherent in the routine (Kristjansson, 2001).

Continuous forethought is like using an inner clock. It governs the implicit planning that, with time, makes activities habitual. This type of planning includes all routines and situations that establish the structure and processes of family life. During busy morning preparations, no one spends hours in the bathroom, since that would interfere with other family members' needs to use the bathroom. Parents who place a high priority on spending time with their child after a whole day away may structure the afternoon in order to make this a 'reunion event'. Instead of playing with a friend next door, having a little snack together may be orchestrated to reunite the family. Young children are rarely allowed to watch films every evening until after midnight, because the future-oriented parent knows that there is an early start the next day.

Such skilled parental regulation teaches children that freedom from demands may be fine, but indulging in immediate pleasures cannot continue to take precedent (staying up late, sleeping all morning, watching cartoons for hours, playing with one's best friend, staying home from childcare). In other words, through repeated experiences of moving between external demands and freedom from them, young children acquire an implicit understanding that there are times when necessities govern what is done and times when pleasures rule.

Everyday routines seem to take on a life of their own, but this stems from a process organized and managed by responsible parenting. Essentially, parents make sure that the child is included in and guided through the temporal fine-tuned series of everyday life episodes with their distinct social relationship patterns. Gradually, young children learn and take an active part in the course and flow of events. Children expect and anticipate what is to be done at different times of day and in different social situations.

Routines that have no implicit or explicit function will probably not develop in a family. The typical day's routines and interactions are constructed in order to meet various developmental needs and purposes. For example, in studying socialization, few have addressed the importance of the temporal aspects in the process. However, by using the everyday temporal routine perspective, this can be done. When young children go through their daily routines, it happens in the same temporal rhythm as other people. As a rule, a child's actions will rarely be purely individual, or out of sync with social events. Without continuous forethought as 'an invisible hand' binding the day's interactions together, everyday life would be socially splintered and fragmented. For example, in extreme individualized families, each family member sits in a separate room watching TV or doing other private things.

Continuous foresight is not only important for socializing; without it fundamental needs will not be fulfilled in the family. Unlike a young child, an experienced parent with continuous forethought knows that one cannot simply continue to reach into the fridge and find one's favourite food on the shelf. Long before the milk is drunk and the cornflake box is empty, 'an invisible hand' has restocked supplies. A further example of continuous forethought is the fact that preparations for the following morning begin the night before (Kristjansson, 2001). The young child's clothes are laid out, the lunchbox is prepared and bags are packed. So continuous forethought is also closely related to managing various practical chores in the family, but it is more than that. Forethought is the basis of evaluation; it organizes and checks whether things happen as planned and as deemed necessary.

In the handling of daily chores, continuous forethought is also reflected in the *distribution of tasks*. Families establish agreements about routines, defining who does the dishes, who cleans the bathroom and who mows the lawn, and when – in fact, all the tasks that need to be done to accomplish the goal of being a proper family.[80] This also brings to mind the dual-earner family as a complex negotiation system – a vital part of the relatively equal gender-sharing role agreements described previously as happening in many contemporary negotiation families (Sommer, 2010).

Admittedly, both renegotiations and agreements have the potential to cause conflict and disagreement. Problems may arise if a couple are unable to agree on sharing household chores, or if they interpret an agreement differently. Although this has not been researched in detail, a gender difference between male and female continuous forethought may exist. Research indicates that fathers prefer to be involved with their young child in here-and-now fun activities (Lamb, 2004). In addition, although gender-based sharing in Scandinavia and other countries has become more pronounced in contemporary dual-earner families, women still do most household chores and, apparently, the least exciting ones (Bonke, 2009). This indicates that paternal and maternal preferences may differ, with fathers having a more here-and-now activity horizon versus mothers having a broader temporal responsibility horizon. If this is so, the following can be pursued as a possible hypothesis. If males and females do not have the same time perspective in their everyday parenting, some conflicts may arise. *Her* overall temporal continuous forethought may collide with *his* here-and-now view, which considers it adequate to be in the helper role with individual chores, when asked, or be engaged with his young child in here-and-now play. She may not only want to include her partner in specific chores but also require him to assume a more general and shared responsibility for running a family. An expectation that her partner as a father must be at the forefront of activities is not met if, ten minutes before bedtime, he involves the child in exciting rough-and-tumble play, which makes it harder to calm the child down in order to reach the expected sleepy mood that usually follows.

Continuous forethought also applies to the *emotional relationship* between parent and child – the construction of fellow feelings, social acceptance and connectedness. Successful parenting is based on the underlying premise that children love their parents and thus accept being socialized and encountering challenges stemming from necessities and not always pleasure. A later section will describe how personalized care is key to understanding that acceptance and connectedness are developed in intimate personal encounters. But in order to encourage intimate relationships, 'creating the right moments', time is needed.

In late modern times with rapidly changing values and individualization as a main reference point, it may seem a paradox that living in small groups is still preferred by many, for instance living in a family with one child or more (Dencik et al., 2008). This may be explained partly by humans' deep-rooted sociality (Tomasello, 2009). Seen in an everyday parenting perspective, however, parents' overall aim may be to generate and organize family coherence. Through their strategies, they socialize a young child into predictability and clarity – continuous forethought is just one strategy to ensure this. As a family counterbalance to divisive centrifugal societal forces, parents' continuous forethought and scheduling create a centripetal force in their making of everyday family life.

Defensive compliance

Defensive compliance is used when parents temporarily lower their expectations for and demands on their young children for some reasons. Compliance is not a particular style, but is a strategy used in specific situations and at different times of the day. Being 'defensive' is a parental strategy used in situations where parents decide to bend and give way from even reasonable age-appropriate developmental demands in order to achieve a higher goal. Defensive compliance is an adapted strategy used by parents with continuous foresight in their efforts to bind together, harmonize routines and make relationships run smoothly. This strategy, as shall be demonstrated, is observable in dual-earner families in the mornings when time is limited and there are many things to do.

As noted in the section on parenting typology, this gives the impression that parents consistently practise a particular style. Parenting, however, is regulated by two moderating factors. On the one hand, the individual parent's long-term sense of what a child at a certain age can be expected to understand, so parents accommodate their parental style accordingly. On the other hand, a parental tendency to adjust style to the current situation. Thus, parenting is not the implementation of a rigid set of rules, instead it is flexible, depending on context. For example, in Western individualistic cultures, parents early on emphasize personal *independence* (Rothbaum et al., 2000).

To ensure that a cultural demand for independence (assuming this is accepted by parents) becomes developmentally functional in a family, it has to be 'converted'. In everyday practice, independence may be transformed into self-governance and resourcefulness. At a certain age, children should be able to brush their teeth and wash themselves, dress themselves, tie their shoelaces. Gradually, children learn to eat without making a mess, and they may be asked to help set the table, keep their room tidy and so on. Demands for independence vary from family to family, but at some point every parent will have to make these requirements. This is an extension of the cultural expectation of individual independence. Demands need to be flexible, however, depending on the time of day. In the morning, with its relatively tight schedule, the child's resourcefulness may be less valued. A child who is too independent may make the morning routines less easy for parents. They may choose, for tactical reasons, to postpone some demands until a time when they know that the child is not sleepy, and a time that allows for lengthy discussions. For example, the child may able to brush their own teeth but the mother does it for them. In doing so, the mother establishes a close relationship, knowing that they will depart shortly for work and childcare, saves time when morning time is short, and the brushing may be more effective. The father of the same five-year-old may be in the kitchen. Despite the child being experienced at setting the table, the father lays the table ready for when child and mother come out of the bathroom. This organization of morning routines and specific parental role-sharing in the family ensures that things run smoothly without too many delays and conflicts.

By applying temporal and context-appropriate defensive compliance, parents can draw on a range of good and bad experiences of how to handle their child in morning situations, for example by considering the young child's mood in the morning and their ability to handle frustration. One motive may be the desire to have a pleasant start to the day – conflict should not be allowed to dominate the brief morning period. Hence, some parents may help their five-year-olds dress and assist them in the bathroom, even though they are capable of doing it themselves. An additional motive can be that it is a way of maximizing time together, which the adult may feel is in short supply during the working week: 'Soon, mummy and daddy will be at work, and you'll be in childcare, so we won't see you until the afternoon.' Later in the day, the same parents may make stricter demands on the child's self-governance and resourcefulness when there is plenty of time.

This type of demand avoidance may sometimes be an example of Baumrind's non-demanding, permissive style, but, interpreted in the parental choreography perspective, can be a case of strategic defensive permissiveness. This means that parents can deliberately choose to be both docile and overly helpful as a short-term solution in a situation where it is not considered helpful to push strict demands (Haavind, 1987). Thus, parental competence is not having the 'right style' by being authoritative, rather competence is seen in the balanced management of the possibilities and limitations inherent in parenting. As choreographers, parents must routinely weigh up conflicting interests in order to maintain harmony in everyday life situations.

Buffering and shielding

The choreography of parenting also involves a substantive buffering and shielding function, which in turn calls for specific strategies. In their complex social worlds, young children may face many difficult challenges. A part of competent, resourceful parenting is to create a buffer, shielding young children from overwhelming stress and pressures inherent in everyday life. Research shows that well-functioning parents are able to buffer 'at-risk' children by circumventing processes that ordinarily lead to developmental disorders (Collins and Roisman, 2006). Extrafamilial conditions may put children under pressure, for example by making social adaptation requirements too high in childcare settings with changing staff. A more general example is the necessary shielding from the demands of the late modern time structure impinging on dual-earner families. In the Nordic study (see above), parents who shield their young children from temporal pressures were observed in the 'how to get the child up' strategies (Kristjansson, 2001). Many strategies were highlighted, but a common denominator was the careful effort not to induce a shock effect by waking children too abruptly. Parents' everyday role and strategies as competent protectors of their children are implicit and perhaps so self-evident that they are rarely reflected upon until the protective shield guarding them from external pressures collapses – or parents themselves become the primary stressors and not protectors.

Shielding strategies can take on a wide variety of forms. Chapter 1 emphasized how individual children have different thresholds when it comes to vulnerability to stressors. Some appear more resilient than others. But the most important individual difference, temperament, is only one ingredient, because the relationships the child are engaged in are vital in enhancing or lowering resilience. From a buffer perspective, successful parental shielding strategies can be understood as an important resilience system in itself. But seen in a dual socialization perspective, direct parental intervention within the family in relation to stressors is only one dimension. External regulation can also be activated if, for example, a parent discovers that some childcare conditions frustrate the child, an intervention may follow by arranging a meeting with the childcare staff in order to solve the problems.

But shielding can be much more. For example, in order to counter-act social fragmentation, a dual-earner family may invent regular family get-togethers. Despite being well known, this micro-cultural routine has been unexplored by research. By designing pressure-free zones, adults and children can enjoy spending time together, watching TV, playing games, eating snacks and chatting.[81] In a hard-working family, the 'Saturday evening feeling' and weekend relaxation can happen, with everybody knowing that the challenges of Monday are far away. Relaxing in a family by 'doing nothing' or watching TV and eating snacks may be an example of consumerism. But from the buffer perspective, in order to interpret some dynamics of the society–family relationship, these relatively undemanding situations can be seen as highly functional. They may be regarded as necessary *compensation strategies* from demanding but rewarding jobs.

DIMENSIONS OF CARING

Caring can be discussed in many ways; however, the intention is not to be comprehensive but selective. This section deals with the everyday cultural aspects of caring. Caring is then defined as a specific relationship quality, and then the importance of personal caring will be presented and underlined. Finally, selected types of relationship quality will be introduced by looking at caring as synchrony and attunement.

Cultural aspects of caring

Child developmental psychology does usually not address caring as a cultural category, but tends to reduce it to a direct adult–child personal relationship.[82] Clearly, caring goes far beyond that. First, caring is closely connected to the way a given culture relates to children. The time-bound nature of beliefs working as interpretative filters was addressed in Chapter 2. Here it was underlined how fundamental ideas about children and caring influence practices with children. The beliefs that parents hold are converted into ways of handling children. Second, caring is not only a personal relationship that is structured, organized and embedded in everyday conditions. According to Harkness and Super (2002), one of the most profound ways in which culture affects the child's development is by imposing conditions, structuring both possibilities and restraints for everyday life. Caring seems to be so deeply affected by culture that few are left unaffected. However, culturally induced conditions should not be seen as deterministic. As referred to in Chapter 3, culture is a product of dynamic processes that arise as a result of human acts and negotiation. If repeated aspects of negotiated culture take over and with time are established as habits, the values and perceptions anchored in them tend to 'freeze' and become relatively resistant to change. This is what Harkness and Super (2002) refer to in relation to culture as a force that frames but does not determine daily family life.

Caring is strongly affected by the weakening of previously stable orientation points as a result of the acceleration of innovation in late modern societies (Dencik et al., 2008). Caring parents may experience a 'state of irrelevance'. This means that they, unlike parents from earlier times, cannot rely on 'ancient wisdom', based on a tradition of caring practices passed down through generations to guide them as carers. Thus, caring in late modernity is not pre-established because in order to work, it has to be functional and useful.

In innovative cultures, fundamental caring and beliefs about what is best for the child seem to change more rapidly than ever before (Cunningham, 1995), which creates a cultural framework of uncertainty and ambivalence that has made caring a growing non-collective and non-intergenerational matter. The Danish study of a child generation showed that caring is experienced as being highly privatized and individual. The involvement of the older generation is more often based on practical help than giving substantial advice on how to provide care (Sommer, 2001). Today, becoming a parent involves reinventing caring, by breaking new ground and relying on personal resources and local advice, experience and knowledge bases, for example reading 'how-to' books on caring, and joining preparation groups of families who face the same challenges.[83]

Despite present cultural and normative ambiguity and the individualization of caring, it cannot take place outside the realm in which the carer is more or less consciously affected by and applies current knowledge about parenting. Developed countries can be characterized as expertise societies, where society and culture have been influenced and transformed by the progress of science. In that sense, folk psychology (Bruner, 1990) coexists with the expertise accumulated in various professions. As cultural systems, they will sometimes be in concert and at other times contradict fundamental ideas about children and the best way to care for them in order to support healthy development. In Chapter 1, it was noted that there is a vast body of up-to-date research on *psychological knowledge* with substantive importance for understanding socialization and caring. Parents do not have to be psychologists or read books in order to offer qualified care, but both popular notions and psychological knowledge affect contemporary caring to some extent (Stern, 2006).[84] However, culture plays a role only as a point of departure, because no cultural standard is a blueprint on child caring. Culture as ideas and ways of expected behaviour has to be processed and transformed into a particular family's unique personal and social reality. Furthermore, young children are individuals and active recipients of caring and do not respond uniformly to culturally mediated ideas that parents seek to implement. Therefore, carers must modify their actions to match children's responses. In the short and long term, attuned modifications affect the practical expression of caring.

Another argument supports the idea that living within the same culture does not mean that individual lives, by necessity, become uniform. Chapter 2's description of late modernity's characteristics of complexity and multiplicity is a central one. The cultural reservoir of caring is much larger and far more complex than anyone can comprehend and apply. So individual mothers and fathers are faced with the necessity of so-called 'complexity reduction' (Sommer, 2010). The products of culture are stored in 'storehouses' of potential ideas and practices that individual people and couples can select from, for example by being attracted to the caring ideas and practices that best fit with one's 'cultural capital' (Bourdieu, 1994). The key point here is that the chosen specific elements of the childcare culture have to *resonate on a personal level* in order to make sense, for instance by either supporting or contradicting the father's or mother's own reflected childhood experiences. In this sense, parental social and personal backgrounds become a crucial factor in determining which cultural prescriptions a parent is inspired by and is willing to transform and implement in caring.

If the cultural framework in itself cannot fully explain the parental approach to caring, where then should we look? Bruner (1990) argues that an essential task is to organize *frames of reference* or *orientation points* that make interactions with the child appear meaningful. In other words, caring is expressed in the specific ways parents organize and make meaningful their interactions with the child in everyday routines. This perspective should be considered essential in an analysis of caring and its implementation, because it clearly emphasizes the limitations of viewing caring as only mother–child and father–child interactions.[85] If the view of caring seen in traditional child developmental psychology was to be converted into guidelines for good caring, it would, in principle, be sufficient for the adequate mother and father simply to *interact with* their young child in prescribed, qualitatively appropriate ways. But evaluated in a broader caring context, it becomes clear that this does not live up to even commonsense folk perceptions of what adequate care is. For example, if a highly involved father of an infant focuses exclusively on his caring interactions, ignoring all else, this would, despite high-quality responsiveness, hardly be considered adequate care. Sooner or later, his ability to interact with the child in a productive way would be undermined. Without using continuous foresight, their interactions would fail to fit into the larger picture and responsibilities of everyday life. Seen in this broader sense, long-term quality caring is closely related to the parental choreography strategies and the ability to establish essential coherent and harmonious daily routines. In competition with many other daily chores and activities, parents must prioritize and find the time and space to express their caring.

Gallimore et al. (1989) proposed an interesting theory to explain how adults include care in their construction of daily routines. The family is depicted as a so-called 'eco-cultural niche' filled with active members who are not simply victims of larger forces of society.[86] An interesting thesis is that parents organize and structure everyday life around a complex selection of values, goals, resources and restraints that apply to them in the close and distant environments of the family.[87] The family's material conditions, income, housing conditions, work and so on, influence the construction of the family as an eco-cultural niche, but cultural values and norms are also essential aspects. Parents draw on these to orient themselves and lead acceptable lives with their children. According to this theory, parents strive to construct and maintain daily routines for themselves and their children, with the aim of forming a life that is perceived as dignified, satisfactory.

The active adaptation within the family is very much based on *basic themes*. These define basic perceptions and particular opinions about caring, upbringing, the obligations of marriage, personal development and so on. The specific basic themes that the individual parent views as particularly important play a key role when this parent constructs interaction routines. For example, a female spouse may see it as a basic life theme to be a good mother and an efficient career woman with a challenging job. Accordingly (and maybe in collaboration with her spouse), she will ensure that she has regular caring times, which meet her desire to be 'a good mother'. When at home, she may establish feeding routines, regularly change nappies and have play sessions. When she is at work, she has, as the good parent she is, arranged acceptable alternative arrangements for the care of her child. This is based on the basic theme of being a good caring mother, which is possible even when she is absent. Thus, quality care goes beyond the specific here-and-now intimate relationships between mother and child and involves responsible actions on behalf of the child when apart. This mother's efforts may be governed by an overarching major goal: being a good mother while also being a successful working woman.

To summarize and in accordance with Gallimore et al. (1989) and Harkness and Super (2002), the expression of care through daily routines is a result of external and internal conditions and possibilities *accommodated by parents*. Even the most intimate aspects of caring are influenced by the external conditions that parents must accommodate and the internal resources and possibilities available within the family. In their efforts to ensure quality care, parents constantly make choices and decisions on behalf of their children, often balancing conflicting concerns. This in itself is a demanding and never-ending process, because of changes in the family eco-cultural niche and in culture and society. Furthermore, the early childhood period is synonymous with alterations that present constantly changing demands, which in turn require parents to accommodate their practices and take the child's developmental process into consideration. The emphasis on the child's needs corresponds well with contemporary child-centred perceptions of children (Sommer et al., 2010).

What is care? The necessary relationship quality

A definition of care is now required. As it is a large subject, focus will be on those aspects of care that are of particular relevance to the understanding of the family in late modernity, as well as the possible relationships that exist between families and public childcare. Leaving aside the previously mentioned critics of parents' significance to children, in developmental psychology, there is general agreement that qualified care is important to children's development. However, one prerequisite for this is to know what characterizes care, and to do this, three questions will be answered: What is care? What is quality care? What is required to guarantee care quality?

Care denotes a particular relation among people whereby one person directs their attention towards another person and acts in a way that fulfils the person's needs and serves their wellbeing. It is fundamental for care to have consideration for another person, showing attention, sympathy and empathy. Care involves kindness, interest and involvement in another person and being ready to act when needed. Thus, the concept of care contains both an attention dimension and an action dimension. You have to be able to *experience* and be psychologically prepared in a particularly empathetic way towards another person; but you also have to be able to *act* in certain ways that realize these attitudes in actual care, for instance comforting the child who is scared and protecting them against danger when necessary. The very definition of care also points to some basic requirements in the carer – the person who directs their attention towards another person. The carer (adult) is responsible for the care offered, thus it is not the receiver's responsibility to provide their own care, or to make others provide it. This is important to emphasize in a sometimes one-sided professional discourse about the 'active child' who is capable of administering their relations to others. As will be apparent later, the placement of the responsibility for care is significant to the assessment of the quality of care in the welfare society's two most important care agencies – the family and childcare.

Consideration for the other is required, that is, a requirement for a psychological 'other orientation' (Bråten, 2007). Empathy requires that the carer let go of their I orientation to be able to use the other person as the starting point. If the basic mental state of empathy is absent, it is called mental care neglect. Care is about interpreting another person's behaviour as a manifestation of their inner mental state, so mind-reading is a prerequisite for care competence. This is gradually acquired by most mothers and fathers, and in relation to small children, most carers eventually learn to interpret their particular way of communicating and expressing themselves.

Developmental psychologists examine the developmental aspects of care and its significance to children and adults, whereas family therapists work with dysfunctional care. Thus theories and practice have been developed, which are directly or indirectly relevant to a detailed understanding of care.

Selected examples are attachment theory's concept of 'internal working models'. Often they do not represent conscious, mental representations (memories) of the care staff or of themselves in relation to them. Mental working models contain the sum of memories about attachment in care, the experience of its quality or lack of it (Bretherton and Munholland, 2008). Stern's interpersonal theory is another example of a relevant theory construction. 'Affect attunement' and 'affect misattunement' in the mother–child relationship demonstrate the fine but decisive differences in how, respectively, quality and less quality care processes proceed (Stern, 2006). A third example is relational family therapy, which has contributed important concepts and methods that are relevant in order to understand how developing and problematic care is created and maintained in social relations, for example different 'family alliances' and the development of 'relationship disorders' (Fivaz-Depeursinge and Corboz-Warnery, 1999; Løvlie, 2005).

Empirical studies also attempt to document the consequences of good and bad care quality – not just in infants and toddlers, but also in adults (Waters et al., 2000a, 2000b). Despite certain differences in how much a given theory focuses directly on care or whether it is developmental psychology or family therapy, one common denominator is that *care is perceived as a particular social and emotional process of relationships* (Fivaz-Depeursinge and Corboz-Warnery, 1999; Stern, 2004, 2006; Løvlie, 2005). The relationship concept has almost become a self-explanatory mantra. However, one should be aware that relationship only denotes a connection between two or more relations. The word is, as such, empty of content and the relation(s) can involve far more than care. The relation's contents are not determined until the moment its special characteristics are mentioned. The definition of care as a particular interpersonal type of relation enables the relation to apply to a specific, close relationship among people where emotional support is central.

Care can also be regarded in a broader sense. According to Hansen et al. (2006), care also manifests itself as:

- *Physical care:* changing nappies, providing food and so on. If this is not included, there is physical care neglect.
- *Pedagogical care:* including the child in common activities with adults and with other children. If this does not happen, it is called pedagogical care neglect.
- *Leaving the child:* alone when they need it, as opposed to overprotection or overdirecting.
- *Planning/organization:* on behalf of the child, with a genuine starting point in the child's interest, which will be beneficial to the child in the short or long term.

In conclusion, care is a multifaceted concept. In an assessment of the quality of care, it is vital to specify which particular aspects of care are involved, rather than talking about the quality of care or care neglect in general terms.

Personalized care

As described above, the role of adults as choreographers is important in order to understand what caring can be. Adults provide structure, coherence and meaning for children, and they care by making arrangements that shield their child from stressors. But it is still not enough to understand caring. *Personalized committed care* is no less crucial to children's development and wellbeing. Young children who spend their lives in several social arenas need to have secure bases where quality care is provided. To engage with many different people every day without experiencing committed and emotionally secure relationships is developmentally threatening. Young children with multiple attachments need *at a minimum* to experience a one-to-one close personal bond with another human being (Howes and Spieker, 2008).[88] Personalized care takes place on a *micro-cultural level*. The close encounters between two people, a child and an adult, are influenced by both cultural and personal features. As can be seen in everyday life, parents and children create their own everyday culture as they develop routines and practices. In other words, although cultural and personal dimensions are not the same, in the analysis of care, they are closely related factors. But what characterizes care as a personal, socioemotional relationship between a young child and their primary adult carer as a micro-cultural phenomenon? This question will be answered in the following.

As discussed earlier, major discrepancies exist between the pre-1960s grand developmental approach and after the paradigm shift, despite the fact that quality care is still considered fundamental to development. Research suggests that *long-term neglect*, when combined with other risk factors, enhances the probability of negative developmental effects (Schaffer, 1990; Rutter, 2008). Studying neglect is not, however, particularly helpful in defining quality care. For example, if all major aspects of neglect risk factors are identified in a family, removing them all would not in itself lead to quality care. So quality personal care is not to be defined as the absence of risk factors, rather a 'positive' definition is needed.

The nuances and fine-tuned tonalities of caring may make it too complex to fit into a standard definition. But certain features are worth highlighting. In post-paradigm shift research, infants are portrayed as relatively active, socially competent and highly capable of affecting their close environment. From very early on in life, infants have a profound influence on their parents. But despite this, few expect infants to care for themselves or others. Early in life a child is not able to regulate its own arousal, the carer plays an important role as an *external regulator*, as a damper or intensifier of the child's internal states of feelings. The terms 'carer' and 'care recipient' imply a central direction in the adult–child relationship, with parents as the responsible part. This suggests an essential *asymmetry* in the relationship between the provider of care and the care receiver. Even in a multiple attachment context, caring has to be distributed in a one-to-one committed relationship. For example, in a mother–infant–father triangular relationship, the one-to-one principle governs because it is not possible for the infant (or the adults) to be highly focused on two or more persons in the same conscious moment (Stern, 2004). Caring in groups of three and four people takes place within shifting one-to-one interactions, now with mother (father watching and smiling) and then with father (mother watching and smiling) (Fivaz-Depeursinge and Corboz-Warnery, 1999).

Care falls outside the normal social rules of quid pro quo, as caring for others means providing care without demanding anything in return. This places considerable demands on an inexperienced young carer. They have to accept the unique 'law of caring' and provide care that is associated with some non-negotiable duties.[89] Offering quality care to someone is a long-term obligation of shouldering the responsibility for someone else's wellbeing.[90] Caring presupposes *empathy*. Empathy is closely related to theory of mind, an ability normally developed in early childhood to adopt another person's perspective and read their mind (Tomasello, 2005, 2009). Mind-reading seems fundamental in the understanding of quality caring. Care, however, also requires helpful and supportive actions based on a sense of what the other person needs. This action dimension in caring will be pursued in the following by selecting synchrony and affect attunement as examples.

Care as synchrony and attunement

Chapter 1 described the old paradigm view of the child as a passive recipient, and how this has been rejected by recent research. Instead, the understanding of caring has to be based on models and theories that can capture the complex dialectics between child and carer. In other words, a dual agency perspective is called for which includes the child as a co-regulator of caring relationships.

An important term in developmental psychology is *interactional synchrony*. In the early 1980s, this referred to the phenomenon that both nonverbal and verbal communication with a child unfolds in finely coordinated and timed sequences. For example, Condon's (1982) research showed that newborn babies move their bodies in *synchrony* with adults' speech patterns. Fluctuations in tone and expression caused finely synchronized responses from the baby in the form of body movements. It has since become common to define interactional synchrony in more general terms as a phenomenon whereby a person actively takes part in mutually coordinated interactions with another, where both parties are influenced by the interaction and are involved in co-regulating the process. Seen over time, the specific developmental 'end result' of interactional synchrony is not a given thing as change takes place as a transactional process.

But how does one person's behaviour in a caring sequence affect the other? According to Fogel's (1993) metaphor, behaviours are not 'exchanged', colliding like billiard balls, nor is care exchanged like gifts, for the simple reason that one person's behaviour does not physically affect the other's behaviour. To speak of *exchanging* smiles is a useful metaphor, but the underlying assumption is that social encounters are made up by two individual 'atoms'. Instead, Fogel describes care as a *creative process* of ongoing mutual information. He uses 'the smile' as an example of a common nonverbal dialogue between adult and child:

> In order for your smile to have an effect on me, in order for it to make me smile in return (another metaphor, since I didn't actually take your smile and give it back to you), I have to perceive the light reflected from the changes in the surface of your face as informative to me. That information may translate into a feeling, and/or another action, like a smile in response. (Fogel, 1993, p. 56)

This little sequence suggests the complicated sensory, psychological and social processes that need to be in place before a young child can participate in their own care process. This will be impossible without a process of reciprocity and synchrony that coordinates and brings the right time flow into the sequence. In addition, synchrony contributes to gluing the pieces of the process together into a whole meaningful event. For example, 'a smile in response' has to come close to the initiating invitation to have a conversation in order to be experienced by the partners as a shared 'now' moment (Stern, 2004). For instance, a five-minute delayed smile will not count as a response.

A related concept that also captures the mutual aspect of care is seen in Stern's (2006) concept of 'affect attunement' – the mutual experience of sharing a feeling with someone else. The point is that it is not necessarily external action or imitation of the other that is important, but rather the partners' shared state of feeling: the three-year-old child swings a toy aeroplane over their head, laughing. The father, smiling and rotating his head, imitates the sound of an aeroplane: 'Yoom, yooom, yoom'. The specific actions and body movements of the child and the father are quite different, but the feelings are shared. Stern (2006) has described in detail the qualities in caring related to attunement. In addition, he also discusses how low-quality caring by parental systematic use of under- and overattunement creates disturbances in the caring relationship. These are types of parental responses that do not match the feelings of the child.

Attunement takes several forms and is not only seen in connection with caring. However, the ability to match someone else's emotional state is crucial to understanding personalized care. For attunement to become a shared experience, *both parties* must be able to engage in emotional reso-nance.[91] According to Stern, infants gradually develop the ability to sense that others are capable of grasping their emotional states. Around the age of nine months, this capacity seems fully present along with the related capacity for grasping others' 'emotional intent' within joint acts (Tomasello, 2005). Attunement may resemble imitation, which the baby is capable of soon after birth. But attunement differs from imitation by focusing on the inner meaning rather than external copying behaviour. The infant does not have to imitate the adult but must understand – and express that they have understood – the underlying emotion of a joint act. For example, if mother and infant are sharing the joy of the mother blowing on the infant's toes, the infant does not respond by blowing on the mother's toes (imitation) but through laughter and eye contact. The infant experiences and reacts to an *emotionally shared moment* with another person, by responding in an infant's preferred ways.

The capacity for affect attunement does not suddenly emerge in the infant but results from an ongoing learning process. In everyday encounters, the child is repeatedly attempting to identify other people's emotions. Being a social human preparing to live in small face-to-face groups, an infant is interested in answering the following question: Are we having and how do we get a 'joint mood'? Repeatedly, the child has to adapt their emotions according to the partner or is engaged in the effort of changing the partner's mood. This implies that attunement is an ongoing process, fine-tuned in the personalized caring relationship. As we have seen, both the adult and the infant initiate everyday social episodes in which attunement is embedded.[92] In everyday life, attunement is not necessarily reserved for specific events, but is woven into other routines.

The relatively fleeting nature of attunement may make it hard to notice when it is there. In addition, attunement has to do with much more than per-sonalized caring. It is also a key to understanding socioemotional relation-ships because it captures the essence of being together, sharing important emotions, feeling sympathy, responding meaningfully, feeling understood, and having an influence on another person by 'editing' their mood states; letting oneself be emotionally influenced by another trusted person. In summary, a quality caring relationship between adult and child seems to develop vital psychological and social competencies required to engage gen-uinely in mutual interactions with others. In other words, the infant develops into an *intersubjective partner* through affect attunement (Stern, 2006).

During early childhood, these basic socioemotional competencies are expanded to include non-family contexts where interpersonal relations are needed, as in the childcare setting. But as argued in Chapter 2, intimacy is not absent in the childcare arena but is less pronounced and individualized than in a family context. There is a 'functional division' between the family and non-family caring contexts. As shown in Scandinavian countries, the late modern family functions as an intimacy zone for young children living in the dual socialization configuration (Sommer, 2001, 2010; Dencik et al., 2008). As documented in Chapter 2, the family has by no means been stripped of its function as a primary developmental arena of care. In the dual socialization context, the young child moves between family and childcare. In many countries, especially in the early years, caring may still be a family matter, because of maternity/paternity leave (Kamerman and Moss, 2009), although the time allowed for parental leave varies greatly across developed nations. However, for many three-year-olds or even younger children, parental care occurs at different times of the day than it typically did when mothers stayed at home 50 years ago. In principle, parental care seems not to be in competition with, but is shared with childcare staff.

5

PARENTING II: EMERGENT FATHER INVOLVEMENT?

Changes in living conditions lead to changes in human perceptions, but some assumptions change slowly, both on a personal and a cultural level. This was demonstrated in Chapter 2 when dealing with beliefs provoked by the rapid changes in early childhood. Sometimes, deep-rooted perceptions resist change, a phenomenon known as 'cultural lag'. If this happens in a professional context, by adhering to paradigms learned once and not since updated, this is 'professional knowledge lag'. For example, perceptions of parental gender-based duties may remain traditional and lag behind the real changes in women's roles in family and society. This applies, as will be demonstrated, to explicit and implicit professional opinions about who, in essence, should be seen as the crucial person in early caring.

Theorizing is double-edged, in that, on the one hand, it constructs the phenomena we 'see' and ascribe meaning to, while on the other hand, it directs our attention away from other phenomena, thereby preventing us from seeing and understanding. Specific types of theorizing within social and developmental psychology have important consequences for whether not only the potential but the actual practising of early father involvement is acknowledged or not. This chapter looks first at how social psychology traditionally portrayed fathers in family theory by instrumentalizing the male role. As will be shown, active father involvement in early childhood has been rendered conceptually wordless until recently and thus defined as invisible and unimportant. It will be noted how, until recently, child psychology has portrayed fathers as breadwinners and mothers as possessing an innate ability to bond with her children. But it will also be demonstrated that new research points to a hitherto unseen paternal caring potential, with important consequences for the child's early development.

PATERNAL INVOLVEMENT?: ABOUT
PATERNAL POTENTIAL

We are, to some extent, bearers of our growing-up histories, which in turn are embedded in a context of cultural history. Buried in our long-term memory are memories of a father who was or was not present in our childhood. This could be the image of the *distant father*, once in a while spending time with his daughter. Walking along hand in hand with his daughter, the father may be engrossed in his own thoughts. Perhaps he has something important to say or is even on the brink of revealing close sentiments towards his daughter. But as they hardly know each other, and perhaps because of the masculine fear of showing intimacy, the father may end up not saying it.

This father bears similarities to what might be called the 'traditional' father image. In the traditional household, the father had a limited role, and the main impression was of a breadwinner. It was accepted that he put so much time and energy into his role that at home he was reserved, sometimes tough and sometimes kind. Typically, the traditional father was respected, perhaps feared by his child, and the two never really got to know each other. This version of fatherhood has deep historical roots. The following processes in particular have affected this perception (Sommer, 2003):

- *The historical separation of home and workplace:* the separation of men's and women's primary domains; home versus work.
- *The polarization of male and female tasks and identity:* the father's role as worker/breadwinner and the mother's primary role as carer; the rational, instrumental man versus the intuitive, emotional woman.
- *The sentimentalization of motherhood and childhood:* the ideological link that bonds mothers and children, leaving little room for early father involvement.

But is there an alternative to this image of the distant father? Yes, as will be apparent later, an emergent trend of late modern early childhood and fatherhood has to do with the child's relationship to a close, playful, involved male: the 'psychological father'. According to research, fathers can play an essential role in the development of infants and young children. But there are many obstacles to such a conclusion, not only from commonsense beliefs but also from 'lessons' from various professional positions.

FATHERS INSTRUMENTALIZED

First, the instrumentalized father idea will be presented and evaluated, showing that there are few concepts and words about early father involvement. The definition of a father's roles and duties 'transport' him out of caring and into the rational sphere of work. Pre-paradigm shift socialization and family theories were based on the reality of the 1950s and 60s. Once again, we see how research was (and is) a product of its time, sometimes uncritically adhering to and reflecting prevailing social practices in society and family and assuming an unintended normative function. Family and socialization research from that period not only described and conceptualized life but also cemented an implicit view of what normal life was like.

In connection with Parsons and Bales' (1955) highly influential theory on primary socialization in the family, it was argued that the primary socialization approach was outdated and a dual socialization configuration was introduced (see Chapter 2). But the gender role implications of Parsons and Bales' theory were not included. Their theory seems to be outdated compared to the drastic changes in women's employment and the rise of the dual-earner family as a growing norm, along with the emergent trend of negotiation families. This all seems to undermine the relevance of Parsons and Bales' theory.

Despite this, the theory clearly represents a way of thinking that, even if it does not explain the actual way many people live today, articulates a common idea: the male as the primary breadwinner. So this classical understanding can be used as an example of the belief in the gender role-divided family. Earlier, it was argued that phenomena such as professional knowledge lag and cultural lag explain resistance to rapid change. Deeply held ideas can survive even when major societal changes occur. Some ideas may change, others may not, and some even become solidified and cherished, as seen in the public debate in Chapter 2. In dealing with the phenomenon of the potential benefits of early father involvement, a complex of highly gendered role expectations will probably be activated.

A resistant idea is that of the instrumentalized father, which is highlighted in Parsons and Bales' perspective, where the separate roles, tasks and functions of men and women are:

- crucial for the survival, functioning and wellbeing of the family
- not attributed equal power and status, although in principle, they are equally important
- polarized – in and outside the family
- based on a hierarchy. Male power is established as a principle. As a spouse and a father, males are supposed to be superior in important family decisions.

In this view, the male role is seen as primarily *instrumental*, that is, rational and logical and not often emotionally involved in caring. When involved, the father's function is to be the rational socializer and role model. Male identity is closely linked to his role as provider. The female's duties lie in her expressive role as having the *integrative function* in the family, binding it together. Characteristics of the female role and identity are emotionality and an intuitive orientation towards close relationships. It is the complementary balance between the instrumental/rational and the integrative/expressive functions that forms the basis of this theory. The natural consequence of this is a clearly gendered differentiation of roles and duties in relation to child-care and parenting.

In addition, the idea has been widely legitimized and naturalized by early bonding and attachment theory (see a later section). There are no words in the instrumentalized male approach to explain growing phenomena, such as a father with tears in his eyes on seeing and touching his first newborn child, a male pushing a pram, a father changing nappies and engaging in a rough-and-tumble play with his toddler. This has all been documented in recent research, undermining the idea of the solely instrumental male, as will be discussed later.

The underlying normative nature of theories is uncovered when the time-bound contexts they were fitted to explain are withering. The normative consequences of the gender polarized paradigm are expressed in two ways:

1. by dichotomizing roles, the idea fails to mention the necessary functions that men and women may represent to varying degrees. Role functions may be loaded with tradition, but role negotiation and remaking duties seem to have potential in changing times.
2. the normal prescription for the instrumental father in a well-functioning family is that of the rational parent.

Seen in a reproductive societal perspective, the father is institutionalized as the family's representative of society, setting standards, offering advice, giving instructions, and being a future role model for his son. The integrative female, by contrast, becomes the child's primary carer through intimacy and close-ness, especially in the early years, being a future role model for her daughter.

Stereotypes have a tendency to become self-fulfilling prophecies. By underscoring the polarity of men and women (men are from Mars and women are from Venus), men's potential disinterest in being involved with their young children is naturalized as well as legitimized. If, by definition, males are exclusively rational and logical, and females intuitive and sensi-tive, a father is, in essence, rendered incompetent to care for infants and young children, especially if the quality of personalized caring discussed in Chapter 4 (that is, synchrony and emotional attunement) characterizes father–child relationships. In this connection, the stereotype imbues a female with the necessary caring qualities, who without further argument is handed the role as the unquestioned expert. The instrumental man paradigm, in turn, makes him fit nicely into the well-ordered, rational employment sphere of society. Thus, the prescription of the instrumental male stereotype 'transports' fathers from early childcare into society.

But the male role is not as rigid as may be thought. Roles are flexible and contextually sensitive. However, in order to discover that, the external environment has to change. If it does not, role change is unlikely. To give a basic example of the importance of functional fitness: basic survival of the family is crucial, and the ecological niche it is embedded in frames how this is best guaranteed. Thus, we have to be aware that the emotional and social relationships between children and fathers can be different in different cultures. This is richly demonstrated in studies of the hunter-gatherer Aka people in central Africa. Here, the *fathers* spend much more time with their infants and young children than in any other society in the world. Observations show that for more than half the time in any given day, the typical Aka father is only arm's length away from his baby or infant. When the child cries, the father is usually the first to pick them up and offer comfort. The fathers' daily contact is more than five times as frequent as in other hunter-gatherer societies (Hewlett, 1992).

The reason for this is that the males and females share the workload equally, hunting, gathering plants and childcare. When the baby travels with the parents on long hunts, the father carries the child, as this would be too strenuous for the mother. Yet even when they return to the village, the father continues to spend time with the infant, and he cares for them many hours each day (Hewlett, 1992). These fathers act as primary carers, and play a key role at a very early stage in the child's life. This is not something they have 'chosen' to be, but their nurturing role comes out of some kind of necessity. Active father involvement seen in other hunter-gatherer cultures enhances the chance of survival. It frees the women to be much more efficient when they leave the village to collect food and bring it home for all to share, especially if the village's male hunters are not very good at shooting game (Hrdy, 2009). This example illustrates the considerable global and cultural variation in gender roles. It serves as a reminder of the adaptability of the human species, and that our (normal) lifestyle is not the only or necessarily the best one for everyone, everywhere.

The naturalization 'blueprint' idea of masculinity and male identity has been weakened by recent historical evidence from role-sharing negotiation families. But it has even been questioned by groundbreaking biological research. This research questions the dichotomous and gender polarized perception that men and women have different, natural abilities for care. Masculinity and femininity seem to be more biopsychological, plastic phenomena than previously presumed. This is shown in two studies of the hormonal consequences of father–child contact (Storey et al., 2000; Berg and Wynne-Edwards, 2001), where fathers' practice with infants – even with dolls – significantly changes the number of important gender-specific hormones. Father involvement reduces the male hormone testosterone while increasing the female hormones oestrogen and prolactin. A so-called 'intimacy effect' is created, that is, direct father–child contact sensitizes while the 'insensitive' masculine side is toned down. This type of research is an example of how the nurture versus nature dichotomy is challenged by the new nurture/multiple nature paradigm (Shenk, 2010). Thus, hormones do not necessarily act as a 'blueprint' by making women sensitive to caring and males non-sensitive, as argued by mother-centric positions. Hormones do not solely regulate behaviour, because human activity can seemingly influence both hormonal processes and quantities in brain and body. Such findings are in line with the recent paradigm of probabilistic epigenesis and the highly transactional nature of brain hormone/environment exchange, presented in Chapter 2.

A contextual approach to the changing nature of gender roles also implies, however, that roles do not necessarily change. If, as in Germany, as opposed to Scandinavia, it is still common for mothers of small children not to work and the spouses to be the breadwinner, then the pressure on father participation in early care will be less. In addition, non-shared role identity can be expected to change fast. The main point is that it is not argued here or in the following that father involvement is *the* global new trend or fashion or a must be. In late modernity with its plural character, a multitude of roles and identities and various ways of being a father can be expected to exist side by side. There are clear signs of emergent father involvement in our times, especially in dual-earner families and more so in those characterized by negotiation relationships. Seen from a historical perspective, a gradual shift in gender traditions towards a growing democratization of gender roles has happened since the Second World War. The old patriarchal set-up with the male as the undisputed head of the family has gradually been eroded. This development towards a more democratic approach also may affect perceptions of fatherhood.

Having extracted some consequences for fathering and father involvement from a classical social psychological approach, it is time to turn to developmental approaches. A critical discussion will follow of selected parts of attachment theory, bonding research and the notion of critical developmental periods. This is done in order to identify some important professional mother-naturalized positions that have hindered an appropriate understanding of the developmental potential of early fathering.

MOTHERS EMOTIONALIZED: ATTACHMENT, BONDING AND CRITICAL STAGES

The fundamental mother–infant monotropic axiom coined by Bowlby can still be seen in some places as definitive attachment theory. For example, in the childcare debate in Chapter 2, this approach clearly fuelled the arguments about the developmental threats of sending a child to a nursery, discarding the fundamental one-to-one relationship with the mother. Particularly in relation to father involvement, claiming a monotropic stance has the subsidiary effect of making potential contributions by the father conceptually invisible. The following offers a closer look at selected, but important roots behind professional knowledge that does not reflect the potential importance of early paternal involvement.

According to Bowlby (1958, 1969, 1973, 1980), mother and child have developed evolutionary and appropriate dynamic processes that ensure the survival and healthy development of the child. On the basis of this assumption, he then developed his influential thesis on children's attachment to a mother figure. Bowlby (1969) defined secure attachment as a strong emotional bond that an infant establishes to another person as well as the concomitant sense of wellbeing, security and trust. On the one hand, understood as an emotional bond, attachment is a construct about inner emotional experiences. On the other hand, inferences about attachment are also based on observations of the infant's efforts to achieve closeness by using the mother as a secure base when frightened. Bowlby sparked controversy within and outside developmental psychology, with arguments for and against his monotropic stance. Over time, he modified his point of view, so it is important to distinguish between the 'early' and the 'late' Bowlby.

Early in his work, Bowlby presented his 'monotropic attachment' concept – an idea that implies a particular developmental sequence in who should be (and not be) the child's primary attachment figure. The main assumption is that to ensure normal development, an intimate relationship with only one mother figure has to be established during the first years of life.[93] Early in his work, Bowlby points out that the absence of the mother figure (maternal deprivation) and early experiences of deprivation will have crucial negative consequences for the child's later psychological development.[94] Influenced by Lorenz's theory on imprinting,[95] Bowlby specified this subsequent negative development as an 'affectless' character disorder in his early writings. This disorder can be traced back to insecure attachment formation to the mother in a particularly sensitive developmental period – a critical stage paradigm as seen in Chapter 1.

If an insensitive mother fails to establish secure attachment with her child, transcending the age-specific critical phase limits, the mother has laid out a subsequent route towards pathology for her child. Inherent in the ontogenetic phase idea of monotropic attachment is this progression: first comes the one-to-one mother–child relationship and after that perhaps the one-to-one father–child relationship. In other words, in the monotropic approach, there are no concepts available to explain these current and observable practices in families with infants:

- in the infants' first year, both mothers and fathers are involved in one-to-one attachments (and other) relationships
- mother–infant–father are regularly observed in triadic relationships (Howes and Spieker, 2008).

At the time, Bowlby's approach was clearly in line with the developmental stage theory and mother-centrism before the paradigm shift.

As paradigms were beginning to shift, such ideas came under attack, and under criticism, Bowlby revised his views. First, he acknowledged that the mother need not necessarily be the child's biological mother. He also seemed to discard his idea about critical phases. Nevertheless, it can be claimed that Bowlby's resistance to a wholehearted revision of his theory about the mother's primary importance has caused his theory still to be used as scientific support for the natural status of the mother–child relationship (Eyer, 1993). Hrdy (2009, p. 124), in her scholarly treatment of the evolutionary benefits of parenting by people other than the mother, concludes:

> Yet scratch him hard and Bowlby's view of infant development was profoundly mother-centred. Through attachment theory's first half century, research focused on infant's relationships with this one other person.

This is to some extent true, but perhaps not entirely fair to Bowlby, as it is largely based on Bowlby's (1951) influential report *Maternal Care and Mental Health* for the World Health Organization. In later writings (Bowlby, 1969, 1973), he explicitly states that 'mother figure', 'maternal' and all terms that contain the word 'mother' can, in fact, refer to other close persons, such as fathers, grandparents and so on. He even cites studies in which children have shown equal attachment to both father and mother. The point is that it is the specific quality of the relationship between adult and child that determines the nature of the attachment, not infants' biological predisposition towards their mother. In a late publication, Bowlby (1988) emphasizes again that both fathers and mothers (and other 'maternal substitutes') may provide a safe base for infants and young children.

It is fair to conclude that Bowlby himself laid the foundation for later research into multiple attachment relationships. This rapidly growing field acknowledges infants' and young children's extraordinary social competencies and defines criteria for quality care in multiple contexts. Bowlby (1988) also abandoned his critical stage thinking and replaced it with the promising idea of 'developmental pathways'. This concept, together with his concept of the attachment working model, has become influential in recent multiple attachment theorizing, among others, by including fathers (Bretherton, 2005). However, such important reformulations came relatively late in Bowlby's work and he did not directly take issue with his earlier theorizing on attachment. This may explain the ambivalence in understanding what Bowlby really meant. It may also explain how 'two Bowlbys' can be found in professional discussions, either used as a legitimization for a pure mother-centric stance or an argument that accepts the importance of early father involvement.

Although Bowlby presented his attachment theory as evolutionary and universal, recent research points to *cultural variations in attachment patterns.*

This has important implications for a wider contextual understanding of maternal and paternal roles. Although there is little doubt among leading culture researchers that the human need for security rests on an evolutionary basis, there is still room for wide cultural variation (Rothbaum et al., 2000). For example, Grossmann et al. (1985) report that children from northern Germany have less secure attachments than US children. One suggested explanation is that German mothers encourage their children to be independent early on in life. Also, German mothers are more likely than their US counterparts to see a child who repeatedly seeks their parents as a safe base as relatively overprotected and spoiled. Sagi-Schwartz and Aviezer (2005) found that only a third of kibbutz children display secure attachment, which is considerably less than normally found in American families, but considered quite normal in Israeli culture.

In traditional Japanese families, where the male is the breadwinner and the female is the domesticated mother and housewife, young children display more anxious/avoidant behaviour, and significantly fewer children display secure attachment to their mothers compared with children in the US (Miyake et al., 1985). In addition, Japanese fathers in traditional families work many hours per day and tend not to be actively involved in the lives of their infants (Shwalb et al., 2004). One suggested explanation of the findings of attachment patterns is that traditional Japanese mothers rarely leave their children alone, so fostering a high degree of dependency in their children. According to the researchers, this in turn reflects a Japanese cultural norm of unconditional family loyalty.

In the research procedure, Ainsworth's classical method, the 'strange situation', was used to measure attachment style. The standard procedure is to place a mother and a child in a playroom equipped with toys, then the mother is asked to leave the room while there is a stranger present. Subsequently, the mother is asked to return, and the child's reunion behaviour will reveal whether they are securely or insecurely attached. When the Japanese mothers returned, their children obviously perceived the situation as far more alarming and threatening than the US children, and they responded in a way that showed insecure attachment.

An interesting point is that the emergent global change towards dual-earner families and early childcare has also come to the East. The relatively new 'Asian dual socialization situation' may have some consequences for mother–child attachments in Japanese families, as infants and young children of *working Japanese mothers* display more similar patterns of attachment with Western children than with Japanese children from traditional families. Research, however, has proved that the traditional distant role of Japanese fathers is still shaped by Confucian principles (Shwalb et al., 2004). New maternal roles, combined with changing values, now pose a challenge to redefine parental roles in a family that is changing.[96]

In relation to cultural differences and perhaps some growing global similarities, it should be noted that research methods may be inherently culturally biased. Markus and Kitayama (1991) reviewed a large number of studies that showed that despite possible growing global similarities, distinct cultural differences in socialization are still dominant. There is wide cultural variation in how parents regulate children's emotions (anxiety, anger, shame and guilt). The classification of infants regarding their attachment clearly departs from the pattern typically observed in Western studies. In particular, many more Japanese infants are classified as having an ambivalent attachment style than Western infants, which could possibly be a result of underlying cultural biases inherent in the way the strange situation procedure is constructed. This procedure is closely related to a belief in the self as independent and so may be unsuitable for evaluating attachment in non-Western cultures (Markus and Kitayama, 1991). Before Lamb's (1976a, 1976b) studies of (Western) father–infant attachment, the strange situation procedure was used mainly with (middle-class) mothers and children. Inadvertently, by not having observation or scoring procedures that encompassed fathers (or other figures), this much used methodology became mother-centric from the start. Today, the strange situation method is used in the study of multiple attachments.

Inspired by ethology, maternal deprivation studies, and Harlow's monkeys that preferred 'contact' over 'milk', research into *maternal bonding* rose in the 1970s. This was a period when developmental psychology was in the midst of its paradigmatic revolution. While attachment theory deals with the infant's establishment of an emotional bond with the mother figure and explains this process in detail, the theory on bonding aims to explain the mother's instinctive bonding with her child. Klaus and Kennell's (1976, 1982) studies attempted to prove that only *a few hours immediately after birth* determine whether the mother will bond with her child or not. Bonding is not activated by merely looking at the child through a window. According to Klaus and Kennell, bonding is established only through close body contact with the newborn child, which in turn triggers the mother's bonding instinct. If body contact is delayed a few hours, which, at the time, was normal hospital practice all over the world, there would be long-term negative consequences to both the child and the mother–child relationship.[97]

This approach has three distinct features:

1. Making a few hours so crucial to normal development of human affection towards the newborn is an extreme version of the 'critical stage' axiom. After a few hours, a mother's instinctive ability to bond with her baby would have reached its point of no return.
2. The 'eliciting' axiom – that an instinctual pattern of emotions and behaviours is dormant in every woman just waiting to be triggered – represents a pure naturalization of motherhood.

3. There is obviously no concept inferring a comparable father instinct to be triggered by close body contact with a newborn.

Being educated within medicine and not child psychology, Klaus and Kennell were unaware that their claims appeared out of sync with growing developmental research. In their publications, there are no references to this research, which undermines their own studies. Not surprisingly, therefore, bonding research has been strongly criticized on the following counts:

- The theory's analogy between animal mothers' (sheep) and human mothers' instincts is simply flawed.
- Others have been unable to demonstrate a bonding trigger mechanism in humans.
- The existence of a critical period has also gone undocumented. On the contrary, it is apparent that mothers have no problem establishing an affectionate bond with their children at later times (Rutter, 2008). Furthermore, adoptive parents can also bond intensely with their child, despite not having had close bodily contact with the child in the hours after birth.
- Long-term negative consequences of a lack of close contact between mother and baby immediately after birth have not been found in other studies (see also Eyer, 1993).

As a consequence of these criticisms, Klaus and Kennell retracted some of their original points and modified others. Despite the many problems, one positive side effect was that the bonding studies revolutionized hospital practice and allowed mothers a rewarding and immediate contact with their newborns. Later on, this practice was extended in many places (despite not being inferred from the bonding research) to include the fathers of newborns. Today, however, bonding as a research field is considered a dead end. Ironically, the bonding paradigm – a classic example of mother-centricity and critical stage thinking in simplified versions – was in its prime at the very time developmental psychology was undergoing tremendous change. As an epilogue to this and a prelude to the next, here is a recent conclusion and wake-up call from a leading attachment researcher:

> studies tend not to identify which of a child's several attachments figures should be considered primary (those that do so tend to find that this role is more often played by the mother). (Bretherton, 2005, p. 17)

This implies that most often the primary attachment figure is the mother, because she usually has the primary role. Bretherton (2005) makes clear that more studies are needed in order to learn about the degree to which individuals develop relationship-specific working models (cognitive representations and memories) of peers, teachers, childcare staff and, not least, fathers.

The primary carer: only a woman?

This may be seen as a highly provocative question. It must be remembered, though, that the questions and answers do not intend to exclude the importance of mothers or women as qualified carers. The infant's evolutionarily developed potential of being intimately related to mothers as well as other humans has been well documented (Howes and Spieker, 2008; Hrdy, 2009). Thus, in light of recent research, the assumption of the child's *all-or-none* mother–child destiny appears dubious. A lasting, personal relationship between child and adult relies more on the quality of the relationship than on the identity and gender of the short- or long-term carer. The care provided needs to be of a certain duration though, and five minutes of intense daily interaction is probably not enough to ensure a stable attachment. Depending on *childcare practices and arrangements,* a child may develop strong feelings for the father, an older sibling or a preschool educator, while the mother may temporarily come second. Young children may at one point in time show strong preference for both mother and father, while at other times cling to the mother. In dual-earner families, periods of intense father attachment are also to be expected. The key point is that the child's preferences seemingly have more to do with daily routine practices within the family than fixed parental gender. As caring routines are divided by gender, attachment will be too; if routines are shared, a dual attachment internal working model will probably develop (Bretherton, 2005).

In his later writings, Bowlby clearly underlines the meaning of his concept of 'mothering'. It is the specific quality of the relationship between a committed adult and a child that determines the nature of the attachment, not infants' predisposition towards their biological mother in particular or a woman in general. In attachment theory, the emotional bond is secured by adult sensitivity and caring qualities, not child characteristics. This is only partly the case, however, because infants and young children are not passive recipients. They are relationship and attachment co-builders with adults. In *A Childhood Psychology* perspective, the child's social agency contributes actively to their own development. At an early stage in life, an infant prefers habitual nonverbal conversation styles with its various interactional partners. For example, a father is 'invited' to engage in rough-and-tumble play, whereas a mother is 'invited' to participate in a peek-a-boo game where they sit close. The child is probably not the inventor of such complex relationships; rather they are based on and elaborated from the child's regular experiences with different father and mother styles.

For more than three decades, the concept of the mother's one-to-one all-inclusive importance to the child's development has been critiqued, reflected in numerous empirical studies, models and theories. Although mothers are extremely important to children, today's developmental research has abandoned the idea that a child's future developmental 'fate' lies only in a mother's arms. If the biological mother dies or becomes unable to care for her child, alternative carers can be substituted, for example fathers and adoptive parents. Multiple factors impinge on development, as highlighted by the new developmental models introduced in Chapter 1. Despite this, the tendency of *mother-blaming* (not father-blaming) continues. Obviously one cannot expect laypeople to read, follow up and draw conclusions from new research, so the new paradigm in developmental psychology may not be very well known. This may apply even to so-called 'child experts', who use their (outdated) interpretative filters on new phenomena. Mother-blaming has, in fact, been a central ingredient in the mother-centric arguments articulated by the debaters presented in Chapter 2, that is, leaving a little child in the care of others is seen as a sign of maternal failure, and having a job that takes her away from her young child, a sign of egotism. But are such examples just selected coincidences? Probably not, as mother-blaming seems to be a phenomenon connected to our times. In a historical analysis of the two faces of fatherhood, Pleck (2004, p. 51) concluded: 'Mothers, especially in the 20th century, were more often blamed for the failings of children than fathers.' An important consequence of the paradigm shift is that there is no longer a professional legitimization of mother-blaming, that is, the idea that children's developmental deficiencies and personality disorders are caused by separation from their mother or early deficiencies in the mother–infant attachment (see Eyer, 1993; Rutter, 2008).

Schaffer (1990) asked: Do young children need a mother? His answer was once 'yes' and twice 'no'. Yes, if it implies that infants and young children need a stable, loving and caring relationship with at least one other person. No, if it implies that this person must be the biological mother, and should she die, no one else can take her place. No again, if caring means a close relationship to a single woman who is considered paramount to the child's wellbeing. A handful of committed people with whom the child is familiar and feels safe around may provide a secure, stable and caring foundation. Both the evolutionary and contemporary benefit of this and the conclusion that parenting by others and not solely mothers and fathers is an intrinsic part of humanity have been researched (Howes and Spieker, 2008; Hrdy, 2009). Following this perspective, the definition of mothering can be seen independently of a specific woman. Instead, *mothering represents the essential human qualities necessary in relationships with children*; for example, a necessary ability to adopt another person's perspective, to sense what the other is feeling, experiencing and needs in order to act accordingly (Tomasello, 2009). To become an active 'psychological parent' – not just having a role or a biological relationship – to a young child seems to be based on actual caring, not governed by genes but learned by practice. Father involvement in early childhood may be one pathway on the road to becoming such a psychological parent.

THE CARING FATHER IDEAL

This section deals with the caring father as an *ideal* held by some but not by others; an ideal that is barely realized in many parts of the world, only slowly emerging in other parts, while perhaps a reality in some places. In discussing the caring father ideal, this is not to be seen as a value statement or an ideology that fathers must always be close carers. But societal tendencies – along with emergent family tendencies and value changes, described in previous chapters – indicate some generational differences in fatherhood. In dual-earner families, the average levels of paternal engagement and accessibility are higher than in families with unemployed mothers (Crouter, 2006). The consequences for child development of this emergent trend need to be explored.

Legislation on behalf of children may be interpreted as a 'secular value signal'. For example, 177 countries worldwide have ratified the UN Convention on the Rights of the Child (UN, 1989), which offers a vision of the child as an individual *and* a member of a family and a community, with rights and responsibilities appropriate to their age and stage of development. Article 18, section 1, states:

> States Parties shall use their best efforts to ensure recognition of the principle that *both parents have common responsibilities for the upbringing and development of the child.* (emphasis added)

On the one hand, this ideal is far from an actual reality in many places. On the other hand, governments would not have signed the convention if they did not agree with the idea of shared parental responsibilities. The point is that an *ideal prescription* on behalf of the child is formulated so both parents have equal upbringing and developmental obligations for the next generation. Although not stated directly above, this can be translated into a 'caring father ideal'.

There will be substantial differences, however, in how such a prescription is interpreted and enacted in various societies in the world. For example, in European developed countries, there is no unitary father model. Instead, the caring father ideal jostles with the economic breadwinner father model (O'Brien, 2004). In Europe and other countries worldwide, legislation regarding paternal leave varies considerably. Scandinavia is closest to the implementation of the caring father ideal, having the most generous maternal and paternal leave. So, is Article 18 on the rights of the child in line with Scandinavian welfare states, with their strong traditions for equal rights for men and women? Here, the answer has to be partly yes and partly no. Partly yes, because it is documented that father involvement is observed in all socioeconomic groups (Sommer, 2010). Haavind (2006) reviewed secular changes in fathering in Scandinavia, identifying three important steps or acts, with Scandinavia now 'in the middle of third act', which means that the father's participation in parenting is more the rule than the exception. Engaged, sensitive caring is now shared more equally between women and men, and the male commitment to children has become a more integrated part of masculine identity. Partly no, because professional discussions on growing equal opportunities for males and females have been rather vague in relation to what these changes mean substantially to a renewed interpretation of fatherhood and male involvement in early childcare and parenting. The new practice is out there, so to speak, but the academic reflections on this revolution are sparse.

Despite being a natural setting for large-scale social experiments, the international research on father involvement did not take off in Scandinavia. In the 1970s, a group of US pioneers abandoned the study of absent fathers and turned their attention to present, involved fathers (for some pioneering work, see Lamb, 1976a, 1976b, 1976c, 1976d; Pedersen, 1980). The idea of growing paternal involvement was founded less on representative statistics than on studies making inferences based on the following (Sommer, 1999):

- Generalizations based on research into the few pioneer fathers, who have chosen to be the primary carers, or (the relatively few) fathers who have shown a particular interest, for example by applying for custody after a divorce.
- Conclusions inferred from an ideology, which emphasizes growing equality between the sexes. Based on this premise, men's and women's attitudes to childcare are expected to change.
- The increasing number of mothers in the labour market and the rise of the dual-earner family. This shift in the traditional division of labour is expected to generate pressure for changes in parenting, with the end result that nurturing fathers are becoming more typical.

These explanations are interrelated, but it is important to distinguish between them in terms of the impact on father involvement. The labour market factor is probably the strongest, as research shows that the more hours the mother works, the more paternal involvement (Crouter, 2006).

THE CARING FATHER: THE SCANDINAVIAN CASE

Studies from nearly all parts of the world and from various ethnic groups within countries have documented an enormous variability in how fathers relate to their young offspring (Lamb, 2004). Consequently, there is no single model available to explain father involvement. The 'new caring father' as proposed by pioneer researchers in the 1970s has to been seen as a specific US middle-class ideal, not realized or wanted in many places. The reason, however, that father involvement is relevant in *A Childhood Psychology* is that rising father involvement in early care and socialization has been witnessed, and this varies with the number of hours mothers work outside the home and whether it is holiday time or not (Crouter, 2006). Although not necessarily typical, this phenomenon and its consequences for early childhood cannot be avoided.

In many EU countries, New Zealand, Australia, the UK, the US and Asia, the participation of fathers in early care does not equal the time spent by mothers, even in dual-earner families (O'Brien, 2004). While there is probably not a 'caring gene' reserved for mothers, cultural and societal variations may explain the malleability of gender roles. Within the social sciences, there is an increasing international interest in Scandinavian welfare societies' pronounced egalitarian norms for gender roles and focus on gender equality. This is manifested in the general consensus seen in society (Esping-Andersen et al., 2003), in men's experience of gender equality and life quality (Holter et al., 2008), in family changes and the negotiation culture (Dencik et al., 2008) and in fathers' increasing involvement in their children's lives (Mikelson, 2008).

The fatherhood revolution was internationally proclaimed in the 1970s by emphasizing the 'new psychologically close father', who increasingly looked after his children (Parke, 1996; Lamb, 2004). The stereotypical gendered rhetoric about the man as the family's rational foreign secretary and the woman as the family's emotional home secretary was replaced by other ways of understanding the genders and their relations. Significant societal changes in Scandinavia, including women's entry into higher education and the workplace, put pressure on the traditional gender roles, with the necessary scientific redefinitions of the family with children (Dencik et al., 2008).

So how are childcare tasks shared in a Scandinavian country? Despite specific differences in Norway, Sweden and Denmark, they share similarities regarding the late modern interchange between the welfare state, the family and children's wellbeing (UNICEF, 2007; Kamerman and Moss, 2009). When inter-Scandinavian research and statistics are unavailable, one country can function as a case example. In the following Danish survey, research with randomly chosen participants on early father involvement in late modern dual-earner families in all socioeconomic groups will be presented. The research showed that nearly all young children are in childcare on a daily basis for eight hours, and that mothers' and fathers' direct interaction time had risen over the past few decades (Bonke and Esping-Andersen,

2009). Among females and males, childcare and companionship are, in general, highly valued. If there is a shortage of time, the standard of household chores is lowered (Bonke, 2009). This seems to imply a 'children first rule', exemplifying a fundamental late modern child-centred cultural belief, discussed in Chapter 2.

Paternal child beliefs

In Norway and Sweden, a few smaller studies have researched fathers' images of their children. In Denmark, however, a longitudinal study of 4,000 fathers living with five-month-olds is available (for further details of the study and results, see Sommer, 2001).

Fathers' experiences of their children are a mixture of cultural influences, their personal views of children and practical experiences with their own child. How a father perceives his child, whether stubborn, demanding, irritable, hard to comfort, or the opposite, plays a significant role in the adult–child interaction. Fathers believe that this infant is equipped with particular characteristics, although they are more likely to be the result of social interaction. However, fathers' attitudes to their child's characteristics regulate their expectations to what it is like to spend time with their infant. Table 5.1 provides the results of a questionnaire where fathers were asked to indicate how well a number of characteristics described their five-month-old baby.

Fathers were asked to comment on the following four dimensions:

- *Active/directed at the surroundings:* Interestingly, fathers perceive their five-month-old baby as active, curious and eager for contact. In this context, there is no notion about a passive, socially distanced creature whose only need is care, food and mother. These fathers' perception of their babies seem to be in line with the new post-paradigm shift research, which highlights that from the beginning of life, humans are active, directed at their surroundings and more socially competent than previously assumed.
- *Calm:* The fathers generally regard their babies as calm, trusting and happy. The majority also believe that the baby is 'gentle and compliant', although they are more divided on this. The fact that the fathers do not perceive their baby as *un*settled and *un*happy, and as one who meets the adult with *mis*trust, makes it easier for the father to develop a happy relationship. Other studies indicate that the typical father–child interaction is characterized by happiness and a spontaneous joy in each others' company.
- *Anxious:* 67% believe that the description 'quiet' and 'cautious' suits their baby badly, while 27% believe that it describes them somewhat or perfectly. Only 12% believe that 'fearful' describes their baby more or less. In other words, by far the most fathers express that they have quite a resilient baby, who does not withdraw or take fright easily. Among other things, this may be connected to how fathers' most frequent interactions are

Table 5.1 *Fathers' perceptions of their baby's characteristics*

	Very true %	Somewhat true %	Note very true %	Untrue %	Don't know %	Answers %
Active						
a. Active, eager	74	24	1	0	0	99
b. Curious	78	20	1	0	1	100
c. Keen for contact	69	28	2	0	1	100
Calm						
d. Calm, trusting	57	38	4	0	1	100
e. Content, happy	81	19	0	0	0	100
f. Gentle, compliant	20	40	24	10	6	100
Anxious						
g. Quiet, cautious	7	21	39	28	3	98
h. Fearful	2	10	26	52	8	100
Demanding						
i. Stubborn	29	32	22	10	7	100
j. Demanding	14	33	33	16	3	99
k. Hard to comfort	2	11	30	56	1	100
l. Irritable	1	8	24	64	3	100
N = 4,023–4,096						

Source: Based on Sommer, 2001

playing with their children (see later). Through the spontaneous father–infant play interaction, the child's handling of fear is tested in a trusting way. The playing is often noisy and a cautious and a quiet child would quickly make the game stop.

- *Demanding:* 61% perceive their baby as 'stubborn', which is not a *stable* personality trait in babies. Table 5.1 also shows that the fathers are evenly split in terms of experiencing their baby as 'demanding'. Are the fathers of modern individualists influenced to 'see' their children as separate individuals, who very early on demonstrate their own will? Other answers in Table 5.1 seem to indicate so: because stubbornness is not connected to negative characteristics in a baby, only to some extent as 'demanding'. When many fathers see their baby as stubborn, it is apparently not a negative term. This interpretation finds support in cross-cultural research. Adults in Western, modern societies, including Scandinavia, view humans as independent individuals with a unique personality and having free will, as compared to other cultures (Markus and Kitayama, 1991; Rothbaum et al., 2000; Chao and Tseng, 2010). Even at the preverbal age, such cultural attitudes begin to apply in the way adults experience and treat their babies, long before they are actually independent people (Morelli and Rogoff, 1992). Both fathers and mothers are carriers of these cultural perceptions. Stubbornness is probably perceived positively by fathers in a Scandinavian culture as a way in which their baby displays individualism and independence.

Early paternal involvement

Studying father involvement with children of all ages is relevant. But the types of direct contact with babies are of special interest because this can test the realities behind the idea of the solely instrumentalized male.

What does contact with infants mean to men's identity as a father? According to Siegel and Lisi (2002), parents develop 'cognitive schemata', which are crystallized from interactions with their children. These mental representations of the relationship with the child become the main source of the inner experience of success or failure as a father. A positive identity as a father is largely based on whether the interaction is perceived as pleasurable, that the father sees his child as fun to be with.[98]

As documented in Table 5.1, most fathers perceive their child as active, trusting, curious, content, happy and eager for contact. This perception is significant to the mood state that a father approaches his child with, and predictably, the drive to spend time with the child is increased. However, the experience of being a father, and the father's perception of his child, does not influence the child directly. Instead, the infant's experience with their father is based on direct contact, both in the *type of interaction* (for example feeding, playing, changing nappies) and in the *frequency* of this interaction. But which type of interaction do fathers have with their five-month-old baby? Let us now examine the 'doing' side, that is, practical paternal involvement, presenting results from the Danish longitudinal study (Table 5.2).

What emerges from Table 5.2 is a rather varied pattern, where in some situations, Danish fathers frequently interact with their babies, and in others, they do so more rarely:

- By far the most frequent form of contact is 'playing with the baby' – 77% play with their baby on a daily basis, and 17% do it often. No fathers say that they never play with their baby
- 48% 'change the baby's nappy' every day and 22% often, while 4% never do it
- 23% 'put the baby to bed' daily and 33% often, that is, they take part in the intimate task of settling a baby down for the night

Table 5.2 *Contact with baby*

	Daily %	Often %	Sometimes %	Never %	Reply %
a. Bathing the baby	8	30	44	17	99
b. Playing with the baby	77	17	5	0	99
c. Feeding the baby	30	21	26	22	99
d. Changing the baby's nappy	48	22	25	4	99
e. Putting the baby to bed	23	33	32	12	100
f. Getting up at night	8	11	36	44	99
N = 4,098					

Source: Based on Sommer, 2001

- 30% feed the baby every day and 21% often, that is, babies who are not exclusively breast-fed
- Only 8% 'bathe the baby' every day and 30% often
- Only 8% 'get up in the night' every night and 11% often.

When interpreting this relatively small number, it is important to remember that mothers in this study are on maternal leave and the fathers are not, so they still need to get up early in order to go to work. In addition, some (not all) mothers are still breast-feeding, therefore only the mother can feed the baby when (and if) they wake during the night. This indicates that a mixture of gender-based feeding procedures and/or 'temporal demands' may structure relatively traditional caring roles during the night.

The study shows that fathers often join the mother in *comforting a crying baby*. This is particularly important, as it requires the sensitivity and empathy inherent in personal care competencies. In the context of a caring relationship, calming the infant is important for the development of secure attachment and trust. The fathers' most frequent comforting strategies, which may occur in the same caring sequence, are (Sommer, 2001):

1. Lifting the baby up and holding against body
2. Talking to the baby
3. Giving the baby a dummy
4. Rocking the baby, in arms and/or bed.

Thus, fathers' caring in order to comfort his baby when crying is based on closeness and sensory stimulation:

1. close body contact
2. verbal contact

3. comforting by 'self-soothing'
4. rhythmic soothing.

The study shows that these methods are frequently used by mothers as well, with more breast-feeding instead of offering the dummy. Thus, if caring quality is based on what mothers typically prefer to do, the four paternal strategies in these families seem to be developmentally important.

Danish fathers, to some extent illuminating Scandinavian fatherhood, are in daily caring relationships with their infants in a number of ways. In accordance with recent theorizing, these relationships probably promote the child's early development, for example by gradually establishing an important attachment bond in the first six months of life. As seen previously, fathers are frequent playmates, but comforting a crying baby may serve as the litmus test in the practice of quality caring. Successfully being able to remove the fears and threats that make the infant cry may serve as a royal road to secure attachment to fathers.

In a Scandinavian context, with its culture of gender equality, this is also evident in the father–child relationship later on. Subsequent analysis documents that father involvement is relatively high and stable over time. In addition, fathers showed no gender-specific preferences in their caring and playing activities with girls and boys. Furthermore, father involvement was not associated, as might be expected, with educational level, an indication that the belief in gender equality has permeated society (Sommer, 2010). In a Scandinavian context, this new trend is supported by Haavind's (2006, p. 691) analysis of the new father phenomenon: 'At first the new father was a middle class phenomenon. Today there are no distinct signs that working class males are less involved in every daily chores with their children.'

It can be concluded that the ideal of the caring and involved father has, to some extent, become a reality in a Scandinavian context, more so than in other countries. This is not explained solely by changing gender beliefs, but by a complex array of interrelated factors. The unique interplay between Scandinavian families and the universal welfare society has been highlighted internationally (Esping-Andersen et al., 2003; UNICEF, 2007; Kamerman and Moss, 2009).

RESEARCH ON FATHER INVOLVEMENT

As part of the paradigm shift in developmental research, father involvement studies have flourished over the past 30 years. As documented in Chapter 2, children can, in principle, thrive by growing up with a wide diversity of experiences with individuals of both sexes. Recent research indicates that the child's social and cognitive competencies develop when the child grows up in close nurturing and trustworthy environments (Hrdy, 2009).

Furthermore, there is ample evidence of a child's early ontogenetic capacities to form multiple attachments and corresponding internal working models (Bretherton, 2005; Sagi-Schwartz and Aviezer, 2005; Howes and Spieker, 2008). So the infant and young child 'are ready' due to their potential and, in this paradigm, father involvement and its developmental consequences become appealing.

The stereotype of the instrumental father and the idealized all-important mother has been particularly strong in relation to the young child, and much of the first wave of father–child research explored this point in ontogeny. Like other pioneer research, father–child involvement research did not emerge in a cultural vacuum, but was influenced by the fact that it had to relate to the prevailing view that only the mother was competent. So maternal competence became the benchmark for evaluating fathers' early caring competence. Much energy was devoted to answering these two questions: Can fathers be said to be competent carers? Do fathers and infants form profound attachments? The answers have the potential to erode some stereotypes about the instrumental man, although they do not assess fathers on their own terms, but from a mother-centric point of view. To move beyond that, one would also have to view fathers as different from mothers, not merely as mother substitutes. This, however, sparks another question: Do fathers and their young children have a particular interaction style, for example play?

Paternal caring competence?

A Childhood Psychology agrees with the NICHD Early Child Care Network (2005) that most modern theories about early child development stress that, through interaction with their mothers and fathers, infants come to know these individuals and trust them as sources of emotional security and knowledge about the world. This group of extremely experienced researchers underline the importance of mothers, fathers and others in early child development. In order to qualify for this, however, some important caring skills are required. Here, the potential caring competencies of fathers are discussed, the focus being on quality rather than quantity.

Are the number of hours spent together synonymous with caring quality and competence? When looking at the amount of time that fathers and mothers spend with their young children on a daily basis, mothers still score higher in most families (Parke, 2002). An important distinction is often blurred, however, as in the rationale that says: 'Fathers do not have as much time to be with their children, so the contact between father and child is poor.' The debate about time allocation will be an issue that concerns couples, but if this is seen from a developmental perspective, the qualitative aspect of the adult–child relationship becomes essential. The definition of caring quality pointed to the ability to 'read' another person's mind. Furthermore, the ability to attune one's own reactions to the child's initiatives is crucial for establishing a lasting personal relationship with a child.

The rules are not simply that the more hours, the higher the quality, rather it is about engaged relationships. Research has demonstrated that many hours are not necessarily a good thing, as fathers forced to be carers because of job loss, and thereby with plenty of time to spend with their child, have a negative impact (Lamb, 2004). Following Parke's (2002) quality time argument, there is a lower time limit where the establishment of quality caring becomes impossible. With this in mind, are fathers able to be competent carers? From a pure mother-centric perspective, to leave a vulnerable, dependent infant in the hands of someone who is not by nature or experience prepared for this task may, for some, be seen as a game of chance. The answer to this question may offer an indication of the potential of early fathering. In fact, research has looked into exactly the qualitative aspects of the judgement of early father competence. This pioneer endeavour began around the mid-1970s and has now grown into a considerable body of research. The initial studies assumed a so-called 'micro-perspective' and explored the content and quality of actual interactions between fathers, babies, toddlers and young children.

Greenberg and Morris (1974) illuminated the profound effects that newborn babies have on their fathers. They use the term *engrossment* to describe the father's relationship to his baby, which describes the phenomenon that fathers participating in the birth of their child became completely absorbed and express strong emotional involvement – feelings of deep joy, awe and wonder. In their initial contacts with their newborn baby, most fathers were very attentive to the newborn's face, eye movements and activity level, and they kissed and gently stroked the baby's face. In other words, fathers spontaneously focused on the facial area that forms the basis of the baby's first social communication. It should be remembered from Field's (1990) pioneering study that babies are able to respond and imitate adults' facial expressions.

Studies of father competence find that fathers communicate with the child in a similar way to mothers when they are placed in a situation where care is expected of them. In addition, there is less specialization between mothers and fathers when fathers are alone with the infant. In situations like that, the full range of paternal caring behaviour that resembles the mother's is present (Lamb, 2004). On a theoretical level, quality caring and caring competence can be defined. On a more heuristic and practical level, however, if a quality blueprint is the typical maternal caring behaviour and the mother–infant relationship, it can be inferred that fathers typically seem to be competent carers (Pedersen, 1980; Parke, 1996, 2002; Day and Lamb, 2004a).

In terms of caring competence, successful bottle-feeding demands a host of fine-tuned relationships between the adult and the baby. Parke and

Sawin's (1976) first pioneering study observed father–infant interaction during bottle-feeding. The fathers adjusted to the infant's sucking rhythm and made subtle adjustments to match the child's sucking pattern, such as pausing in order to let the infant breathe. Fathers correctly understood when the child was full or when it was time to burp. The infant, lying calmly in the father's arms, actively responded with sucking, close eye contact and eventual babbling.

Although the situation of the father as the primary carer and the mother as the primary breadwinner is quite rare, Pruett (1983) documented high child wellbeing and development in this context. But although studies conclude that fathers have a high degree of competence, not all fathers may seem equally competent. Field (1978) studied fathers who she categorized as either 'primary' or 'secondary' carers. At that time, many fathers were, in fact, secondary carers due to being the primary breadwinners. Unsurprisingly, the findings showed that fathers who were the primary carer typically displayed a significantly higher degree of carer competence than fathers who were a secondary carer. This variation in male carer competence indicates that it is more of a function of experience and daily practice with an infant than an issue of gender. The example of the Aka fathers bears this out (Hewlett, 1992), as does Hrdy's (2009) investigation of the evolutionary advantages of having more carers than just mothers. If so, caring competence becomes an acquired skill that seems to be a case of 'practice makes perfect'. As documented previously, practice with caring (even with dolls) causes an increase in male hormonal production of oestrogen and prolactin, which in turn may influence fathers' nurturing behaviour.

However, research into father involvement has also shown that involvement per se is not necessarily positive for the child. Context is important, for example where negative life circumstances, such as a sudden loss of job, makes father involvement forced and perhaps not desired. Both research and real life offer examples of inadequate paternal carer competencies. Fatherhood has historically had two faces – the 'good dad–bad dad' complex. Pleck (2004) has researched this in various historical periods in the US, and highlights that the designations are dependent on what the dominant ideas of male and female roles in society and the family were at a specific time.

Studying inadequate male caring competencies may perhaps add to the 'bad dad' aspect, if higher father involvement is a more or less a hidden agenda. However, should a sharp gender role division be the preferred idea, such as where men are the primary breadwinners, inadequate paternal care competencies are not that devastating. In fact, underlying roles, beliefs and identities seem to influence the way fathers relate to their young children. This was first studied by Heath (1978), who observed a sample of *highly career-oriented fathers* in care situations. Compared to other fathers, they appeared significantly less attentive, less responsive and, in general, less competent in father–child relationships. For example, when in the same room with their child, they were responsible, but preferred mostly to be 'distant' from the child by reading the newspaper or watching TV. This not only points to an important link between work and family life, it also illustrates more specifically the important consequences of male attitudes and identity.

The fathers in this study strove to establish their career position in a workplace culture with little regard for children as a key part of male identity. Additionally, they were in a phase of their life where family and childcare made large and conflicting demands on their roles and involvement. These families appeared to 'resolve' this conflict through a gender-specific distribution of tasks. The fathers were not required to engage in childcare, they might once in a while have a supervisory function when the mothers were out of sight, and these fathers were relatively mentally absent in the presence of their children. Seen in a family dynamic perspective, this 'who-takes-care-of-what' arrangement depends on the complementary roles of the spouse. So the direct relationship between a father and infant is latently influenced by decisions and role negotiations stemming from the spouse. In addition, research shows that male networks, for example the attitudes of workplace colleagues, have an important influence on father involvement in both negative and positive ways (Riley, 1990).

Observational research has demonstrated that fathers can be nurturing and competent early carers. The quality of early father involvement, however, is modified by career factors, as well as gender role division, beliefs, social networks, male identity and role negotiations.

Father–child attachments and fathers as emotional guides

In Chapter 2, the multiple attachment paradigm and empirical research was introduced. In short, multiple attachments are not only an early human capacity. Both during the history of humankind and today in the late modern dual socialization configuration, it is the typical situation for many infants and young children. Here, father–child attachment research will be presented and conclusions drawn.

As demonstrated by Greenberg and Morris (1974), fathers show strong feelings of affection at the birth of their child, as captured by the term 'engrossment'. But do infants and young children form emotional bonds with their fathers?

In the 1970s, Lamb (1976b, 1976c, 1976d, 1977a, 1977b, 1980) conducted some groundbreaking studies by using the same procedures as when measuring mother–infant attachments, both in the laboratory and in the family setting. In non-stressed, family situations, an active father seems to be on an equal footing with the mother as an object of the child's affection. We see that the child's secure attachment with a father relies more on the quality of the relationship than the number of hours spent together. Admittedly, this was studied in relaxed, non-threatening settings, whereas real attachment develops in unfamiliar situations where the child becomes upset and starts to seek a secure base. Is father attachment relevant in these situations? It seems so. Father-attached children are significantly less anxious in unfamiliar situations than the monotropic mother-attached child.

Kotelchuck (1976) reviewed of a number of studies and concluded that under twos who have only been cared for by the mother show an intense crisis-like reaction when they are left alone with a stranger. Children who have also formed an attachment with their father, however, either do not protest at the separation, or do so to a lesser extent. For example, the transition to childcare seems less traumatic for the dual attached young child. From the child's perspective, they appear to be more secure when having more than one trusting attachment figure to rely on. This may also make it easier for the child to generalize and be open to making further attachments with others. It seems that the infant can distinguish between their various relationships with people, on the basis on the actual conventional way of being together (Stern, 2006). Thus, being with their father is sometimes like being with their mother and at other times is not. This is highlighted by Bretherton's (2005) discussion of the implications of Bowlby's working model concept of attachment relationships in light of recent longitudinal studies. In light of the fact that for many children early childhood is synonymous with multiple attachments, the possibility exists that the child can form both secure and insecure attachment relationships with various people, such as a secure attachment to the mother and an insecure one to the father or visa versa (not to mention attachment in childcare contexts). Interestingly, studies on fathers show that: 'two secure relationships predicted better child outcomes than two insecure relationships, with intermediate results when one parent–child relationship is secure and the other insecure' (Bretherton, 2005, p. 17).

In other words, a secure mother–infant attachment alone does not seem optimal for child development, whereas two secure relationships are, indicating the independent (positive/negative) influence of father–child attachment. In the formative early years, infants seem to construct an integrated self-model while participating in two (and more) qualitatively different attachment relationships in daily life. So one cognitive working model, storing memories and experiences of being with a father, may be developed as well as one model for being with a mother. Or perhaps a general attachment construct may be the case, but this is not known (Bretherton, 2005).

Another theme that negates the non-involved, instrumentalized male stereotype deserves attention, that of fathers as potential emotion regulating guides. Fathers who have established a close relationship with their children can play an independent role by influencing children's emotional competence. For instance, fathers' supportive dialogue regarding their five-year-old child's anger and sadness was connected to the child's social competence when they were eight. Children were likely to show anger and other negative emotions when they found themselves in stressful situations if their fathers were negatively affected and stressed when their children displayed negative affect or were controlling and directing in conflict situations. But children whose fathers were supportive and gave problem-solving guidance, with an emphasis on the child, handled stressful situations better. These children were described by nursery staff and teachers as non-disruptive/non-aggressive (Parke and O'Neil, 2000).

Furthermore, the next section will show that fathers play more physically with their small children than mothers do. This relatively strong physical interaction seems – when it is appropriate to the child's age and tempera-ment – to contribute to the young child's early control of emotions, underlin-ing the father's significance as an emotion guide for children. This research illuminates the role and potential of fathers in children's relationship learn-ing, especially the regulation of the emotional aspects of social relationships. Fathers seem to contribute to searching the limits of emotions because of the wide scope of emotional intensity, in addition to the unpredictable character of their special playing relationship (Parke and O'Neil, 2000). So the father's role in the family as an emotion guide and developer of children's social competencies is important – both positively and negatively. As regards the negative aspect, clear correlations have been found between fathers' style of bringing up children with behaviour problems: when fathers are predom-inantly critical, angry and controlling during everyday interactions, their children find it difficult to control their own negative feelings (Parke and O'Neil, 2000).

But is emotional regulation only linked to father involvement? One of the principle problems in studying whether mothers and fathers are separately important is this: they both seem to be. But to claim this without further argument is problematic. If a child thrives with an involved father, the rea-son may be that the relationship with the mother is good as well. Thus, we do not know if the father is important in himself. Another challenge has been that the study of fathers' importance has focused mainly on infants and less on older children. Amato (1994) has attempted to address both of these issues, by looking at the importance of the mother–child relationship and the father–child relationship in 471 adolescents. They were interviewed about their experiences of closeness to both parents, their psychological wellbeing, stress and general happiness. The study showed that, for adolescents, a close relationship to both parents was important to their psychological wellbeing and overall happiness. Even at a time when youngsters were distancing themselves from their parents, the sense of closeness remained intact.

Close relations to both a father and a mother also serve to reduce stress. Furthermore, it was interesting to note that both boys and girls were pos-itively affected by having a close relationship to their father. Thus, fathers matter not only to sons but to daughters as well. Independent of the relationship to the mother, an overall finding was that the closer young daughters and sons were attached to their father, the happier, more satisfied and the less stressed they were. Fathers, seemingly, make important and independent contributions to children's mental health (Amato, 1994).

It has been documented that males, in principle, are capable of providing care and forming close attachment relationships with infants and young children in a way that denies the one-dimensional image of the instrumental man. In addition, involved fathers appear to be important emotional regulators who guide their young children in how to balance emotions in everyday life encounters.

The playing father: a distinct paternal interaction style?

Although research indicates a range of similar behaviour patterns in fathers and mothers, there are differences as well, although there is a tendency that the more equality there is in family roles, the smaller the differences. In his review of the (limited) cross-cultural evidence of types of father involvement, Parke (2002) asks if there is a universal father play style. Parents in the US, England and Australia show gender differences in relation to play, whereas in Sweden and in Israeli kibbutz families, short-term observational studies seem to show no differences between the sexes. Other evidence from Chinese, Malaysian, Taiwanese and Thai mother and father self-reports indicate that they rarely engaged in physical play with their children. In Indian families in New Delhi, fathers (and mothers) are more likely to display affection while holding their infant rather than playing (Parke, 2002). This seems to show that father play is not a universal but rather a cultural phenomenon.

In Western families, the few examples of non-parental differences have been explained by the tendencies towards more 'egalitarian arrangements'. Yet this cannot explain why father play is a key characteristic of some egalitarian Western societies. For example, in equality oriented Danish families, 'father as a playmate' characterizes the father–infant relationship. Earlier, it was documented that in a sample of 4,000 Danish fathers, randomly selected from all socioeconomic levels and in full employment, 77% reported that they played 'daily' with their infants and 17% that they did it 'often'. No one said they 'never' played with their child, and only 5% did it 'sometimes'. In addition, an overwhelming majority of these fathers believed that their babies were 'active/eager' and 'keen for contact'; presumably a belief rooted in their numerous daily playful relationships full of humour and laughter. This indicates that despite emergent trends towards relatively more equality beliefs and roles in late modern dual-earner families (thus not accounting for all families or all cultures), the playing father still seems to stand out in some places as a distinct feature, showing that a father–child relationship is not simply an extension of the maternal relationship, because mothers are less involved in such types of play (Lamb, 2004).

With some cultural exceptions, from the very beginning of father involvement, studies point out that the two sexes offer the child different types of experiences, at least in Western societies (Lamb, 1976, 2000, 2004; Pedersen, 1980). Thus, in this context, and with some variations, fathers supposedly have a unique developmental role in the lives of infants and young children. *Idiosyncratic play* seems to be a characteristic developmental arena for the father and child, with the father being involved in physical, rough-and-tumble, imaginative play, far from the cool, distant, logical approach associated with the instrumentalized male role. Mothers predominantly seem to provide primary care in a more toned-down style, and when playing, they employ more culturally conventional games, such as peak-a-boo. Fathers' spontaneous engagement with children in a playful style is assumed to be developmentally important, as play during infancy is essential to the child's personality development (Lamb, 2004). Father–child play also appears to be important to the construction of a father's beliefs and his relationship with his spouse. The NICHD Early Child Care Research Network (2005) found that father sensitivity, when involved in play sessions, was higher when fathers held less traditional child-rearing beliefs, and reported more marital intimacy. The latter points to the fact that father involvement is not isolated, rather it is situated in and influenced by broader family system contexts.

CONCLUSION: FATHER INVOLVEMENT IN ITS BROADER CONTEXT

In child psychology, there has been a long tradition of studying mothers at the expense of fathers.[99] In this book, it has been labelled mother-centrism, but as demonstrated many times, this situation has changed considerably over the past few decades, partly because pioneering research has focused on father involvement. Although this has been necessary, there is not much progress in moving from one isolated dyad (mother–child) to another isolated dyad (father–child), albeit they have proved important to the child's development. Therefore, father involvement has to be seen in its broader context.

In Chapter 4, the family was portrayed as a complicated social and reciprocal system with various roles and relationships. Tetrads, triads and dyads were related on different levels, denoting that all family members have some impact on others and are themselves influenced by others. This also goes for the understanding of the mother's relative developmental influence on her children, as well as for the influence and importance of father involvement. The rule is simply that, although important, no one has the ultimate effect ιild's present and subsequent development. As reported earlier,)08), in a research review, concludes that longitudinal studies show that early types of attachment to the mother only explain 5% of later adult psychological functioning. Yet by taking multiple factors into consideration (among these mother and father influences), the probability for guessing how later development will turn out is markedly enhanced (Sameroff, 2000, 2006). This means that fathers (and mothers) are part of a family system, which makes it meaningless to judge whether the 'new involved father' is a threat to the mother role or whether a trend towards close fathering is 'better' or 'worse' than mothering. The gendered competitive question 'who is most important to the child?' will, in a systems approach, have to be answered with 'they both are' – in similar and different ways.

The challenge for future research is to enhance our understanding of how the family as a whole is constituted as a myriad of all participants' beliefs, interpretations and relationships. In addition, the family is influenced by external systems in society, culture and our rapidly changing times. Despite an emerging trend in some contexts towards more father involvement, men's 'marriage' to their jobs remains an important male identity rooted in deep-seated cultural gender codes. Furthermore, this 'marriage' has been strengthened in recent years, as countries adapt to rapidly changing global labour markets. In some respects, this may in the future lead to a 'fatherless society', where more men become job oriented, driven by external necessity and perhaps inner motivation. The future is hard to predict and while this may be an exaggerated perspective, there is little doubt that the role of the father has come under a great deal of pressure since the global financial crisis started in 2007–08. The consequences of this for families are unknown. However, the roles of fathers (and mothers) are influenced by historical and global changes (Parke, 2002; Lamb, 2004), and future research has to explain in which ways. Seen in the contextual perspective of *A Childhood Psychology*, research on father–child involvement is important, but insufficient if pursued in isolation.

6

EARLY EMERGENCE OF THE SELF: SOCIOAFFECTIVE COMPETENCIES

A revolution has happened in the understanding of humans' early manifestations of social and emotional competencies. A competent young child (not in absolute, but in relative terms) with a very early organized mind who lives in an expanded social and cultural world is the focus of this book. However, the paradigm shift highlighted in this book has, until now, been based mainly on extrapolations of groundbreaking empirical studies and the presentation of various conceptual models, rather than on a coherent developmental psychological theory. As mentioned previously, since the demise of the grand developmental era, a coherent, unifying understanding is rare and domain-specific theorizing and empirical work has dominated. Yet some have tried to contribute to a more comprehensive understanding, and in this chapter, leading individuals who have made new contributions have been selected.

Consequently, the focus is now on important recent psychological theorizing that has not only understood the consequences of the new paradigm, but also significantly contributed to it. Stern's (1985, 1991, 1995, 2004, 2006) pioneering and synthesizing theory about early development of self as a relationship product will function as a leading voice in this chapter, with an emphasis on the latest contributions.[100] Because *A Childhood Psychology* is not a typical textbook, but a long reflective argument, theory will not only be presented, it will also be discussed and evaluated in relation to the book's main endeavour: the understanding of young children who live in new contextual realities that have altered development in late modernity and challenged previous understandings.

In his theory, Stern tries to combine previously isolated professional traditions: the revolution in new research ('the observed child') with clinical practice and reflections ('the clinical child'). In so doing, he offers unique interpretations of humans' early social and experiential capacities; for example, that a sense of self is developed very early in life, before language is in place. This is in sharp opposition to the previously held idea that self presupposes and emerges with symbolic functioning. This chapter will demonstrate how the adoption of such a theory, supported by other selected thinkers, can be incorporated and 'visualize' the child competence paradigm in *A Childhood Psychology*.

As it is impossible to provide a comprehensive review of Stern's complex theory, this chapter presents Stern's thoughts about typical development, not the many implications for the theory of psychotherapy. Selected preverbal dimensions of the self will be addressed, that is, the period from birth to the age of seven to nine months, because in this area Stern has made particularly original contributions to our understanding of human development. Important aspects of the theory have to be omitted from this chapter, due to space constraints; one is the infant's perception of a subjective, verbal and narrative self. To remedy this, readers may turn to *The Interpersonal World of the Infant* (Stern, 2006). (For example, see the table on page 32 'Sense of the self'. Here all self-formation types are presented and related to age. On page 33, a model comprising all the domains of how the child is related to other people is presented.)

In the understanding of development, the gulf has clearly widened between psychotherapeutic, psychoanalytically oriented interpretations versus the type of developmental psychology that is based on behavioural research. For example, the classical psychoanalytical concept of the ultimately vulnerable child and the dominance of the ontogenetic past have been replaced by the relatively resilient and socioaffective competent child who lives in changing developing systems (Luthar, 2006; Masten, 2007). Stern is clearly positioned in this new orientation.

Furthermore, starting life with some basic socioaffective competencies (a spontaneous readiness for creating and participating in relationships) also indicates that influences other than what happens in ontogenesis are probably in play. In other words, the new paradigm builds on a markedly reshaped understanding of the evolutionary roots of human sociality (Tomasello, 2009).

WHERE DOES SOCIALITY COME FROM?: AN EVOLUTIONARY APPROACH

A Childhood Psychology is to a large extent inspired by recent research that combines *Homo sapiens'* history with the developmental relationship paradigm. Stern (2004) explains humans' deeply relational nature as the reason for *Homo sapiens'* success. This casts doubt on the pseudo-Darwinian idea that the strong male with his dominant aggressive genes is supposedly the reason why the human species has survived. Instead, the small group and its psychosocial relationships are presented as the explanation for the human species' evolutionary advantages. The strong dominant individual existed in the primeval tribe, but their position is hard to understand without a theory about humans' original social and relational nature. According to Turner (2000), power and status only occur, in principle, in a hominid group if it is to the advantage of the group. The basis for social hierarchies therefore needs to be found in cooperative status rather than in muscular individuals' brutal fight for power within the group.

Stern (2004) describes human beings as the most hypersocial and independent of all mammals, which reflects his discovery of new research: Trevarthen's empirically based theory about human beings' innate primary intersubjectivity and amazingly early ability to enter into so-called 'protoconversations' has revolutionized our perception of the hereditary foundation of relationships (Trevarthen and Aitken, 2001). The child's ability to enter into relationships was traditionally considered as something that only occurs through socialization.[101] According to this view, relationship competence is solely an acquired social ability. However, in light of more recent research, there are now substantial reasons to claim that basic communicative skills are to some extent innate (Trevarthen and Aitken, 2001). A Childhood Psychology's view on where 'the sense of relationship' originates from is inspired by this perspective on phylogenesis – the human source of primary social competence. But how far back in the species' history do we have to look in order to find the origins of this?

Fogel (2004) outlines this in 'The History (and Future) of Infancy'. Human beings originate from a small population of hunter-gatherers. There are indications that the population has its origins either in the Pleistocene period in Africa more than 1.5 million years ago, or from several groups developed independently of each other in different parts of the world.[102] Homo sapiens hunter-gatherers came into existence about 100,000 years ago. About 35,000 years ago, groups of Homo sapiens sapiens hunter-gatherers had spread over Europe and Asia. In this period, a 'community' consisted of small groups of around 25 individuals, who sustained life by hunting and collecting wild plants and roots.[103] Generations lived their whole life within this small sphere of people in a relatively small area. The hunter-gatherer culture is believed to have been the only type of human society throughout the Pleistocene period. Unfortunately, these people left no trace to indicate how they raised their children (Wenke, 1990). Bowlby (1969) has, in his theory about attachment, called the human, ecological context during this long period the 'environment for evolutionary adaptation'. In the Pleistocene environment, the care relationship developed as a strong emotional parent–child relationship over a million years. This was a necessary adaptation to a dangerous environment where there was a constant threat from predators.

As the reproduction of the species maintains the survival of the next generation, the development of emotional ties in the small group was apparently
an effective way of ensuring this. The small tightknit community could not
function as a unit unless individuals developed socially sensitive competencies, so the development of the ability to read other people's verbal and
nonverbal expressions and signals, positive/negative facial expressions and
friendly/intimidating physical attitudes was useful (Tomasello, 2009).

As individuals, humans were relatively defenceless and the group func-
tioned as a safe haven. Individuals who searched for food and shelter on the
savannah and in the jungle were constantly in danger. As compensation for
our weak physique, the brain gradually developed and made possible planning, understanding symbols (language) and other advanced mental capacities.[104] According to Dunbar (1998), socioemotional factors played a direct
role in the development of humans' cognitive abilities. In addition, there was
the invention and use of tools for hunting and everyday chores (artefacts and
primitive technology), which significantly increased the chances of survival
and reproduction (Cole, 1996). The offspring's observation and imitation of
adults was the beginning of culture, that is, transferring traditions and habits
from one generation to the next. As a compensation for humans' inferior
physique and other deficiencies, the species' chances of survival were guaranteed through the development of a number of social abilities. The ability
to read the intentions and emotions of others makes possible an extremely
flexible coordination of group communication and actions. Within the
group, the ability to have fast and easy communication, through the use
of intentional movements, signals and language, improves the group's effi-
ciency and capability to act, that is, its ability to adapt (Stern, 2004).

According to *A Childhood Psychology*, humans are the social species par
excellence, directed at social contact from the beginning. As seen in Chapter
2, even the disposition to enter into relationships seems innate.[105] This foundation is not learned but must be maintained, extended and refined in the
child's long developmental process.

Anthropological and intercultural studies have documented humans'
ability to adapt to a multitude of situations – maybe they should be called
Homo opportunus? Humans' pronounced predisposition for sociality and their
sense of relationships are difficult to understand without including humans'
unique openness and adaptation to close and distant situational conditions.
So a small community consisting of strong, inner-controlled individuals –
equipped with fixed personality traits – would hardly have been very
adaptively functional.[106] After his lifelong research into human social psychology, Zimbardo (2004) concludes that humans are so incredible that they
can adapt to any imaginable external environment to survive, create and
destroy, if necessary. Humans are not born with the tendency to do either
good or bad, but with a capacity to do both, more amazingly and more
destructively than ever before. Only by acknowledging that the individual

is not an island, but that we are all a part of the same common human life conditions will humility precede unfounded pride in recognition of our vulnerability when faced with situational forces (Zimbardo, 2004).

But how does the potential for destruction go together with the fundamental assumption of the evolutionary (and actual) primacy of human sociality? This is a complex question to answer, but in dealing with why we cooperate, Tomasello (2009) has a point. The growing acceptance among recent evolutionary thinkers about the primacy and survival benefits of being social make it crucial to explain the fact that the history of humankind is infused with cruelty and destructiveness. The 'in-group' versus 'out-group' mentality may be an explanation:

> Of course, humans are not cooperative angels; they also put their heads together to do all kinds of heinous things. But such deeds are not usually done to those inside 'the group'. Indeed, recent evolutionary models have demonstrated what politicians have long known: the best way to motivate people to collaborate and think like a group is to identify an enemy and charge that 'they' threaten 'us'. (Tomasello, 2009, p. 99)

Interestingly, and somewhat paradoxically, asocial and even cruel behaviour towards others is explained as a consequence of the fundamental social nature of humans. The deep wish to belong to a group activates actions against those who, whether a reality or not, are assumed to threaten this. Today, humans live predominantly in small groups and in social situations. Family, work, friends and other groupings involve several prototypical purposes and activities, usually within the framework of acceptable behaviour. Even an isolated individual's thoughts and life may be strongly influenced by groups. To stay outside a community requires that an individual masters a number of 'social avoidance strategies', that is, they influence social relations in such a way that it leads to social exclusion.[107]

To accept the basic idea that nature has equipped the human child with a particular social directionality has consequences for a professional understanding of relationships. It is hardly a relationship if nature/nurture is perceived as a polarity. Discussion has sometimes unproductively focused on whether this or that human trait is either innate or acquired.[108] It seems to be both/and. Recent research on infants has shown that basic innate sociality and primary relationship competencies both organize and open up infants' ways of interacting with adults. Stern (2006) has called this a 'human alphabet'. Infants respond – spontaneously and in harmony with the situation – with their body and gestures to their mother's social invitations. Furthermore, infants become – as proved in the 'blank face' study – frustrated when their mothers do not react to their interaction initiative. Thus, the child quickly expects 'give-and-take' patterns with another person (Meltzoff and Moore, 1998; Trevarthen and Aitken, 2001). It is still debatable whether such studies are actual proof that basic innate social predispositions organize early interaction. If not, then this must be a very early and fast ability to learn to enter into harmonious relations.

FROM PSYCHOANALYSIS TO DEVELOPMENTAL PSYCHOLOGY: STERN'S THEORY OF SELF

Stern's theoretical journey is a rare professional example of a start in classical psychoanalytic circles and a move to developmental psychology, still as a psychotherapist. His journey is not only a vivid example of the paradigm shift that happened at the same time, but also a contribution. Metatheory of psychoanalysis, with its developmental implications, has become noticeably weakened over the past few decades as a result of new child research from many disparate sources. The discrepancies between the 'research child' and the 'psychoanalytic child' have become more and more obvious, a situation Stern has greatly contributed to. Thus, it would be difficult to assess Stern's unique influence on developmental psychology without addressing the major disagreements within the theoretical field of psychoanalysis that he is also rooted in. It has provided him with ideas and inspiration, but in many ways he has also abandoned it. As has been repeatedly demonstrated in this book, in the history of child psychology and other disciplines, experts have offered clear examples that conceptualizations reflect underlying time-specific and culture-specific ideological perceptions of the child. According to Stern (2006), particularly strong criticism has been raised against the ideological, mythological and inherently normative character of psychoanalysis. On vital points, Stern diverges strongly from psychoanalysis, which makes his critique of classic psychoanalytic theory, especially Mahler's, particularly important. Seen in a broader perspective, this debate goes to the very heart of the 'true nature' of the infant and young child.

Classical psychoanalytical theory, together with more recent object relations theory, regards the first years of life as particularly crucial; here, the infant is sensitive to internal impressions (fantasy), and infancy, in particular, is characterized by absolute dependency and lack of any cognitive and individual social processing (Klein, 1952; Freud, 1963; Mahler and Fuhrer, 1968; Mahler et al., 1975). In relation to Stern, Mahler is especially interesting. According to Mahler, the separation of self and environment gradually takes place through the first year of life, starting with a fused relationship with the mother. Like most psychoanalysts after Freud, Mahler was not interested in the progressive character of the developmental process, but bases much of her work on interpretations of adults' childhood memories – the regressive stance. This method departs from a scientifically based child and developmental psychology, whose primary focus is to describe and explain prospective changes in ontogenesis. Mahler's *separation-individuation* theory (the individual's gradual psychological separation from another person) rests on the following developmental sequence (Mahler and Fuhrer, 1968; Mahler et al., 1975): the infant progresses from a normal symbiotic phase in which they perceive themselves as one with their mother within the larger environment, to an extended phase (separation-individuation), which consists of stages in which the infant slowly comes to distinguish themselves from their mother, and then, by degrees, discover their own identity, will and individuality. These are some speculative premises concerning child development:

1. In the first few weeks, the infant is in a 'normal autistic' stage, with no self-organizing or self-perceiving processes.[109]
2. This stage is maintained by a 'stimulus barrier' – surrounding the child as a cocoon which protects it from all environmental stimuli.
3. The infant lacks the competence to distinguish between itself and others.
4. The infant's entire 'psychological birth' (epistemologically, emotionally and socially), the separation-individuation phase, develops from the symbiotic relationship between mother and infant. The infant's early development is characterized as being one with the mother.
5. The earlier a negative experience occurs, the more potential harm. Infancy is a critical period for all later development.
6. The human infant is a particularly at-risk organism. Hence, the key professional words of early development are dependency, vulnerability, trauma, harm, deficiency and protection.

In light of overwhelming new research, the above fundamental perceptions of the infant can be identified as a 'psychoanalytic projection of the infant' stemming from the pre-paradigm period. In other words, a child who exists in the eyes of the beholder, but rarely in reality. Stern (2006) differs substantially from Mahler on the above key points and thus departs from the classic psychoanalytical child interpretative filter. He points out that a stimulus barrier obviously does not exist and that if 'normal autism' (a term Mahler later abandoned) means that a baby does not register any external stimuli, then recent data indicates that this is not so. And 'the capacity to have merger- or fusion-like experiences as an adult is only secondary to and dependent upon an already existing sense of self and other' (Stern, 1985, p. 70).

Peterfreund (1978) and Cushman (1991) point to the historical fact that the metapsychology of psychoanalysis grew out of a 19th-century vitalist, biological and scientific paradigm. As a consequence, fundamental child beliefs are rooted in a period that puts the child in the 'Procrustean bed', as introduced in Chapter 1. Used in a contemporary context, however, such an interpretative filter fails to explain recent interdisciplinary insights about the infant. Stern argues in the same vein. Empirical infant research has contributed with such overwhelming knowledge about early emerging capacities of sociality, cognition and emotion that the fantasy-ridden, cut-off-from-the-world infant of psychoanalysis has been replaced by a baby engaged with the outer world from the beginning of life. In his criticism of the classic psychoanalytical stance on development, Stern (2006) notes the following major problems:

- Psychoanalytical theories on development carry a heavy legacy from Freud, in that development is assumed to take place in *stages*; not only being a specific stage in the development of ego and super-ego from id but a specific phase is also closely connected to specific risks of developmental deficiencies (oral, anal, phallic phase disturbances).
- In the construction of individual ontogenesis, psychoanalysis works backwards in time by using the so-called retrospective clinical method. This approach encourages adults to recall suppressed childhood experiences. So in order to understand a human being in the present, previous experiences and past events are the principal developing agents.
- Psychoanalysis, in essence, depicts 'normal development' by extrapolating this from a psychopathology theory. For example, with a quirky form of logic, Mahler assumed that severe mental disorders in adults (for example 'pathological' autism) had their roots in typical childhood phases where these problems were a completely normal part of development ('normal' autism). Thus, disorders of the adult mind are, by their nature, 'infantile', being involuntary regressions to childhood.

However, to base our understanding of normal childhood development on classic psychoanalytical premises leads to what Peterfreund (1978) labelled 'adultomorphic thinking', by which he meant that adult characteristics are attributed to infants and young children. In addition, assumed theoretical constructs drawn from descriptions of mentally ill adults are thought to offer valid information about early childhood development. Despite the fact that the existing phenomenon of preverbal amnesia (our inability to recall experiences from our preverbal period) implies that early infancy is the least accessible territory for a clinician to grasp, psychoanalysis (and Mahler) bases a preverbal stage theory on an adult perspective. In other words, Mahler's infant becomes adultomorphic, a 'projection screen' for adult life problems and themes. Such thinking is also an example of what, in Chapter 1, was called a pure top-down approach in developmental psychology.

In addition, such a conceptual fallacy may be characterized as an example of the 'pathologization of childhood'. But it is difficult to derive the principles of normal developmental processes based on developmental deficiency and deviation. This transferability is questionable because a population of people with mental disorders can hardly be assumed to be typical of a population without disorders. The vulnerability versus resilience research supports this point. Particularly vulnerable children (and adults) are more likely to develop disorders than the more resilient, in other words, different individuals have different stress thresholds (Masten and Gewirtz, 2006; Sameroff, 2007). Hence, knowledge derived from experience and practice with individuals in therapy is not to be generalized to general developmental principles. Furthermore, psychopathological theories descend into developmental reductionism by emphasizing only conflict-sensitive themes. In so doing, a carer's (mother's) primary role is shaped, making her the prime *protector* against potential dangers and one that should shield her infant's contact with the environment. Non-conflict-ridden themes, for example the joyful experience of father–infant play, and several others that should be considered more relevant to our understanding of normal developmental processes are ignored.

As introduced in Chapter 1, until the 1960s, the perception of children's development was dominated by psychoanalytical thinking. So does Stern offer a real departure from psychoanalysis? It may be relevant to include the 'social constructivist debate' between Cushman (1991) and Stern (2006) in order to answer this question. Cushman (1991) criticizes Stern for simply seeking to 'modernize psychoanalysis' by giving it its much needed scientific legitimization through observational research studies. In addition, Stern is criticized for not considering the possibility that his theory is more of a cultural construction (a narrative) than objective science. The latter point will be pursued later, but does Stern only adapt psychoanalysis to modern times? No, he doesn't; Cushman (1991) misses three crucial points in his characterization of Stern's work in contrast to classical psychoanalysis:

1. Unlike the psychoanalytical approach, Stern's departure is to describe and explain typical, normative self-development and then let these insights form the reference point for the understanding of pathogenic forms – not the other way around as psychoanalysis does.
2. He has a view of development by applying a prospective rather than a retrospective stance. Thereby, he is in line with recent non-clinical developmental psychology.
3. Drives and non-conscious fantasies are not viewed as the sine qua non of development; this role is attributed to the infant's interpersonal relations and experiences in real-life interactions. Consequently, mental representations of the mind are reality-oriented products, not innate fantasies.

These three key properties (and more) fully secure Stern's position as one of the few psychoanalysts in the field of contemporary child and developmental psychology.

From a purely empirical point of view, some behavioural researchers may consider the self a dubious concept – perhaps even a 'mentalist fiction' (Nyborg, 1994). Admittedly, Stern's concepts of the sense of self and the preverbal experience of mental coherence, organization and structure are hypothetical constructs based on his therapeutic knowledge and rather bold interpretations of observations of infants. In this sense, the theory clearly has an imaginative touch and is in need of empirical support. However, a multitude of new ways of studying the infant and young child, previously unthinkable, have become available. In addition, current standard text-books on child and developmental psychology state that self-development holds a key position in the discipline (for example Berk, 2009). But the recent studies and theorizing within cross-cultural and contextualist research (see Bornstein, 2010) are hardly represented in Stern's theory, perhaps limiting it to a Western theory of self-development rather than a universal one. As will be discussed later, this raises some problems for the theory.

Preverbal selves: early socioaffective competencies

Stern's main intention is to obtain insight into an infant's subjective experi-ence, and he pursues this by making the *sense of self* the focal point (Stern, 2006). Even though cognition plays an important role in the infant's psycho-logical development, Stern does not situate himself in a cognitive tradition. With his emphasis on the self as a sense, a subjective experience, he is closer to phenomenology. If the sense of self as subjective organization is the cen-tral aspect of the self, then thinking and memory may still be necessities, but they will not appear as such to the infant. Self is sensed, not reflected upon. Cognitions, actions and perceptions related to the self do not, as such, exist for an infant. All experiences become recast as patterned constellations of the infant's basic subjective experience.

In order to see the uniqueness in this way of arguing, a classical defini-tion of the self may be appropriate. Here self is a conscious phenomenon, an idea that is philosophically rooted in rationalism. Self is an expression that is used to describe when experience or consciousness takes on a reflective character, as when one is aware that one is aware. In other words, there must be a thinking person, and traditionally the self emerges with the capacity for symbolic representation that allows for metacognition. Even within a phenomenological orientation ('awareness'), this clearly places self within a cognitive tradition. In addition, self does not emerge from the begin-ning of life; by definition, the self cannot be a part of the preverbal mind. Stern differs radically from this classical view of the 'self as self-reflection' and 'awareness-of-awareness'. Instead, his definition of the self positions it as subjective existence, intentionality and as a very early organization of the mind. The infant's self is seen as a *pervading attention pattern* evident in the infant's actions and mental processes. Spending time with a young infant soon makes it clear that social exchange is not only governed by the adult, the child is actively focused, for example through eye contact. Early imitation of facial expressions together with the infant's coordinated social responses also point to some kind of an inner organizer of attention and behaviour. The pervading attention pattern exists long before the infant becomes aware of being aware.

Consequently, an infant does not process the environment in a random or chaotic manner, but possesses a very early form of organization. Here the paradigm of the competent child is clearly in contrast to previous ideas that a baby is born only with reflexes, a 'blank slate' or driven by innate 'impulses'. The organizing subjective experience is the preverbal, existential counterpart to the objectifiable, self-reflective self. Thus, the self exists long before the development of conscious self-awareness, and the self is present in multiple ways as an intuitive, preconscious mental activity. According to Stern (2006), emergent, preverbal forms of self can be identified from observation of the infant's patterned behaviours right from birth (and probably in the later periods of gestation) – an assumption that clearly sets Stern apart from other theorists (for example the Mead tradition, see Mead 1934), and even from the tradition within recent developmental psychology (Berk, 2009).

A common notion – based on symbol function as necessary for self-development – is that language creates the self as a reflective activity (Damon and Hart, 1991). Without language, there is no self-development, which means that self and language development are twin aspects of the same process. Stern's (2006) argument is radically different: neither self-reflection nor language are the source of the most basic parts of the self. But self-reflection and language may be important tools in the child's 'self-disclosing' and 'self-transforming'. For example, for a four-year-old, language gradually makes metacognition possible. This in turn enables the child to think of themselves as someone who is thinking, thus being in better conscious contact with one's self. Language and self-reflection emerge long after the child has established a coherent experience of a self. The later emerging verbal self, however, can to some extent be helpful in the unpacking and transforming of the subconscious senses of self that exist preverbally. However, language can also alienate and dissociate experiences formed in the period before language – precisely because of their preverbal mental organization in memory.

Stern (2006) views the infant's sense of being both *separate* and *autonomous* (against the background of togetherness with others) as an early characteristic of the self. He also assumes that this infant actively and wilfully is engaged in the environment from a very early age. So early, in fact, that autonomy cannot be seen as emerging in accordance with a specific developmental stage, as claimed by Erikson (1950, 1972). Autonomy utterances by a baby are clearly different from those of a toddler, being in the 'no' mode. For example, turning the head away in order to avoid intrusive interaction with a non-attuned father may be a sign of early autonomy. This is one of many examples of how Stern departs from classical stage theorizing. Instead, he advocates a layered model:

> In contrast to the conventional stage model(s) whereby each successive phase of development not only replaces the preceding one but also essentially dismantles it, reorganizing the entire perspective, the layered model postulated here assumes a progressive accumulation of the senses of the self, socio-affective competencies and ways-of-being with others. No emerging domain disappears; each remains active and interacts dynamically with all the others. (Stern, 2006, p. xi)

Sharing some similarities, although not identical to the notion of parallel mental processing – for example that infants own two different, parallel mental systems for making sense of the different laws that govern the physical and the social world – this idea of layered development is clearly a radically new way of understanding human ontogenesis.

Just as the layered model is a critique of stage models, so is Stern's concept of *life themes*. Life themes may occur throughout the life span in varying qualitative expressions, without necessarily taking on particular importance at any given stage. An infant who voluntarily directs the adult's attention by protoconversational pointing is just one example of an active, independent action occurring long before the occurrence of Erikson's autonomy stage. As a life theme, autonomy is not specific stage that disappears with age. In old age, for example, autonomy may be a fight to maintain personal dignity in a situation where disability may demand institutionalized care.

By defining the self primarily as a relatively autonomous entity (although in relationship with others), Stern does not deal much with whether this relatively sharp boundary between the self and the environment is a historically and culturally specific phenomenon. It is seen rather as a universal phenomenon:

> The self and its *boundaries* are at the heart of philosophical speculation on human nature, and the sense of self and its *counterpart*, the sense of other, are *universal phenomena* that profoundly influence all our social experiences. (Stern, 2006, p. 5, emphases added)

Furthermore, Stern presents the self as a coherent inner mind entity:

> There is the sense of a self that is a single, distinct, integrated body; there is the *agent* of actions, the *experiencer* of feelings, the *maker* of intentions, the *architect* of plans, the *transposer* of experience into language, the *communicator* and *sharer* of personal knowledge. (Stern, 2006, p. 5, emphases added)

In the first definition, self is seen as a counterpart to the sense of others, thus perhaps inadvertently downplaying the important relationships between them and the salience of others in self-development. In addition, this is seen as a universal phenomenon. In the second clarifying definition, the self as actor is dominant, with many active names given (see italics). (As will be discussed later in more detail, it is somewhat problematic that the above defined self is clearly intended to be synonymous with the 'Western self' and not necessarily a universal feature.) However, some aspects of the self – especially in infancy – seem to be universal, for example the body's importance to the formation of a self. This idea of the *embodied self* is added to Stern's new introduction in *The Interpersonal World of the Infant* (2006). Here, the sense of self is not anchored in history and culture but to some extent in the body. Where the body is located becomes the point of departure for the perceiving person. An African and a European infant in a cot (or a culturally similar artefact) experience the features of the room quite differently from when they are carried around by an adult. This embodiment probably represents related biological mind features of self-formation that apply to all humans (Fogel, 1993).

Furthermore, as a universal given, it will be assumed that people in all cultures and historical eras sense and perceive 'a self' (with more or less reflection) as some sort of coherent organization of sensations, emotions and acts. It will be discussed later how and to what extent culture influences self with regards to the boundaries and the degree of individual autonomy.

Amodal perception and vitality affects

Does a baby have a self at birth and during the first few months of life? Contrary to common theory of self, Stern argues that this is indeed the case: around the age of two months, the infant gradually develops a sort of emergent sense of self and others. Not a firm, stable core but a sense of having motivations for action and an interest in exploring the world – testing it. This view is quite different from the structuralist Piagetian tradition (1977), which seeks to explain development as a *product* of integrative and organizing processes. In this tradition, various sensations are thought to be integrated and coordinated by practice and subsequently combined to form a more comprehensive perspective (cf. Piaget's concept of the sensorimotor stage).[110] In contrast to this view, Stern emphasizes the *process*: the infant does not simply use an organization that has already been formed, but instead senses the formation process itself. Here, two ways of organizing experiences are particularly important: amodal perception[111] and vitality affects.

The concept of *amodal perception* positions Stern (2006) squarely in opposition to the notion of sensation as modality specific (for example that the infant's visual impressions have no connection to tactile impressions). Amodal perception refers to the baby's ability to transfer experiences from one sensory modality to another during the first weeks of life. The following example may serve to explain what amodal perception is. In their revolutionary study, Meltzoff and Borton (1979) gave 29-day-old babies a dummy (without letting them see it) to suck, either one with a rough nipple or one with a smooth nipple. Afterwards, the babies were presented with big coloured pictures of the two dummies. The babies spent significantly longer looking at the dummy they had sucked on, suggesting that even very young babies are capable of transferring information from one sensory modality to another. In this example, experience from the oral tactile sense about texture was transferred to vision. Meltzoff and Borton (1979, p. 404) draw some far-reaching conclusions from their study:

> A basic assumption of Piagetian theory is that infants begin life with independent sense modalities that gradually become intercoordinated with development. Our findings, however, show that neonates are already able to detect tactual-visual correspondences, thereby demonstrating an impressive degree of intermodal unity.

The crucial point is that repetitive sensory-specific practice, where the baby builds and integrates schemata, by seeing, sucking, touching and perhaps even hearing the dummy's ring clicking – is not necessary. Infants recognize the dummy whose texture they had previously only explored with their mouths. Traditional theory of the acquisition of knowledge about the physical world, which states that cognitive schema are established through sensorimotor operations on objects, is unable to explain this phenomenon, as the infants had no previous experiences to link tactile sensations to visual information. Stern's bold thesis is that the infant has the ability to switch back and forth between the sensory modalities (such as touch, vision, hearing), and that this is an innate competence (Stern, 2006). Stern points to the surprisingly early occurrence of amodal perception as circumstantial evidence for the notion that the capacity is innate. Nevertheless, the early ability to switch between more sensory modalities does seem to be reasonably well founded. For example, the ability to transfer between hearing and sight (audiovisual transfer) seems to be present in babies who are only a few weeks old (Berk, 2009). Furthermore, infants appear to be particularly sensitive to timing, for example the sense of the temporal choreography of interactions (see the section Care as synchrony and attunement in Chapter 4). This remarkably early competence to sense temporal patterns may explain why even very young infants are able to engage in finely attuned and synchronized sequences of events with their carers – a phenomenon of key interest to developmental theory.

According to Stern, there are two organizing principles from the beginning of life of how we form experiences: *perceptual unity* and the *supramodality* of experiences. Perceptual unity means that human infants perceive their environment as sensory wholes. This relies not only on the ability to transfer between sensory modalities but also on the global nature of sensations.

The supramodal nature of sensory experiences refers to the idea that sensory experiences are stored as abstract versions of *sensory qualities*. A sensory experience is not only related to a particular sensation (for example a visual impression) but should be understood as a holistic essence. Sensations, therefore, consist of all the activated senses, which merge to form an experience. In interactions with others, the perception of *intensity* (the emotional dynamics of social events), the *holistic nature of shapes and persons* (for example that mother is not a breast but a person), and *temporal regularities* are three examples of sensory qualities that organize infants' experiences of their environment.

This point of view has radical implications. Not only does it negate Piaget's theory on the integration of separate parts of experience (cognitive schemas) through sensorimotor practice and coordination, but psychoanalytical theory is also rejected, including Klein's (1952) assumption of the 'good' or 'bad' breast. Infants do not originally perceive their parents as partial objects, but as complete persons (gestalts), who are able to express a range of affects, not just being categorically good or bad.

The time from birth until around two months is strongly influenced by the infant being in an *affective domain*. Describing the principles of how sensations work for humans who perceive the world is the subject of study for perception psychology. Yet dealing with perception and sensation without the accompanying, perceived affective qualities is more an expression of a scientific conceptualization than a real expression of how an infant's mind works. Stern suggests that the self as a subjective sense originally springs from infant emotion, that is, an 'affective core' containing fleeting moods and tones and this should be seen as a precursor of the self. This should not be understood as a reference to innate fantasies in a classic psychoanalytical way, as Stern is a 'naturalist'. Instead, it refers to very early emotions that feed on and are orchestrated by real-life experiences in relationships with others.

Research into affects and emotions in infants has seen a renaissance in recent decades. Radical research suggests that infants are born with the capacity to express *categorical affects* (for example anger, joy, discomfort, comfort, sadness) (Berk, 2009). During development, these basic affects are intermingled with social experiences, which add differentiation and nuance to the infant's repertoire of basic emotions. Interestingly, this type of research has uncovered basic emotions even in newborn babies. The problem is, however, that our knowledge of basic emotions does not address a large number of more subtle important emotions. More or less fleeting moods and tones account for important parts of the experiential worlds of adults and children alike. An adult's experience of a sunset, a Beethoven symphony, a rock concert, love-making or a walk in a wood can activate a range of fleeting emotional qualities that it would be difficult to call categorical affects. Stern (2006) uses the term *vitality affects* to describe such complex emotional qualities in human experience, for instance those evoked in the infant in connection with changes in motivation, appetite, arousal and personal relations. Some everyday dynamic terms capture the character of the vitality affects that can be present in the infant, for example surging, fading away, fleeting, explosive, crescendo, decrescendo (Stern, 2006). In *The Diary of a Baby* (Stern, 1991), a beautiful sequence of varying vitality affects is described – going from an almost physically painful hunger storm to a blissful state of satiety. Together, six-week-old Joey and his mother create vitality affects by performing a well-choreographed pas de deux through their cooperative efforts to still Joey's hunger. One example of a vitality affect may be the rush of anticipation in Joey when his mother responds to his hunger cries by unbuttoning her blouse.

Vitality affects are essential to our understanding of the earliest development of the self in humans. Together with amodal perception, vitality affects form the infant's early ways of organizing self experiences. The social and physical world seems to be perceived with a myriad of changing moods and emotional tones by the infant until there is a gradual understanding of the regularities that characterize the world. The role of vitality affects in the organizing efforts of the self are further evident in the way that they can function as a sort of 'common currency': vitality affects are able to connect even very different events if they arouse a similar affect in the infant. Thus the 'rush' of anticipation comes not only from the mother in feeding her baby, but may be activated in other social situations and link otherwise unrelated events, with the vitality affect as the common denominator.

EMERGENT SELF AND CORE SELF: PRIMARY CONSCIOUSNESS AND THE SENSE OF CONSTANCY AND TOGETHERNESS

From birth until approximately two months, a baby's sense of self and the world is organized by their sense of an *emergent self*. In his revised theory, Stern now acknowledges that even at this very early time of life, there is a sort of primary consciousness – a revolutionary idea in comparison to earlier assumptions of human nature. But which type of consciousness is it? Primary consciousness is not self-reflective, not verbalized and only lasts during a 'present moment' that is 'lived now' (Stern, 2004; 2006, p. xvii). Posture, muscle tone, proprioceptive feedback, activation and affects (vital background input from the body) are sensed by the infant as a kind of background music, the affective dimensions of which are vitality affects. This is a part of the emergent self, or protoself, but can also be linked to a state of mind in the mode of present awareness. The early mind is characterized as 'having' an intentional object. The intentional object is whatever the mind is 'stretching towards', that is, what the infant notices here and now. Thus primary consciousness consists of connecting the intentional object and the vital body input in a present moment (Stern, 2006).

Around the age of two months, so many changes happen that the period from two to six months represents perhaps the single biggest change in the human life span. Infants now increasingly engage in interpersonal relations that make them feel as if there is an 'integrated sense of themselves as a distinct and coherent body, with control over their own actions, ownership of their own affectivity, a sense of continuity and a sense of other people as distinct and separate interactants' (Stern, 2006, p. 69). In the active co-creation of an interpersonal world, the infant forms a sense of a *core self* and *core others*.

The core self as a sense of separation is closely linked to senses of *constancy*, called 'self-invariants'. With just a glance, the external environment seems shifting, complex and confusing. A key tendency of the human mind is to counteract this with bringing in some kind of orderliness. Infants readily display the tendency to put some order into the world by seeking invariants.

Self-invariants

Stern emphasizes four relatively invariant experiences as crucial to the creation and maintenance of the infant's sense of a core self:

1. *Self-agency:* the self as the author of action. This aspect relates to the infant's experience of being the volitional source of communication with others; a sense of being in control of actions that originate from the infant. Thus, activity and volition are fundamental aspects of the function of the core self.
2. *Self-coherence:* the self as a sense of coherence. 'What are the invariant properties of interpersonal experiences that may specify that the self versus the other is a single, coherent, bounded physical entity? And what are the infant's capacities to identify them? Without a sense of self and other as coherent entities unto themselves, a sense of a core self or core other would not be possible, and agency would have no place of residency' (Stern, 2006, p. 82). Some experiential features contribute to establishing a sense of self-coherence:
   - *unity of locus* – infants can tell that others' behaviour comes from somewhere other than their own behaviour.
   - *coherence of motion* – things that move together in time probably belong together, for example a person seen moving through the room or observed against a stationary background.
   - *coherence of temporal structure* – limbs, body and face tend to move in one common temporal structure (also referred to as 'self-synchrony').

- *coherence of intensity structure* – the variation in loudness of vocalization in an angry outburst is generally matched by the variations in the forcefulness of accompanying movements and vice versa.
- *coherence of form* – the form (or configuration) of the other is an obvious property that 'belongs' to someone and can serve to identify that person as an enduring and coherent entity (Stern, 2006).

3. *Self-affectivity:* the self as a sense of affectivity is important. The infant has countless experiences of how many basic affects (for example anger and joy) have a relatively stable association with certain acts. Furthermore, the infant learns that even if certain affects (for example joy) can occur in widely different social dynamics, three types of feedback are constant, despite changes in context: feedback from the face (for example a smile), inner mobilization of tension (arousal) and the subjective quality of the affect (for example joy).

4. *Self-history:* the self as personal history. The individual's own developmental history provides a sense of coherence and identity, a feeling of being the same over time. Perhaps living between two and six months seems a very short period compared to the human life span, but an infant who lives in the here and now will have had thousands of engaging and emotionally important experiences in that time, experiences that create a growing fount of personal history with others. Our personal history is the crucial feature that distinguishes interaction from relationship. If humans fail to establish a reasonably meaningful and coherent perception of themselves (being an unreflecting core self feeling or a metacognitive narrative self), then a mental anchor is missing as an inner point of reference. This will render personal encounters with other people disturbing. In contrast to his earlier writings, Stern argues that it is sufficient to operate with three of these self-invariants: agency, self-coherence and self-history (continuity), as he now considers self-affectivity subordinate to the concept of continuity.

Self with other

Stern (2006) now seems to emphasize the very early social nature of the self much more strongly than in his 1985 book. His basic definition of the self as subjectively separate from the other(s) is still acknowledged as the way of experiencing the world. But the new perspective implies a different emphasis on an individual's relationship with others. As argued previously in this chapter, humans are evolutionarily equipped with the capacity for sociality. After birth, primary intersubjectivity organizes the infant's social encounters (Trevarthen and Aitken, 2001). For example, babies who are only a few hours old can be observed to imitate and mirror facial expressions – tongue protrusion, looking surprised (Berk, 2009) – a competence so complex that it seems to be more than simply reflexive. The paradigm of early sociality in human nature indicates that even the most 'private' and subjective sensations, moods and experiences always have an interpersonal dimension. What is remembered, felt and thought springs from previous, current and potential future experiences in relationships with significant others.

Previously, Stern (1985) believed that genuine intersubjectivity did not develop until the age of nine months. But newer research has made him aware that humans have the capacity for intersubjectivity almost from the beginning of life (Stern, 2006, p. xxii). In addition, the discovery of so-called 'mirror neurons' and 'adaptive oscillators' suggest a neurobiological basis for social interactivity. The social human seemingly owns a social brain. Mirror neurons in the premotor cortex of primates activate (fire) when an individual carries out an intentional act, such as a hand gesture. This is not too surprising. What is surprising is that a similar firing pattern happens in the individual's brain when someone else is *observed* carrying out an intentional act. The brain seems to respond to other people's social and intentional actions, as if we were carrying them out ourselves. The social acts of others (for example gestures and facial expressions) appear not only to activate the brain, but are also involved in creating a sense of self. The sense of some sort of separation or distinction between one's self and others may be obvious, but in this paradigm, the very notion of an 'I' is unthinkable without the presence and influence of 'you', 'we' and 'them'.

This has obvious implications for our understanding of the social nature of humans, for example for imitation, empathy and the capacity to achieve emotional consensus with someone else, so-called 'affective resonance'. As argued earlier, the capacity for reciprocity and cooperation seems to have a biological basis as a result of humankind's long evolutionary history. Smart but physically weak humans could not have survived on their own, if survival had not been based on adaptation and the development of skills for living in small groups. Therefore, over the millennia, humans developed social competencies, which seem to be founded on a neurobiological basis (see Frith and Frith, 2001 for a discussion of the biological and neurological basis of social interaction). This new and intriguing look at man's fundamentally social nature is also one of the pillars of *A Childhood Psychology*. We are not being forced into sociality through socialization, because it is already there from the beginning.

The paradigm of the infant's basic social nature does not mean, however, that innate communicative capacities come fully developed. Innate capacities seem to be essential, but are only the point of departure for human development. As elaborated in Chapter 3 about culture acquisition, it is a long-term process to learn how to navigate in a complex social world. Relatively more experienced adults and older peers function as mediators by including the infant and young child in an expanding field of culturally appropriate ground rules. There is a vast array of cultural rules for so-called 'normal expected' social behaviour, which infants and older children have to learn, and which explains, in part, why the childhood period is markedly extended in humans compared to other species. The new child competencies approach, however, has documented and argued that this seems to be founded on some basic social skills that are in place very early in ontogenesis.

The RIG system

One of Stern's major contributions to our understanding of early mental function is the RIG system (Stern, 2006). RIG stands for *R*epresentations of *I*nteractions that have been *G*eneralized. What does this mean? RIGs are a vital part of the memory where, in principle, all the infant's experiences from everyday social contacts are recorded in the RIG system. A specific RIG should not be imagined as an inner image, icon, or a fantasy, for example of the mother; instead RIGs are mental representations of real relationships that occur in everyday life, for example a mother nursing her baby.[112] Such socioaffective experiences enter into the RIG system, but a RIG is not a specific memory from yesterday or today. Over time, during regular social routines, the baby's diverse experiences with nursing gradually become generalized into a 'nursing RIG'. Father–infant play similarly creates a RIG containing this type of experience. RIGs are to be seen as relatively flexible structures that represent a kind of average of numerous specific relationship experiences. Thus RIGs are *generalized prototypes*. This is not only true of the RIG for nursing and father–infant play, but of all social experiences. In memory, a large number of RIGs are gradually distilled, based on a multitude of everyday routines. The RIG system allows the infant to preserve and activate relationship partners mentally, whether they are currently present or not. Stern uses the term 'evoked companion' about perceiving someone who is not present. The function of the evoked companion may be soothing, for example an infant in childcare recalls the experience of being with a parent, even when they are not around. So 'out of sight' is not necessarily, as previously thought, 'out of mind', as in this paradigm, the phenomenon occurs even relatively early in infancy.

This implies that humans store encounters that they have actively participated in, a point that is essential to our understanding of the infant's self-perception. RIGs include attachment experiences, but are much more than that. The total sum of RIGs preserves the infant's personal history, sensed by being together with someone else; thus an individual's personal history is constructed as social experiences. Countless experiences of 'being with others' gradually construct the RIG system and, by the same token, the individual's self-perception. In the revised edition of *The Interpersonal World of the Infant* (2006), Stern's theory about the RIG system has been left unchanged since the first edition in 1985, and he used the idea in *The Motherhood Constellation* (Stern, 1995). Experiences of 'self with others' create a complex experiential system that can be activated in new situations. Over time, subjective expectations of what happens accumulate and enable the individual to add personal flavour to a relationship. In clinical cases, repeated negative experiences (maltreatment) stored as generalized RIG relationships can lay the foundation of distorted perceptions about how a good caring reality is not to be expected, as, in principle, it does not exist.

But what role do good or bad experiences play long term? The answer lies in the weighing of positive or negative loaded and felt experiences. If, for example, the baby has had a number of pleasant prototypical experiences that are similar, they feel and expect that 'nursing is good'. Seen like this, some unpleasant experiences will probably not have a negative impact. Perhaps some 'misattunements' between mother and baby, when feeding does not always go so well, will lead to an internalization of the interaction as a partially negative nursing RIG that 'nursing is not always good'. That may happen, for example when mother is tired, stressed after returning from work, or when the baby has a cold and is irritable. However, the many dominant previous good experiences with nursing will be reactivated, resulting in the dominant perception that 'nursing is usually good'. If, however, the baby's predominant experience is misattunement, this will result in a growing general and negative expectation when in a relationship with others. As the development process continues, accumulated RIGs have an increasing influence on the infant's subjective expectations of being with others.

The myriad of relationships that an infant has had *with the same person* are represented by person-specific generalized prototypical memories. So there seem to be as many person-specific relationship RIGs as the actual number of people the child engages with – mothers, fathers, siblings, grandparents and childcare staff. Socially competent children are 'mentally multipersonal' from early in life, although, of course, not all relationships have equal importance for the child. This is another example of how the view of the child since the paradigm shift transcends the mother-centric idea. Yet it is unclear to what extent prototype experiences specific to a particular person are generalized to others. Research shows that infants can develop an insecure attachment to their mothers and a secure one to their fathers or vice versa (Howes and Spieker, 2008). Using this on the RIG model, it seems to indicate that the infant does not generalize its insecure relationship with the mother to the father, or at least that the father together with his infant is able to confirm and continue their positive relationship.

RIGs as preservers of personal history

Leaving infancy for a moment, some principal consequences of the RIG model for the understanding of past, present and future memories need to be drawn.

Psychoanalysts have not been able to document that adult memories reflect real events in early childhood. When adults memorize past experiences, their childhood can be reconstructed under the influence of the current situation and mental state. This point of view finds some support in studies of depressed and post-depressed adults. Depressed adults associate key childhood experiences with more profound negative feelings than they do six months later when they have recovered from their depression; the memories of the past are now clearly less negative (Nielsen, 1990). Thus childhood events seem to be filtered by later experience. As a result of the 'narrative turn', a sceptical stance is now taken of the notion of early childhood memory as autobiographical realism. A person's history becomes established through the personal narrative that is based on fragments of real events, but not necessarily the factual truth.

Human individual development occurs in three dimensions of time: past, present and future. Psychoanalysis believed that the explanations of development are buried in the past (infancy and early childhood). Past experiences may to (a minor) extent play a part in ontogenesis, but there seems to be a complex interplay between the experienced past, present and future affecting human development. So it is vital to include a present and future perspective in addressing the impact of past events in an individual's life. This is illustrated in Figure 6. 1.

Figure 6.1 shows Stern's middle position; on the one hand, rejecting a purely narrative idea of a complete transformation of memory influenced by the later development process, while on the other hand, being critical of the psychoanalytic assumption about the principal importance of the personal past. As discussed in the RIG model, original memories and their connected

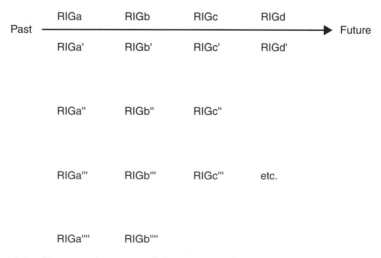

Figure 6.1 Ontogenetic temporal dimensions of memory

affects may consist of generalized essences of *real-life* situations in childhood. Therefore, some reality basis of early (and present) memory probably exists. However, as time goes by, such memories are subject to shifts in perspective, which leaves room for autobiographical reconstruction. In Figure 6.1, this is reflected in the fact that every RIGa over time may become RIGa', RIG'', RIGa''' and so on. However, they are still somewhat different versions of RIGa, as they do not become a RIGb or a RIGc. An original and prototypical RIGa, for example, may represent the newborn baby's profound repeated sensory experience of 'being together with mother', starting with lying skin to skin on her body just after birth. RIGa' may be togetherness experienced in the light of the two-year-old's desire for autonomy, after exploring the world by returning to mother's arms for rest and approval. A RIG'' may be the school child's verbal way of talking about the nice feelings of intimacy with the mother. RIG'' may be influenced by RIGa and RIGa', but not usually in a conscious way, as they are stored as different sensory, perceptual and preverbal prototypes. It is difficult for the verbally coded RIG'' experiences to connect with a RIGa acquired during the earliest part of life. Thus, if this period of life is to be 'revisited', it cannot be done directly, but either during a *reconstruction* of past experiences and sensations through a verbal narrative or – to get closer to the original sensations and related affects – an application of unconventional nonverbal memory techniques.

THE THEORY OF SELF AND CONTEXTUALISM

A basic approach in *A Childhood Psychology* is contextualism. Contextualism, however, is not a single body of theory about infant and child development; rather, the paradigm characterizes a series of related assumptions. As suggested in Chapter 1 and elsewhere in this book, the basic point is that a perspective on the development of action and mental activity should be seen as embedded in a historical, societal and physical context. As a consequence, a theory about self-development will benefit from being anchored in such contexts. However, Stern's theory of self emphasizes the sense of self as separate from sense of other, essentialism (self as core, a whole entity) and universalism (self as the same for all, dependent on age). All these ideas seem in opposition to contextualism. At first glance, then, Stern cannot be considered a contextualist, and as will be apparent, this is also the point of Cushman's criticism, presented next.

The critique from social constructivists and an answer

To a certain extent, a constructivist view can be helpful in the evaluation of developmental psychology by pointing to some inherent self-evident, but overlooked and underlying basic assumptions (see Burman, 2008a). One does not necessarily have to be a full constructivist in order to use some arguments from that approach as a tool in the investigation and discussion of important underlying assumptions in Stern's theory of self.

The declared constructivist Cushman (1991) strongly criticized Stern, who, he believed, describes humans as separated atoms relating to each other. This criticism is central as it challenges the underlying features of Stern's theory. In summary, Cushman described Stern's theory of self as:

- *ahistorical:* it claims to be equally applicable to Stone Age infants and today's infants
- *ethnocentric:* despite its clearly universalist character, it will not be applicable to cultures other than the West
- *organismic:* despite attributing great importance to the development of the self, Stern emphasizes innate unfolding properties in the preverbal infant.

As for the ahistorical and universal character of the theory, this is simply taken for granted and not much discussed by Stern. In his ambitious new endeavour to integrate the psychoanalytical interpretation of the subjective life of the infant ('the clinical child') with the behavioural descriptions from developmental empirical research ('the observed child'), he combines two fundamentally divergent traditions. Stern argues that the clinical and the observed child are to be seen as complementary paradigms rather than mutually exclusive, thus opening new avenues for integration.[113] A common denominator is that both rely on universalism, describing assumed general developmental principles, and thus being non-historic traditions.

Stern replies to this challenge in the introduction to the second edition of *The Interpersonal World of the Infant* (Stern, 2006). On some points, he agrees with Cushman (and thus with the social constructivists) that culture, history and ideology are essential. However, Cushman's criticism goes too far and becomes unproductive in its either/or rhetoric. This happens especially with the social constructivists' claim that culture is completely decisive for development, a complete social narrative, implying that humans have no real evolutionary history to establish socioaffective competencies. Stern certainly does not think that culture is the only source:

> There are not an infinite number of variables through which any culture can be enacted early in life such that they will be perceivable by the infant. The repertoire comprises facial expressions, or the lack thereof; visual regards, or their avoidance; vocalizations, or silences; body orientations; physical distances; gestures; ways of being held; the rhythms, timing and duration of acts and activities; and so on. No other human alphabet for socio-cultural contextualisation exists. To continue the

analogy: Different cultures can make different sentences with this same alphabet, but first we must examine how such an alphabet can (not must) work. (Stern, 2006, p. xxvii)

Thus, in Stern's opinion, there is a complex relationship between the 'human alphabet' and the specific culture and era in which a person grows up. Stern chooses to study the universal basics of human competencies, emphasizing the socioaffective domains. This 'both/and' paradigm statement may appear academically clear: culture is based on the common repertoire of *Homo sapiens*. But the cultural and historic meanings and interpretations of facial expressions, visual regards, vocalizations, body orientations, gestures, ways of being held, rhythms and timing of activities can be different. These key elements of the human alphabet of social relationships and practices can probably be observed in all cultures, although cultural developmental science shows that there is still remarkable variance in cultures worldwide (Bornstein, 2010). In his reply to Cushman, Stern maintains that his *first priority* is to research developmental regularities across cultures. There is no doubt that Stern acknowledges the importance of the cultural context, but it is futile to look for the role of culture in self-development. Despite the reply to the social constructivists, some basic understandings, for example the very definition of self, become somewhat problematic when evaluated in light of recent research on the impact of culture on self-development. A later section focuses on this issue.

Another social constructivist argument, partly related to the organismic critique of Stern's approach, is that there is no such phenomenon as a specific type of self, depending on age-governed experience and social relationships. Instead, selves are not only constructed but vary with the many roles people play. Should we, then, see the human mind as a composite – a 'kaleidoscope of selves'? Stern rejects this notion, believing that humans have a coherent mode of experience. The principal difference between Stern's position and a social constructivist position is illustrated in Figure 6.2.

Social constructivism (Cushman, 1990; Hermans et al., 1992) has attempted to transcend the concepts of individualism and objectivism[114] that characterize Western psychology by adopting the idea of relative and amorphous *multiple selves* embedded in and inseparable from the many relations between person and environment. The social constructivists thus abandon Stern's separation of two inner universes with separate RIGs (for example the mother's and the young child's) that reach across the subjects through social relationships.

As suggested, Stern's idea of the baby sensing a core self as a coherent entity between two to six months has an element of essentialist thinking and of being oneself. Seen in an ontogenetic perspective, however, the theory does operate with multiple 'senses of self' (emergent self, core self and so on), but in an age-related sense. So, while a true contextual view will highlight

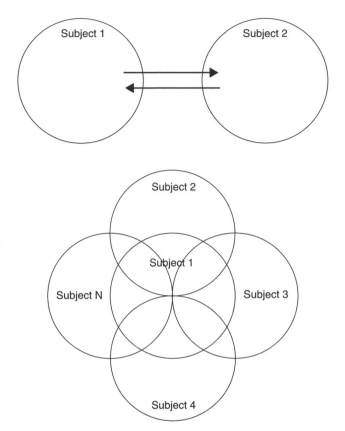

Figure 6.2 Stern's core self versus the multiple selves of social constructivism

the variability and fluctuations of self, an essentialist point of view (Stern's) implies that the self has unity and substance (Palmer and Donahoe, 1992). Again, however, the social constructivist either/or rhetoric becomes unproductive. The idea of multiple selves (where roles mistakenly become identical with selves) creates a problem: How do individual children manage to perceive themselves as 'the same' across time and changing situations while being a situation-specific, non-connected bunch of selves and roles? Without some integrating and organizing capacities, what prevents the individual from becoming completely fused with the environment? Certain central inner processes that create coherence and continuity should be assumed to hold the person together as an 'I'.

Constructivist theories claiming that the individual's many social roles resemble multiple selves have great difficulty explaining how individuals perceive their roles as a separate part of 'me' – the same person. Being a 'child in childcare' means playing different roles than the roles at home being a 'family child'. The same goes for the different roles played when with peers and other adults. Everyday routines require many different roles. Despite daily life demands, a multitude of unconnected roles are learned and practised, but it is unusual to confuse them. But even when being 'me', practising a particular role and practising a different role later on does not necessarily mean than the self is fragmented and embedded in all such roles. If the self is seen as submerged in its own constantly changing social life or as one with it, what then keeps us from claiming that human essence is constantly variable? That we change who we are from one second to the next dependent on the environment (Broughton, 1987)? Stern's arguments are important for the infant's sense of self-continuity, as they prevent such extreme views.

Social constructivism does offer some refreshing perspectives in its more moderate version, but generalized and used on all science, it poses serious inherent logical problems (see Collin, 1998). The notion that some cultural, societal and psychological phenomena are constructed narratives has been convincing. Yet not all aspects of reality are constructed through narratives. Take the human 'body'. Clearly there are a wide variety of historical and cultural narratives about the body, detailed in ancient and modern medicine/science books, leading to numerous interpretations of the body. However, it does not dissolve the body or other physical phenomena and turn them into sheer discourse or historically dependent knowledge. For example, some key aspects of the emotional self are not based merely on narratives, but on bodily sensations and brain processes, although others certainly are. Indeed, in his revised model, Stern acknowledges this by introducing a so-called 'narrative self' alongside the verbal self. Prior to that there are preverbal selves and here a complex of inner bodily emerged sensations and emotions play a vital role to the sense of self – coined by the term 'embodied self'.

The following offers a closer look at the potential applications of his theory in relation to the contextual framework of *A Childhood Psychology*, with the caveat that these are this author's own extrapolations, to be regarded as a sketch. A 'good theory' is an interpretation that works well in the specific time–space context in which it is used. This is in line with the functionalist principle laid down previously in this book. Then one might ask: Is there a hidden correspondence of latent value assumptions in Stern's theory and our times in a Western culture, which the theory functionally validates? This seems to be the case; Stern's theory is based on the interpretation of a large body of evidence arising from both therapy experience and behavioural research in a Western context. Observations of children of various ages in contemporary Western culture may be meaningful when interpreted through Stern's perspective; for example, the early emphasis on independence as a cultural value in parental practice, and in recent developmental and educational theory (including Stern's). Furthermore, important parts of Stern's discussion of the socioaffective competent self-regulating infant may be adapted – sometimes, but not always about a universal infant – but can explain the functioning of infants and young children in Western, late modern societies as autonomous, independent individuals. His theory is useful in explaining self-development in the emergent negotiation families, presented in Chapter 4. The point is that the same social structures and processes have influenced the late modern self and the construction of theories about that self. Therefore, Stern's theory on infants' early socioaffective competencies is valuable as a 'local theory' that attempts to understand child development in our era and culture.

It may be claimed that Stern is a contextualist because context is referred to, both in his own work (Stern, 2006) and in previous work published with colleagues. This is, however, only used in a narrow sense of the term, typically applied in observation research. Here, the context is the parent–infant relationship (Zeanah et al., 1989). But as argued in this book, several other contexts are necessary to explain child development. Interestingly, however, another part of Stern's framework allows for that. Earlier, it was noted that Stern's work is based on *real-life everyday interaction episodes*, from which can be inferred that when the child has regular contact outside the parent–child context, this can be explained developmentally, for example the development of a RIG for daycare staff experiences and RIGs for various peers in childcare. In other words, self-development takes place in natural relationships. If this is combined with cultural psychological ideas and broader contexts that influence the young child, the theory will also be combinable with the broader contextual stance proposed in this book (to be elaborated on in Chapter 7).

The role of culture in self-development

This section will deal with culture and self, discussing Stern's concept of self in relation to that. First, some important points must be made. The following is not an attempt to relaunch old 'anthropological tropes' about, for example, *the* Mayan mother, *the* Japanese mother and *the* American mother, thus implicitly outlining normal standards or stereotypes. However, recent empirical evidence shows real cultural differences in perceptions of socialization into self–other relationships, and how early care is practised. On the other hand, there are cultural commonalities: there are efficient practical ways of nursing that work, for example soothing an infant by holding them close to one's body is functional in stopping crying. Here, the evidence presented of cultural differences will be interpreted as showing relative cultural preferences and emphases rather than being seen in one culture and totally absent in another culture.

What is the role of culture in relation to self-development? On the basis of a considerable body of cross-cultural research, Kitayama and Markus (1994) concluded that people in different cultures have some different constructions of self, of others and of their mutual relations. They view the following definition of self as highly cultural: that self is a separated, unique, more or less integrated motivational and cognitive universe, a dynamic centre containing consciousness, emotion, discernment and action organized as a whole that stands in clear contrast to other such entities (Kitayama and Markus, 1994). This stands out as a Western monopoly of self psychology, which ignores the fact that the notion of a core self probably emerged as a product of individualization in the West. This type of professional knowledge seems to have spread widely to future psychologists and child professionals in many cultures, partly through the distribution of classical American textbooks of developmental psychology (for example Berk, 2009). Stern's core definition of the self, with its relatively sharp boundaries and as an experiential counterpart to the sense of others as a universal given, is clearly in line with the above definition. Perhaps much of the appraisal and fascination of Stern's theory stems from the fact that it so clearly represents a modern Western humanistic and progressive ideology about the infant's competent, bounded and feeling self.

Western culture is full of signals of individualism and the inviolable self. In Chapter 4, this feature was identified in late modern parenting tendencies, for example negotiation families appreciate and respect their young children's early independent opinions in everyday practice, reflecting the parents' culturally influenced developmental beliefs and goals, which include the early promotion of autonomy and independence. Despite the increasing number of these families, this should not be considered a universal prototype, to be generalized worldwide.

The crucial influence of variations in cultural practices on the formation of the self from birth is indicated in Morelli and Rogoff's (1992) cross-cultural studies of sleeping arrangements.[115] They compared the ways that middle-class US families and Maya Indians handled bedtime routines from birth until the child was around six months old. (The Maya people constitute a diverse range of Native American people of southern Mexico and northern Central America.) Results showed that few of the US babies slept in their mother's bed right from birth; instead they slept in a cot, either in the parents' bedroom or their own bedroom. Between the age of three to six months, most had moved to their own bedroom. All the Mayan children, however, slept in their parents' bed. The US mothers seemingly wanted to foster personal independence from the start, whereas the Mayan mothers wanted to be close to their babies. In the Western independent context, 'transition objects' are commonly used in order to ease separation, such as dummies and soft toys. To minimize the feeling of separation, extended bedtime routines are quite common. For example, in Scandinavia with its belief in individualism, the study 'Childhood, Society and Development in the North' demonstrated this. The study recorded a whole day's social routines (Kristjansson, 2001). At bedtime, young children and their parents were involved in sometimes lengthy transition routines – not playing, holding hands, reading a bedtime story, speaking softly and so on – obviously with the intention of helping the child to go to sleep and to ease sleeping alone in their own bed. This was not the case for Mayan children and those with similar sleeping arrangements. Thus, from the beginning of life, the cultural requirement for developing a bounded self is expressed in child-rearing practices in some cultures, while not in others.

Similar cross-cultural differences in development patterns are highlighted in reviews of Asian and Western research, building on decades of empirical studies (for example Markus and Kitayama, 1991; Rothbaum et al., 2000; Kitayama, 2000; Fogel, 2000; Lewis, 2000; Tobin, 2000; Greenfield et al., 2006; Menon and Fu, 2006). Unlike Stern, a self is documented as having more than one core definitional status. There seems to be an Asian more *interdependent* self than the Western *independent* self. A consequence of this is that the latter definition of self does not account for how billions of people in principle sense their self.

Independence is a characteristic of Stern's autonomous infant: bounded, whole, continuous, the seat of action, the author of their own actions. But this is not an adequate characterization of the *interdependent self, as it changes relatively easily with the changing social context*. For instance, the Japanese word for self refers to 'one's share of the common life space' (Markus and Kitayama, 1991). The self is not considered a constant entity but as pulsating with no fixed boundaries, either between individuals or inside the individual; the self changes readily over time by reflecting adaptation to external situations. This springs from Japanese culture and its tradition for social relativism. Stern (2004, 2006) does not address this vital cross-cultural discussion. As mentioned, the independent self – a term that Stern does not use, but which has a clear parallel to his concept of the core self – stands out as a universal phenomenon.

Some of Stern's self-concepts might be combined with a cross-cultural perspective to steer Stern away from a collision with the growing evidence from cross-cultural studies of self. Using Stern's perspective, the argument may be that children's emerging sense of self – existing before the core self – is characterized mainly by interdependence. If we assume that this interdependence has a panhuman evolutionary basis, then culture splits development into specific directions. The content of relationships relevant to self-development seems to vary across cultures, but interdependent self-formation remains universally common for *Homo socius*. However, right from birth, culture begins to influence self-construction in important ways by *accentuating* certain adaptation strategies more than others. The term 'accentuating' implies that the process reflects some differences in cultural emphasis rather than the complete absence or presence of certain features or a dichotomy between cultures.

Different 'cultural lenses' affect the developmental path of the interdependent basis for sociality in culturally specific ways. Metaphorically speaking, cultures are like prisms that bend the light to produce different hues (Rothbaum et al., 2000). In a research review, Rothbaum et al. discuss the far-reaching implications of a substantial body of cross-cultural research into close human relationships. With this evidence, it is now possible to construct culture-specific developmental models. Rothbaum et al. (2000) constructed a model illustrating some different ways in which the different lenses in the East and the West (exemplified by Japan and the US) channel the 'biological substrate of relationships' (see Figure 6.3).

In the West, the interdependent basis for sociality is refracted through an *individuation lens*. In this culture, early in life, children encounter demands from parents, carers and others for early independence and individuality. Remarks like 'standing on one's own feet', 'the right to raise one's own voice' and 'where there's a will, there's a way' indicate an emphasis on an autonomous self. At the same time, there are contradictory cultural norms concerning togetherness, intimacy, loyalty and acceptance of dependence. These different cultural expectations create a fundamental tension in parenting and socialization. Rothbaum et al. (2000) point out many implications of this generative tension for the making of theory in Western culture. No wonder concepts like ego-drive, self-determination and individual intentionality are needed in this context.

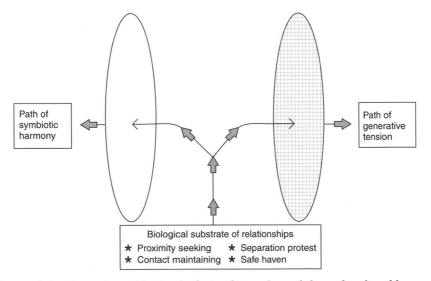

Figure 6.3   The universal basis of relationships refracted through cultural lenses
Source: Rothbaum et al., 2000

In order not to be pure individualism, it has to be complemented by sociality. In a normal life, the pressure on individuality is in constant competition with social considerations. A young child's too much 'I' and 'me' behaviour – expressed as insufficient self-restraint and emotional regulation – may cause a loss of intimacy and social appraisal if cultural ground rules, for example tolerance and respect for others, are violated. Perhaps this inherent tension between the individual and others is a natural, unquestioned part of child-rearing in Western cultures. The parenting beliefs contributing to this tension have been documented in Scandinavia. A group of Danish mothers and fathers with children aged three and a half declared 'independence' as the most important quality to be developed by their children, while the second priority was 'consideration for others' (Sommer, 2008b).

Classical developmental theorizing has incorporated this tension into culturally biased general concepts, not realizing that a 'local theory' is presented. One example of this is Erikson's (1950) well-known stage theory. Here there is a specific phase for independence versus shame/doubt, where the positive outcome is willpower and self-restraint – clear examples of the culture-specific tension. Erikson also has a phase for individual initiative versus guilt, where the positive outcome is the development of intentionality – the Western ideal of an autonomous, wilful and goal-oriented individual, of whom self-restraint and impulse control is also required. This may serve as one example of developmental theories that are inadvertently ethnocentric. Now, it can rightfully be claimed that Erikson (1950, 1972) actually acknowledges that culture plays a key role in development. Indeed, he describes how approaches to child-rearing in various Indian tribes foster distinctly different personality features. In introducing his stage theory, however, the scene changes when a universal neopsychoanalytical theory is presented.

This discussion also has a practical and applied side. Theories that more or less assume that independence is a preferred early goal in successful parenting should not be applied to other cultures without careful consideration. For example, various Western conceptualizations are probably not useful for understanding parenting among immigrants in various ethnic groups who live in Western societies. Greenfield et al. (2006) focus on this issue and discuss the practical importance of the new cultural research for parents, paediatricians and other practitioners. By focusing on late modern young childhood and children's dual socialization situation, *A Childhood Psychology* can also offer relevant advice to various practitioners.

This brings us to the other cultural lens and the special way it refracts the panhuman substrate. According to Rothbaum et al. (2000), the so-called Eastern cultural lens filters the biological essence towards social accommodation. Studies have shown that Japanese culture has a stronger emphasis on so-called *symbiotic harmony* than Western culture. This means that as a cultural ideal, childcare and parenting practices place a high priority on dependence and adjustment. A prototype of symbiotic harmony is the way Japanese mothers 'spoil' and 'dote' on their children, as seen from a Western perspective. The young child's *amae*, that is, complete dependence on the mother, is seen as primary. Independent and volitional behaviour would be ignored, meeting with no encouragement and little approval. However, *amae* means that a mother offers her child a guarantee against the frequent frustration of needs. The mother knows what the child wants, even before the child has become aware of it. Thus, such children do not have to suffer frustrations and express demands to their mother. This bolsters the children's dependency and restricts the individuation process (Rothbaum et al., 2000). In time, this develops the culturally specific development of an interdependent self. A strong norm for children to learn *omoiyari* (empathy) helps promote the formation of this interdependent self. *Omoiyari* has priority in the moral hierarchy in Japanese culture (Lebra, 1994).

Back to Stern and the discussion of how to incorporate his theory of self in a cross-cultural framework. The above implies that Stern's concept of core self can be, to a large extent, incorporated as a culturally specific theory of infants in Western societies. This does not mean, however, that young children in other cultures do not perceive themselves as somewhat distinct from others. There probably will be a sense that their own actions spring from them, while they remain closely linked to others. However, the individual's autonomous influence on their environment does not receive as much support in certain cultures as it does in the West, so infants' early sense of themselves as a core, separated from others, seems to be less profound in the more collectively oriented cultures than in the more individually oriented cultures. The most we can say at this point is probably this:

1. The emphasis and accent on individual independence/dependence and autonomy (the balance between interdependence and independence) is culturally conditioned.
2. The basic and initial constitution of the self per se is probably panhuman and characterized by interdependence in any culture.

CONCLUSION

Stern's theory holds promising basic elements that can be embedded in a contextual perspective. *Vitality affects* are an interesting invention in Stern's work, as the choreography of these emotions can be explained within a contextual theory on self formation in history, society and culture. The *RIG system* represents a challenge for researchers who are interested in mental functions in infancy and early childhood. As suggested, the RIG system develops from real-life, everyday relationships. This is also the premise of culture acquisition, and thus, in an expanded form, the RIG system may be seen as a way to 'preserve' culturally influenced relationship experiences. This makes the RIG system applicable in *A Childhood Psychology* and when used in a broader developmental context.

Affective attunement (and misattunement) is another useful concept, as attunement can be viewed both as a personalized relationship between infant and carer and a culturally specific way of choreographing relationships. Affective attunement, however, does not necessarily only take place in real life where people can be observed doing this or that. If development is viewed in a full cultural perspective, much happens behind the scenes. Both emotions and vitality affects may be studied in 'interactive silence', that is, in the shared everyday routines where 'nothing' appears to be happening. People are often together without doing much, because well-known situations and routines are full of meaning that can create an inner sense of togetherness and shared moods. This is characteristic of many everyday routines in families, where infants do not interact directly with adults (see Chapters 3 and 4). If interviewed, people can talk about such phenomena. In this context, Stern's theory may be expanded to include concepts from anthropology about implicit culture. In conclusion, it is possible to incorporate many of Stern's points of view about infants' self-development as important elements in a late modern contextual childhood psychology.

7
A CHILDHOOD PSYCHOLOGY: CONCLUSIONS AND FUTURE PERSPECTIVES

This chapter begins by summarizing the core differences between the pre- and post- paradigm shift worldviews. Then a model about what influences the young child living in late modernity is presented and its implications are discussed. From the start, *A Childhood Psychology* has argued for an interdisciplinary conversation, by presenting various concepts and models as potential platforms mainly drawn from contextual childhood psychology. In this chapter, specific preliminary ideas are put forward and discussed in order to pursue this idea further, providing food for thought. Some may believe that this threatens their own professional turf. So it is important to say what interdisciplinarity can be. Learning about the young child using various professional perspectives does not necessarily infer eclecticism. Sociologists, anthropologists, educationalists, health and social care professionals and psychologists do not have to give up the foundation in their specific subject. In an interdisciplinary approach, the disciplines remain important as the vertical pillars of knowledge, and the *inter* can be seen as the horizontals that help us to reach an understanding of the complexities of young children's lives in our rapidly changing times. Building an interdisciplinary framework is an endeavour beyond the scope of this chapter, but some promising paradigmatic and conceptual similarities will be pointed to and their interdisciplinary potential (between selected childhood sociologies and a childhood psychology) will be discussed.

Finally, reflections are made on what affects young children's development in the long term. A life span model is presented in order to illuminate how young childhood is related to other important developmental periods during the whole human life span.

MAIN DIFFERENCES BEFORE AND AFTER
THE PARADIGM SHIFT

A Childhood Psychology can briefly be defined as the scientific study of human development seen in its cultural, historical and individual dimensions. We have seen that before the paradigm shift, among various theories, the psychoanalytic axiom was prominent in highlighting the developmental significance of the personal past. Today, this seems to be a part of the history of developmental psychology. There has been a shift in focus from a 'regression' stance towards a life span, here-and-now and future-oriented approach, with the developmental past as one influential factor among many. Another characteristic of the pre-paradigm shift era was the strong belief in teleology and finality. Science was considered capable of explaining the child's future with stage theories. At the time, this was a common view in both social sciences and psychology. However, such 'prior knowledge', extrapolating from an individual's past and present experiences to the future, turned out to be problematic. *A Childhood Psychology* reflects a paradigm whereby the individual life path is seen as a personal journey and an integrated part of a larger social and cultural historicity.

This book has consistently argued that the focus of theory and research is to explore and explain the existing and changing developmental conditions for young children. A range of new concepts have been proposed and old ones have been discarded. The rapid changes in late modern society that have impinged on young children's lives, as documented in Chapter 2, have challenged deeply held commonsense and professional beliefs. But change also offers new opportunities, stimulating a public debate and moving theory and method forwards.

As said at the beginning, *A Childhood Psychology* is to be seen as one of many possible readings of some (not all) vicissitudes of late modern early childhood and child development from a researcher's point of view, in an attempt to offer a fresh interdisciplinary perspective. However, the reflections in this book are not merely private musings. As evident from the references, they take their inspiration from new international psychological research relevant to the understanding of today's young children and their childhoods. A sea change, based on decades of extensive research, has occurred in the study of human development, which has led to the paradigm shift. Looking at this evolving developmental landscape, even after studying it, it still stands out as a fragmented influx of new studies and domain-specific theories. In the wake of the general, universal developmental era, a single universal perception of the discipline has not been achieved. As Chapter 1 concluded, such a vision remains elusive, although systems theory and contextualism show promising potential as metatheoretical unifiers. But after the criticisms of the grand developmental idea, the utopian dream of a single, universal theory has faded.

An important element in this process was the loss of faith in the teleological nature of knowledge, for example that development can be conceptualized as step-like stages from childish immaturity to adult maturity. Even today, in order to achieve scientific status, some child psychology claims to be value free, by being purely objective and rejecting notions of hidden, underlying values; for example, when development is presented as a natural decontextualized phenomenon studied by the neutral scientist apparently unaffected by cultural assessments. The child may also be perceived as a miniature scientist, the cool cognitivist seeking to discover the patterns and constancy in the world through their manipulation of objects. Or the child is perceived to be in the grip of age-specific, stage-determined development that unerringly organizes the child's relationship to the environment. Or parents are portrayed as objective constants who have specific effects on the child, regardless of their own perspectives or the changes they might undergo in life. Or objective conditions exercise control over the family in important ways. As discussed in Chapter 1, neutral, value-free knowledge about development, unrelated to time and context, was an idea that dominated before 1960, but this approach is also evident in some of today's developmental research.

This book has consistently argued for a major paradigm shift in order to understand young children's development in our changing times, presenting *A Childhood Psychology* as a specific approach. But is it really so essential to distinguish between approaches that dominated before the 1960s and 70s and the present? Box 7.1 illustrates why a distinction matters, because the two are closely related to substantially different types and approaches to knowledge. This book has repeatedly stated that the term 'pre-paradigm shift' was related to historically embedded academic ideas coined during the 20th century until the 1960s and 70s. This is seen in the left-hand column of Box 7.1. Axioms that have become fundamental since the paradigm shift, spelled out thorough *A Childhood Psychology*, are seen in the right-hand column.[116]

Box 7.1   Main themes before and after the paradigm shift

SHIFT IN PARADIGM – MAIN THEMES

From the grand developmental era	*To A Childhood Psychology*
Strong tendency towards dominating psychological 'schools'	One among many approaches. An interdisciplinary stance. Systems theory and contextualism as potential unifiers
Universal, top-down knowledge. Few, nearly all-encompassing deductive principles and concepts. Once learned, in principle, always usable	Culturally and historically situated knowledge. Recurrent updating of knowledge base is required as the subject under study is constantly changing

Teleology and finality	The future is difficult to predict. Influenced but not determined by past, present and future
Monocausal, deterministic tendency	Multicausal, probabilistic and transactional approach
Primary/secondary socialization	Dual socialization
Family-centricity	The child's actual network relationships
Mother-centricity	The child's multipersonal world
The fragile child	The relatively fragile and resilient child
The incompetent child	The relatively competent child
The passive-receptive child	The child as an active meaning-maker
Stage development	Development of functional cultural, social and personal skills and competencies

If, for a moment, the new domain-specific character of knowledge originating from developmental research is ignored, and a common denominator is extracted, the following picture emerges. Research, which began in the 1970s and continues today, has provoked this fundamental shift in thinking, with implications for the image and future of a discipline navigating in an ever-changing world.

A CONTEXTUAL APPROACH

Everyday social life is a crucial developmental level because it is here young children meet their 'developers' in relationships. But activity on other levels is potentially developing as well. Regarding the relationship between society, culture and the young child, some conceptually distinct, but intrinsically related levels are illustrated in Figure 7.1.[117]

Models are constructs and do not 'exist' as such, but they can be helpful in clarifying what is important. In this model, one can start, in principle, at every level, not necessarily at the top. But if starting there, the macro-level denotes conditions that develop culture and society, conditions that also structure and frame childhood in important ways. This framing is twofold in that it constrains some possibilities, while expanding others. At the macro-level, however, a host of conditions do not impinge on children or interfere with their development. Thus we have to focus specifically on conditions that directly and indirectly affect young children, and this is achieved by giving special relevance to 'childhood architects', that is, specific people

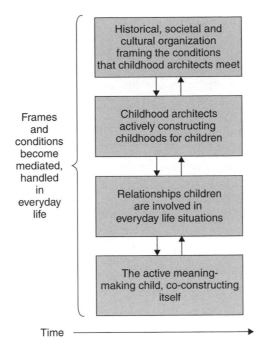

Frames
and
conditions
become
mediated,
handled
in
everyday
life

Time

Figure 7.1   A level perspective of children's integration into society and culture

who are actively involved in shaping the conditions under which children grow up. The 'design', for example, of the socialization arena of childcare for young children may be the deliberate or unintended result of adult decision-making. Sometimes such decisions are made in the best interests of the children. But at other times, necessity, for example economic pressure, is the reason behind such decisions. Or perhaps the explanation lies in the shift in the motivation of educated women to have a career, along with their male counterparts. Important young childhood architects in late modernity are:

- parents and other family members involved in structuring childhood
- individuals in culturally important organizations involved in structuring childcare, upbringing and education, for example legislators, planners, media people, politicians, nursery teachers, educators.

Macro-conditions do not 'affect' a child directly; they have to be *mediated* in order to be transferred into the child's life world (Cole, 1996; Cole and Cagigas, 2010).[118] In the model, adult–child relationships seem to be developmentally most powerful. As noted above, parents and people involved in care, upbringing and education shape childhood in ways that are essential to a child's culture acquisition and development. As specific childhood makers, they modify, utilize and transform 'given' conditions that frame (not deter-mine) the meaning and function of children's interactions. Thus the child enters and performs in various 'arenas' that adults construct, and in these arenas, cultural and societal conditions are transformed, converted as they are into culturally attuned affordances. As an agent, a child participates in the co-creation of themselves as a social person. Thus young children make essential contributions to their own development. Figure 7.1 illuminates the indirect, but important impact of cultural and societal organization levels that in many ways construct childhood, as well as the ways in which close and distant adults directly and indirectly *structure the child's life.* For example, the childcare revolution restructured young childhood as a consequence of mothers joining the workforce.

The model highlights how not everything is open to negotiation, as one might think based on the position of micro-level cultural production. For instance, few children are, in principle, allowed to choose to attend child-care or stay home. This decision is taken by parents on behalf of the child, and may be based on necessity (for example parents going out to work) as well as adults' priorities and choices on behalf of the child. In addition, the young child's involvement is often based on routines and customs that the child has not been involved in negotiating. However, children use their options to reshape and modify their relationships to their childhood makers. Children engage in creating social interactions and 'negotiate' the direction and content of their everyday relationships.

Time

Time permeates all levels, institutions, networks and relationships in Figure 7.1. This means that, in the long run, very little – society, culture, childcare, social networks, carers, relationships – constitutes 'developmental constants' in relation to the young child. Although daily routines are regu-lar, over a longer time period they will also change slowly or quickly. As the infant grows older and begins to talk, for example, parents and children are increasingly involved in taking conversational turns, and having a new sib-ling necessitates a renegotiation of routines and relationships in families. On an institutional level, in childcare, meeting and leaving peers is regulated by time, for example entering at three years of age (or younger) and later leaving for school. In addition, educational ideas and fundamental beliefs about what a child is and should be change over time, as demonstrated ear-lier in this book. On a societal and cultural level, living in a late modern, global world entails being influenced by historical and rapid changes. One example of this is the global financial crisis, which started around 2007–08 and has had, and will continue to have, worldwide consequences for many families and children.

The idea of developmental constants was, nonetheless, a common idea in earlier child psychology. It implies that only the child develops, surrounded as they are by mature, fully developed adults. This was seen in the classical socialization idea and the unidirectional, passive-receptive developmental model presented earlier. But studies within the life span approach have demonstrated that the image of the 'constant adult' does not match reality, as parents react to major life events, for example job change, unemployment, divorce, having a second child. So it may be more realistic to hold a multiple developmental stance – adults on their developmental track change over time with new experiences, while they are carers for a young child on their own developmental track. Simultaneously, everybody lives in a society and in institutional environments that are not constant, subject as they are to change. This makes the understanding of young children's development multifaceted and difficult to formulate, but it may be a first step in understanding the complex realities of living in late modernity.

Thus, it is vital to understand that a parent is affected by various *life transitions* before, during and after becoming involved in bringing up children. Life transitions bring qualitative changes to a relationship (Baltes et al., 2006). In other words, both the child *and* the adults close to the young child are involved in their respective lifelong developmental processes. Interestingly, this is in line with the transactional idea presented in Chapter 1.

Developmental levels

Figure 7.1 has other implications for the understanding of development, by illustrating the fact that the child is embedded in societal and contextual levels. A key theoretical point here is that different levels, both separately and in combination, play important developmental roles, ranging from the material, social and ideological conditions within culture and society, institutions, social network environments through to family, childcare and personal social episodes. The most important level concerns the relationships the young child is actively engaged in and how the child subjectively experiences them. Each level is defined by its own sets of properties and dynamics, and although it is influenced by other levels, it cannot be reduced to another level.

As constructed 'maps', thinking in terms of levels, for both scientific and pragmatic reasons, can be useful. Promising suggestions have been seen for integrative level models and worldviews, ranging from Bronfenbrenner's (1979) ecological model to life span theorizing (Baltes et al., 2006) and indeterminism in systems theory (Fogel, 1993; Sameroff, 2000, 2006; Fogel et al., 2006, 2009; Witherington, 2007). Regardless of differences, level models (including Figure 7.1) have certain common features. They express a more or less clearly stated critique of developmentally reductionist 'monocausal' explanations in child and developmental psychology. For example, the claim that early *dyadic interaction* (for example between mother and infant) fully explains security/insecurity of attachment, or *a single factor* (for example the family) explains children's behaviour, or *a specific condition* (for example divorce) can alone explain developmental change.

Another key point is that models based on levels with their reciprocal nature do not necessarily restrict the professional and practitioner to choose between this or that particular theory; in fact, sphere and level models encourage inter-theoretical thinking. In a preliminary stage, a model may help identify important life arenas for infants and young children that a given theory should adhere to. The functions of such a model (for example Bronfenbrenner's and Baltes') may be to sketch out and visualize the 'topography of childhood', that is, specifying all potential *real-life environments and persons* that contemporary children may (or may not) encounter. This also includes 'distant systems' that are transformed and mediated for the child by adults – material, cultural and social conditions in society that the child encounters indirectly.

The importance of experience in the context of childhood

Level models may be suitable as reference systems that underlie the expert's grasp of potential direct and indirect, close and distant influences on the young child. A theoretical point elaborated in Chapters 3 and 4 was that families and thereby children are affected by developments within society at large. But variations in the parents' cultural and personal resources and the way they *relate to* outside influences mean that family life shows considerable variation, even when families are exposed to the 'same set' of external conditions. Introducing the concept of agency, the way that people address and actively respond to structural conditions negates an image of family, children and parents, as mindless puppets governed by outside forces.

A cautious word about the use of level models is needed, however. It is unwise to draw direct inferences from social and cultural levels as explanations of individual development. In other words, deducing mainly or exclusively from macro-sociological conditions to explain what goes on in a family or a child will result in a 'sociologization' of the child. From an interdisciplinary perspective, sociology is an important voice, with its detailed explanation of the societal and cultural characteristics of late modernity. In fact, childhood sociology has been a inspiration for *A Childhood Psychology*, and has matured to the extent that it now has its own handbook (Qvortrup et al., 2009). Among a range of new insights, the sociological approach to childhood has raised doubts about the universality of development in the critique of the grand developmental stance in psychology. However, the child in sociology remains an abstraction: 'in a sociological optic, children – even as actors – become generalized as "bearers", "producers", and "reproducers" of social, societal and cultural categories' (Sommer et al., 2010, p. 72).

In fact, the consequence is that the baby is thrown out with the bathwater as its experiential and personalized meaning-making is overlooked in the sociological perspective. The mind becomes a kind of empty box but not an individual experiencing self. Even micro-sociological observations of play in childcare have a tendency to interpret direct observations of what children *do* as mere 'culture reproduction' (Corsaro, 2009), Instead, recent developmental psychology offers detailed conceptualizations and observational studies of how the mind is externalized and internalized in relationships. When *A Childhood Psychology* leans on its psychological leg, both an 'inner' (mind) and 'in-between' (relationship) axiom forms a basic ground. Regarding the inner – the mind – dimension, individual experience and meaning-making is at the forefront. From the start, presenting his groundbreaking ecological model, Bronfenbrenner (1979) emphasized the *phenomenological* core in his concentric model. In so doing, he avoided the 'sociologization' of the child, by calling attention to the fact that although living in presumably similar childhood conditions, individual children can still experience them in dissimilar ways and pursue different developmental pathways. In addition, in his critique of natural science-inspired designs, Bronfenbrenner called for a more pronounced child perspective in developmental psychology. To achieve better ecological validity, he formed the 'correspondence principle', that is, that the intentions of researchers' studies should be understood and in line with the child's experience of what is happening in the experiment. Thus, a psychological child perspective represents an adult's successful attempt to see and understand a child's unique way of perceiving, understanding and experiencing. So the interpretation of the mind and actions of the other that corresponds with theirs is a key competence in a child perspective approach.

It is important to distinguish between a child perspective and children's perspectives. The latter represents the child as a subject who experiences and makes personal meanings. This subject is what a child perspective-oriented adult (parent, teacher, researcher) strives to understand by interpreting the child's acts and verbal statements (for more on the child perspective approach, see Sommer et al., 2010). So in order to avoid the 'sociologization' of the child, a child perspective and a children's perspective are important underlying core axioms in Figure 7.1.

At first glance, the late modern changes in young children's developmental conditions, documented in Chapter 2, may give the impression that children are confronted with 'new' fragmented social lives, but this is not the case. Although it is not a reality for all children throughout childhood, as a *base*, regular, trusting relationship experiences with adults, in principle, form a fundamental safeguard (Howes and Spieker, 2008). In Chapter 4, this was called the *buffer function* of the modern family. These trusted, safe home and childcare bases may be generalized, stimulating a young child's social competencies and curiosity in meeting new people and environments. Here, a key point is that the child's repeated personal experiences of social encounters with other people are generalized to become represented in the mind as 'being together prototypes'. They are recast to become proto-typical experiences with other people and part of the child's RIG system (*R*epresentations-*I*nternalized-*G*eneralized) (see Chapter 6). This system provides a flexible store of memories and experiences that the child uses to construct and interpret new and old social contacts. What is important is – and it applies to both the child and the adult – that what happens in encounters is experienced and thus interpreted. So there is no direct route from what people do together and a memory representation in the mind. RIGs are not cold cognitions, but as essences of human encounters, they are charged with personal meaning and corresponding positive or negative emotions. Once again, the importance of children's perspective (and the adult's perspective) is highlighted.

INTERDISCIPLINARITY: FUTURE PERSPECTIVES

A Childhood Psychology has repeatedly suggested and hinted at interdisciplinary collaboration, but this has not been pursued in detail. How relevant is the paradigm presented here for childhood sociology for example? Some important differences between, for example, childhood *sociology* and the childhood *psychology* paradigm of this book have already been highlighted. But this does not mean that future conversations are doomed. In fact, it will be suggested here that the two stances may be complementary and thus (after much future work) can contribute to a more complete understanding of contemporary childhood. This includes the anthropological and ethno-graphic interpretative method used by some childhood sociologists. The following is a presentation of some ideas of common 'platforms' or 'stepping stones' that may stimulate future interdisciplinary work. These should be seen as suggestions, not as final statements or dogma.

Interdisciplinarity requires a relaxation from theoretical purism and 'ter-ritorial thinking', but this does not mean losing the understandings from one's own particular discipline. The tendency should be avoided, however, to dig into disparate schools and instead work with the potential strengths that other child and childhood disciplines may contribute.[119] A leading researcher concludes that what is much more important than maintaining professional territory is that we remain aware of the body of knowledge out-side our own discipline that can be relevant to our research efforts (Luthar, 2006). *A Childhood Psychology* is clearly in favour of the interdisciplinary approach, realizing that this opens up a much broader and more compre-hensive picture of the young child's socialization and development in late modernity, as well as posing problems. For example, how valid will it be to combine disparate research and domain-specific theory from inside and outside psychology that is grounded in different traditions of how to study the phenomena under investigation? This complex problem calls for future clarification in order to avoid eclecticism. In this book, the problem has only partly been solved, by using an umbrella-like contextual approach in combination with systems theory and by presenting various conceptualizations and models that invite interdisciplinary thinking. Others have suggested this, for example Woodhead and Montgomery (2003), but much more future work is clearly needed. Some preliminary suggestions follow on how to start an interdisciplinary collaboration (a more elaborated version can be seen in Sommer et al., 2010, Part I). There will be an analysis of some integrative potentials in selected conceptualizations taken from the new paradigm in child psychology as well as childhood sociology.

Challenges raised by childhood sociology for a childhood psychology and vice versa

How can sociology and psychology enrich each other? Let us briefly consider this in a larger perspective. The notion of an individual that can be studied independently of society and culture has been rendered obsolete, and childhood sociology is able to offer child psychology a much broader view of children's everyday cultural and societal existence. Sociology can provide invaluable knowledge about the huge social and cultural variations in children's living conditions, and raise doubts about the universality of development, which developmental psychologists have taken (and some continue to take) for granted. Still, as pointed out earlier, the child in sociology remains an abstraction; in a sociological lens, 'children – even as actors – become generalized as "bearers", "producers" and "reproducers" of social, societal and cultural categories' (Sommer et al., 2010, p. 72). In a psychological sense, the child seems to be thrown out with the bathwater. Sociology has a modest interest in the variation in individual children's responses, perceptions and experiences within the 'same' macro- or micro-cultural context. As will be seen later, psychological phenomena are more or less implicitly *assumed*, for example 'self' and 'mind'. In macro-sociology, such categories are perceived from an 'outside' societal point of view, and in micro-sociology reflected in what children *do*, interacting as subjects in everyday cultural encounters. This omits *what children in fact experience* – the phenomenological dimension. But seen in a complementary way, sociology offers a detailed explanation of the societal conditions of children's actions and how they, for example, reproduce culture, while child psychology offers more sophisticated and detailed explanations of the particular ways children mentally process, experience and orient themselves in relation to society and everyday life. In child psychology, individuals are influenced by, but not totally reducible to, group living. This is also seen in everyday social practice. For example, carers know that June and Peter experience, make meaning and act in idiosyncratic ways even when growing up in socially and culturally similar environments.

But despite differences in the ways that sociology and psychology approach children, the 'common object and subject' is child, children and childhood. If it is accepted that no single discipline has access to the full knowledge of its object of study, it may be more promising to move the spotlight from differences and instead turn it to potential similarities or complementary dimensions. The next sections will try to identify specific, promising common conceptual platforms.

Children as intentional, meaning-making actors: common conceptual platforms

In childhood sociology, children are clearly portrayed as *actors in their own and society's development* and they are *co-constructors*, not passive objects of adult and institutional socialization (Qvortrup, 2002). Corsaro (2005) considers the concept of the active child as a cornerstone in his theory: children *acquire, rediscover, negotiate, share, create* and *reproduce* culture. According to James and Prout (1990) and James et al. (1998), children are *social actors in their own right*, involved in their *own construction, possessing agency*, which is attributed to the *subjects' own volition*.[120] This is similar to other recent paradigmatic views of the child, seen in interpretive and sociocultural approaches (Cole, 1996; Hundeide, 2003; Rogoff, 2003) and in Pramling-Samuelsson and Asplund-Carlsson's (2003) theory of developmental pedagogy, to mention a few. However, the agency perspective has to support the interpretation of children's social acts so it enhances adults' understanding of children's perceptions and experiences of their life world. Thus, it is not sufficient to stipulate children as active creators of, for example, mini-cultural meaning if their actions are not followed by detailed conceptualizations of *children's specific phenomenological constructions of meaning and intentions*. Nevertheless, the agency perspective offers a promising common platform for an emergent interdisciplinary approach. This will be pursued further.

The heading of this section introduces three key terms that characterize children in recent paradigms across disciplines: intentionality, meaning-making and actor. How are they to be understood? What is their mutual relationship?

Intentions represent inner urges (desires and assumptions), while *intentional acts* refer to purposeful activities with a present or future goal. Thus, intentions are essentially phenomenological in nature (inside the mind), but they are 'public' as well, shown in behaviour and adjusted to other people's intentional acting.[121] Intentions function as a kind of engine that drives and targets actions in social contexts. But young children cannot function in tune with other people without continuously decoding their motives and intentions (Stern, 2004). To pursue their intentions effectively, a young child has to be able to act in socially regulated ways in everyday relationships involving many different people. This means that children develop a 'theory' that humans possess *mental states.*

In their understanding of social practices, micro-oriented childhood sociologists do not refer to intentionality or specific mental states. However, children's active expression of intentions and purposes, and their understanding of other people as intentional beings, constitute the foundations for all types of human social communication (Tomasello, 2005). If children, engaged in Corsaro's (2005) 'culture reproduction', are unable to understand and interpret others' intentions and read their minds, they will act outside the realm of humankind. So socially coordinated activity requires an ability to *mind-read* — to understand others' communicative intentions. This important dimension is not dealt with in Corsaro's theory, so here child psychology can make a contribution. The gradual development of children's understanding of their own and others' intentions is researched within theory of mind (ToM) – a rapidly expanding topic within social cognition (Harris, 2006). In relation to a childhood-in-context approach, however, a problem with ToM research is its decontextualized basic research. Nevertheless, essential insights from ToM research may prove useful in childhood sociological and cultural theory, explaining in detail how the active and meaning-making child uses mind-reading as an effective relational competence.

As evidenced earlier in this book, the fundamental condition for our ability to understand others' intentions is the ability to discriminate people from objects, knowledge that is in place in a surprisingly early period of ontogenesis. The key difference is that 'living objects' have relatively complex and unpredictable behaviours compared with 'dead objects' that simply adhere to the laws of nature (Legerstee, 1992). A characteristic of living objects is their spontaneous agency and relative unpredictability. As children gradually learn to interpret other people's intentions, their acts become meaningful. The insights from basic psychological empirical research into human intentionality add flesh and blood to James et al.'s 'agent', Qvortrup's 'co-constructor' that 'chooses', Corsaro's 'negotiator' and 'creator', and other agency-related concepts in childhood sociology. Children affect others (and are affected by them) by communicating intentions, which they adjust on the basis of their readings of others' intentions in everyday cultural practices.

An approach that holds promising integrative power is the developmental psychologist Allan Fogel's and colleagues relational social and cultural theory (Fogel, 1993; Fogel et al., 2006, 2009). According to this theory, children construct their interpersonal selves and simultaneously create and reconstruct culture in everyday verbal and nonverbal dialogues. Clearly in line with this is Bruner (1990, 1996), whose main point is that the mind is essentially *situated*, that is, constructed in the social context, where it is created and shaped through active participation. Making sense and finding coherence are characteristically human urges from the beginning of life. The search for meaning is closely linked with children's inherent and inexhaustible urge to 'wonder' and 'take an interest' (Gopnik et al., 1999). Bruner (1990) links the paradigms of agency and intentionality, saying that agency implies the conduct of action under the sway of intentional states. Action, activity and intentionality are seen as fundamental human characteristics. Bruner does not ignore that children's experience, sense and perception of their world can be idiosyncratic. The emphasis, however, is moved from the child's individual phenomenology to the interpersonal and cultural construction of knowledge and meaning. The 'mind' manifests itself in action contexts.

Promising integrative potential lies in analysing the relationships between the paradigm of intentionality, activity and sense-making in children's everyday life. Will it be beneficial to link developmental psychological research of mental states/intentionality with the agency paradigm in childhood sociology? Yes, if the *external agency* concept from childhood sociology is combined with the complex *external/internal agency* concept from recent parts of developmental psychology. Sense-making and the creation of intentions take place in social groups as well as within subjects, since one would be unthinkable without the other. Empirical research using a contextual relationship framework can also demonstrate and explain how mental processes, as desires, beliefs, volition, expectations, experiences within the child, manifest and thus become observable in children's social activity with peers (Sommer, 2003, Ch. 6). Thus, using alternative interpretive filters, observing a young child's 'same' social actions may be seen as a sign of 'culture reproduction' as well as an expression of 'materialized intentions'. The micro-sociological and the child developmental interpretation will be just as 'true' as the other.

The inner psychological space of the self

In James et al.'s (1998) sociological analysis of children in society, their approach to the child as a subject holds the following promising concepts:

- *the inner psychological space of the self*
- the notion of *subject identities*
- *the experience of being a child.*

These are interesting constructs about the presumed phenomenology of subjects that even hint at psychology. However, on a closer reading, this inner psychological self appears as an empty box when it comes to understanding children's experiences and identities. Nevertheless, the concepts are of integrative value, in that the existence of something 'mental' is recognized – promising a possible common platform and a link between micro-oriented childhood sociology and recent theories of self in psychology. The sociological 'self' is nicely connected to society but has to be complemented with a richer phenomenological understanding. This will be pursued by introducing a few theories of self that explain the important relationships: how a subject's *inside* environment – mediated by an *in-between side* – is inextricably linked to the subject's *outside* environment.

Perceiving a person's relationship with the environment as a *dichotomy* – 'inner versus outer', 'subject versus object', 'self versus other' – is seen in classical, Western, Descartes-inspired philosophies. This has perhaps crept into James et al.'s (1998) term 'the inner psychological space of self'. In child and developmental psychology, however, theoreticians have, relatively independently of each other, moved the focus from the 'inner' individual to interpersonal relationships. This shift has been essential for understanding childhood socialization, parenting and learning, as shown in this book. In some (not all) developmental psychology, the traditional split between individual and environment has been acknowledged as highly problematic, and has led to the emergence of a discipline called the developmental psychology of personal relationships (Mills and Duck, 2000). This approach acknowledges that people live in both *changing and stable relationships.* But what professional terms support the relational notion of the self as a non-isolated inner space? Let us take a brief look at three theories of self from psychology.

Fogel (1993) developed a systemic theory about the *dialogical self.* The self emerges in the earliest pre-symbolic period, long before G. H. Mead and other proponents of classical socialization theory talked about an emerging self. In sociology leaning on the classical approach, the self is not established before symbolic and language-based reflections are in place. But according to Fogel, the infant is socially and communicatively competent. The self is a continuous result of communicative processes in verbal and nonverbal dialogues between people. Thus, the position of the self is located *between people* more than within the individual:

> The dialogical self is not an objectively specifiable entity. The self is not entirely 'in' the individual, since it embodies the positions of others and can imagine itself in times and places that are not here and now. (Fogel, 1993, p. 141)

Fogel calls the ongoing communicative adjustment between actors *co-regulation.* Co-regulation, in verbal or nonverbal dialogue between two interlocutors, takes place in ways that make it difficult to predict a developmental or socialization outcome of the dialogue. One adjusts to the other's input and vice versa, and unexpected incidents may also occur that may radically alter the interaction. Obviously, this model rejects fixed goals of socialization and development. For that, the myriad interactions that people engage in during a lifetime are too unpredictable. In this respect, it is in line with the transactional approach introduced in Chapter 1. However, it should be emphasized that dialogues rarely follow a free or chaotic course, since according to Fogel (1993), they take place within *consensual frames*, that is, the actors' relative agreement on 'what we are doing is what we usually do in situations like this', that is, purpose, topic and meaning. A consensual frame contains cultural as well as personal meanings and it regulates the situationally relevant and attuned communicative behaviour. So *customs and everyday routines in a culture* provide structure and meaning and typify communicative relationships. This is a basic understanding in *A Childhood Psychology* (see Chapter 3). In subsequent encounters, the socially experienced young child does not have to start from scratch. The child applies (and through socialization has become familiar with) a large number of cultural customs for when and how we interact, and the meaning of different types of conversations. Corsaro's (2005) micro-sociological theory of 'culture reproduction' explains how this happens in culture reproduction, and Fogel (1993) adds a personal meaning framework as well. Bruner's (1990) theory of the *distributed self* has similarities with Fogel's dialogical self. 'Distributed' means that the self is created, distributed and maintained through daily social and cultural practices. Self-perception is distributed as a social product in children's various socialization arenas. In Bruner's universe, culture and self are simply two different but internally related sides of socialization.

Stern's theory of self expresses a relational perspective as well (Stern, 1985, 2004, 2006). It explains in detail how distinct formative life periods are related to qualitative *ways of being with others* (the theory of self was discussed in Chapter 6). In Stern's theory, the child's self-construction is essentially relational when it comes to the understanding of the child's inner mental representation (internal objects) of a personal world:

> Such internal objects are not people; nor are they aspects of others. Rather, they are constructed from the patterned experience of the self in interaction with another: What is inside (i.e. represented internally) comprises interactive experiences. (Stern, 1985, p. xv)

If we link the theories of self presented above with James et al.'s (1998) theses on the subject (for example 'the inner psychological space of the self' and 'subject identities'), we can pursue this a step further. A relationship can now be established between the social/cultural 'outside' in mediation with the 'in-between side' and the child's psychological 'inside'.[122] James et al.'s (1998) empty box is not only filled up with analytical content, their metaphor of the self as an 'inner psychological space' (that is, a situated place) needs rephrasing. James et al.'s (1998) empty box concept of self and identity has to be filled with much more detailed and specific content. Here, Stern

(1985, 2006) provides a description of children's formative periods from the beginnings of life.

More integrative potential: suggestions

Previous sections have discussed potential common platforms for future interdisciplinary conversations. The main aim has been to stimulate an integrative holistic understanding of the *interrelatedness* of childhood, children, society, culture and individual minds. But there seem to be more opportunities. Here, just a few will be examined:

- *The relationship between the use of language/symbols, 'psychological realities' and children's micro-cultural reproduction:* Such phrases from Corsaro (2005) need to be elaborated, for example the view of the role of language in relation to what he coined 'psychological realities'. Many of Corsaro's observations of Italian and American five-year-olds reveal that the analysis of *language dialogues* are the key to understanding what is going on. Linguistics, the acquisition and function of language and symbolic thinking, has long been a vital part of psychological developmental cognition research (for example Gleason and Ratner, 1998). A future challenge lies in embedding selected parts of such linguistic research in a culturally contextualist approach. However, future work remains to be done in order to use this growing knowledge in an interdisciplinary way.
- *'Volition' and the 'by-choice' argument:* James et al. (1998) attributed children with the ability to initiate acts based on volition. Qvortrup's term 'by-choice' also suggests this capacity, but without pursuing these interesting terms. But these are meaningful topics in relation to the previous discussion of children as intentional, active sense-makers.

On a more general level, these notions may also help us answer the following question: Where are the boundaries of children's 'free will' and human potential for change? The macro-oriented and micro-oriented approaches in childhood sociology produce different answers to this question. So we need a more in-depth analysis of the *relationships between the macro- and micro-oriented approaches* and their links to subjects' potential free will and agency. Seen through micro-sociological, anthropological and ethnographical lenses, children are able not only to incorporate, but reproduce and create culture. From a macro-sociological perspective, childhood is sometimes described as having a structuring effect that leaves little room for acting; like adulthood, childhood is an age-specific category with its own characteristics, not dealing with children living their everyday lives (for example Qvortrup, 2009). In Corsaro's and James et al.'s theorizing, an impression is that macro-level and micro-level analysis are separated, even having their own chapters. This indicates that a 'macro-child' and a 'micro-child' in sociology do not work well together. How the integration of analytical levels may be linked is wide open as a future area of research.

Studies in the humanities have a long tradition and scientific interest in 'self', 'volition', 'volitional acts' and 'consciousness' as phenomena. This is not the exclusive domain of either sociology or psychology, and thus offers a potential for establishing common platforms for future research.

The above is an invitation to interdisciplinary conversation. One hope is that theoretical purism may gradually give way to creative collaboration – that new combinations are formed from elements taken from different theories or far-reaching revisions of the original basis for a given theoretical position, necessitated, for example, by new empirical findings and/or changes in children's living conditions. Some have already helped with this by their harsh criticism and deconstruction of developmental psychology (for example Broughton, 1987; Walkerdine, 1993; Morss, 1996; Burman, 2008a, 2008b). Despite some reservations concerning an apparent lack of nuance and some generalizations, this has inspired this author in the orientation towards the possibilities of a paradigm shift. But the next step towards interdisciplinarity still seems to be lacking.

Another example of the feasibility of an interdisciplinary approach without eclectic vagueness and lack of theoretical substance can be illustrated by some interdisciplinary researchers:

- Tomasello (1999, 2005, 2009), with his combination of developmental psychology with an evolutionary approach to humans, cognition, sociality and culture.
- Stern (2006, 2004), developmentalist and clinical psychologist, who uses philosophy, holistic functional perception theory, empirical evidence, clinical practice and even some selected psychoanalysis.
- Bruner (1990), Cole (1996), Cole and Cagigas (2010) and Rogoff (1990, 2003), who creatively combine cognition, human development, learning and culture.
- The transactional approach is also relevant when used as a promising metatheoretical unifier (Sameroff, 2000, 2006; Sameroff and MacKenzie, 2003; Smith and Thelen, 2003; Fogel et al., 2006, 2009; Witherington, 2007).

Although *A Childhood Psychology* is not specifically about *practice*, there are clear links to important practice areas that hold similar paradigmatic understandings of young children and their childhoods. To mention a few:

- in Sommer et al. (2010, Part I), the basic understandings in *A Childhood Psychology* have been related to a *child perspective* approach seen in the context of *children's rights*

- *a humanistic, interpretative approach to the care of young children* (Hundeide, 2003, Part II)
- *early childhood education* (Pramling-Samuelsson and Asplund-Carlsson, 2005, Part III).

Another example of the benefit of using new childhood sociological and psychological understandings is seen in Woodhead's (2006) paper contributing to UNESCO's 'Education for All' ambition, discussing global policy and strategy regarding children's rights and early childhood education. This also includes Woodhead and Moss (2007).

Child research may, by being communicated on a broader public basis, prove both useful and educational. In contrast to natural science, it has the potential to 'change' the very subject under study:

> Whether we intend it or not, the general educational nature of the work is inescapable. The process has already begun and is accelerating to alter the general view of the infant held by most people. Once parents see a different infant, that infant starts to become transformed by their new 'sight' and ultimately becomes a different adult. (Stern, 2006, p. 276)

So child science is not a pure detached academic matter in our information society. Empirical research and theorizing about children, like other cultural knowledge, actively contribute to the *production* of interpretative filters of 'how children are' and how we should relate to them. This in principle alters the object of study that the selfsame discipline sets out to investigate.

WHAT AFFECTS DEVELOPMENT IN THE LONG TERM? FINAL CONCLUSIONS

What 'here-and-now' incidents, social episodes and relationships hold potential for later psychological function? This is a complex issue previously addressed in this book. Some conclusions will be drawn here. For instance, will a single trauma or a few disturbing experiences in early childhood determine future development? Mainly yes, if pre-paradigm shift theorizing is used. No, if later explanatory models and empirical studies are taken into consideration. In summarizing state-of-the-art knowledge, the answer is that numerous influences are interwoven, and monocausal explanations of developmental issues should be treated with the utmost scepticism. For example, the 'early trauma myth' was a consequence of a time when the classic psychoanalytic regression axiom dominated. This idea holds that *traumatic incidents* in early infancy and childhood are the main route to later psychopathology (see Chapter 1). Other notions of developmental determinism are seen in the belief that *loss* and *deprivation* following the break-up of a family are the main reasons why children from broken families will display later psychological and behavioural problems. But this hardly seems to be a law-like case, as the connection between such early negative developmental turning points and later functioning has proved to be relatively weak (Rutter, 2008). Instead, the joint results of accumulated incidents seem to be a more realistic way of depicting the probabilities of future development.

Four decades of resiliency research have repeatedly demonstrated that a complex of cumulative risk and protective influences offer a better explanation of children's future development than any single incident or main effect (Luthar, 2006; Masten and Gewirtz, 2006; Masten, 2007). For example, the accumulation of a wide range of risk factors might in time lead to the development of disorders. However, it remains hard to predict the course of development by extrapolating all relevant knowledge about a child from one point in time into the future.[123] The 'lived present moment' holds developmental potential when it occurs (Stern, 2004), as well as 'future becoming moments', which may have some unforeseen impact on the child's course of development. In a time of global crisis, worrying about the future can be very real for many families. If, for example, a parent is worried about what's going to happen after being fired, this has the potential to be mediated through parent–child relationships and thus negatively influence the child.

But there's a life after childhood. Research of lifelong development may provide a much needed answer to the fundamental question: What is the relative importance of the childhood period as part of the total human life span? This is a complex question to answer, but it seems that a life span perspective is needed. Perhaps the future study of children will be better integrated in the rapidly expanding research field of *life span developmental psychology*. This interdisciplinary approach to human development started some decades ago (for an early introduction, see Datan and Ginsberg 1975; Hetherington et al., 1988). The life span perspective is about ontogenetic development, and thus is truly future oriented. It attempts to map possible, probable and available futures with an ambition to follow the same humans from gestation to death.[124] This approach attempts to describe and explain human development as it progresses through life from conception to death. Seen in this perspective, childhood is one of many periods in human life, with its own milestones and sharing with other periods its relative contribution to human development (see Figure 7.2).

Figure 7.2 is shaped like an upside-down funnel. This suggests that developmental changes remain possible throughout human life, but that infancy and the subsequent childhoods hold particularly large potential. Figure 7.2 also illustrates the relatively limited duration of these childhood periods. In many late modern societies, the life expectancy for girls is more than 80 years, a little less for boys. So a woman who has formally past her childhood and adolescence has at least 60 more years to live. In this perspective, would

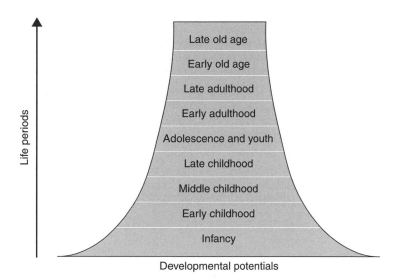

Figure 7.2   Human life periods in the life span

it not be problematic to claim that personality is more or less fully formed and fixed during childhood and adolescence, leaving most years in human lifetime to minor adjustments?[125]

In a positive sense, pre-paradigm shift theories of child psychology have emphasized, in various ways, the overwhelming importance of the childhood period – the younger the child, the more crucial. This stimulated decades of research. However, as evidenced in this book, research has shown that the early theories, in a deterministic way, overstated this importance. Thus adult psychological functioning can only be explained partly with reference to reaction patterns acquired in infancy and early childhood.[126]

The horizontal lines in Figure 7.2 suggest gradual transitions from one life period to another, but they also imply that each period builds on the preceding one(s). However, the periods should not be seen as stages, with separate, built-in and fixed developmental issues.[127] The model deliberately avoids this, as core issues can hardly be derived as top-down general developmental principles. Some may be – which is far from well known – because some developments are panhuman and common to *Homo sapiens* (Tomasello, 2009; Sommer et al., 2010, Part IV.) To a large extent, however, developmental issues in any of the specific -hoods of the life span can vary considerably, depending on the historical, cultural and personal ways in which the environment structures childcare and child-rearing. Placing a specific life span period within sharp age limits is not realistic either, seen in a global context. Although age in developmental psychology is still important in the timing of developmental milestones (not stages) (Berk, 2009), Rogoff (2003) calls attention to the fact that such 'metrics of development' are deeply related to cultural practice, values and goals. To this could be added various historical periods. The content and developmental tasks of the life periods of an individual will be framed by practices that are culturally common and expected as 'givens'.

To conclude, childhood is one of many life periods explaining human development; important, but with no determining later developmental influences. But how is the relative importance of childhood on the whole life span to be understood? Perhaps we will know more about that when the child has lived through its subsequent -hoods and reaches old age. Child and childhood research has been unable to answer this question, because it only studies children. In the future, childhood research may prosper by being a part of the growing interdisciplinary approach of life span development.

NOTES

INTRODUCTION

1. First, the 'new reality' axiom does not imply that it is impossible to deduce general and even universal principles for children's development. It is more a matter of the point of departure of the discipline – should it be a deductive or an inductive enterprise? The axiom here is that the discipline of child psychology originates from the realities in which the child's life is embedded. The next step, then, is to carry out and compare studies done in historical and cultural contexts in order to reach conclusions concerning some general characteristics of human development. Second, 'new reality' does not imply that *A Childhood Psychology* offers a reality-based applicability – a 'how-to-use' or a 'how-to-decide' guide for practitioners. Instead, hopefully, it will live up to Bruner's words 'that there is nothing as practical as a good theory'. For example, the fundamental paradigm of children, together with the reality orientation that forms the basis of this book, has a number of indirect practical implications, which in turn may affect decisions and actions concerning children's welfare on many levels of society.
2. The view of contemporary society held by this book is inspired by Giddens (1990), who is sceptical of the term 'postmodernism'. Instead, he prefers the term 'radically modern age', and the related term 'late modernity'. The benefit of this term is that it does not suggest a categorical shift away from the mechanisms that have driven the development of classical modernity. However, conditions in contemporary society have been 'condensed' and are so different from high modernity in the classic era that it is fair to talk about a 'late' version of modernity. Thus, 'late modernity' is the term consistently used in this book. Selected characteristics that are especially relevant to young childhood are presented in Chapter 2.
3. Procrustes was a Greek robber, nicknamed 'the stretcher'. He lured his victims onto a torture bed and stretched those who were too short and cut inches off those who were too tall. As a metaphor, a Procrustean bed refers to the attempt to tweak a phenomenon to make it fit a conceptual matrix.
4. Reference books and dictionaries provide nominal definitions of given academic terms and concepts. But such knowledge (in order to be updated) reflects relatively current perspectives, which are not necessarily timeless and universal. Even within the same time period, there may be differences in how a subject is defined. Another description of child psychology as a discipline in a Scandinavian context can be found in the *Danish Encyclopedia*, vol. 3. Berk's (2009) bestselling textbook provides another.

5. The criticism of stage theories does not imply that aspects of children's development cannot be conceptualized in terms of stages, as long as these stages are not
   seen as real entities per se. Sometimes, a 'stage notion' seems a meaningful metaphor for competencies that are valued and expected in specific age periods in
   a given culture. Seen in that way, underlying and manifest cultural expectations
   construct developmentally appropriate 'stages' (see Chapter 1).

CHAPTER 1

6. The term 'grand theories' refers to psychological perceptions that have profoundly
   affected child psychology, and explain children's development universally on the
   basis of general concepts.
7. Attachment research may serve as an example of this trend. Attachment came
   on the agenda as a result of the growing interest in emotional development in
   the 1970s and 80s, known as the 'cognitive era'. Nevertheless, this research is an
   example of the specificity of the new theories: they study one single aspect (albeit
   an essential one) of the infant–environment relationship. It should be noted that
   the study of emotional ties alone does not offer a complete or comprehensive
   explanation of early development.
8. According to Parke (1989), the paradigm shift is driven exclusively by research.
   But this is an inadequate explanation. Researchers are affected by trends in
   contemporary social development, philosophy and worldviews. The paradigm
   shift must be driven by the complex interaction of at least two factors. First, the
   consequences of the Western world's transition from an industrial society to an
   information society and the conceptual implications this has for the research
   community. Second, the rich empirical research, which is sensitive to cultural
   variations.
9. Family-centricity has been evident not only in professional theory, but also in the
   public debate. Chapter 2 examines both areas in depth.
10. In parts of Scandinavia, for example Denmark, the influence from psychodynamic
    and clinical approaches to normal development seems to have prevailed even
    after this period.
11. Perhaps the socialization concept should be abandoned and replaced with con-
    cepts that place greater emphasis on the child's agency. Chapter 2 offers a dis-
    cussion of this aspect and presents a definition that corresponds with the 'new
    realities' of early childhood.
12. This claim may seem unfair in relation to the type of child psychology, for exam-
    ple Piagetian theory, that acknowledges children's role as active participants and
    the consequent crucial role of childhood. However, if such a theory in its general
    approach regards the childhood period as mainly immature where the develop-
    mental goal is to reach maturity (the adult condition), then the critique is relevant.
    If we describe development as age stages with a more or less implicit finality and
    ends–means thinking, then Näsman's point of view is relevant.
13. For example, the many types of psychological tests, standardized or not, should
    not be considered objective instruments for assessing a child's development, and
    probably few insightful psychologist would attempt this. Instead, psychological
    tests may be considered 'cultural instruments' that aim to assess a child's personal,
    social and cognitive competencies in light of certain specific psychological refer-
    ence systems and cultural standards. Standardized tests reflect expected criteria
    for children's typical development in their real-life environments. Thus, skills
    and competencies are not necessarily universal entities but qualities embedded in

cultural assessments, expectations and requirements to children. Viewed as specific psychological, cultural instruments, tests may be useful.

14. It is suggested here that knowledge from the social sciences and the humanities is an embedded part of the time–place context that is being studied. It is also suggested that this makes professional knowledge an active part, which even has the power to affect its own object of study (the child). For example, new knowledge about young children may change well-intentioned parents' and teachers' perceptions of children, which in turn may affect and alter the relationship between adults and children. Knowledge from childhood psychology based on systematic methods and in-depth analyses can offer a specific type of context-dependent knowledge, a source of insight that differs from other types of knowledge about children, its preliminary character notwithstanding.

CHAPTER 2

15. The percentages do not reflect either the quality or local availability of the services offered.

16. As underlined in Chapter 1, those designations do not imply that families are unimportant and mothers irrelevant. They indicate that explaining development only on the basis of family and maternal factors is misleading to an understanding of the child's actual social encounters in daily life.

17. Children are not an influential group per se. Instead, professionals, politicians, government administrators and practitioners may claim to campaign on behalf of children. Divergent ideologies and interests may also be found along the dimensions of social class distinctions between the well-educated middle class and groups with less education; sometimes referred to as the 'cultural capital' of the middle class.

18. As a member of the Early Childhood Advisory Group on Early Child Care for the Child Commissioner in New Zealand, this author has followed some heated debates and controversies regarding early childcare. Interestingly, they look surprisingly similar, in their for and against arguments, to the debates in Scandinavia 20 years ago. In Scandinavia, with more than 50 years' experience of universal childcare, recent discussions are seldom about family/mothers versus childcare, but how to ensure and strengthen the quality of childcare.

19. In order to avoid misunderstandings, the criticism of mother-centrism does not discard mothers as highly important carers for the child. But the total network of relationships, with their relative developmental importance, has to be accounted for if the contemporary young child's social reality is to be understood, for example fathers, grandparents, siblings and childcare relationships.

20. Biddulph's book *Raising Babies: Should under 3s go to Nursery?* has sold more than 4 million copies worldwide and has been referred to in several written and electronic media. In addition, UNICEF (2008) cites paragraphs from the book. This interpretative filter works as a 'developer' of ideas and beliefs of childhood and is therefore relevant in presenting challenged and challenging beliefs.

21. Like Biddulph, Gerhardt's interpretative filter has been extensively quoted in the public debate.

22. For a description of the scope, methods, publications, findings and so on of this study, see http://secc.rti.org/.

23. With the large sample in mind, it should be pointed out that even small differences between groups will become significant. So, even potential non-findings are important.

24. With regard to the family being the normal cortisol distribution benchmark, the afternoon drop for children at home is expected because morning levels are higher. But some of the fall from morning to afternoon may be the result of too little stimulation, the child being alone, watching TV or being relatively inactive. This is not known from the studies, but does question what 'normality' is.

25. Stress is not only related to childcare. In families with a depressed parent or with violence, high stress levels in children will result (Hart, 2006).

26. See Mead (1934), page xvii, footnote.

27. In Chapter 5, research about the father as an influential potential developer will be presented.

28. The butterfly model was constructed in the project 'Childhood, Society and Development in the North' (see Haavind, 1987; Denick et al., 1988; Langsted and Sommer, 1992; Kristjansson, 2001). The model focuses on the family–childcare matrix. But contemporary young children's developmental ecology, with its direct and latent pathways, is even wider.

29. This framework may prove fruitful in childcare debates, ensuring that important relationships between the two socializing arenas are kept in mind, and in discussions including the relative importance of family childcare. The same goes for its use in social work and policy. In research, the model may be used as a starting point for empirical studies in both domains, and to guide holistic interpretations of findings from only one of the arenas.

CHAPTER 3

30. The paradigm is seen in questions seeking ultimate explanations of how the environment governs children's learning and development. It is related to the view that through systematic organized learning programmes, it is possible to teach the young child a range of desired qualifications. For example, the 'early start' position that claims that early scholastic stimulation in childcare will provide children with a head start that will endure later in life. An optimistic view like that is easy to explain in the passive-receptive paradigm.

31. The model is from Sommer (2010).

32. The idea about complementary integration signifies that childcare pedagogy is not exclusively based on children's interactions. For instance, learning a complex language does not happen in children's interactions, but in dialogue with adults.

33. The issue of self-development in early childhood is discussed in Chapter 6.

34. In this context, focus is on strengthening the child's language skills to enable the child to enter into more complex dialogues and negotiations with adults and other children. Nonverbal modes of communication and body language are also important. In group interactions among two-year-olds, a number of important nonverbal ways of expressing intentions and motives can be observed. Bringing children into situations that let them acquire everyday cultural norms and rules (explicit and implicit) is an important means of culture acquisition. Everyday activities in childcare, with and without adult regulation, hold obvious possibilities.

35. The structure of everyday life, its actions, demands, expectations and considerations, become the foundation of development. However, it is difficult to make everyday life the object of reflection. Routines and interactions are culturally integrated and familiar, and they are stored as experiences that elude systematic reflection – they represent tacit knowledge. Practitioners and scientists who study everyday life may be well aware of this phenomenon: when asked to reflect on observations of children's culture acquisition, it is difficult to find words and concepts that go beyond mere trivial descriptions.

36. The 'buffer' concept refers to something or someone acting as a protector against the forces in late modern society that may have negative effects on children. Here, meaningful everyday routines are seen as a buffer that protects children from the impact of rapid changes.
37. This explains the phenomenon of boredom, a not uncommon experience even in our culture of information abundance. Rigid routines may lead to boredom, whereas flexible routines may open up new prospects.
38. Plain traditions are idiosyncratic routines that have developed through practices and negotiations. They are not the same as major social traditions such as Christmas, Ramadan or collective transition rituals.
39. Routines are crucial for the survival of cultures and societies. In early human communities, the development of social routines were just as essential as finding sustenance. For example, greeting routines help strengthen friendly relations and reduce hostility.
40. Humans seek meaning in all events, even in apparently senseless events such as murders and natural disasters. When failing to grasp the meaning of events, they are categorized as 'senseless', thus becoming part of a meaning system.
41. However, a sense of alienation in relation to cultural routines reflects a lack of inner motivation and maybe even a protest. Youth gangs, for example, express alienation in relation to late modern society and its institutions. In response, they establish their own counterculture, with rules, habits and routines that they find meaningful.
42. Highly ritualized routines may be an indication of relationship disorder in families.
43. The purpose of this section is to offer real-life examples of certain types of interaction competencies. The point is not to offer a comprehensive description of this concept. This section is based on the project 'Childhood, Society and Development in the North', which, among other things, studied five-year-olds' peer interactions in Nordic childcare. Space does not allow a description of the systematic selection criteria and methodology applied in the project; interested readers are referred to Sommer, 2003, Ch. 6.
44. The following examples are taken from five-year-olds' interaction and play in Nordic childcare. Thus, the interaction competence is expressed in the behaviour displayed by five-year-olds in interactions with peers, without adult involvement.
45. Musatti (1986) refers to studies by Mueller and Lucas, which found that children with frequent peer interactions displayed social interactions that were both more complex and of longer duration, compared with children without frequent peer interactions.
46. Not all children are curious and interested in learning. In light of the above-mentioned principle about primary interest in learning, it may be that these children's learning environments (family, childcare institution, school and so on) have not been adequately challenging, or they have destroyed the children's drive to learn something new.
47. It is almost impossible for human beings to avoid learning. Even a negative experience is to some extent educational, hence the saying: 'Let that be a lesson to you'. Over time, negative experiences, along with the positive ones, become life experience.
48. The 'frequency sucking' method is applied here, as you cannot interview infants. When nothing happens, the infant either does not suck or does so relatively calmly. However, when new objects are introduced, they suck considerably faster. This is seen as a sign that the child is experiencing something interesting.
49. Depending on the theory, this is called 'scripts', 'mental representations', 'working models'. However, these terms share the limitation that they have a tendency

to mentalize small children's knowledge, which, to a large extent, is physically embedded. Fogel's (1993) concept 'embodied cognition' encapsulates this physically embedded knowledge of experience.

50. Parents and other adults function as mediators between the child's private world and the culture's conventional (symbol) world by 'denoting' objects and events.

51. For Martin to call an inanimate phenomenon (a rainbow) dead must mean that the rainbow is 'alive' when it is in the sky. Such vitalization of a physical phenomenon is called 'animistic thinking', although it is doubtful this applies to Martin. His reaction is more like a creative, playful and spontaneous suggestion connected to the strong visual colour impressions he experiences.

52. If the father is a physicist, he could, in principle, have explained the phenomenon with a number of formulas. This is not the case, so he adjusts to what Martin can understand.

53. The example is a condensed extract from the study 'Children's Relationship Patterns' (Sommer, 2003, Ch. 6).

54. This demonstrates the social context's importance in what children say and do not say.

55. The bottom-up perception is a paradigm about how humans 'learn in depth'. This basic view applies not only to small children, as even teaching principles at university can be based on the bottom-up approach (Biggs, 2003).

56. 'Pure versions' mean that a certain pedagogy does not necessarily appear in its ideal shape in practice. Still, professionally, it is important to examine its basic pedagogical view.

57. In the US, there is a huge market for learning programmes that promise great progress, which childcare institutions and ambitious parents can buy.

58. Self-assertiveness is obviously not an ideal in East Asia or other cultures in the world in which connectedness to the group is more important. In Chapter 6, cross-cultural research on the independent self and interdependent self will be presented and discussed.

59. Again, the relative character of these claims should be kept in mind. These are not universal competence requirements but rather a general outline of future requirements in Western, late modern societies.

CHAPTER 4

60. This provoked a fierce debate between conservatives, who believe in family-centrism, marriage and the classic family model, against liberals who advocate accepting the inescapability of multiple family types in society.

61. This theme will be followed later in this chapter, because of its relevance to the understanding of an emerging trend in later modern parenting of so-called 'negotiation families'.

62. This does not mean that male superiority in some societal domains and in families has vanished and power is shared equally. Three points are worth highlighting: this documents a trend that is more prominent today than ever before; connects this with recent changes in late modern society; and draws some important theoretical consequences to the understanding of a contemporary type of family – the negotiation family.

63. Children's growing influence on decisions in the family is already being exploited commercially. For example, some companies have conducted family surveys, which showed that children have a major influence on daily food shopping.

In response to this, supermarkets now address (exploit) children as active consumers.

64. Changes in legislation offer insight into changes in the cultural perception of fathers' authority in relation to children. There has been a fundamental shift in the father's position from what might be called legal supremacy in family issues to subordination to the overriding principle of children's welfare and interests.

65. In his concept of 'cultural capital', Bourdieu (1994) stresses that societal settings such as families, schools and workplaces function as developers of skills that are functionally needed in society, which, in this context, includes early childhood childcare. The point is that a contemporary society based on democracy and its rules for balancing conflicting powers has a functional need for a type of family that (mostly intuitively) on a daily basis practises negotiation and cooperative skills with the next generation.

66. The following should be seen as extrapolations and hypothesis, as there is little empirical research on the relationship between 'negotiation'–socialization in late modern families and young children's social negotiation behaviour in non-family contexts. These reflections, along with the dual socialization configuration, may stimulate new research.

67. Countries experiencing the turmoil of rapid social change may face debates about a spoiled next generation. As noted in Chapter 2, rapid change will provoke deeply held interpretative filters and expose these in public debates.

68. This book is not about school education. However, developmental projects may be launched with the goal of creating educational approaches that match the needs and qualities of negotiation children.

69. It should be noted here that Baumrind's typology deals with 'pure' forms or essences. Few parents behave as her model suggests; most will be somewhere on a continuum in relation to Baumrind's categories. However, as a template of different types of parenting, it works. A model is a simplified version of reality; however, it is this simplification that enables it to capture and refine certain aspects of reality.

70. Baumrind's research points to a key aspect of this type of late modern parenting: the parents' inclusion of the child and their encouragement for the child to participate in and influence decisions in the family.

71. In a polarized Danish debate about competent child-rearing, some claim that parents must 'set boundaries' for the late modern child who has no respect for authority. On the one hand, there are demands for the demarcation of clear behavioural standards to promote the child's development. On the other hand, the need is seen to respect children's rights, and not hamper their natural maturing potential. Baumrind's model includes both as necessary conditions for competent parenting.

72. The permissive parenting style resembles the so-called 'laissez-faire' approach in pedagogy, which believes that controls and setting behavioural limits will damage children, so their inner potential cannot be realized.

73. This book is about typical trends in late modern early childhood. It does not deal with parental strategies that negatively influence children's psychopathology.

74. In the following, some examples of this will be presented. Further research is needed to explore and conceptualize real-life parenting strategies.

75. This section is based on family analyses of everyday parenting routines within the Nordic project 'Childhood, Society and Development in the North' (see Haavind, 1987; Kristjansson, 2001).

76. Young children acquire knowledge about a wide range of social regulations without adult interference. The focus on parenting as an intervention has deflected

attention from children's acquisition of social rules through everyday experiences outside active adult control.

77. The balance also has to do with the child's age. Families with older children display few direct, explicit signs of active parenting. As the code of social conduct is gradually internalized, direct intervention becomes less necessary. However, infants also acquire codes of moral and social behaviour through their participation in planned routines. Within a given routine and activity, they will comply with direct requests from the adults that are justified by the situation. Familiar routines organize parenting behaviour and ethical codes.

78. An exception is Haavind (1987), who described and conceptualized a number of gender-specific parenting competencies.

79. Analysis of everyday time structure and routines in the project 'Childhood, Society and Development in the North' on dual-earner families with a child in childcare showed remarkable similarities. In families with comparable work hours, the timing of routines in the mornings, for example, were quite similar (Kristjansson, 2001).

80. 'Continuous forethought' usually emerges as the result of numerous experiences with living in a family relationship. However, no Danish researchers have studied whether Danish women/mothers are more likely than their male counterparts to develop this competence because women feel that they have the overall responsibility for making the family work. There are certainly signs of gender-specific differences, as fathers' involvement is more ad hoc, helping out with minor tasks, while the women/mothers still shoulder the main responsibilities.

81. This sort of relaxing family time may not be as undemanding as one might think. Simply spending extended periods of time together requires self-control, as illustrated by a conversation with a foster parent who described how difficult it was for their foster child to spend time with them, just relaxing. This child was so restless that he could not sit still and relax with the others for very long.

82. It has been difficult to find research about childcare from a cultural analysis perspective. Therefore, the following section is pieced together with inspiration from the theorists who were also addressed in Chapter 3. Thus, care has been embedded in this everyday culture approach. This chapter also introduces additional contributions, most notably Gallimore et al. (1989) and Stern (2006).

83. The global boom in parental advice literature shows that parents need help with their how-to-do quality caring. It is an indirect signal that information from old caring wisdom is probably not sufficient or is not used.

84. Professional knowledge is becoming increasingly influential. The influence of preschool educators is one example of professional perceptions of children that affect many parents. In conversations with parents, the educator uses jargon from child psychology and education. Some parents are affected by this and begin to take an educational approach themselves, buying educational toys and so on, to promote the child's development. The health visitor is another example of a practitioner with professional knowledge about children whom the parents encounter at a crucial time in the child's life.

85. To avoid misunderstanding, this is not to say that the personal relationship between child and carer is not important, because it is, as the next section demonstrates. The point is to challenge the overly interactionist perception of childcare in psychology, as if nothing matters besides the close adult–infant relationship. However, childcare is more than just the time spent together; care is also expressed in the planned and organized actions by adults who care about their children as they take steps to create an everyday structure that makes good care possible.

86. Gallimore et al. (1989) make it possible to apply this paradigm within the parameters of the basic perspective of this book.

87. This point of view is in accordance with my own view of parents as actors who structure everyday life based on the existing possibilities and constraints. Thus, it is within the parameters of everyday life that we should conclude whether today's families can be said to struggle with the personal and cultural demands of providing care. Global analyses of family and society often fail to grasp this actor perspective. As mentioned earlier, general psychological theories also fail to grasp fully late modern parents, families and the relationship with adults outside the family. Chapter 3 established the theoretical perspective that is applied in this chapter.

88. Here, it should be said that care is not the exclusive domain of mothers. Children have fathers, and late modern children meet many other carers throughout their young childhoods. I am attempting here to define the basic qualities that characterize childcare. The criticisms against the one-sided mother–child focus are addressed in more detail in Chapter 5.

89. This is one among many reasons why some men who have just become fathers may experience the initial period with the newborn baby as stressful and demanding. In terms of the 'payoff', of course, it is an important 'reward' for parents to see that the child is thriving. The point is, however, that they cannot expect this from the child.

90. The need to be responsible points to one of the dilemmas of the late modern family. Parents (often mothers) may be caught in a conflict between their dual responsibilities towards children and work. The balance between work and childcare can become imbalanced if the alternative childcare options are inadequate (maternity/paternity leave, childcare outside the home).

91. Here, Stern differs from traditional psychoanalytical views that tend to give the mother the main responsibility for caring dysfunction. If, like Stern, we accept the infant's role in establishing the nature and quality of the relationship, the attention can be directed at the relationship rather than the mother as a person. This also lets us look for any neurological or psychological deficiencies in the infant that might cause or contribute to a dysfunctional caring relationship.

92. In my youth, with little experience of children, I trained in a nursery. This gave me ample opportunity to learn how infants were able 'to test' a new carer, for example by checking whether the adult was able and willing to share emotions. I recall an incident with one infant as I changed her nappy. First, she looked at the new adult (me), then she knocked the mobile with her hand, making it swing, and then turned to me with a big smile. The first time I missed the point, but soon after the child repeated the action. This time, when she looked at me again (to check my response), I laughed and gave the mobile a push. Then we laughed together. As a young, inexperienced carer, I thought (then) that the influences were governed by the adult. My 'infant teacher' taught me that children have a substantial impact on the personalized caring process.

CHAPTER 5

93. Although not relevant in developmental thinking today, a denial of the relevance of fathers to their infants stems from psychoanalysis. Here the importance of the father was not conceptualized before the Oedipal conflict solution. Up to three years of age, a close relationship to more than the mother was seen as a threat to the mother–child symbiosis.

94. After criticism, Bowlby later revised his point of view and in principle also allowed the possibility of the infant bonding with other people besides the biological mother.

95. As an ethologist, Lorenz studied the way goslings were imprinted on their mother instantly after hatching (birth), as she was usually the first living creature the goslings saw. In a modified form, Lorenz's experiments were seen as Nature's model for the human attachment process. An infant's attachment to their mother was viewed as a longer and more complex process, but the inappropriate bird analogy was maintained. This provided mother-centricity with a biological rationale. Embarrassingly, in their rush to naturalize the mother–infant relationship, child psychologists missed this obvious point: Lorenz's experiments showed also that the gosling would bond with him – a man with a big beard – if he was the first moving target they saw after hatching. Lorenz had grown-up geese that followed him to his lectures and left with him when the lecture was over.

96. From a professional meeting with Japanese developmental and social scientists, discussing emergent trends and problems facing Japanese child families.

97. Klaus and Kennell's research revolutionized childbirth practices in hospitals worldwide, a great step forward from previous practices. Ironically, these improvements were based on research that later proved to be flawed, erroneous and ideologically biased.

98. This can perhaps account for the psychological reason why practically all fathers prefer to play, while most avoid the 'necessary' care routines with the child. Added to this is the significant consequences of the family's decision that the mother, and not the father, takes maternity leave. When the child is five months old, the father works full time, while the mother is at home. However, studies have shown that as the mother's working hours increase, the father's involvement also increases (Crouter, 2006). This can also be expected to happen in Danish families.

99. If a mother–child biological bond is synonymous with quality parenting – a mother always just 'has it in her naturally' – then it is difficult to explain cases of maternally induced violence, neglect and abuse that are seen in every society.

CHAPTER 6

100. Stern's revolutionary book *The Interpersonal World of the Infant* was first published in 1985, followed by a paperback edition in 2003 (the latest 2006 reprint is used in this chapter). Stern chose not to revise the original text. Instead, the paperback edition has an extensive and interesting introduction, in which Stern discusses the changes and developments in his thinking since the first edition. In this connection, he also responds to his critics. When it has been judged particularly relevant, the key changes in Stern's theory are addressed in this chapter.

101. It certainly is. Much is learned and experienced through interaction. The new element is that humans are apparently equipped with some protosocial species-specific characteristics of a fundamental and relational nature.

102. This is a good example of the disagreement in research. The 'out of Africa' hypothesis places the human cradle in Africa. Over time, humans migrated to other parts of the world. The 'multiregional' hypothesis states that the human species came into existence separately in Eurasia and Africa.

103. A group of *Australopithicus afarensis*, who died together 3.2 million years ago, were found in Hadar, Ethiopia. The discovery indicates that prehistoric humans lived in social groups. Researchers have called this group of fossils 'the first family'. However, these people were far from being as advanced as later species.

104. A big brain in a big body is not necessarily a sign of intelligence. For instance, a lion has a bigger brain than a cat, but is hardly cleverer. Apparently, the correlation between brain size and body mass is more important. Promising new research calculates a so-called 'EQ' (encephalization quotient), defined as the correlation between brain–body mass. In this connection, humans excel by having an exceptionally large brain in comparison to their body size. This implies that the brain developed to compensate for our modest physique.

105. However, this does not mean that newborns are familiar with social conventions. Morals probably exist early in life in a protoform. But a culture's complicated system of rules needs to be learned in childhood.

106. The inner, self-controlled individual is a Western, historical perception of humans. It is more of a cultural construction (fiction) than a global reality (Triandis et al., 1990).

107. The apparent paradox that asociality is also socially related became apparent in my study of five-year-olds' peer play in Nordic nurseries. For further information about the study, see Sommer, 2003, Ch. 6.

108. It can be called science's categorical logical discourse. In the search for an ultimate truth, the substantial part that can explain everything is sought in a genuine platonic manner. In contrast, the idea of relations influences a number of factors regarding heredity/environment and innate/acquired development in complex ways.

109. Mahler's concept of 'normal' autism is oxymoronic. It is best explained by the fact that Mahler's theory of child development was created on the basis of adult pathological concepts that were transferred to mental states in infants.

110. Piaget's structuralism suggests an organism that under universal laws is applicable to all living creatures: accommodation and assimilation regulate the relationship between the organism and its surroundings.

111. This phenomenon is actually called 'cross-modal perception', and empirical studies use that name. By calling it amodal perception, Stern calls attention to theoretical implications of what may be going on in the child's mind, for example that external information probably is not bound to a specific sense modality.

112. RIGs are not about the infant's lived experience of the world. RIGs do not exist as such, but are a researcher's perspective of the cognitive organization of the infant's acquisition of experiences.

113. This point of view, however, raises a number of methodological and conceptual issues, which are only addressed sporadically in the first edition of *The Interpersonal World of the Infant*. Space constraints do not allow an in-depth look at the question.

114. Objectivism claims that the world consists of separate objects, each with their characteristic properties, and that these objects are capable of interacting.

115. Sleeping arrangements and parents' rationales for them constitute important everyday routines that offer insights into parenting strategies and values. These arrangements reflect intentions that are expressed in practice, with important consequences to the child's self-development.

CHAPTER 7

116. It should be noted that this summary deliberately simplifies the complex and gradual development of the paradigm shift. However, this sacrifice of complexity may be justifiable in a summarizing chapter. Readers who want

documentation or more details may turn to Chapter 1, as well as the literature that this chapter is based on.

117. The model was constructed in the project 'Childhood, Society and Development in the North' (see Haavind, 1987; Kristjansson, 2001).

118. This is why there are no arrows going from the macro-level directly to the child level outside the in-between levels

119. The idea of professional purism is a historical throwback from the classic modernity period. Defining the 'core' identity of developmental psychology was done by counter-defining and establishing boundaries to other disciplines that may have the child as object of study. Such strong purism has faded in late modernity, with a growing openness towards more eclectic and interdisciplinary approaches. In building on an ecological basis, *A Childhood Psychology* is to be seen as an example of this.

120. Qvortrup (2002) has a 'by-choice' phrase. This also suggests that children have real choices in childhood. Having choices presupposes volition, and that brings us close to the discussion about the more or less free will of the individual. However, this is not addressed in Qvortrup's macro-sociological theory.

121. It is important to note that intentions often 'start' from the outside, derived from an interpersonal process, and then within the child as an intrapsychological category that might both drive and direct new behaviour.

122. In relational self psychology, the child's self is not seen as a 'nucleus' but a relational experiential product. The existence of multiple selves is a possibility, although this is still being debated (see Chapter 6).

123. This point is especially important but perhaps troublesome for child practitioners in a situation where it is urgent to make decisions regarding disadvantaged children. Resilience research, however, has presented principles and guidelines for how to use intervention by practitioners (Masten, 2007).

124. The use of longitudinal designs has been a major method in the life span approach. Here the same people are followed as they develop over years.

125. According to classical psychoanalysis, the fundamentals of the child's personality are developed around six years of age.

126. This is not to say that childhood is an unimportant period of life. In that case, it would hardly seem justifiable to write a book about childhood psychology. Childhood experiences are relatively important later in life. Here, however, childhood is placed in a larger life span sequence, by stressing that the developmental importance of events occurring after the childhood period should also be acknowledged.

127. This has been inspired by Stern's (2006) concept of 'life themes'. Life themes are not limited to a particular developmentally active stage where a particular psychological issue is all-important and should be addressed. As the term suggests, life themes are lifelong issues, for example the psychological sense of 'intimacy'. Intimacy has different meanings to a newborn baby, a teenager, a middle-aged person and an octogenarian, but it is more or less always there. Another life theme can be how to regulate aggression. The experience or lack of intimacy or difficulties in handling aggression, however, remain crucial issues for the individual's problems or wellbeing throughout life. In certain psychological states, the qualitatively different experiences of intimacy that characterize the different life stages may fuse. Thus, life themes cut across and connect the various human life periods.

REFERENCES

Amato, P. R. (1994) 'Father-Child Relations, Mother Child-Relations, and Offspring Psychological Well-Being in Early Adulthood', *Journal of Marriage and the Family*, 56, 1031–42.

Andersson, B.-E. (1989) 'The Importance of Public Day-Care for Preschool Children's Later Development', *Child Development*, 60, 857–66.

Andersson, B.-E. (1992) 'Effects of Day-care on Cognitive and Socioemotional Competence of Thirteen-year-old Swedish School Children', *Child Development*, 63, 20–36.

Baillargeon, R. (1994) 'How Do Infants Learn about the Physical World?', *Current Directions in Psychological Science*, 3, 133–140.

Baltes, P. B., Lindenberger, U. and Staudinger, U. M. (2006) 'Life Span Theory in Developmental Psychology', in R. M. Lerner (ed.) *Handbook of Child Psychology*, vol. 1: *Theoretical Models of Human Development*. Hoboken, NJ: John Wiley & Sons.

Baumrind, D. (1978) 'Parental Disciplinary Patterns and Social Competence in Children', *Youth and Society*, 9(2): 239–76.

Baumrind, D. (1988) 'Rearing Competent Children', in W. Damon (ed.) *Child Development Today and Tomorrow*. San Francisco: Jossey-Bass.

Baumrind, D. (1991) 'Effective Parenting During Early Adolescent Transition', in P. A. Cowan and E. M. Hetherington (eds) *Advances in Family Research*, vol. 2. Hillsdale, NJ: Lawrence Erlbaum.

Baumrind, D. (1993) 'The Average Expectable Environment is not Good Enough: A Response to Scarr', *Child Development*, 64, 1299–317.

Beck, U. (1977) *Risikosamfundet [Risk Society]*. København: Hans Reitzels Forlag.

Bee, H. and Boyd, D. (2007) *The Developing Child* (11th edn). Boston: Pearson.

Berg, S. J. and Wynne-Edwards, K. E. (2001) 'Changes in Testosterone, Cortisol and Estradiol Levels in Men Becoming Fathers', *Mayo Clinic Proceedings*, 76, 582–92.

Berk, L. (2009) *Child Development* (8th edn). Boston: Allyn & Bacon.

Bertram, H. (2006) *Overview of Child Well-being in Germany: Policy Towards a Supportive Environment for Children*, Working Paper. Florence: UNICEF Innocenti Research Centre.

Biddulph, S. (2006) *Raising Babies: Should under 3s go to Nursery?* London: Harper/Thorsens.

Biggs, J. (2003) *Teaching for Quality Learning at University* (2nd edn). Maidenhead: Open University Press/Blackwell.

Block, J. H. and Block, J. (1980) 'The Role of Ego-Control and Ego Resilience in the Organization of Behaviour', in W. A. Collins (ed.) *Minnesota Symposium on Child Psychology*. Hillsdale, NJ: Lawrence Erlbaum.

Bonke, J. (2009) *Forældre, udgifter af tid og penge på deres børn [Parents, Expenditure of Time and Money on Their Children]*. DK: University Press of Southern Denmark.

Bonke, J. and Esping-Andersen, G. (2009) *Family Investments in Children: What Drives the Social Gap in Parenting?* Study paper, no. 26. Copenhagen: Rockwool Foundation.

Börjeson, B. (1995) 'Det ideologiskt omstridda barnet' ['The Ideological Contested Child'], in L. Dahlgren, and K. Hultqvist (red.) *Seendet och seendets villkor* [*Viewing and the Conditions of Viewing*]. Stockholm: HLS-Förlag.

Bornstein, M. H. (ed.) (2002a) *Handbook of Parenting* (2nd edn). Mahwah, NJ: Lawrence Erlbaum.

Bornstein, M. H. (ed.) (2002b) *Handbook of Parenting*, vol. 4: *Social Conditions and Applied Parenting* (2nd edn). Mahwah, NJ: Lawrence Erlbaum.

Bornstein, M. H. (ed.) (2010) *Handbook of Cultural Developmental Science*. New York: Psychology Press.

Bourdieu, P. (1994) *Af praktiske grunde: omkring teorien om menneskelig handlen* [*Of Practical Reasons: Theorizing about Human Action*]. København: Hans Reitzels Forlag.

Bowlby, J. (1954) *Maternal Care and Mental Health*. Geneva: WHO.

Bowlby, J. (1958) 'The Nature of the Child's Tie to his Mother', *International Journal of Psychoanalysis*, 39, 350–73.

Bowlby, J. (1969) *Attachment and Loss*, vol. 1: *Attachment*. New York: Basic Books.

Bowlby, J. (1973) *Attachment and Loss*, vol. 2: *Separation: Anxiety and Anger*. New York: Basic Books.

Bowlby, J. (1980) *Attachment and Loss*, vol. 3: *Loss: Sadness and Depression*. New York: Basic Books.

Bowlby, J. (1988) *A Secure Base*. London: Routledge.

Boyd, D. and Bee, H. (2010) *The Growing Child*. Boston: Pearson.

Bråten, S. (ed.) (2007) *On Being Moved: From Mirror Neurons to Empathy*. Amsterdam: John Benjamins.

Brembeck, H. (2000) 'Det nordiske barn' ['The Nordic Child']. *Filiokus, 3*.

Bretherton, I. (2005) 'In Pursuit of the Internal Working Model Construct and its Relevance to Attachment Relationships', in K. E. Grossmann, K. Grossmann and E. Watters (eds) *Attachment from Infancy to Adulthood: The Major Longitudinal Studies*. New York: Guilford Press.

Bretherton, I. and Munholland, K. A. (2008) 'Internal Working Models in Attachment Relationships: Elaborating a Central Construct in Attachment Theory', in J. Cassidy and P. R. Shaver (eds) *Handbook of Attachment* (2nd edn). New York: Guilford Press.

Brinkmann, S. (2006) *John Dewey: en introduction* [*John Dewey: An Introduction*]. København: Hans Reitzels Forlag.

Bronfenbrenner, U. (1979) *The Ecology of Human Development*. Cambridge, MA: Harvard University Press.

Broughton, J. M. (ed.) (1987) *Critical Theories of Psychological Development*. New York: Plenum Press.

Brown, R. (1965) *Social Psychology*. New York: Free Press.

Bruner, J. (1990) *Acts of Meaning*. Cambridge, MA: Harvard University Press.

Bruner, J. (1996) *The Culture of Education*. Cambridge, MA: Harvard University Press.

Bukato, D. and Daehler, M. W. (2004) *Child Development: A Thematic Approach* (5th edn). Boston: Houghton Mifflin.

Burman, E. (2008a) *Deconstructing Developmental Psychology* (2nd edn). London: Routledge.

Burman, E. (2008b) *Developments: Child, Image, Nation*. London: Routledge.

Cairns, R. B. and Cairns, B. D. (2006) 'The Making of Developmental Psychology', in R. M. Lerner (ed.) *Handbook of Child Psychology*, vol. 1: *Theoretical Models of Human Development*. Hoboken, NJ: John Wiley & Sons.

Carroll-Lind, J. and Angus, J. (2011) *Through Their Lens: An Inquiry into Non Parental Education and Care of Infants and Toddlers.* Wellington: Children's Commissioner's Office.

Cassidy, J. and Shaver, P. R. (eds) (2008) *Handbook of Attachment* (2nd edn). New York: Guilford Press.

Chao, R. and Tseng, V. (2010) 'Parenting in Asians', in M. H. Bornstein (ed.) *Handbook of Parenting*, vol. 4. Hillsdale, NJ: Lawrence Erlbaum.

Charman, T. (2006) 'Imitation and the Development of Language', in S. J. Rogers and J. G. Williams (eds) *Imitation and the Social Mind.* New York: Guilford Press.

Cicchetti, D. and Garmezy, N. (1993) 'Prospects and Promises in the Study of Resilience', *Development and Psychopathology*, 5, 497–502.

Clarke-Stewart, A. and Allhusen, V. D. (2005) *What We Know About Child Care.* Cambridge, MA: Harvard University Press.

Clarke-Stewart, A. and Dunn, J. (eds) (2006) *Families Count.* Cambridge: Cambridge University Press.

Cole, M. (1996) *Cultural Psychology.* Cambridge, MA: Harvard University Press.

Cole, M. and Cagigas, X. E. (2010) 'Cognition', in M. H. Bornstein (ed.) *Handbook of Cultural and Developmental Science.* New York: Psychology Press.

Collin, F. (1998) 'Socialkonstruktivisme og den sociale virkelighed' ['Social Constructivism and the Social Reality'], i M. Järvinen and M. Bertilsson (red.) *Socialkonstruktivisme: bidrag til en kritisk diskussion* [*Social Constructivism: Contributions to a Critical Discussion*]. København: Hans Reitzels Forlag.

Collins, W. A. and Roisman, G. I. (2006) 'The Influence of Family and Peer Relationships in the Development of Competence during Adolescence', in A. Clarke-Stewart and J. Dunn (eds) *Families Count.* Cambridge: Cambridge University Press.

Condon, W. S. (1982) 'Cultural Microrhythms', in M. Davis (ed.) *Interaction Rhythms: Periodicity in Communicative Behaviour.* New York: Human Sciences Press.

Corsaro, W. A. (1997) *The Sociology of Childhood.* Thousand Oaks, CA: Pine Forge Press.

Corsaro, W. A. (2005) *The Sociology of Childhood* (2nd edn). Thousand Oaks, CA: Pine Forge Press.

Corsaro, W. A. (2009) 'Peer Culture', in J. Qvortrup, W. A. Corsaro and M.-S. Honig (eds) *The Palgrave Handbook of Childhood Studies.* Basingstoke: Palgrave Macmillan.

Crouter, A. (2006) 'Mothers and Fathers at Work: Implications for Families and Children', in A. Clarke-Stewart, and J. Dunn (eds) *Families Count.* Cambridge: Cambridge University Press.

Cunningham, H. (1995) *Children and Childhood in Western Society Since 1500.* London: Addison Wesley Longman.

Curtis, W. J. and Nelson, C. A. (2003) 'Toward Building a Better Brain', in S. S. Luthar (ed.) *Resilience and Vulnerability.* Cambridge: Cambridge University Press.

Cushman, P. (1990) 'Why the Self is Empty: Towards a Historically Situated Psychology', *American Psychologist*, 45(5): 599–611.

Cushman, P. (1991) 'Ideology Obscured: Political Uses of the Self in Daniel Stern's Infant', *American Psychologist*, 6(3): 206–19.

Dahlgren, L. and Hultqvist, K. (1995) *Seendet och seendets vilkor* [*Seeing and the Conditions of Seeing*]. Stockholm: HLS-Förlag.

Dam, D. (1999) 'Børns selvforvaltning: mål eller middel' ['Children's Self-management: Goal or Means'], *Vera*, No. 8.

Damon, W. and Hart, D. (1991) *Self-understanding in Childhood and Adolescence.* Cambridge: Cambridge University Press.

Danish National Encyclopedia [Den Store Danske Encyklopædi] (1995) *Børnepsykologi* [*Child Psychology*]. København: Gyldendal, bind 3.

Datan, N. and Ginsberg, L. H. (eds) (1975) *Life-span Developmental Psychology: Normative Life Crisis.* New York: Academic Press.

Day, R. and Lamb, M. (eds) (2004a) *Conceptualizing and Measuring Father Involvement.* Hillsdale, NJ: Lawrence Erlbaum.

Day, R. and Lamb, M. (2004b) 'Conceptualizing and Measuring Father Involvement: Pathways Problems, and Progress', in R. Day and M. Lamb (eds) *Conceptualizing and Measuring Father Involvement.* Hillsdale, NJ: Lawrence Erlbaum.

Dencik, L. (1999) 'Fremtidens børn: om postmodernisering og socialisering' ['Children of the Future: About Postmodernization and Socialization'], in L. Dencik, and P. S. Jørgensen (eds) *Børn og familie i det postmoderne samfund* [*Children and Family in Postmodern Society*]. København: Hans Reitzels Forlag.

Dencik, L. (2008) 'Modernisering: individualisering og fællesskab' ['Modernization: Individualization and Togetherness'], in L. Dencik, P. S. Jørgensen and D. Sommer *Familie og børn i en opbrudstid* [*Family and Children in a Time of Change*]. København: Gyldendal Academic/Hans Reitzel.

Dencik, L. Backstrom, C. and Larsson, E. (1988) *Barnens tva varldar* [*The Child's Two Worlds*]. Stockholm: Esselte Studium/Almquist & Wiksell.

Dencik, L., Jørgensen, P. S. and Sommer, D. (2008) *Familie og børn i en opbrudstid* [*Family and Children in a Time of Change*]. København: Hans Reitzels Forlag.

Douglas, J. D. (1970) *Understanding Everyday Life.* Chicago: Aldine.

Dunbar, R. I. (1998) 'The Social Brain Hypothesis', *Evolutionary Anthropology*, (6)5: 179–90.

Dunn, J. and Brown, J. (1991) 'Relationships, Talk about Feelings, and the Development of Affect Regulation in Early Childhood', in J. Garbner and K. A. Dodge (eds) *The Development of Emotion Regulation and Dysregulation.* Cambridge: Cambridge University Press.

Eisenberg, N. and Valiente, C. (2002) 'Parenting and Children's Prosocial and Moral Development', in M. H. Bornstein (ed.) *Handbook of Parenting*, vol. 5. Hillsdale, NJ: Lawrence Erlbaum.

Ellegaard, T. (1995) 'Børnehaveforskerens blik' ['The Eye of the Childcare Researcher'], *Dansk Pædagogisk Tidsskrift*, Nr. 1.

Erikson, E. H. (1950) *Childhood and Society.* New York: Norton.

Erikson, E. H. (1972) *Growth and Crisis of the Healthy Personality.* Harmondsworth: Penguin.

Esping-Andersen, G., Gallie, D., Hemerijk, A. and Myles, A. (2003) *Why We Need a New Welfare State.* Oxford: Oxford University Press.

Eyer, D. E. (1993) *Mother-Infant Bonding: A Scientific Fiction.* Yale: Yale University Press.

Feeney, P. and Porter, L. (2009) 'Nought to Five: The Daycare Experiment', *North and South*, April, 47–54.

Field, T. (1978) 'Interaction Behaviours of Primary Versus Secondary Caretaker Fathers', *Developmental Psychology*, 15(6): 601–7.

Field, T. (1990) *Infancy.* Cambridge, MA: Harvard University Press.

Fischer, K. W. and Bidell, T. R. (2006) 'Dynamic Development of Action and Thought', in R. M. Lerner (ed.) *Handbook of Child Psychology*, vol. 1: *Theoretical Models of Human Development.* Hoboken, NJ: John Wiley & Sons.

Fivaz-Depeursinge, E. and Corboz-Warnery, A. (1999) *The Primary Triangle: A Developmental Systems View of Mothers, Fathers, and Infants.* New York: Basic Books.

Floccia, C., Christophe, A. and Bertoncini, J. (1997) 'High-amplitude Sucking and Newborns: The Quest for Underlying Mechanisms', *Journal of Experimental Child Psychology*, 64, 175–98.

Fogel, A. (1993) *Developing Through Relations: Origins of Communication, Self, and Culture.* New York: Harvester Wheatsheaf.

Fogel, A. (2000) 'Developmental Pathways in Close Relationships', *Child Development*, 71(5): 1150–2.

Fogel, A. (2004) 'The History (and Future) of Infancy', in G. Bremner and A. Fogel (eds) *Blackwell Handbook of Infant Development.* Oxford: Blackwell.

Fogel, A., Lyra, M. C. and Valsiner, J. (eds) (2009) *Dynamics and Indeterminism in Developmental and Social Processes.* New York: Psychology Press.

Fogel, A., Garvey, A., Hsu, H.-C. and West-Stromming, D. (2006) *Change Processes in Relationships.* New York: Cambridge University Press.

Freud, A. (1963) *Normalitet og patologi i barndommen [Normality and Pathology in Childhood].* København: Hans Reitzels Forlag.

Freud, S. (1975) 'An Outline of Psychoanalysis', in J. Strachey (ed.) *The Standard Edition of The Complete Works of Sigmund Freud.* London: Hogarth Press.

Friedman, D. (2010) *An Unsolicited Gift.* London: Telegraph Books.

Frith, U. and Frith, C. (2001) 'The Biological Basis of Social Interaction', *Current Directions in Psychological Science*, 10(5): 151–5

Frønes, I. (1994) *De ligeværdige [The Equals].* København: Forlaget Børn & Unge.

Fuller, B. (2008) *Standardized Childhood: The Political and Cultural Struggle over Early Education.* Palo Alto, CA: Stanford University Press.

Furedi, F. (2001) *Paranoid Parenting.* Harmondsworth: Penguin.

Gallimore, R., Weisner, T. S., Kaufmann, S. Z. and Bernheimer, L. P. (1989) 'The Social Construction of Eco-cultural Niches: Family Accommodation of Developmentally Delayed Children', *American Journal of Mental Retardation*, 94(3): 216–30.

Gerhardt, S. (2004a) *Why Loves Matters: How Affection Shapes a Baby's Brain.* New York: Brunner-Routledge.

Gerhardt, S. (2004b) 'Cradle of Civilisation', *The Guardian*, 24 July.

Gibbs, N. (2009) 'What Women Want Now', special issue, The State of the American Woman, *Time*, 14 October.

Giddens, A. (1990) *The Consequences of Modernity.* Cambridge: Polity Press.

Gleason, J. B. and Ratner, N. B. (eds) (1998) *Psycholinguistics* (2nd edn). New York: Hartcourt Brace.

Globalisation Council [Globaliseringsrådets Rapport] (2006) *Progress, Innovation and Cohesion: Strategy for Denmark in the Global Economy: Key Initiatives.* København: Statsministeriet.

Goodnow, J. J. (2002) 'Parent's Knowledge and Expectations: Using What We Know', in M. H. Bornstein (ed.) *Handbook of Parenting*, vol. 3. Hillsdale, NJ: Lawrence Erlbaum.

Goodnow, J. J. and Collins, W. A. (eds) (1990) *Development According to Parents: The Nature, Sources, and Consequences of Parent's Ideas.* Hillsdale, NJ: Lawrence Erlbaum.

Gopnik, A. (2009) *The Philosophical Baby.* London: Bodley Head.

Gopnik, A., Meltzoff, A. N. and Kuhl, P. K. (1999) *The Scientist in the Crib: What Early Learning Tells Us About the Mind.* New York. HarperCollins.

Gottfried, A. E., Gottfried, A. W. and Bathurst, K. (2002) 'Maternal and Dual Earner Employment Status and Parenting', in M. H. Bornstein (ed.) *Handbook of Parenting*, vol. 2. Hillsdale, NJ: Lawrence Erlbaum.

Gottlieb, G. (2003) 'Probabilistic Epigenesis of Development', in J. Valsiner and K. Connolly (eds) *Handbook of Developmental Psychology.* Thousand Oaks, CA: Sage.

Gottlieb, G. (2007) 'Probabilistic Epigenesis', *Developmental Science*, 10, 1–11.

Greenberg, M. and Morris, N. (1974) 'Engrossment: The Newborns Impact upon Father', *American Journal of Orthopsychiatry*, 44(4): 520–31.

Greenfield, P. M., Suzuki, L. and Rothstein-Fisch, C. (2006) 'Cultural Pathways Through Human Development', in W. D. Damon and R. M. Lerner (eds) *Handbook of Child Psychology*, vol. 4: *Child Psychology in Practice*. New York: John Wiley & Sons.

Grossmann, K. E., Grossmann, K. and Watters, E. (eds) (2005) *Attachment from Infancy to Adulthood: The Major Longitudinal Studies*. New York: Guilford Press.

Grossman, K. E., Grossmann, K. E., Spangler, G. et al. (1985) 'Maternal Sensitivity and Newborn's Orientation Responses as Related to Quality of Attachment in Northern Germany', in I. Bretherton and E. Waters (eds) *Growing Points of Attachment Theory and Research*. Chicago: Chicago University Press.

Grunewald, R. and Rolnick, A. (2007) 'A Productive Investment: Early Child Development', in M. E. Young and L. Richardson (eds) *Early Child Development: From Measurement to Action*. Washington, DC: World Bank.

Haavind, H. (1987) *Liten og stor [Small and Big]*. Oslo: Universitetsforlaget.

Haavind, H. (2006) 'Midt i tredie akt? Fedres deltakelse i det omsorgsfulle foreldreskap' ['In the Middle of Act Three? Fathers' Participation in Caring Parenting'], *Tidsskrift for Norsk Psykologforening*, 43, 683–93.

Haavind, H. and Magnusson, E. (2005) 'The Nordic Countries: Welfare Paradises for Women and Children?' *Feminism and Psychology*, 15(2): 227–35.

Hansen, M., Thomsen, P. and Varming, O. (2006) *Psykologisk-Pædagogisk Ordbog [Psychological-Pedagogical Wordbook]* (15th edn). København: Hans Reitzels Forlag.

Harkness, S. and Super, C. H. (2002) 'Culture and Parenting', in M. H. Bornstein (ed.) *Handbook of Parenting*, vol. 3. Hillsdale, NJ: Lawrence Erlbaum.

Harris, J. R. (1998) *The Nurture Assumption: Why Children Turn Out the Way They Do*. New York: Free Press.

Harris, P. L. (2006) 'Social Cognition', in R. M. Lerner (ed.) *Handbook of Child Psychology*, vol. 2. New York: John Wiley & Sons.

Hart, C. H., Newell, L. D. and Olsen, S. F. (2003) 'Parenting Skills and Social-communicative Competence in Childhood', in J. O. Greene and B. R. Burleson (eds) *Handbook of Communication and Social Interaction Skills*. Hillsdale, NJ: Lawrence Earlbaum.

Hart, S. (2006) *Betydningen af samhørighed: Om neuroaffektiv udviklingspsykologi [The Meaning of Being Related: About Neuroaffective Developmental Psychology]*. København: Hans Reitzels Forlag.

Harwood, R., Miller, S. A. and Vasta, R. (2008) *Child Psychology: Development in a Changing Society*. New York: John Wiley & Sons.

Heath, D. H. (1978) 'What Meaning and Effects Does Fatherhood Have for the Maturing of Professional Men?', *Merrill-Palmer Quarterly*, 24(4): 265–78.

Hermans, H. J., Kempen, H. J. and van Loon, R. J. (1992) 'The Dialogical Self: Beyond Individualism and Rationalism', *American Psychologist*, 47(1): 23–33.

Hetherington, E. M., Lerner, R. and Perlmutter, M. (eds) (1988) *Child Development in Life-span Perspective*. Hillsdale, NJ: Lawrence Erlbaum.

Hewlett, B. S. (1992) 'Husband-Wife Reciprocity and the Father-Infant Relationships Among Aka Pygmies', in B. S. Hewlett (ed.) *Father-Child Relations: Cultural and Biosocial Contexts*. New York: Aldine de Gruyter.

Holter, Ø. G., Svare, H. and Egeland, C. (2008) *Likestilling og livskvalitet 2007. [Equality and Quality of Life 2007]*. Research Report: Norden, NIKK, AFI and WEI.

Howes, C. and Spieker, S. (2008) 'Attachment Relationships in the Context of Multiple Caregivers', in J. Cassidy and P. R. Shaver (eds) *Handbook of Attachment* (2nd edn). New York: Guilford Press.

Hrdy, S. B. (2009) *Mothers and Others: The Evolutionary Origins of Mutual Understandings.* Cambridge, MA: Harvard University Press.

Hundeide, K. (2003) 'Becoming a Committed Insider', *Cultural Psychology*, 9(2): 107–27.

Jackson, J. F. (1993) 'Multiple Caregiving Among African Americans: The Need for an Emic Approach', *Human Development*, 36(2): 87–102.

James, A. and Prout, A. (1990) *Constructing and Reconstructing Childhood.* London: Falmer Press.

James, A., Jenks, C. and Prout, A. (1998) *Theorizing Childhood.* Cambridge: Polity Press.

Jenks, C. (1996) *Childhood.* London: Routledge.

Jensen, A.-M. (2009) 'Pluralization of Family Forms', in J. Qvortrup, W. A. Corsaro and M.-S. Honig (eds) *The Palgrave Handbook of Childhood Studies.* Basingstoke: Palgrave Macmillan.

Jerlang, E. and Jerlang, J. (2001) *Pædagogisk-Psykologisk Opslagsbog [Educational-Psychological Referencebook].* København: Gyldendal.

Johansen, J.-B. and Sommer, D. (eds) (2006) *Oppdragelse, danning og socialisering i læringsmiljøer [Upbringing, Education and Socialization in Learning Environments].* Oslo: Universitetsforlaget.

Joseph, J. (2003) *The Gene Illusion: Genetic Research in Psychiatry and Psychology under the Microscope.* Ross-on-Wye: PCCS Books.

Kagitcibasi, C. (2007) *Family, Self, and Human Development Across Cultures* (2nd edn). Hillsdale, NJ: Lawrence Erlbaum.

Kail, R. V. (2007) *Children and Their Development* (4th edn). Upper Saddle River, NJ: Pearson/Prentice Hall.

Kamerman, S. B. and Moss, P. (2009) *The Politics of Parental Leave Policies.* Cambridge: Polity Press.

Karmiloff-Smith, A. (1995) 'Annotation: The Extraordinary Cognitive Journey from Foetus through Infancy', *Journal of Child Psychology and Psychiatry*, 36(8): 1293–313.

Karmiloff-Smith, A. (2010) *Mental Capital and Wellbeing: Making the Most of Ourselves in the 21st Century.* London: Government Office for Science.

Katzenelson, B. (1994) *Homo Socius: Socialpsykologisk grundbog [Homo Socius: A Social Psychological Primer].* København: Gyldendal.

Kitayama, S. (2000) 'Collective Construction of the Self and Social Relationships: A Rejoinder and Some Extensions', *Child Development*, 71(5): 1143–7.

Kitayama, S. and Markus, H. R. (1994) 'Culture and Self: How Cultures Influence the Way we View Ourselves', in D. Matsumoto (ed.) *People: Psychology from a Cultural Perspective.* Pacific Grove, CA: Brooks/Cole.

Klaus, M. and Kennell, J. (1976) *Maternal-Infant Bonding: The Impact of Early Separation or Loss on Family Development.* St Louis: Mosby.

Klaus, M. and Kennell, J. (1982) *Parent-Infant Bonding.* St Louis: Mosby.

Klein, M. (1952) *Developments in Psychoanalysis.* London: Hogarth Press.

Kojima, H. (2003) 'Historical Contexts for Development', in J. Valsiner and K. Connolly (eds) *Handbook of Developmental Psychology.* Thousand Oaks, CA: Sage.

Kotelchuck, M. (1976) 'The Infant's Relationship to the Father: Experimental Evidence', in M. Lamb (ed.) *The Role of the Father in Child Development.* New York: John Wiley & Sons.

Kristjansson, B. (2001) *Barndomen och den sociala moderniseringen [Childhood and Social Modernization].* Stockholm: HLS Förlag.

Krøjgaard, P. (2002) '"Jeg ved hvad du vil!" Om udviklingen af børns forståelse af sig selv og andre mennesker som intentionelle væsener' ['"I Know What You

Want!" About the Development of Children's Understanding of Themselves and Other People as Intentional Beings'], in M. Hermansen and A. Poulsen (red.) *Samfundets børn* [*Society's Children'*]. Aarhus: Forlaget Klim.

Laird, R. D., Pettit, G. S., Bates, J. E. and Dodge, K. A. (2003) 'Parents' Monitoring-relevant Knowledge and Adolescents' Delinquent Behavior: Evidence of Correlated Developmental Changes and Reciprocal Influences', *Child Development*, 74(3): 752–68.

Lamb, M. and Ahnert, L. (2006) 'Nonparental Child Care: Context, Concepts, Correlates, and Consequences', in R. M. Lerner (ed.) *Handbook of Child Psychology*, vol. 4. New York: John Wiley & Sons.

Lamb, M. (ed.) (1976a) *The Role of the Father in Child Development*. New York: John Wiley & Sons.

Lamb, M. (1976b) 'Interactions between 8-month-old Children and their Fathers and Mothers', in M. Lamb (ed.) *The Role of the Father in Child Development*. New York: John Wiley & Sons.

Lamb, M. (1976c) 'Twelve-months-olds and their Parents: Interactions in a Laboratory Playroom', *Developmental Psychology*, 12, 237–44.

Lamb, M. (1976d) 'Effects of Stress and Cohort on Mother- and Father-Infant Interaction', *Developmental Psychology*, 12, 435–43.

Lamb, M. (1977a) 'Father-Infant and Mother-Infant Interaction in the First Year of Life', *Child Development*, 48, 167–81.

Lamb, M. (1977b) 'The Development of Mother-Infant and Father-Infant Attachment in the Second Year of Life', *Developmental Psychology*, 13, 637–48.

Lamb, M. (1980) 'The Development of Parent-Infant Attachments in the First Two Years of Life', in F. A. Pedersen (ed.) *The Father Infant Relationship*. New York: Praeger.

Lamb, M. (2000) 'The History of Research on Father Involvement: An Overview', *Marriage & Family Review*, 29, 23–42.

Lamb, M. (2004) *The Role of the Father in Child Development* (4th edn). New York: John Wiley & Sons.

Langsted, O. and Sommer, D. (1992) *Småbørns livsvilkår i Danmark* [*Young Children's Growing Up Conditions in Denmark*]. København: Hans Reitzels Forlag.

Lebra, T. S. (1994) 'Mother and Child in Japanese Socialization: A Japan-U.S. Comparison', in P. Greenfield and R. Cocking (eds) *Cross-cultural Roots of Minority Child Development*. Hillsdale, NJ: Lawrence Erlbaum.

Legerstee, M. (1992) 'A Review of the Animate Inanimate Distinction in Infancy: Implications for Models of Social and Cognitive Knowing', *Early Development and Learning*, 1(2): 59–67.

Leira, A. (1992) *Welfare States and Working Mothers: The Scandinavian Experience*. Cambridge: Cambridge University Press.

Lerner, R. M. (2006) 'Developmental Science, Developmental Systems, and Contemporary Theories of Human Development', in R. M. Lerner (ed.) *Handbook of Child Psychology*, vol. 1: *Theoretical Models of Human Development*. Hoboken, NJ: John Wiley & Sons.

Lerner, R. M., Rothbaum, F., Boulos, S. and Castellino, D. R. (2002) 'Developmental Systems Perspective on Parenting', in M. H. Bornstein (ed.) *Handbook of Parenting*. Hillsdale, NJ: Lawrence Erlbaum.

Lewis, C. C. (2000) 'Human Development in the United States and Japan: New Ways to Think about Continuity', *Child Development*, 71(5): 1152–5.

Little Treasures (2009) 'Aggressive and Anxious?', 1 November.

Løvlie, S. (2005) *Relationer i psykologien: et dialektisk perspektiv* [*Relationships in Psychology: A Dialectical Perspective*]. København: Akademisk Forlag.

Luthar, S. S. (2006) 'Resilience in Development: A Synthesis of Research across Five Decades', in D. Cicchetti and D. J. Cohen (eds) *Developmental Psychopathology*, vol. 3: *Risk, Disorder, and Adaption* (2nd edn). New York: John Wiley & Sons.

Luthar, S. S., Cicchetti, D. and Becker, B. (2000) 'The Construct of Resilience: A Critical Evaluation and Guidelines for Future Work', *Child Development*, 71(3): 543–62.

McCrone, J. (2009) 'Daycare Debate', *The Press* (New Zealand), 31 October.

Maccoby, E. E. (1992) 'The Role of Parents in the Socialization of Children: An Historical Overview', *Developmental Psychology*, 28(6): 1006–17.

Mahler, M. S. and Fuhrer, M. (1968) *On Human Symbiosis and the Vicissitudes of Individuation*. New York: International Universities Press.

Mahler, M. S., Pine, F. and Bergman, A. (1975) *The Psychological Birth of the Human Infant*. New York: Basic Books.

Majdan, M. and Schatz, C. J. (2006) 'Effects of Visual Experience on Activity-dependent Gene Regulation in Cortex', *Nature Neuroscience*, 9, 650–9.

Markus, H. R. and Kitayama, S. (1991) 'Culture and Self: Implications for Cognition, Emotion and Motivation', *Psychological Review*, 98(2): 224–53.

Masten, A. S. (2007) 'Resilience in Developing Systems: Progress and Promise as the Fourth Wave Rises', *Development and Psychopathology*, 19, 921–930.

Masten, A. S. and Garmezy, N. (1985) 'Risk, Vulnerability, and Protective Factors in Developmental Psychopathology', in B. Lahey and A. Kazdin (eds) *Advances in Clinical Child Psychology*. New York: Plenum.

Masten, A. S. and Gewirtz, A. H. (2006) 'Vulnerability and Resilience in Early Child Development', in K. McCartney and D. Phillips (eds) *Blackwell Handbook of Early Childhood Development*. Oxford: Blackwell.

Mead, G. H. (1934) *Mind, Self and Society*. Chicago: Chicago University Press.

Melson, G. F., Ladd, G. W. and Hsu, H.-C. (1993) 'Maternal Support Networks, Maternal Cognitions, and Young Children's Social and Cognitive Development', *Child Development*, 64, 1401–17.

Meltzoff, A. N. and Borton, W. (1979) 'Intermodal Matching by Human Neonates', *Nature*, 282, 403–4.

Meltzoff, A. N. and Kuhl, P. K. (1990) 'Faces and Speech: Intermodal Processing of Biologically Relevant Signals in Infants and Adults', in D. J. Lewkowicz and R. Lickliter (eds) *The Development of Intersensory Perception: Comparative Perspectives*. Hillsdale, NJ: Lawrence Erlbaum.

Meltzoff, A. N. and Moore, M. K. (1998) 'Infant Intersubjectivity: Broadening the Dialogue to Include Imitation and Intention', in S. Bråten (ed.) *Intersubjective Communication and Emotion in Early Ontogeny*. Cambridge: Cambridge University Press.

Menon, T. and Fu, H.-Y. (2006) 'Culture and Control: How Independent and Interdependent Selves Experience Agency and Constraint', *National Culture and Groups: Research on Managing Groups and Teams*, 9, 21–51.

Mercer, J. (2010) *Child Development: Myths and Misunderstandings*. London: Sage.

Mikelson, K. (2008) '"He Said, She Said": Comparing Father and Mother Reports of Father Involvement', *Journal of Marriage and Family*, 70, 613–24.

Milardo, R. M. and Duck, S. (eds) (2000) *Families as Relationships*. New York: John Wiley & Sons.

Mills, R. and Duck, S. (eds) (2000) *The Developmental Psychology of Personal Relationships*. New York: Wiley.

Miyake, K., Chen, S. and Campos, J. J. (1985) 'Infant Temperament, Mother's Mode of Interaction, and Attachment in Japan', in I. Bretherton and E. Waters (eds) *Growing Points of Attachment Theory and Research*. Chicago: Chicago University Press.

Morelli, G. A. and Rogoff, B. (1992) 'Cultural Variation in Infants' Sleeping Arrangements: Questions of Independence', *Developmental Psychology*, 28(4): 604–13.

Morss, J. (1996) *Growing Critical: Alternatives to Developmental Psychology*. London: Routledge.

Musatti, T. (1986) 'Early Peer Relations: The Perspectives of Piaget and Vygotsky', in E. Mueller and C. Cooper (eds) *Processes and Outcome in Peer Relationships*. New York: Academic Press.

Näsman, E. (1995) 'Vuxnas interesse av att se med barns ögon' ['Adults' Interest in Looking with the Eyes of the Child'], in L. Dahlgren and K. Hultqvist (edd) *Seendet och seendets villkor [Seeing and Its Terms]*. Stockholm: HLS Förlag.

NICHD Early Child Care Research Network (eds) (2005) *Child Care and Child Development: Results from the NICHD Study of Early Child Care and Youth Development*. New York: Guilford Press.

Nielsen, T. (1990) *Depression*. København: Dansk Psykologisk Forlag.

Nyborg, H. (1994) *Hormones, Sex and Society*. Westport, CT: Greenwood Publishing.

O'Brien, M. (2004) 'Social Science and Public Policy Perspectives on Fatherhood in the European Union', in M. Lamb (ed.) *The Role of the Father in Child Development* (4th edn). New York: John Wiley & Sons.

Ochs, E. and Shohet, M. (2006) 'The Cultural Structuring of Mealtime Socialization, *New Directions for Child and Adolescent Development*, 111, 35–49.

OECD (n.d.) *OECD Family Database*. OECD Directorate for Employment, Labour and Social Affairs, www.oecd.org/els/social/family/database.

Oppliger, P. (2007) 'Effects on Gender Stereotyping on Socialization', in R. W. Preiss, B. M. Gayle, N. Burell et al. (eds) *Mass Media Effects Research: Advances Through Meta-analysis*. Hillsdale, NJ: Lawrence Erlbaum.

Palmer, D. C. and Donahoe, J. W. (1992) 'Essentialism and Selectionism in Cognitive Science and Behaviour Analysis', *American Psychologist*, 47(11): 1344–58.

Papalia, D. E., Olds, S. W. and Feldman, R. D. (2002) *A Child's World: Infancy through Adolescence* (9th edn). Boston: McGraw-Hill.

Parke, R. D. (1989) 'Social Development in Infancy: A 25-year Perspective', *Advances in Child Development and Behaviour*, 21.

Parke, R. D. (1996) *Fatherhood*. Cambridge, MA: Harvard University Press.

Parke, R. D. (2002) 'Fathers and Families', in M. H. Bornstein (ed.) *Handbook of Parenting*, vol. 3. Hillsdale, NJ: Lawrence Erlbaum.

Parke, R. D. and Buriel, R. (1998) 'The Influence of Significant Others on Learning about Relationships: From Family to Friends', in N. Eisenberg (ed.) *Handbook of Child Psychology* (5th edn). New York: John Wiley & Sons.

Parke, R. D. and O'Neil, R. (2000) 'The Influence of Significant Others on Learning about Relationships', in S. L. Rosemary and S. Duck (eds) *The Developmental Psychology of Personal Relationships*. New York: John Wiley & Sons.

Parke, R. D. and Sawin, D. B. (1976) 'The Father's Role in Infancy: A Re-evaluation', *The Family Coordinator*, Special Issue, 25(4): 365–71.

Parsons, T. and Bales, R. F. (1955) *Family: Socialization and Interaction Process*. New York: Free Press.

Pedersen, F. A. (ed.) (1980) *The Father Infant Relationship*. New York: Praeger.

Peterfreund, E. (1978) 'Some Critical Comments on Psychoanalytic Conceptualizations of Infancy', *International Journal of Psychoanalysis*, 427–41.

Phoenix, A., Woolett, A. and Lloyd, E. (eds) (1991) *Motherhood: Meanings, Practices and Ideologies*. London: Sage.

Piaget, J. (1977) *The Development of Thought: Equilibration of Cognitive Structure*. New York: Viking.

Pianta, R. C. (ed.) (1992) 'Beyond the Parent: The Role of Other Adults in Children's Lives', *New Directions for Child Development*, 57, 61–80.

Pickens, J. and Field, T. (1993) 'Facial Expressivity in Infants of Depressed Mothers', *Developmental Psychology*, 29(6): 986–8.

Pleck, E. (2004) 'Two Dimensions of Fatherhood: A History of the Good Dad-Bad Dad Complex', in M. Lamb (ed.) *The Role of the Father in Child Development*. New York: John Wiley & Sons.

Pramling-Samuelsson, I. and Asplund-Carlsson, M. (2005) *Det legende lærende barn i en udviklingspædagogisk teori* [*The Playing Learning Child in a Developmental-Educational Theory*]. København: Hans Reitzels Forlag.

Pruett, K. D. (1983) 'Infants of Primary Nurturing Fathers', *Psychoanalytic Study of the Child*, 38, 257–77.

Quinn, P. C. and Oates, J. (2004) 'Early Category Representation and Concepts', in J. Oates and A. Grayson (eds) *Cognitive and Language Development in Children*. Oxford: Blackwell.

Qvortrup, J. (2002) 'Sociology of Childhood: Conceptual Liberation', in F. Mouritsen and J. Qvortrup (eds) *Childhood and Children's Culture*. Odense: University Press of Southern Denmark.

Qvortrup, J. (2009) 'Childhood as a Structural Form', in J. Qvortrup., W. A. Corsaro and M.-S. Honig (eds) *The Palgrave Handbook of Childhood Studies*. Basingstoke: Palgrave Macmillan.

Qvortrup, J., Corsaro, W. A. and Honig M.-S. (eds) (2009) *The Palgrave Handbook of Childhood Studies*. Basingstoke: Palgrave Macmillan.

Ramey, S. H. (2005) 'Human Developmental Science Serving Children and Families: Contributions of the NICHD Study of Early Child Care', in The NICHD Early Child Care Research Group (ed.) *Child Care and Child Development*. New York: Guilford Press.

ReadyWeb Virtual Library Archives (n.d.) *Curriculum and Assessment*, http://readyweb.crc.uiuc.edu/virtual-library/1994/sreb-gsr/cur-ass.html.

Reddy, V., Hay, D., Murray, L. and Trevarthen, C. (1997) 'Communication in Infancy: Mutual Regulation of Affect and Attention', in G. Bremner, A. Slater and G. Butterworth (eds) *Infant Development: Recent Advances*. Hillsdale, NJ: Lawrence Erlbaum.

Reese, H. W. (1991) 'Contextualism and Developmental Psychology', in H. W. Reese (ed.) *Advances in Child Development and Behaviour*. San Diego: Academic Press.

Rescorla, L., Hyson, N. C. and Hirsch-Pasek, K. (eds) (1991) 'Academic Instruction in Early Childhood: Challenge or Pressure?', *New Directions for Child Development*, 53, 39–45.

Riley, D. (1990) 'Network Influences on Father Involvement in Childrearing', in M. Cochran, M. Larner, D. Riley et al. (eds) *Extending Families: The Social Networks of Parents and Children*. Cambridge: Cambridge University Press.

Rogoff, B. (1990) *Apprenticeship in Thinking: Cognitive Development in Social Context*. Oxford: Oxford University Press.

Rogoff, B. (2003) *The Cultural Nature of Human Development*. Oxford: Oxford University Press.

Rollo, S. (2010) 'Nannied Boys "Likely to be Womanisers"', *Daily* Telegraph, 20 March.

Rosier, K. B. (2009) 'Children as Problems, Problems of Children', in J. Qvortrup, W. A. Corsaro and M.-S. Honig (eds) *The Palgrave Handbook of Childhood Studies*. Basingstoke: Palgrave Macmillan.

Rothbaum, F., Pott, M., Azuma, H. et al. (2000) 'The Development of Close Relationships in Japan and in the United States: Paths of Symbiotic Harmony and Generative Tension', *Child Development*, 71(5): 1121–43.

Rutter, M. (1972) *Maternal Deprivation Reassessed*. Harmondsworth: Penguin.

Rutter, M. (1991) 'A Fresh Look at Maternal Deprivation', in P. Bateson (ed.) *The Development and Integration of Behaviour*. Cambridge: Cambridge University Press.

Rutter, M. (2008) 'Implications of Attachment Theory and Research for Child Care Policies', in J. Cassidy and P. R. Shaver (eds) *Handbook of Attachment: Theory, Research, and Clinical Applications*. New York: Guilford Press.

Rutter, M. and Rutter M. (1993) *Developing Minds: Challenge and Continuity across the Life Span*. Harmondsworth: Penguin.

Sagi-Schwartz, A. and Aviezer, O. (2005) 'Correlates of Attachment to Multiple Caregivers in Kibbutz Children from Birth to Emerging Adulthood', in K. E. Grossmann, K. Grossmann and E. Watters (eds) *Attachment from Infancy to Adulthood: The Major Longitudinal Studies*. New York: Guilford Press.

Sameroff, A. J. (1987) 'The Social Context of Development', in N. Eisenberg (ed.) *Contemporary Topics in Developmental Psychology*. New York: John Wiley & Sons.

Sameroff, A. J. (1991) 'Neo-environmental Perspective on Developmental Theory', in R. M. Hodap, J. A. Burack and E. Ziegler (eds) *Cognitive and Language Development in Children*. Oxford: Blackwell.

Sameroff, A. J. (2000) 'Developmental Systems and Psychopathology', *Development and Psychopathology*, 12, 297–312.

Sameroff, A. J. (2006) 'Identifying Risk and Protective Factors for Healthy Child Development', in A. Clarke-Stewart and J. Dunn (eds) *Families Count: Effects on Child and Adolescent Development*. New York: Cambridge University Press.

Sameroff, A. J. (2007) 'Biopsycosocial Influences on the Development of Resilience', in B. M. Lester, A. Masten and B. McEven (eds) *Resilience in Children*. New York: Annals of the New York Academy of Science, vol. 1094.

Sameroff, A. J. and MacKenzie, M. J. (2003) 'Research Strategies for Capturing Transactional Models of Development: The Limits of the Possible', *Development and Psychopathology*, 15, 613–640.

Scarr, S. (1992) 'Developmental Theories of the 1990s: Developmental and Individual Differences', *Child Development*, 63, 1333–53.

Scarr, S. and Dunn, J. (1987) *Mother Care/Other Care*. Harmondsworth: Penguin.

Schaffer, R. (1990) *Making Decisions about Children*. Oxford: Blackwell.

Shantz, C. U. (1983) 'Social Cognition', in J. H. Flavell and E. M. Markman (eds) *Handbook of Child Psychology*, vol. 3: *Cognitive Development*. New York: John Wiley & Sons.

Shenk, D. (2010) *The Genius in All of Us*. London: Icon Books.

Shulman, S. (1993) 'Close Friendships in Early and Middle Adolescence: Typology and Friendship Reasoning', in B. Laursen (ed.) *Close Friendship in Adolescence*. San Francisco: Jossey-Bass.

Shwalb, D.W., Nakazawa, J., Yamamoto, T. and Hyun, J.-H. (2004) 'Fathering in Japanese, Chinese, and Korean Cultures: A Review of the Research Literature', in M.E. Lamb (ed.) *The Role of the Father in Child Development* (4th edn). New York: Wiley.

Shweder, R. A., Goodnow, J., Hatano, G. et al. (2006) 'The Cultural Psychology of Development: One Mind, Many Mentalities', in R. M. Lerner (ed.) *Handbook of Child Psychology*, vol. 1: *Theoretical Models of Human Development*. Hoboken, NJ: John Wiley & Sons.

Siegel, I. and Lisi, A. V. (2002) 'Parent Beliefs are Cognitions: The Dynamic Belief Systems Model', in M. H. Bornstein (ed.) *Handbook of Parenting*, vol. 3. Hillsdale, NJ: Lawrence Erlbaum.

Signorelli, N. (1989) 'Television and Conceptions about Sex Roles: Maintaining Conventionality', *Sex Roles*, 21, 341–60.

Singer, D. G. and Singer, J. L. (eds) (2001) *Handbook of Children and the Media*. Thousand Oaks, CA: Sage.

Slater, A. and Butterworth, G. (1997) 'Perception of Social Stimuli: Face Perception and Imitation', in G. Bremner, A. Slater and G. Butterworth (eds) *Infant Development: Recent Advances*. Hillsdale, NJ: Lawrence Erlbaum.

Smånyt [Small News] (1996) København: Center for Småbørns-forskning, nr. 13.

Smetana, J. G. (1994) 'Parenting Styles and Beliefs about Parental Authority', in J. G. Smetana (ed.) *Beliefs About Parenting: Origins and Developmental Implications*. San Francisco: Jossey-Bass.

Smith, L. B. and Thelen, E. (2003) 'Development as a Dynamic System', *Trends in Cognitive Sciences*, 7, 343–8.

Smith, L. and Ulvund, S. E. (1999) *Spedbarnsalderen [Infancy Age]*. Oslo: Universitets forlaget.

Sommer, D. (1999) 'Faderskab i den radikaliserede modernitet: En undersøgelse af fader-spædbarn-relationen' ['Fatherhood in a Radicalized Modernity: A Study of the Father-Infant Relationship'], in L. Dencik and P. S. Jørgensen *Børn og familier i det postmoderne samfund [Children and Family in the Postmodern Society]*. København: Hans Reitzels Forlag.

Sommer, D. (2001) *At blive en person: Forældreskab og børns tidlige følelser [Becoming a Person: Parenthood and Children's Early Emotions]*. København: Hans Reitzels Forlag.

Sommer, D. (2003) *Barndomspsykologiske facetter [Childhood Psychological Facets]*. Kapitel 6: *Børns samværsmønstre [Children's Relationship Patterns]*. København: Systime Academic.

Sommer, D. (2008a) 'Familie og børn: tal og tendenser' ['Families and Children: Numbers and Tendencies'], in L. Dencik, P. S. Jørgensen and D. Sommer *Familie og børn i en opbrudstid [Family and Children in a Time of Change]*. København: Gyldendal Academic/Hans Reitzel.

Sommer, D. (2008b) 'Børnefamilien: dynamik og relationer' ['The Child Family: Dynamics and Relationships'], in L. Dencik, P. S. Jørgensen and D. Sommer *Familie og børn i en opbrudstid [Family and Children in a Time of Change]*. København: Gyldendal Academic/Hans Reitzel.

Sommer, D. (2010) *Børn i senmoderniteten [Children in Late Modernity]*. København: Hans Reitzels Forlag.

Sommer, D. (2011) 'Hvad er resiliens?' ['What is Resilience?'], in J. Sørensen (ed.) *Mønsterbrud i opbrud [Pattern-breaking in Flux]*. Frederikshavn: Dafolo.

Sommer, D., Pramling Samuelsson, I. and Hundeide, K. (2010) *Child Perspectives and Children's Perspectives in Theory and Practice*. New York: Springer.

Spelke, E. S. and Kinzler, K. D. (2007) 'Core Knowledge', *Developmental Science*, 10(1): 89–96.

Spelke, E. S., Phillips, A. and Woodward, A. (1995) 'Infants Knowledge of Object Motion and Human Action', in D. Sperber, D. Premack and A. Premack (eds) *Causal Cognition: A Multidisciplinary Debate*. Oxford: Oxford University Press.

Spelke, E. S., Breinlinger, K., Macomber, J. and Jacobsen, K. (1992) 'Origins of Knowledge', *Psychological Review*, 99, 605–32.

Statistisk Årbog (2007) [Statistical Yearbook]. København: Danmarks Statistik.

Statistics Denmark (2006) 'Nyt fra Danmarks Statistik ['News from Statistics Denmark'].

Statistics Denmark (2007) 'Nyt fra Danmarks Statistik' ['News from Statistics Denmark'].

Stern, D. N. (1985) *The Interpersonal World of the Infant: A View from Psychoanalysis and Developmental Psychology*. New York: Basic Books.

Stern, D. N. (1991) *The Diary of a Baby*. London: Fontana.

Stern, D. N. (1995) *The Motherhood Constellation*. New York: Basic Books.

Stern, D. N. (2004) *The Present Moment*. New York: W.W. Norton.

Stern, D. N. (2006) *The Interpersonal World of the Infant: A View from Psychoanalysis and Developmental Psychology* (2nd edn). New York: Karnac.

Storey, A., Walsh, C. J., Quinton, R. L. and Wynne-Edwards, K. E. (2000) 'Hormonal Correlates of Paternal Responsiveness in New and Expectant Fathers', *Evolution and Human Behaviour*, 21(2): 79–95.

Sylva, K., Melhuish, E., Sammons, P. et al. (2003) *The Effective Provision of Pre-school Education (EPPE) Project: Findings from the Pre-school Period*. London: Institute of Education.

The Family in America (2003) 'Fear in the Blood', 17(10), online, http://www.profam.org/pub/nr/nr_1710.htm.

Thelen, E. and Smith, L. B. (2006) 'Dynamic Systems Theories', in R. M. Lerner (ed.) *Handbook of Child Psychology, vol. 1: Theoretical Models of Human Development*. Hoboken, NJ: John Wiley & Sons.

Tobin, J. (2000) 'Using "The Japanese Problem" as a Corrective to the Ethnocentricity of Western Theory', *Child Development*, 71(5): 1155–9.

Tomasello, M. (1999) *The Cultural Origin of Human Cognition*. Cambridge, MA: Harvard University Press.

Tomasello, M. (2005) 'The Item-based Nature of Children's Early Syntactic Development', *Trends in Cognitive Sciences*, 4, 156–63.

Tomasello, M. (2009) *Why We Cooperate*. Cambridge, MA: MIT Press.

Tomasello, M., Carpenter, M., Call, J. et al. (2005) 'Understanding and Sharing Intentions: The Origins of Cultural Cognition', *Behavioural and Brain Sciences*, 28, 675–735.

Trevarthen, C. and Aitken, K. J. (2001) 'Infant Intersubjectivity: Research, Theory, and Clinical Applications', *Journal of Child Psychology and Psychiatry and Allied Disciplines*, 42(1): 3–48.

Triandis, H. C., McCusker, C. and Hui, C. H. (1990) 'Multimethod Probes of Individualism and Collectivism', *Journal of Personality and Social Psychology*, 59(5): 1006–20.

Turner, J. H. (2000) *On the Origins of Human Emotions*. Stanford: Stanford University Press.

UN (1989) Convention on the Rights of the Child. New York: UN.

UNICEF (2007) *Child Poverty in Perspective: An Overview of Child's Well-Being in Rich Countries*. Innocenti Report Card 7. Florence: UNICEF Innocenti Research Centre.

UNICEF (2008) *The Child Care Transition*. Florence: UNICEF Innocenti Research Centre.

Valsiner, J. (1987) *Culture and the Development of Children's Actions*. New York: John Wiley & Sons.

Valsiner, J. (2000) *Culture and Human Development*. London: Sage.

Verhave, T. and Hoorn, W. (1981) 'The Temporalization of the Self', in R. M. Lerner and N. A. Busch-Rossnagel (eds) *Individuals as Producers of their Development*. New York: Academic Press.

Vermeer, H. J. and van Ijzendorn, M. H. (2006) 'Children's Elevated Cortisol Levels at Child Care: A Review and Meta-Analysis', *Early Childhood Research Quarterly*, 21(3): 390–401.

Walkerdine, V. (1993) 'Beyond Developmentalism?' *Theory and Psychology*, 3(4): 451–70.

Ward, C. W. (2003) *Modernizing the Mind: Psychological Knowledge and the Remaking of Society*. Westport: Praeger.

Waters, E., Hamilton, C. E. and Weinfield, N. S. (2000a) 'The Stability of Attachment Security from Infancy to Adolescence and Early Adulthood: General Introduction', *Child Development*, 71(3): 678–83.

Waters, E., Merrick, S., Treboux, D. et al. (2000b) 'Attachment Security in Infancy and Early Childhood: A Twenty-year Longitudinal Study', *Child Development*, 71(3): 684–89.

Wenke, R. (1990) *Patterns in Prehistory: Humandkind's First Three Million Years.* Oxford: Oxford University Press.

Werner, E. E. and Smith, R. (1977) *Kauai's Children Come of Age.* Honolulu: University of Hawaii Press.

Werner, E. E., Bierman, J. M. and French, F. E. (1971) *The Children of Kauai Honolulu.* Honolulu: University of Hawaii Press.

White, S. H. (1983) 'The Idea of Development in Developmental Psychology', in R. M. Lerner (ed.) *Developmental Psychology: Historical and Philosophical Perspectives.* Hillsdale, NJ: Lawrence Erlbaum.

Witherington, D. C. (2007) 'The Dynamic Systems Approach as Metatheory for Developmental Psychology', *Human Development*, 50, 127–53.

Woodhead, M. (2006) 'Changing Perspectives on Early Childhood: Theory, Research and Policy', *International Journal of Equity and Innovation in Early Childhood*, 4(2): 1–43.

Woodhead, M. (2009) 'Child Development and the Development of Childhood', in J. Qvortrup., W. A. Corsaro and M.-S. Honig (eds) *The Palgrave Handbook of Childhood Studies.* Basingstoke: Palgrave Macmillan.

Woodhead, M. and Montgomery, H. (2003) *Understanding Childhood: An Interdisciplinary Approach.* Chichester: John Wiley & Sons.

Woodhead, M. and Moss, P. (eds) (2007) *Early Childhood and Primary Education.* Milton Keynes: Open University.

Woulfe, C. (2009) 'Home Best for Babies says Doctor', *Sunday Star-Times* (New Zealand), 7 June.

Young, M. E. and Richardson, L. (eds) *Early Child Development: From Measurement to Action.* Washington, DC: World Bank.

Zeanah, C. H., Anders, T. F., Seifer, R. and Stern, D. N. (1989) 'Implications of Research of Infant Development for Psychodynamic Theory and Practice', *Journal of the American Academy of Child and Adolescence Psychiatry*, 5(28): 657–68.

Zimbardo, P. G. (2004) 'A Situationist Perspective on the Psychology of Evil: Understanding how Good People are Transformed into Predators', in A. Miller (ed.) *The Social Psychology of Good and Evil: Understanding our Capacity for Kindness and Cruelty.* New York: Guilford Press.

Zukow-Goldring, P. (2002) 'Sibling Caregiving', in M. H. Bornstein (ed.) *Handbook of Parenting*, vol. 3. Hillsdale, NJ: Lawrence Erlbaum.

NAME INDEX

Subject Index